Dedication

To Michael

Associate Editor

Anna Yallop

Acknowledgements

Jonathan Smythe, Steve Wilson and Geraldine Onslow at Blackfriar
Publications Ltd (can't wait for '96)

Steve Lake and all the staff at Allsport

Contributors

TED AVES ● SIMON BAKER ● STUART BARNES ● IAN BEER ● ANNIE BRIGGS ● PETER BROOK
COLIN BROWN (CANADA) ● RAY CAIRNS (NEW ZEALAND) ● GREG CAMPBELL (AUSTRALIA)
JONATHAN CAVENDER (FRANCE) ● ROBERT COLE ● MATTHEW COOPER (NEW ZEALAND) ● FRANKIE DEGBE
(ARGENTINA) ● PETER DOWNIE ● RODERICK DYMOTT ● ANNMARIE FEENEY ● CLIVE FORTNUM
JOHN GATES (AUSTRALIA) ● DAVID GRAHAM & ASSOCIATES ● EDWARD GRAYSON QC ● CARLOS
GUARNA (ARGENTINA) ● TONY HALLETT ● JONATHAN GOZLETT (SOUTH AFRICA) ● DAVID HINCHCLIFFE MP
DAVID LAWRENSON ● PETER MCMULLAN (CANADA) ● ANDREA PASSARINI (ITALY)
QUINTUS VAN ROOYEN (SOUTH AFRICA) ● KEITH ROWLANDS (IRFB) ● BRIAN SKIRROW &
JILL WATKINS (RWC 95) ● ANDY SUTHERDEN ● JOHN WHITTAKER ● DILLON WOOD
LUCY YALLOP ● FLETCHER YALLOP

The *International*
RUGBY
ALMANACK

1995

Edited by DEREK WYATT and NICHOLAS KEITH

BLANDFORD

A Blandford Book

First published in the UK 1994
by Blandford, a Cassell imprint
Villiers House, 41–47 Strand, London WC2N 5JE

Cataloguing in publication data for this title is available
from the British Library

ISBN 0-7137-2515-X

Design and Typesetting by Blackfriar Publications Ltd
303 The Plaza, 535 King's Road, London SW10 0SZ
Telephone 0171 376 8853. Fax: 0171-352 7082
Colour and mono reproduction by Colour Solutions, London
Printed and bound by Stephens & George, Merthyr Tydfil

INTRODUCTION

Rugby Union is the world's fastest growing team sport. Everyone associated with the game needs a regular reminder of the facts and figures of the national and international tournaments, the many changes taking place in the rules and administrative structure, and – perhaps most important – the traditions and diversities which have made the game great.

The *International Rugby Almanack* is designed for the players, administrators and supporters of the modern game. It reflects the game's vitality, recognises its problems, acknowledges success and aims to contribute to the necessary debate which will keep the sport healthy. The *Almanack* will become as much a part of your love of the game as a Rory Underwood try, or Phillippe Sella breakaway, or an All-Black forward rush, or your own team holding a trophy aloft.

THE EDITORS

DEREK WYATT played rugby for a variety of clubs in the late 1960s and early 1970s before breaking into the big time with first Bedford and then Bath.

At Bedford he set an all time record scoring 145 tries in 152 games and scrambled a cap for England as substitute in 1976 in the Calcutta Match at Murrayfield. At Bath he equalled the existing try scoring record of 29 tries in his first and second seasons in 1978-79 and 1979-80 and played four times for the Barbarians. He left Bath for Oxford University to read for an M.Sc. in Management Education and gained a Blue as a 32-year-old in the centenary Varsity match in 1981. in 1987 he was awarded a Special Commendation by the United Nations for his work on sport and apartheid.

He writes for the *Financial Times* on rugby. He and is a Major Stanley's Trustee at Oxford University. His next book, *Rugby Betrayed,* will be published shortly after the 1995 Rugby World Cup

NICHOLAS KEITH is a former rugby reporter for and sports editor of *The Times*. In the last 10 years he has been involved in editing and producing sports and leisure publications, including: the 3M Guide to the Olympic Games in 1984 and 1988; A series of 10 *Sportsviewers' Guides*, published by David & Charles; *The Ashes* magazine, 1990-91, published for Sky Television by Murdoch Magazines; and recently as editor of *Sports* Magazine, published by SLM.

Contents

A very warm welcome back. Ieuan Evans takes the accolades for the victory in the Five Nations. It was later reported that he even managed a smile...

Editor's Notes

Welcome to the second edition of the *Almanack*. Rugby has continued to grow in world importance although it still needs a world body more responsive to the demands now placed on every sector of the game. Otherwise, the game will break apart into professional and other ranks.

It has been a long season, too long perhaps. But there is the great prospect ahead of the third World Cup in South Africa in 1995. The northern hemisphere was visited by arguably the two best sides in the world – Australia and New Zealand. Australia left with plaudits, New Zealand with fleas in their ears. Both sides were watched by record crowds throughout France, England and Scotland.

The season closed with South Africa in New Zealand. The South Africans pose problems because their game is too violent. They need to grow as a country before this will be irradicated. The failure of the International Rugby Football Board (IRFB) to stamp its authority on the game is also worrying. We repeat our call for a world authority with teeth.

The IRFB's position has been severely undermined by the decision of the International Olympic Committee (IOC) that, if the Millennium Olympic Games in Sydney favour rugby as a show sport, the Fédération International de Rugby (FIRA), not the IRFB, will be the organisers. This means that the millions of pounds (sterling) available to rugby through the Olympic Solidarity funds will be channelled via FIRA not IRFB. This is an absurd situation but it gives the French a tremendous bargaining position.

Juan Samaranch, the IOC president, is a skilful politician, a man the world of rugby lacks. He will not be IOC president in 2000. The chances are that either Dick Pound of Canada or Kevan Gosper of Australia will be. It is time the IRFB appointed a full-time officer to monitor the Olympics if they are serious about making it an Olympic sport.

As for the French, they have stolen the IRFB's thunder for the moment. Since Marcel Martin is on the RWC 1995 board this suggests that the French Fédération de Rugby do not like either the role he has undertaken to date or the way the IRFB works.

Throughout the 1993-94 season, rugby was in danger of dividing into several camps, on different fronts.

THE LAWS: There was the on-going row about the turnover law: the New versus the Old.

WORLD CUP: There was the British-led campaign to try to move the 1995 Rugby World Cup from South Africa to back home.

NORTH v SOUTH: There was the feeling as the season developed that countries in the southern hemisphere were moving faster than their northern counterparts. The quality of play of the national sides from South Africa, Australia and New Zealand bore this out. Only England presented any serious challenge to their hegemony, and in a strictly restricted way.

PROFESSIONALISM: There was growing concern over the professionalism at the upper echelons of the game; this was another example of the north-south divide.

REFEREES: As standards of refereeing around the world sank to new depths, there was a call for the establishment of a small elite group of referees to be paid for their work, rather like the system that operates with the leading tennis umpires. Other equally important issues included:

● Illegal drugs continued to pervade the game, especially in South Africa.

● The law of the land has begun to make its presence felt in various countries. In New South Wales the Australian Rugby Union did not contest a case from Brett Papworth, a former Rugby League player who wanted to return to play Union again. Stuart Evans, a former Welsh Union player who turned League and wants to return to the "amateur" game, was still battling to be reinstated as we went to press in July. He was threatening to sue the IRFB.

● The status of the IRFB which now looks as if it has decided against policing the game.

● The lack of public accountability with regard to financial matters.

● The change in the television market-place. (*See Review, Section 6*)

KEEP TAKING THE TABLETS

The IRFB is the law-making council for the world-wide game, although no players or coaches sit on the Board. A sub-committee on the laws makes recommendations to the main board, which seems to make changes largely because of the pressure on the game from Rugby League in New Zealand and Australia.

Two years ago, a law was changed that has altered the game so much that Union has become a laughing stock – especially and ironically among the Rugby League community. This is the "turn-over" law. If a player is caught in possession and cannot go down on the ground to create a ruck, the referee must call a scrum and the put-in goes to the opposition. Even if the player has gathered a ball and made 15 metres, if he cannot release it, he is penalised.

As a result, fly-halves have become more predominantly kickers. The ball is won at the line-out, and kicked up in the air in the general direction of the opposing full-back. He is engulfed and prevented from playing the ball and so the attacking team win the scrum.

In fairness, this has been compounded by a change to the penalty law. Now teams are penalised twice for one offence: first, a penalty kick is awarded against them; if the ball is kicked into touch, the other side has the throw-in at the line-out as well. So a side can control a game by playing the line-outs and kicking from the fly half. Calamity!

Both laws should be withdrawn immediately. The turn-over law is an affront to natural justice; the side making every attempt to go forward should win the scrum. The old penalty law should be re-instated. If a side continues to infringe a law, the referee should be allowed to give a penalty in front of the posts, irrespective of where on the field the offence took place.

Unfortunately, the laws remain on the statute book until after the 1995 World Cup.

THE 1995 RUGBY WORLD CUP

There was a concerted attempt by rugby writers in the UK during the latter part of 1993 to try and move the rugby World Cup from South Africa.

This chorus of disapproval – combined with some violent scenes in the run-up to the South African General Election – bounced the IRFB into action. On the day before England arrived in South Africa in May 1994, and only two days after Nelson Mandela had been inaugurated as the first democratically elected President of South Africa, the IRFB announced that the alternative venue for the 1995 Rugby World Cup would be split among the four Home Unions – England, Ireland, Scotland and Wales – with the final at The National Stadium, Cardiff. They gained no marks for diplomacy and tact.

England's Stuart
Barnes. Definitely
NOT just another
kicking fly half

SOUTHERN HEMISPHERE V NORTHERN HEMISPHERE V BRITISH LIONS

Traditionally, the game has always been stronger in the southern hemisphere, in South Africa, New Zealand, and, more recently, Australia. Occasionally, France could claim some ascendancy in the north but nearly every time she toured she came unstuck. Wales had fine traditions at home but also struggled Downunder. England promised to deliver but seldom did so – despite historic wins in the early 1970s against South Africa and New Zealand and again in South Africa in June 1994. Only Australia, in the last decade, has caught up with her southern "neighbours".

One problem was that British Lions tours interfered with the developments of the northern sides. There may yet be a place for the Lions tours – but, for me, they are an anachronism.

The Lions effectively prevented the development of individual nations in the Home Unions. When the All Blacks or the Australians toured, they never played four Tests against the British Lions. They met the four Home Unions individually.

The Four Home Unions committee no longer serves the interests of the wider world. It probably never did. When England rightly asked for more money from the treasury chest of the television rights, Ireland, Scotland and Wales took umbrage. Yet, in the end England won because the argument against her was not strong.

England may have the odd hiccup in the Five Nations Championship – Wales and Ireland away in 1993, Ireland at home in 1994 – but she has set the standards for the past five years in the north. And to go on achieving, England must start to ask some hard questions about how they will take the game up to the Millennium?

Does England need the Five Nations? Or do

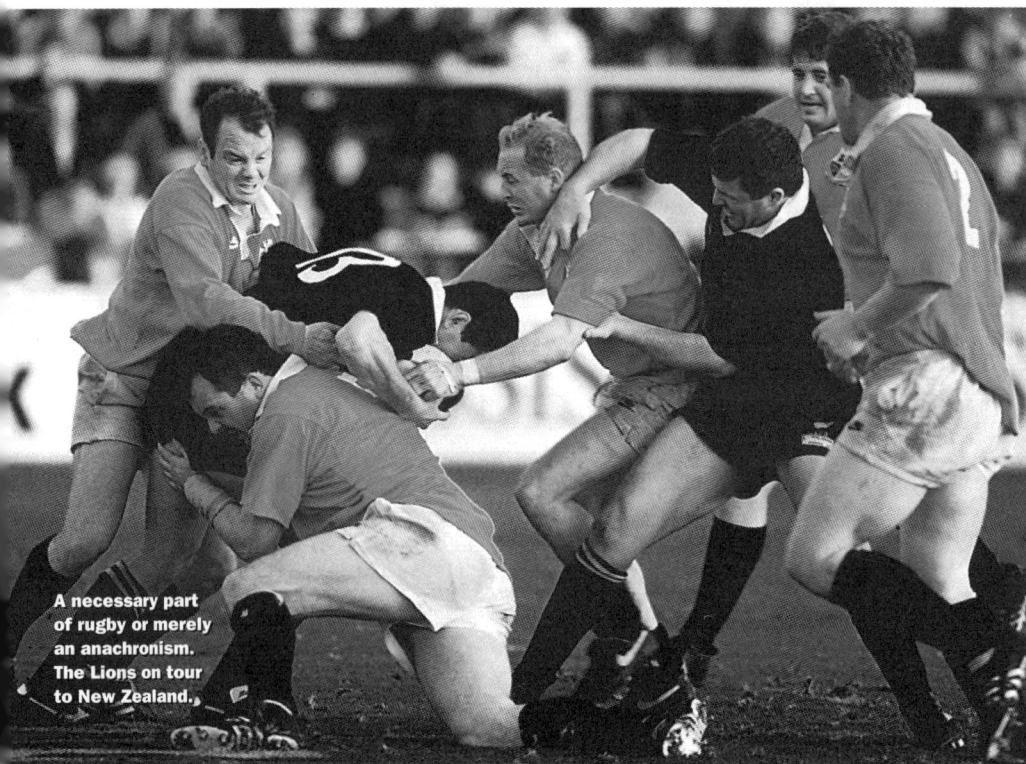

A necessary part of rugby or merely an anachronism. The Lions on tour to New Zealand.

the Five Nations need her more? Should she withdraw from the cosy cartel of the Four Home Unions and arrange her own incoming tour pattern? It may have been in the Four Home Unions interests to have signed a television contract for three, rather than a five, years; in retrospect it was certainly better for England. In 1998, they could and should go it alone.

PROFESSIONALISM

As the IRFB does not police the game world-wide, the nature and scale of the development of professionalism differs from one country to another. This may be unfair, but that's how it is. Could it be any other way? The IRFB is worried about its rights as the protector of the game in law. Around the world each union has a different atitude to what legally breaks the amateur code, and a sort of professional anarchy rules.

Talk to the players in New Zealand and Australia and the last thing on their mind is how much money they are making. Of course, they are glad to have some help from sponsors and supporters, considerable help in some cases. But the one thing they are united on is that they are thrilled that they are not one of the myriad run-of-the-mill League players running around scratching a living.

Rugby Union in both NSW and Queensland has positioned itself quite brilliantly. Players have immense status and have become household names. Children want to emulate them. This careful packaging has much to commend it.

In the Four Home Unions the situation is blurred and confused. This can only be to the detriment of the game. In France, all the international squad for 1993-94 had to sign a contract giving the French Fédération de Rugby the rights to exploit their name alongside that of the FFR. In England and Wales most of the leading players have agents. This situation should not have been allowed to develop; it does not serve the best interests of the game.

Since squash has gone "open" (and before it the likes of cricket, soccer, tennis) payment to a few leading players has not prevented us enjoying our league games or our friendlies. Has the game of squash been sullied by professionals – the Jonah Barringtons and Khans of this world? No, the game is better. Perhaps points are disputed over more frequently and the notion of winning has become more important than behaving with grace at the amateur level. But we are all richer for having a professional profile of the sport.

Would it matter if the leading rugby players were paid – despite all their protestations they do not want money for actually playing? They seem not to want to be paid; I am sure they do really. The game would change, and it would be for the better. Uncertainty, hypocrisy and "shamateurism" are themselves bad for the game, for the players and for the spectators.

At the moment rugby is the best team game in the world. Its spirit and culture make rugby people friends the world over within minutes of meeting. Would we put this at risk if players were paid? I can't see any danger. Another fear is that paying players would automatically make it possible for Rugby League players to play Union. Do we want this? Yes!

From my point of view, Rugby League is a good game. Their set piece occasions at the Wembley Cup finals are almost always marvellous spectacles of tough sport and sporting crowds. The 1994 final when Wigan beat Leeds was a superb game – and completely outshone the

> ## Would it matter if the leading rugby players were paid – despite all their protestations they do not want money for actually playing? I doubt it . . .

Jon Callard sports what could have been a career ending injury. Empowering the referees, with the aid of television, will help eradicate foul play and violence whilst allowing spectators a fuller understanding of the referee's decisions

dull and desperately disappointing Pilkington Cup final between Bath and Leicester. Rugby players should be allowed to speak the same language – to each other – and it is ridiculous that players are banned from Union if they play amateur League after the age of 18. This Union hypocrisy must be buried. We do need the IRFB to be in control of the Union game world-wide – more than the MCC who are merely upholders of cricket law. This may take another four or five years before the IRFB are given the powers to do so. Into this vacuum may yet step professional rugby, Packer-style circuses. Let us hope not.

> # It is a sad indictment of modern sport that making it more professional opens the door for cheats...

vision microphones so that their decisions can be relayed to commentators who can then best interpret them to the television audience.

Lucky them. Meanwhile, the luckless paying spectators are left completely in the dark.

Other sports – American football, baseball and even cricket – have used television cameras to help as an additional arbiter, but rugby is stalled in the slow lane. We need greater experimentation; we congratulate the RFU's Don Rutherford on his work in this area to date and trust it will bear fruit.

We must give unions the chance to use two referees per game, wire them up for the spectators, as per American football, and give them access to the television. Finally, we must pay a fully professional troupe of referees to ensure the best referees referee.

REFEREEING

The *1994 Almanack* was remiss in not addressing the problem of international refereeing. Where are the best administered sports in the world? In America. The National Football League has set all the modern day parameters – contracts, television coverage, professionalism, medical back-up, ownership, franchises and media friendly administrators and players.

Baseball, basketball and ice-hockey have all followed the NFL pattern. Indeed, the National Basketball Association has done so well it has lifted the game into second place in America behind the American Football.

However, Rugby Union is so poorly administered that it is no surprise that the game has failed to take advantage of television. At international level, rugby has the most players on the field at any one time (30) of any game in the world. It also is the only game of its numbers with one single arbiter – the two linesmen can intervene but their role is restricted.

In some countries, rugby referees wear tele-

DRUGS & THE LAW

It is a sad indictment of modern sport that making it more professional opens the door for cheats. It has always been the case since the 19th century, when boxers and cyclists used to take drugs to aid their endurance; and even going back to athletes in the ancient Greek Olympic Games.

Now, especially in South Africa, drugs are allegedly a currency among top rugby players. Testing to Olympic standards (post 1984) must be an integral part of the 1995 Rugby World Cup. If any player is found using a banned substance, his **team** must be disqualified.

Rumours about drug-taking is part of the culture of sport. Where one drug taker is found guilty there are normally another 10 or so participating. Rugby must be vigilant so that it does not go the way of American football, or Athletics. If the IRFB is to grow as a truly world body then it must be brave and start to bring all the constitutions in line with natural justice. Vernon Pugh QC is the new chairman of the IRFB and, hopefully, he will bring his presence to bear. Without question the game of rugby needs one set of laws for the sport to be universally agreed.

THE IRFB AND VIOLENCE

Philip de Glanville did not enjoy having his face violently re-arranged in the SW England fixture against the All Blacks. Jonathan Callard suffered a severe gash to his cheek playing for England against Eastern Province when he was raked twice by a brutal boot: the wound required a total of 25 stitches. The fuss over these incidents and the protracted row that ensued should have been settled by an IRFB mechanism. It is clearly daft to restrict complaints from either side having to be made within 48 hours.

Ian Beer, President of the RFU, was present when Callard was injured and Tim Rodber was sent off in South Africa against Eastern Province. Rodber should have received an automatic one match ban; after all some sides have banned their players for six weeks to a year for being sent off in a club game!

England refused to face the music and they were deservedly beaten in the second Test. Aparently, behind the scenes, the players made clear that if Rodber was suspended, they would not play the second Test. The RFU should have stood up and said, "so be it". They no longer can claim they run the game or occupy the high ground. The power has passed to the players; a quite disgraceful situation.

TOURS TO THE HOME UNIONS

The end-of-tour fixture between the Barbarians and the touring team should stop. Let's make that fixture worth something and allow the tourists to play the Lions, with a proper period of preparation for both sides.

Cricket tourists to England start at Arundel by playing a Duke of Norfolk's XI. Let's allot the opening fixture of a rugby tour to a charitable fund for a match at Twickenham between the tourists and the Penguins or a Past & Present Oxford & Cambridge XV.

AND FINALLY...

We apologise for some of the errors that crept into our first edition. Some were our fault, some were not – in a few instances we were provided the names of club officers from the wrong years or even before they had been elected. Apologies none the less. We hope by changing our system this year that we have put right last year's mistakes.

Please keep writing. We have enjoyed your letters. We have been most heartened by the overseas interest in the *Almanack* and we hope you will notice the subsequent improvement in information.

This year's Order of the Brown Nose goes to the BBC for giving the England XV the Team of the Year Award. All they did was lose to Wales and Ireland, even if they did beat the All Blacks. Consider poor old Wigan – a mere six Rugby League premier titles, four combined premier and Challenge Cup wins and three trebles – championship, premier and cup – in five years, and that was before this year's treble! And what about the women's England cricket team who won the World Cup?

Wish of the Year for 1995...? That all Rugby Unions make their accounts available to the general public; accountability is the key for our sport if we want to retain its unique spirit.

Enjoy your rugby in World Cup year.

Derek Wyatt
London
August 1994 ■

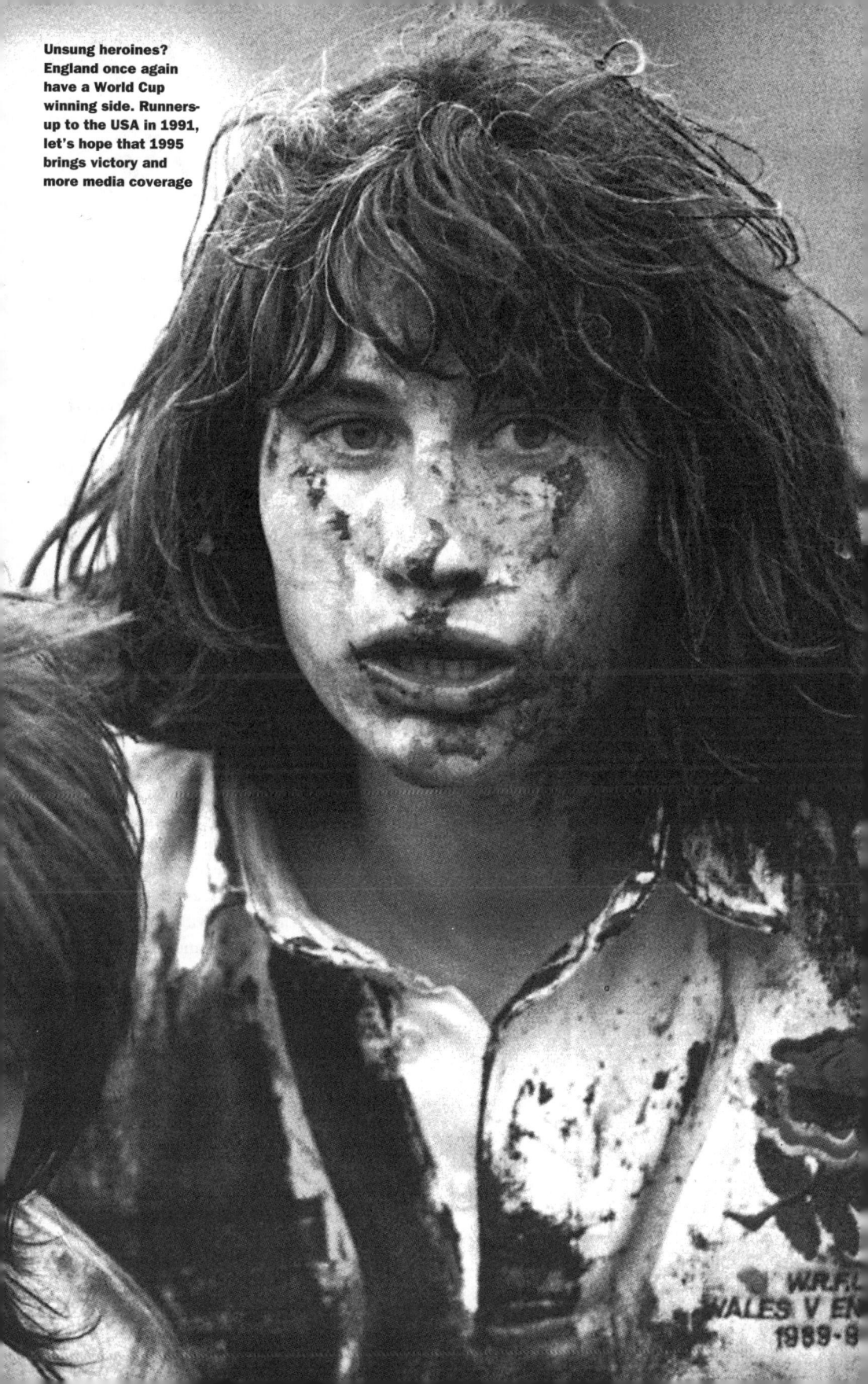

Unsung heroines? England once again have a World Cup winning side. Runners-up to the USA in 1991, let's hope that 1995 brings victory and more media coverage

WR.FU
WALES V EN
1989-9

1994-95 Awards

In soccer it is no longer a novelty for a player to win a century of caps; in rugby it has never been done before until that remarkable Agen centre, Philippe Sella, accomplished it on 26 June 1994. We offer to him our heartiest congratulations and have no hesitation in making him one of our Players of the Year. This year, four of the players are backs; and three of them are fly-halves. Michael Lynagh's bones may be creaking and his brain may be beginning to hurt but his game just gets better and better as those of us who were lucky enough to see his performance in Paris against France can confirm. Eric Elwood and Gareth Rees are by comparison relative newcomers but share that common bond of brilliance that can change a game in a trice.

Dean Richards is much like cricketer David Gower in his approach to the game – if not his physique – both men prefer to play rather than attend nets or practice. How Richards has played over the past decade. When he is missing from the England pack, it tends to lose or play well below par. When he plays it is as if he is everywhere the ball is, as if there are really two Richards' playing in the same game ■

PLAYERS AND TEAMS OF THE YEAR

Philippe Sella

Agen & France

ONE OF THE GREATEST rugby players of all time, Philippe Sella became the world record holder for caps in 1993 and won his 100th cap against New Zealand in June 1994.

Born on St Valentine's Day in 1962, he was spotted by Agen and played in their championship winning team at the age of 20. He started as a full back and scored a try in his first game.

First capped against Romania in 1982, Sella scored two tries on the right wing in his second international against Argentina. His first match in the Five Nations was against England at Twickenham in January 1983. Between 1982 and 1987 he played in 45 consecutive games for his country and, in winning 67 caps up to 1990, he only missed one international. Subsequently he has made his name as a centre and his 16-game partnership with Cordoniou for France was one of the all-time great pairings.

There were two milestones: in 1986, when he scored a try in every Five Nations game, and, when he was a member of the first French team to beat the All Blacks. In the following year he helped France achieve a Grand Slam and reach the final of the World Cup.

His colleagues know Sella as the ultimate team player who possesses great humility for a man of his considerable talents. He plays the game for the joy of it. Sella is a magnificent all-rounder; in attack he makes a break or appears in support with equal facility, while in defence his covering and tackling are formidable.

Michael Lynagh

Benetton Treviso, Queensland University and Australia

MICHAEL LYNAGH took most of the 1993 season off. He missed Australia's games against New Zealand and the Tests against South Africa. A difference in diagnosis was what caused the likeable Lynagh to take time out.

In Italy it was something muscular which was not so far off the mark; in Australia it was found to be a hernia. He returned in time, thankfully, for the Australian tour to North America and France as captain. 'Noddy' Lynagh is not a natural leader. He is a quiet and reflective character away from the game and lets his passing and kicking do the talking – and how it has talked.

Lynagh has been the central part of Australia's remarkable 10-year domination of international rugby. What will they do when he retires, as he will surely do after the 1995 Rugby World Cup?

Once restored to the Australian side he saw them through wins (just) against America, and more easily against Canada. After a disappointing first Test in Bordeaux, he contributed completely to the rout of the French in Paris with a devastating display of running rugby. That's right, running rugby, despite the craziness of the current laws.

Bob Dwyer devised a set of tactics that could win by playing an attacking game. The French were astounded. Back home, he saw Queensland home in the SuperTens final against Natal and then led Australia to a comprehensive two-Test victory against Ireland. He played in the first game of their close run series win against Italy, though injury prevented him from playing in the second Test.

Lynagh is a year round player who spends increasing amounts of time in Treviso, Italy, playing for Benetton.

Eric Elwood

Lansdowne and Ireland

ERIC ELWOOD burst on the scene in the middle of the 1993 Five Nations season and had an immediate impact on the Irish fortunes, helping them to a win away at the Arms Park. Then he steered them to a brilliant win against a tired looking English side. He kicked assuredly from the hand and seemed to revel in the additional pressure of place-kicking which he took in is stride.

He must have been mortified when he found out that the two Lions fly-halfs places went to Barnes and Andrew. Yet, this didn't stop him leading a motley collection of Irish sevens players to the semi-finals of the World Sevens where they should have beaten their old enemy, Australia.

It is customary for a player to enjoy one season of the Five Nations and then find he is a marked man. Not Elwood. His second season was equally successful even if he was prone to kick too much in the opening encounter against France at the Parc – though that was probably under orders.

Against England at Twickenham he was magnificent. Here is a fly half playing most of the time behind a retreating set of forwards but still stamping his authority on the game.

He is set to be one of the all-time greats but needs to take his considerable talent to a club side in France or England. At international level he is always likely to be playing behind a struggling pack.

Dean Richards

Leicester and England

IF RUGBY UNION internationals had their own players' association, the man who would continually come top of their poll for being the players' player would be Dean Richards, the very much larger than life copper from Hinckley, Leicestershire.

Richards was first capped in 1986, scoring two tries on his debut against Ireland. Since then he would have been most people's first choice but a recurring injury to his shoulder has stopped him from gaining even more caps. He went on the Lions Tours of 1989 and 1993 and played in all six Tests.

He has an uncanny knack of always being where the ball is. He may not have the build of a truly great Number 8, and he's never found training a very stimulating exercise, but he is simply the best. It would be sad for the game if he could not find the personal inspiration to make the RWC 1995 in South Africa.

Gareth Rees

Oxford University, Oak Bay Castaways, Newport and Canada

MUCH HAS ALREADY been documented about Gareth Rees because he was educated at Harrow and played in a Cup Final for Wasps against Bath while still at school. But he was born in Duncan, in British Columbia and attended St Michael's University School before winning a sixth form place in England.

He failed to gain a place at a British University and so plumped instead for the University of Victoria back on Vancouver Island. He kept his contacts with Oxford University open and played for the Major Stanley's XV in 1989; by 1993 he was a post-graduate. In the meantime he had also graduated to the full Canadian side and played in the World Cups of 1987 and 1991. He has earned his place in history for it was his last-second kick at the Arms Park against Wales in November 1993 that gave Canada their first win against Wales by 26-24.

He is probably the best built fly half in the world and has basketball-like skills and a vision that will make him one of the most talked about players in the game. He has that touch of arrogance which is so critical to a player in his position and delights in taking conversions from the right side of the pitch with his left foot and from the left side with his right foot. Talent indeed.

In the Summer of 1994, he kicked all 18 points to see Canada record their first victory against the French by 18-16 and he also kicked all of Canada's points a week later when they succumbed to Wales 15-33.

Wales

Winners Five Nations Championship '94

HIP HIP HOORAY, THE WELSH ARE BACK.
Who would have doubted it? Well, if you were Welsh watching the national side fumble to defeat against Canada in November you would have pondered whether they would beat Spain in the play-offs for the 1995 World Cup in May 1994.

Confidence has come back in bundles and, while their reserve forward cover is slight, how good it has been to see them playing

more like their old selves. They played brilliantly in their defeat of France, and poor Scotland got their deserved come-uppance.

Wales went to Twickenham with the chance of a Grand Slam and, although somewhat out-gunned by England on the day, they bravely kept the score down so that they won the Five Nations Cup with a superior points difference.

In the Summer recess, they beat Portugal and Spain comprehensively before setting their sights a little higher with wins against Canada, Fiji, and Tonga; although they lost, at the end of an exhausting tour, to Western Samoa, the one game they would have loved to win.

Bath

League and Cup Double '94; Middlesex Sevens Winners '94

BATH BID GOOD-BYE to their coach Jack Rowell with yet another double, to go alongside those won in 1989 and 1992. And for good measure, they also won the Middlesex Sevens.

Their league result was never really in doubt but the Cup victory was a dour game in front of a record crowd of 68,000 for a club game. The spectators deserved better.

Brian Ashton now assumes the mantle. In my view, Bath really needed someone of the calibre of Pierre Villepreux or Bob Dwyer to take the side up another notch. Still, they have set the trends for a decade and have only been matched by Liverpool FC, Wigan RFL and Essex CCC. Some company.

Dunvant

Promoted to Premier League, Wales 1993; retained membership 1994

DUNVANT NESTLES just outside Swansea. It has always had a strong rugby tradition but to be fair has always lived in the shadows of the big clubs. Indeed, that's where it would still be but for the introduction of leagues in Wales which have helped revitalise Welsh rugby. (Even so it is felt that too much club rugby is still being played).

In the first few home matches, the traffic jams were frequently two miles long as the demand grew to see a little bit of history . In the end, and just by a whisker, Dunvant stayed up having hovered near the bottom of the league for most of the season. This gallant small club has shown that anything is possible.

New Zealand (7-a-side)

Winner, Unofficial World Championship, Hong Kong '94

FOR A LONG TIME the Southern Hemisphere countries – Fiji, Tonga, Western Samoa, New Zealand and Australia – saw Sevens as a game for fast-track whippets. When they entered the field, it became their territory, except for that beautiful day at Murrayfield in 1993 when a scratch England side beat everyone to lift the World Cup. In

the 1994 Hong Kong Sevens New Zealand and
Australia contested the final. NZ won with a brand
of power Sevens of their own. Jonah Lomu, like
Martin Offiah who graced the tournament for the
Penguins in 1986, became the darling of the
crowd in 1994 with his precocious skills.

Toulouse

Winners French Championship '94

TOULOUSE ARE the great Beziers/Narbonnes sides of the 1960s rolled into one. They play an expansionist game with great flair. How sad it is that in the increasing politicisation of the game in France they are not flavour of the month and as a result, few of their players are selected at international level.

Even after France's magnificent series win in New Zealand in Summer 1994, the game is confused in some quarters. It may not be too long before the Jean-Pierre Rives/Denis Charvet/Pierre Villepreux axis comes to power. Then, and only then, will the French side blossom continuously.

In the meantime take time out to see this wonderfully friendly club side.

Dudley Wood

Secretary, RFU
1995 Administrator of the year

IN 1995 at the end of the Rugby World Cup, Dudley Wood retires from his position of Secretary of the Rugby football Union – or "president" as Henri Bru, rugby correspondent of *L'Equipe* put it.

He has created a profile for rugby that has at times had the media eating out of his hands. One of the funniest after-dinner speakers in the world, never volunteer to speak before him, he has taken the firmest grip on English rugby and of Twickenham itself.

It would a tribute to his stewardship if the odd 'gong' came his way. It would be a tribute, too, if the RFU named an aspect of the West Stand after him.

He may not have always endeared himself to the current England players for his stance over professionalism but he has been speaking for a much wider constituency who do not want to see the game change.

Vernon Pugh d.c.

Chairman, Welsh RU 1993-4

VERNON PUGH (above) has become an overnight success story in Wales but it has taken him 30 years to achieve such status. His own rugby career was modest when compared to the traditional figures that have reached the dizzy heights of Chairman of the WRU.

Pugh's rugby background embraced Amman Grammar School, Amman United, Downing College, Cambridge, and Leicester FC. He began life as a centre, though sometimes played fly-half, and his career ended playing for Cardiff High School Old Boys (now Cardiff Harlequins), St Peter's Cardiff and Pontypridd.

He retired in 1979 to spend "more time with his family" but you sense that the opportunities this presented – a diet of shopping and gardening – was never going to be sufficient for him. And sure enough, in the mid 1980s he began coaching CHSOB.

Sandwiched in-between this small love affair for the game was Pugh's own burgeon-

ing legal career. He was called to the Bar in 1969 and took Silk in 1986.

In 1991-2 he wrote the Pugh Report about the South African fiasco that split the Welsh Rugby Union. He has seen through the ups-and-downs of the various secretaries helping Wales through a very difficult period.

Further challenges beckon as he takes on the mantle of Chairman of the International Rugby Football Board.

Bob Dwyer

Australian National Coach 1981-4 and 1988-95

BOB DWYER (below) eats and sleeps rugby. Its been the making of him as a player and as of a man. He is easily the leading thinker on rugby today. Dwyer played 18 years at Randwick and took them to three successive premier-

ships in 1979, 1980 and 1981. He produced most of the players of the Grand Slam in 1984, including the Ella brothers who were from his own club, but Alan Jones was, by then, coach. After, Australia failed to win the inaugural World Cup in 1987, he replaced Jones, and Australian rugby has never looked back.

VISIONS OF RUGBY FOOTBALL

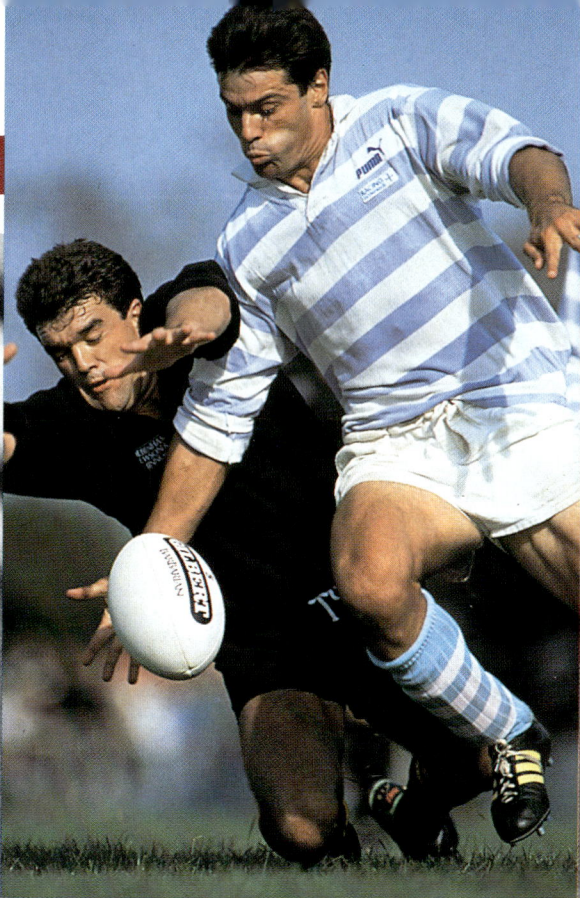

1994 WINNERS

PLAYERS
Neil Back – Leicester
Nick Farr-Jones – Sydney University & Australia
Andrew Harriman – Harlequins & England
Ben Clarke – Bath & England
Jean-Baptiste Lafond – Racing Club de France & France

CLUBS
Bath – League Champions, England
Llanelli – Cup and League Double, Wales
England 7s – winners Rugby World Sevens

France – winners Five Nations Championships
New Zealand – winners Lions Tests & Bledisloe Cup

COACH
Jack Rowell - Bath

ADMINISTRATORS
Steve Tshwete – South Africa ANC National Organiser
Bernard Lapasset – President French Federation de Rugby

SPECIAL AWARD
Derek Limmage – Leicester Groundsman

Will English fans have more to cheer about in the 1995 World Cup to be held in South Africa?

2. The World Cup

From a less than wholehearted beginning, the Rugby World Cup has transformed the image and worldwide status of the game. DEREK WYATT traces its development 10 years ago and looks forward to the 1995 event in South Africa

THE TREK TO THE TOP OF THE WORLD

The initiative for the Rugby World Cup came from New Zealand and Australia in 1984-85. They presented their case to the International Rugby Football Board (IRFB) who were less keen. It's worth remembering that in those far off days that England thought they were the centre of "everything rugby", whereas Wales **knew** they were at the centre of "everything rugby".

The IRFB was an undemocratic body – and still is today, even though there has been a movement to embrace Canada, Japan, Argentina and Italy. Then, it comprised England, Wales, Ireland, Scotland, France, Australia, New Zealand and South Africa (though she was *persona non grata* in almost every other sport in the world and had been banned from the Olympics in 1973).

The first World Cup was eventually given the green light though there were misgivings from the Scottish, the Irish and the English

> While no-one can doubt the success of both World Cups to date, the professional organisation of them has left a bad taste

Unions as to whether or not this would advance professionalism rather than the true cause of the game. So, the World Cup was successfully ambushed from the two unions Downunder. Australia needed a solution to prevent their best players from going League, and were also keen to keep the successful Grand Slam side of 1984 intact. They wanted a carrot for their players and a way for them to earn money, legitimately, from it. New Zealand did not fear the League game as much (how times have changed) but wanted to be the first country to host the final.

The organisation of the first World Cup in 1987 was difficult and compounded by the lack of a decision-making machine within the IRFB. Eventually, two companies bid to manage the event – West Nally and IMG. West Nally won by four votes to three. It was ultimately to contribute to their downfall and, after the cup was over, the company went into liquidation. The company established to run the competition was Rugby World Cup 1987 Pty, but has never

Rumours that it made a profit of £1.6 million simply do not add up...

made its accounts public.

Rumours that it made a profit of £1.6 million simply do not add up. In the early part of 1989, Rugby World Cup Ltd (the company formed for 1991) apparently had to seek "loans" from the then organisers, CPMA, to run the Italian pre-qualifying tournament and, it is alleged, for the deposit on the IRFB's new headquarters in Bristol.

While no-one can doubt the success of both World Cups to date, the professional organisation of them has left room for improvement. The accounts of the 1991 World Cup have also never been made public. Before rugby can become a truly global game its professional administrators need to be more accountable.

The second World Cup in 1991 raised the profile of the game considerably. Australia played a brand of rugby that made them many friends and they were popular winners. They also understood how the media operated and they worked with them. The All Blacks, the pre-World Cup favourites, certainly lost the media game by a land-slide.

The appointment of the company Keith Prowse Associates, which was eventually to be renamed CPMA, to run the 1991 Rugby World Cup, took the sports marketing and sponsorship companies completely by surprise. KPA was a small company which was "given" the rugby World Cup. At the beginning of 1989 it was tied-in to the larger Keith Prowse Agency. KPA had little experience of world sport, and certainly no experience of rugby, although it had run the Bell's Scottish Open golf tournament.

What compounded the situation was that in the middle of this hiatus it emerged that KPA/CPMA had received a piece of paper from John Kendall-Carpenter, the Chairman of RWC 1991, which apparently awarded them the rights to the World Cups for 1995, 1999 and 2003. Backstage, there has been much manoeuvring to try to ascertain the legal status of this letter. Unfortunately, we shall never know what was behind the motives of Kendall-Carpenter because he died in 1990.

Furthermore, the Keith Prowse Agency then went into receivership only weeks before the Cup began; it had been "awarded" the ticketing and hospitality rights. The company was already in a very serious financial position when it won the contract for the ticketing in the first place. The RWC 91 public relations company was Rushman Communications, which was awarded the rights, again against strong opposition. It was bought by CPMA later on.

We shall probably never know what happened off-the-field during the lead up to the 1991 World Cup. However, the IRFB made two critical errors for which rugby is still paying. One was to create a separate holding company for the rights to the World Cup for legal and taxation reasons; the other was to allow the organisers of the 1991 World Cup, CPMA, to hold future rights in the game.

All this was compounded when the 1995 World Cup was awarded to South Africa, a country that had been unable to participate in the 1987 and 1991 Cups because of the political stance of its minority government. It was a sop by the IRFB to Dr Danie Craven, its longest serving member. South Africa should have been made to wait its turn. Fortunately, democracy has now arrived in South Africa and it looks as though the Cup will go ahead without incident.

The paternalistic style of the IRFB meant that it would never have dreamt of offering the cup to Argentina, or accepting a combined bid from France and Italy, or Japan. FIFA, the equivalent soccer world authority, agreed to its World Cup going to America in 1994 and will probably award it to Japan in

2002, although neither country has a long tradition of the game.

Japan may have blown its only hope of hosting the Rugby World Cup. Shiggy Konno, the president of the Japanese Union, is very much yesterday's man in rugby circles. He may speak fluent English (he was brought up there) and believe the game is amateur in Japan, but that doesn't explain how the Ian Williams's of this world make a living in Japan, especially when the Japanese company these players are working for just so happens to have a rugby club in the premier division? Japan is no different from the rest of the world when it comes to creeping professionalism and it is time for Mr Konno to take action.

SOUTH AFRICA 1995

South Africa under the National Party was a secret country. Go and look at any map of the country and see how many townships you can find. Check if Soweto, just to the west of Johannesburg, is there. It's a city of five million people.

On second thoughts, don't bother, because you won't find Soweto. For some extraordinary reason, cartographers round the world have conspired to ensure that the view presented to you was for whites only. Our enquiries at the South African Embassy for such a map in July 1994 were referred to South Africa itself but, alas, none existed.

Of course, it would be asking too much to expect of our rugby administrators to be adept politicians. Yet on the day before England were due to arrive in South Africa, a mere eight days after the first democratic elections, they announced that if the World Cup had to be moved it would come back to the Four Home Unions. How many of them had been in South Africa during the election period? How many of them had studied the summary reports from the Human Rights Committee of South Africa on Repression?

South Africa is on a long upward learning curve. Its white, particularly its Afrikaner community has much to learn in the main because, sadly, it has been so ignorant of the rest of the world. In rugby, despite the formation of one union to cover all its people, there is a danger that its President, Louis Luyt, might use it as a play thing, rather like his predecessor, Danie Craven.

The game has been driven by an inept bureaucracy; its players have been paid for playing; drug-taking has been a feature and gone largely unchecked; and we must remember that the 1989 Centenary celebrations led to overseas players being paid £30,000 to represent the President's XV. All of this has also gone by, without public comment, the International Rugby Football Board.

The World Cup will be an overwhelming success, however. The reason? Television.

The animosity that exists between the various provinces makes *Straw Dogs* seem a picnic by comparison

Australia and New Zealand, are between eight and 12 hours ahead of GMT, but South Africa is only one hour ahead and two hours ahead of BST. Thus, its schedule of games in the afternoon and evening and at the weekends will ensure large audiences throughout Europe.

It may be too successful; in which case it will have hastened the day when the top echelon is fully professional. Certainly, if South Africa does not qualify for the final stages, we can expect the cheque book to come out to attract the top players to come and play for their provincial sides.

This would be the death knell for rugby there. The animosity that exists between the various provinces makes *Straw Dogs* seem a

In the European qualifiers, Wales achieved cricket scores of over 100 points against Portugal and a half-century against Spain

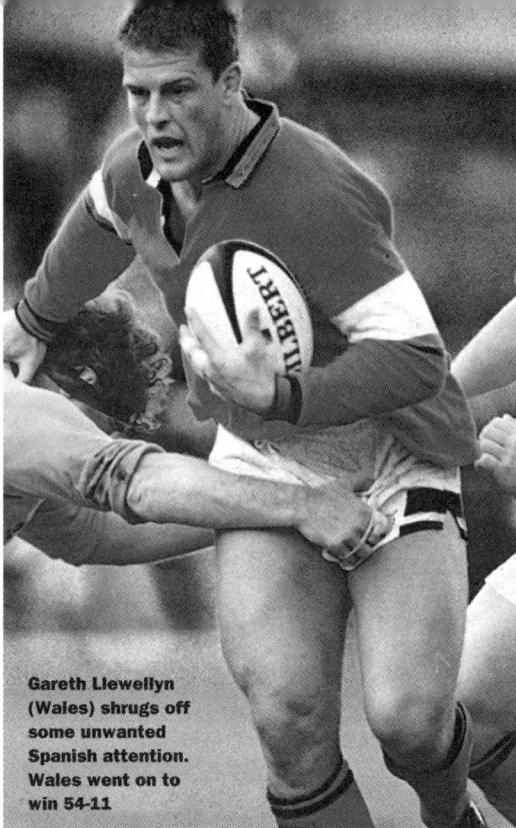

Gareth Llewellyn (Wales) shrugs off some unwanted Spanish attention. Wales went on to win 54-11

picnic by comparison. South Africa needs a strong club base to progress at international level.

The most important requirement for South Africa is for it to develop its rugby in the townships; by development we mean a long term financial commitment to secure the establishment of the game there. Short-termism is not the answer.

THE ROAD TO SOUTH AFRICA

The pre-qualifying games for the RWC 1995 began quietly in Andorra in October, 1992. The matches took the organising committee by surprise. We know that Andorra, Switzerland and Denmark turned up; we know that Luxembourg could not afford to travel and we know that Switzerland won the group.

Given that the profits of RWC 1991 were supposed to be over £6 million, why was Luxembourg denied the chance to play because its own union hadn't the money? Let's hope this sort of thing is not part of RWC 1999.

Altogether, 41 countries took part in the pre-qualifying tournament. From these, seven qualified for the finals to join the nine seeds. The seven were drawn from Europe (Wales, Italy and Romania), the Americas (Argentina), Africa and the Gulf States (Ivory Coast), Pacific Rim (Tonga), and the Far East (still to be decided).

Three countries who were present in 1991

lost out: the United States, because only one position was available in the Americas once Canada had pre-qualified; Fiji, who lost on points to Tonga in a two-game series (which was deeply unsatisfactory and we must hope that for 1999 two positions are made available); and Zimbabwe, who, like Namibia, just lost out to the Ivory Coast.

In 1999 only three countries will be automatic qualifiers, the two 1995 finalists and the winner of the play-off for third place. The host country will also be granted a place and should they have finished in the top three, there will only be three automatic qualifiers. Without Knowing the mechanics of the 1999 draw, the groups and the proposed itinerary of matches, it is too early to predict the demise of Lions tours or the Five Nations tournament, but clearly RWC 1999 will involve more matches.

It was premature to decide for 1999 that there would only be three, or possibly four seeds. The disparity between the old IRFB countries and the rest would make a mockery of the results and act as a disincentive to the game. The best solution would be to keep the seedings to eight – based on Tests from 1996-98 – and extend the tournament to 24 countries.

The 1995 World Cup started with Group 1, in Europe, where Switzerland pre-qualified to join Portugal, Spain, and Belgium in a four-way play-off with the first two going forward. From this group Portugal and Spain joined Wales in a three-way play-off in May 1994. This was convincingly won by Wales – with a cricket score of over 100 points against Portugal and a half-century against Spain. The Welsh still have to play the other two group winners in Europe to determine seeding.

In Europe Group 2, Germany and Russia emerged from their pre-qualifying groups to join Romania, who claimed their place in the finals. In Group 3, Israel, the Netherlands, and Czech Republic pre-qualified but could not stop Italy from going forward. So the seedings' play-offs in Autumn 1994 are:

Romania v Wales (17 Sept)

Italy v Romania (1 Oct)

Wales v Italy (12 Oct)

The winner will be seeded 11; the runner-up 15; and third place will be seeded 16.

In the Americas, Argentina pre-qualified to meet the United States, who had only to beat Bermuda. Argentina won the home and away play-offs and are seeded 10.

The Pacific Rim involved Tonga and Fiji. Tonga won through and are seeded 12. In Africa, Ivory Coast pre-qualified and go forward as 13th seeds. In Asia the ties between Taiwan, Hong Kong, Japan, South Korea, Sri Lanka, Thailand and Malaysia will be in Kuala Lumpur from 22-29 October, 1994. The winner will be seeded 14.

SEEDING FOR 1995

01. Australia

02. England

03. New Zealand

04. Scotland

05. France (9 points & 3 wins in 91)

06. Ireland (7 points 2 wins 1 loss; points difference 51)

07. W. Samoa (7 points 2 wins 1 loss; points difference 20)

08. Canada (7 points 2 wins 1 loss; points difference 12)

09. South Africa (host)

10. Argentina

11. Europe 1 (decided on 12 Oct)

12. Tonga

13. Ivory Coast

14. Asia (decided on 29 Oct)

15. Europe 2 (decided on 12 Oct)

16. Europe 3 (decided on 12 Oct)

Pool A is in Cape Town – at sea level – and involves top seeds Australia, with Canada, South Africa and seed 16 from the European play-offs between Wales, Italy and Romania. The first game of the finals on 25 May 1995 could be one to remember, South Africa v Australia.

England are top of Pool B, which is in Durban and is also at sea level, with Western Samoa, Argentina and seed 15 from Europe. England's first outing, on Saturday 27 May, is an early evening match against Argentina; while Scotland will have started against the Africa qualifier on the previous evening.

Then we climb 6,000 feet to Johannesburg for Pool C where we find New Zealand, Ireland, the winners of Europe play-offs (probably Wales) and seed 14 from Asia. Ireland and New Zealand meet in their first pool match on the opening Saturday.

Pool D, in Pretoria, is also 6,000 feet above sea level and puts together Scotland, France, Tonga and seed 13 from Africa. The critical element is that afternoon kick-off times will definately favour southern hemisphere sides. Games need to begin in the cool of the evenings. It looks to me as if the kick-off times have been scheduled for television's convenience not the players' ∎

1995 RUGBY WORLD CUP FORM GUIDE

AUSTRALIA

1987, finished 4th; 1991, winners

International Record 1993-4 v USA (a) w 22-18, v Canada (a) w 43-16, France (a) L 13-16; v France (a) w 24-3; v Ireland (h) w 33-13, v Ireland (h) w 32-18; v Italy (h) w 23-20; v Italy (h) w 20-7;

Number of clubs: 350+

Registered players: 12,000+

Suffered only four defeats since 1991: two to New Zealand in the Bledisloe Cup matches of 1992 and 1993 (though they won the 1992 series 2-1); South Africa (but won series 2-1) and one to France (drew series 1-1). Re-built the 1991 side though much still depends on Michael Lynagh; this will be his and David Campese's last world cup. Struggled to find a rhythm of any sort in 1994 and their itinerary leading to the finals will not have been taxing.

ENGLAND

1987, QF; 1991, runners up

IR 1993-4 v NZ w (h) 15-9; v Scotland (a) w 15-14; v Ireland (h) L 12-13; v France (a) w 18-14; v Wales (h) w 15-8; v SA (a) w 32-15; v SA (a) L 9-27;

Number of clubs: 1750+

Registered players: c400,000

They keep beating the best in the world - New Zealand, France and South Africa; they have avoided Australia since the 1991 World Cup final. However, against apparently lesser opposition, they have lost - to Wales and Ireland (twice). Jack Rowell has less than a year and only six matches to impose his authority as manager/coach.

NEW ZEALAND

1987, winners; 1991, third

IR 1993-4 v Scotland (a) w 51-15; v England (h) L 9-15; v France (h) L 8-22, v France (h) L 20-23;

Number of clubs: 1020+

Registered players: c190,000

There is a vulnerability about their play of late though on their day they are the best side in the world. They have lost five internationals since 1991 to Australia (twice), England, and France (twice).

SCOTLAND

1987, QF; 1991, fourth

IR 1993-4 v NZ (h) L 15-51; v Wales (a) L 6-29; England (h) L 14-15; v Ireland (a) D 6-6; v France (h) L 12-20; v Argentina (a) L 15-16 v Argentina (a) L 17-19

Number of clubs: 290

Registered players: 26,000

Lucky that their form in 1991 gives them fourth seed status which makes a mockery of their current world position; they have struggled to maintain any sort of consistency over the past three years and some of their best players are well past their sell-by-date.

IRELAND

1987, QF; 1991, fifth

IR 1993-4: v Romania (h) w 25-3; v France (a) L 15-35, v Wales (h) L 15-17; v England (a) w 13-12; v Scotland (h) D 6-6; v Australia (a) L 13-33; v Australia (a) L 18-32

Number of clubs: 60+

Registered players: c12,500

Ireland have been brave enough to tour both New Zealand and Australia since 1991 but have come away empty-handed; they always play above themselves in World Cups and could be a surprise though they may have to beat a resurgent Wales to qualify for the QF round.

WESTERN SAMOA

1987, not invited; 1991, sixth

IR 1993-4: v New South Wales L 23-25, v Waikato w 32-18, v Auckland w 15-13, v Natal L 26-48 (all SuperTen fixtures); v Wales w 34-9

Number of clubs: 90+

Registered players: c4,000

Desperately short of international competition despite being the success of the 1991 RWC; although they beat Wales at home in June 1994 they will have to beat Argentina and probably Italy to qualify for the QF. Difficult to predict.

FRANCE
1987, runners–up; 1991, seventh

IR 1993-4 v Romania (h) w 51-0; v Australia (h) w 16-13, v Australia (h) L 3-24; v Ireland (h) w 35-15; v Wales (a) L 15-24; v England (h) L 14-18; v Scotland (a) w 20-12; v Canada (a) L 16-18; v NZ (a); v NZ (a)
Number of clubs: c1,800
Registered players: 220,000+

France have much to prove but time is running out for them. They are in the weakest pool but will have to adjust to playing at altitude though their own training facilities at Font Romeu should stand them in good stead. A difficult side to predict – as they proved in June when they won a Test in New Zealand for the first time in 25 years and then took the series 2-0 by winning the second Test in July.

CANADA
1987, 1st Round; 1991, eighth

IR 1993-4 v Australia (h) L 16-43; Wales (a) w 26-24; v France (h) w 18-16; v Wales (h) L 15-33
Number of clubs: 230
Registered players: 12,000+
Tour plans 1994-5: Ireland, Wales, England, Scotland, France & Italy
Poor Canada, they have come on leaps and bounds since 1987 but have the toughest pool and will be lucky to survive the opening round.

SOUTH AFRICA
1987, not invited; 1991, not invited

IR 1993-4 v Argentina (a) w 29-26; v Argentina (a) w 52-23; v England (h) L 15-32; v England (h) w 27-9:
Number of clubs: 1,000
Registered players: c80,000
If the rugby World Cup has any pointers in its short history it is that the host sides do well; New

Zealand won it in 1987 (Australia trailed in fourth) and England were runners-up in 1991 (with Scotland fourth). Thus South Africa must stand a good chance of reaching the final. If they can tame their inherently violent attitude when the chips are down, they could win the tournament.

ARGENTINA
1987 1st Round; 1991 1st Round

IR 1993-4 v SA (h) L 26-29; v SA (h) L 23-52; v Chile (h) w 70-7; Uruguay (a) w 19-10; Paraguay (h) w 51-3; v USA (a) w 28-22; v Scotland (h) w 16-15; v Scotland (h) w 19-17; USA (h) w 16-11
Number of clubs: 200
Registered players: c17,000
Tour plans 1994-5: South Africa
Still struggling to maintain a presence in world rugby, Argentina will want to get past the first round for the first time and may just have the side to do it.

WALES
1987, 3rd Place; 1991, 1st Round

IR 1993-4 v Japan (h) w 51-0; v Canada (h) L 24-26; v Scotland (h) w 29-6; v Ireland (a) w 17-15; v France (h) w 24-15; v England (a) L 8-15; v Portugal (a) w 102-11; v Spain (a) w 54-0; v Canada (a) w 33-15 ; v Fiji (a) w 23-8; v Tonga (a) w 19-9; v Western Samoa (a) L 9-39
Number of clubs: 180
Registered players: 40,000+

Can a side have been better prepared than Wales who have played more internationals and blooded more players, except South Africa, since 1991? They now know their limitations and have game plans for different opposition, so that there is just a chance they might proceed to the QF in what for them could be a tough draw if they win the European play-offs in September and October.

TONGA
1987, 1st Round; 1991, didn't qualify

IR 1993-4 – toured NZ no Test played; v Wales L 9-18
Number of clubs: 70+

A Romanian player is shown the finer points of English tackling and stripped of the ball

Registered players: 2,500

Tonga, having missed out in 1991, are thrilled to be back in the big time, but they suffer like all the Pacific Island sides from a dearth of international competition.

IVORY COAST

1987, not invited; 1991, didn't qualify

IR 1993-4 v Morocco (a) w 15-3, v Tunisia (a) w 19-16, v Zimbabwe (a) w 17-10 , v Morocco (a) L 9-17, v Namibia (a) w 13-12;

Number of clubs: 15

Registered players: 2,700+

The surprise qualifier for the 1995 tournament, the Ivory Coast will have underdog status and be popular wherever they go; their success has to be built on for 1999 and for the game in Africa generally as it moves beyond the old colonial boundaries.

ITALY

1987, 1st Round; 1991, 1st Round;

IR 1993-4 v Czech Republic(h)w 104-8 (new RWC record), v Netherlands (h) w 63-9, v Australia (a) L 20-23; v Australia (a) L 7-20

Number of clubs: 270

Registered players: 15,000

Italy do not travel well unless it is to a country that shares their way of life. They have still to make the break-through in world terms but their tour to Australia must have given them a huge fillip.

ROMANIA

1987, 1st Round; 1991, 1st Round

IR 1993-4 v Ireland (a) L 3-25; v France (a) L 0-51; v Germany (h) w 60-6, v Russia (h) w 30-0

Number of clubs: 100

Registered players: 3,000+

Alas, Romania is still struggling to come to terms with her past and rugby has suffered. If she finishes last in the European play-offs she will qualify for Pool A and have to contemplate South Africa, Canada and Australia.....

THE QUALIFYING COMPETITION

LET THE GAMES BEGIN...

EUROPE

England, Ireland, Scotland & France qualified automatically (as quarter-finalists in 1991). Andorra, Luxembourg, Switzerland, Denmark, Portugal, Spain, Belgium, Germany, Lithuania, Russia, Wales, Latvia, Romania, Poland, the Czech Republic, Georgia, Hungary, Israel, The Netherlands, Sweden and Italy were all involved in the play-offs for three places.

The three qualifiers from Europe – Wales, Italy, and Romania – play one another to determine seedings for the finals in October, 1995. The winner is seeded 11th, the runner-up 15th, and the remaining country 16th.

ROUND 1: OCTOBER 1992, ANDORRA

ANDORRA, SWITZERLAND, LUXEMBOURG AND DENMARK.
Denmark 0 Andorra 3; Denmark 8 Switzerland 3;
Switzerland 14 Andorra 0
Luxembourg could not afford to attend; the winner was Switzerland who qualified for Round 2.

ROUND 2: 11-16 MAY, 1993, LISBON

PORTUGAL, SPAIN, BELGIUM AND SWITZERLAND
Spain 40 Switzerland 0; Belgium 3 Portugal 8;
Belgium 3 Spain 67; Portugal 32 Switzerland 0;
Belgium 42 Switzerland 3; Spain 37 Portugal 15
Portugal and Spain qualified for Round 3.

ROUND 3: 18, 21 MAY 1994, LISBON & MADRID

PORTUGAL, SPAIN AND WALES
Portugal 11 Wales 102; Spain 0 Wales 54;
Spain 35 Portugal 19

Wales qualified for the 1995 finals (but must play off against the other two European qualifiers to determine the seedings).

ROUND 4: 1, 8, 29 MAY 1993, BERLIN, RIGA & SIAULIA

GERMANY, LATVIA AND LITHUANIA
Germany 31 Lithuania 5; Latvia 5 Germany 27;
Lithuania 6 Latvia 7
Germany qualified for Round 6.

ROUND 5: 25-29 MAY 1993, GDANSK, POLAND

RUSSIA, GEORGIA AND POLAND
Russia 15 Georgia 9; Poland 23 Georgia 6;
Russia 41 Poland 5
Russia qualified for Round 6.

ROUND 6: 2-7 MAY 1994, ROMANIA

ROMANIA, RUSSIA AND GERMANY
Romania 60 Germany 6; Russia 67 Germany 5;
Romania 30 Russia 0
Romania qualified for the 1995 finals but must play off against the other two Pool winners to determine seedings.

ROUND 7: 30 MAY 1993, BUDAPEST

HUNGARY, ISRAEL
Hungary 8 Israel 67
Israel qualified for Round 8.

ROUND 8: 31 OCT – 6 NOV 1993, AMSTERDAM

ISRAEL, NETHERLANDS, CZECH REPUBLIC, SWEDEN
Netherlands 31 Sweden 6; Netherlands 56 Israel 0
Czech Republic 6 Netherlands 44;
Czech Republic 38 Israel 0;

Czech Republic 34 Sweden 7; Israel 10 Sweden 26

Netherlands and The Czech Republic went through to Round 9.

ROUND 9: 15 – 21 MAY 1994, ITALY

ITALY, NETHERLANDS, THE CZECH REPUBLIC

Netherlands 33 Czech Republic 9; Italy 104 Czech Republic 8; Italy 63 Netherlands 9

Italy qualifies for the 1995 finals but must play off against the Pool winners of Rounds 3 & 6 to determine the final seedings. Winner seeded 11th, runner up seeded 15th, third place seeded 16th.

SEEDINGS FIXTURES

17 Sept: Romania v Wales, Bucharest
1 Oct: Italy v Romania, Italy
12 Oct: Wales v Italy, Cardiff

THE AMERICAS

Canada qualified as quarter finalists in 1991.

26 SEPT – 23 OCT 1993

CHILE, PARAGUAY, URUGUAY, ARGENTINA, AMERICA & BERMUDA

Chile 24 Paraguay 25; Paraguay 3 Uruguay 67; Uruguay 14 Chile 6; Argentina 70 Chile 7; Argentina 51 Paraguay 3; Uruguay 10 Argentina 19; Bermuda 3 USA 60

FINALS:

USA 22 Argentina 28 (Long Beach California, 28 May 1994); Argentina 16 USA 11 (Buenos Aires, 16 June 1994)

Argentina qualified, seeded 10th.

ASIA

One qualifier, seeded 14th.

22-29 OCT 1994, KUALA LUMPUR

TAIWAN, HONG KONG, JAPAN, SOUTH KOREA, SINGAPORE, SRI LANKA,

THAILAND AND MALAYSIA.

In 1991, Japan won through; South Korea reached the 1993 World Sevens finals

PACIFIC RIM

Australia, New Zealand & Western Samoa qualified as quarter finalists in 1991.

FIJI AND TONGA: 12 JUNE 1993, SUVA; AND 17 JULY 1993, NUKU'ALOFA

Fiji 11 Tonga 24; Tonga 10 Fiji 15

Tonga qualified and were seeded 12th.

AFRICA

South Africa qualified as the host country, seeded 9th.

POOL 1: 3-10 JULY 1993, NAIROBI, KENYA

KENYA, THE GULF STATES, ZIMBABWE, NAMIBIA, TUNISIA, MOROCCO AND THE IVORY COAST

Kenya 7 Zimbabwe 42; Namibia 64 Gulf States 20; Kenya 9 Namibia 60; Zimbabwe 50 Gulf States 21; Namibia 44 Zimbabwe 16

Namibia and Zimbabwe qualified for the final Africa round to be played in Casablanca.

POOL 2: 26-30 OCTOBER 1993, TUNISIA

Tunisia 16 Ivory Coast 19; Tunisia 5 Morocco 6; Ivory Coast 15 Morocco 3

The Ivory Coast and Morocco qualified for the final Africa round.

FINAL AFRICA ROUND (In Casablanca)

Ivory Coast 17 Zimbabwe 10; Morocco 16 Namibia 16; Ivory Coast 13 Namibia 12; Morocco 9 Zimbabwe 21; Morocco 17 Ivory Coast 9; Namibia 25 Zimbabwe 20.

Ivory Coast will play in pool D of the World Cup alongside Scotland, France and Tonga. They start their World Cup campaign against Scotland on Friday 26 May. Morocco could have qualified by beating Namibia in the last game; they levelled the score after being 0-16 down, but were let down by their kicking.

THE FINAL POOLS

Pool A (Cape Town): *Australia, Canada, South Africa and seed 16 (Europe 3)*

Pool B (Durban): *England, Western Samoa, seed Argentina and seed 15 (Europe 2)*

Pool C (Johannesburg): *New Zealand, Ireland, seed 11 (Europe 1) and seed 14 (Asia 1)*

Pool D (Pretoria): *Scotland, France, Tonga and Ivory Coast*

THE EDITOR'S PREDICTIONS

QUARTER FINALS:
Argentina v Western Samoa
France v Wales
England v South Africa
New Zealand v Scotland

SEMI-FINALS:
Australia v France
South Africa v New Zealand

FINAL:
Australia v South Africa

WORLD CUP FIXTURES FOR 1995

THURSDAY 25 MAY
Pool A: Australia v SA, 14.30, Cape Town

FRIDAY 26 MAY
Pool A: Canada v Europe 3 Qualifier, 15.00, Port Elizabeth,
Pool D: Scotland v Ivory Coast, 16.00, Rustenburg; France v Tonga, 18.00, Pretoria

SATURDAY 27 MAY
Pool B: Western Samoa v Europe 2 Qualifier, 13.00, East London; England v Argentina, 17.00, Durban
Pool C: Europe 1 Qualifier v Asia, 15.00, Bloemfontein; New Zealand v Ireland, 20.00, Johannesburg

TUESDAY 30 MAY
Pool A: South Africa v Europe 3 Qualifier, 14.30, Cape Town
Pool B: Western Samoa v Argentina, 12.30, East London
Pool D: France v Ivory Coast, 18.00, Rustenburg; Scotland v Tonga, 20.00, Pretoria

WEDNESDAY 31 MAY
Pool A: Austalia v Canada, 13.00, Port Elizabeth
Pool B: England v Europe 2 Qualifier, 17.00, Durban
Pool C: Ireland v Asia, 15.00, Bloemfontein; New Zealand v Europe 1, 20.00, Johannesburg

SATURDAY 3 JUNE
Pool A: Australia v Europe 3 Qualifier, 1500, Stellenbosch; Canada v South Africa, 20.00, Port Elizabeth

Pool D: Tonga v Ivory Coast, 13,00, Rustenburg; Scotland v France, 17.00, Pretoria

SUNDAY 4 JUNE
Pool B: Argentina v Europe 2 Qualifier, 13.00, East London; England v Western Samoa, 20.00, Durban
Pool C: New Zealand v Asia, 15.00, Bloemfontein ; Ireland v Europe 1 Qualifier, 17.00, Johannesburg

QUARTER FINALS; SATURDAY 10 JUNE
(E) Winners Pool D v Runner-Up Pool C, 13.00, Durban
(F) Winners Pool A v Runner-Up Pool B, 15.00, Johannesburg

SUNDAY 11 JUNE
(H) Winners Pool B v Runner-Up Pool A, 13.00, Cape Town
(G) Winners Pool C v Runner-Up Pool D, 15.00, Pretoria

SEMI FINALS; SATURDAY 17 JUNE
Winners E v Winners F, 14.30, Durban

SUNDAY 18 JUNE
Winners G v Winners H, 14.30, Cape Town

THIRD PLACE PLAY-OFF
Thursday 22 June, 14.30, Pretoria

FINAL
Saturday 24 June, 1430, Johannesburg

WORLD CUP RESULTS 1987 & 1991

1987

Held in New Zealand and Australia from 22 May to 20 June

Pool 1

23 May
Sydney
Australia 19 England 6

24 May
Brisbane
US 21 Japan 18

30 May
England 60 Japan 7

31 May
Brisbane
Australia 47 USA 12

3 June
England 34 USA 6

3 June
Sydney
Australia 42 Japan 23

Pool 2

24 May
Napier
Canada 37 Tonga 4

25 May
Wellington
Wales 13 Ireland 6

29 May
Palmerston North
Wales 29 Tonga 16

30 May
Dunedin
Ireland 46 Canada 19

3 June
Brisbane
Wales 40 Canada 9

3 June
Brisbane
Ireland 32 Tonga 9

Pool 3

22 May
Auckland
New Zealand 70 Italy 6

24 May
Hamilton
Fiji 28 Argentina 9

27 May
Christchurch
New Zealand 74 Fiji 13

28 May
Argentina 25 Italy 16

31 May
Dunedin
Italy 18 Fiji 15

31 May
Dunedin
New Zealand 46
Argentina 15

Pool 4

23 May
Auckland
Romania 21 Zimbabwe 20

23 May
Christchurch
Scotland 20 France 20

28 May
Wellington
France 55 Romania 12

30 May
Dunedin
Scotland 60 Zimbabwe 21

2 June
Auckland
France 70 Zimbabwe 12

2 June
Dunedin
Scotland 55 Romania 28

Pool 1 Final Table 1987

	P	W	D	L	F	A	Pts
Australia	3	3	0	0	108	41	6
England	3	2	0	1	100	32	4
US	3	1	0	2	39	99	2
Japan	3	0	0	3	48	123	0

Pool 2 Final Table 1987

	P	W	D	L	F	A	Pts
Wales	3	3	0	0	82	31	6
Ireland	3	2	0	1	84	41	4
Canada	3	1	0	2	65	90	2
Tonga	3	0	0	3	29	98	0

Pool 3 Final Table 1987

	P	W	D	L	F	A	Pts
New Zealand	3	3	0	0	190	34	6
Fiji	3	1	2	0	56	101	4
Italy	3	1	0	2	40	110	2
Argentina	3	1	0	2	49	90	2

Pool 4 Final Table 1987

	P	W	D	L	F	A	Pts
France	3	2	1	0	145	44	6
Scotland	3	2	1	0	135	69	4
Romania	3	1	0	2	61	130	2
Zimbabwe	3	0	0	3	53	151	0

Qtr FINALS

6 June
Christchurch
New Zealand 30
Scotland 3
(NZ: Tries - A Whetton, Gallagher; Conv - Fox 2; PG - Fox 6. Scotland: PG - G Hastings)

7 June
Sydney
Australia 33
Ireland 15
(Aus: Tries - McIntyre, Smith, Burke 2; Cov - Lynagh 4; PG - Lynagh 3.

7 June
Sydney
France 31 Fiji 16
(France: Tries - Laporte 3, Rodriguez 2, Lorieux, Lagisquet; Pens - Laporte 2; DG - Laporte. Fiji: Tries - Qoro, Damu; PG - Koroduadua)

8 June
Brisbane
Wales 16 England 3
(Tries – Roberts, Jones, Devereux; Conv: Thorburn 2. England: PG - Webb)

Semi FINALS

13 June
Sydney
France 30 Australia 24

*(France: Tries – Lorieux,
Sella, Lagisquet; Conv –
Camberabero 4; Pens –
Camberabero 2. Australia:
Tries: – Campese, Codey;
Convs – Lynagh 2; Pen –
Lynagh)*

13 June
Brisbane
New Zealand 49
Wales 6
*(NZ: Tries – Kirwan 2,
Shelford 2, Drake, A
Whetton, Stanley, Brooke-
Cowden.Convs – Fox 7;
Pen- Fox.)*

Third Place

18 June
Rotorua
Wales 22 Australia 21
*(Wales: Tries – Roberts, P
Moriarty, Hadley; Conv
– Thorburn 2; Pens –
Thorburn 2. Aus: Tries -
Burke, Grigg; Conv -
Lynagh 2; Pens - Lynagh
2; DG - Lynagh.)*

FINAL

20 June
Eden Park, Auckland
New Zealand 29
France 9
*NZ: Tries - Jones, Kirk,
Kirwan; Conv - Fox; Pens
- Fox 4; DB - Fox
France: Tries - Berbizier,
Camberabero; Pen - Cam-
berabero.
Teams: NZ: Gallagher;
Kirwan, Stanley, Taylor,
Green; Fox, Kirk (capt);
McDowell, Fitzpatrick,
Drake; Pierce, G Whetton,
A Whetton, Jones, Shelford.
France: Blanco; Camber-
abero, Sella, Charvet, Lag-
isquet; Mesnel, Berbizier;
Ondarts, Dubroca (capt),
Garuet; Lorieux, Condom;
Champ, Erbani,
Rodriguez.
Ref: K Fitzgerald (Aus).
Total attendance: 604,500*

1991

**Held in the UK, Ireland and
France from 3 Oct to 2 Nov**

Pool 1

3 Oct
Twickenham
England 12
New Zealand 18

5 Oct
Otley
Italy 30 USA 9

8 Oct
Gloucester
New Zealand 46 USA 6

8 Oct
Twickenham
England 36 Italy 6

11 Oct
Twickenham
England 37 USA 9

13 Oct
Leicester
New Zealand 31
Italy 21

Pool 2

5 Oct
Murrayfield
Scotland 47 Japan 9

6 Oct
Lansdowne Road
Ireland 55 Zimbabwe 11

9 Oct
Lansdowne Road
Ireland 32 Japan 16

9 Oct
Murrayfield
Scotland 51
Zimbabwe 12

12 Oct
Murrayfield
Scotland 24 Ireland 15

14 Oct
Belfast
Japan 52 Zimbabwe 8

Pool 3

4 Oct
Llanelli
Australia 32
Argentina 19

6 Oct
Cardiff
Wales 13
Western Samoa 16

9 Oct
Pontypool
Australia 9
Western Samoa 3

9 Oct
Cardiff
Wales 16 Argentina 7

12 Oct
Cardiff
Wales 3 Australia 38

13 Oct
Pontypridd
Western Samoa 35
Argentina 12

Pool 4

4 Oct
Béziers
France 30 Romania 3

5 Oct
Bayonne
Canada 13 Fiji 3

8 Oct
Grenoble
France 33 Fiji 8

9 Oct
Toulouse
Canada 19 Romania 11

**POINTS SYSTEM FOR TABLES:
WIN = 3 POINTS; DRAW = 2 POINTS; LOSE = 1 POINT**

Pool 1 Final Table 1991

	P	W	D	L	F	A	Pts
New Zealand	3	3	0	0	95	39	9
England	3	2	0	1	85	33	7
Italy	3	1	0	2	57	76	5
US	3	0	0	3	24	113	3

Pool 2 Final Table 1991

	P	W	D	L	F	A	Pts
Scotland	3	3	0	0	122	36	9
Ireland	3	2	0	1	102	51	7
Japan	3	1	0	2	77	87	5
Zimbabwe	3	0	0	3	31	158	3

Pool 3 Final Table 1991

	P	W	D	L	F	A	Pts
Australia	3	3	0	0	79	25	9
W Samoa	3	2	0	1	54	34	7
Wales	3	1	0	2	32	61	5
Argentina	3	0	0	3	38	83	3

Pool 4 Final Table 1991

	P	W	D	L	F	A	Pts
France	3	3	0	0	82	25	9
Canada	3	2	0	1	45	33	7
Romania	3	1	0	2	31	64	5
Fiji	3	0	0	3	27	63	3

David Campese, of Australia, scored the most tries during the 1991 World Cup. He also made the odd tackle or two...

(NZ: Try – Little; Pens – Preston 3. Scot: Pens – G Hastings 2)

FINAL

2 Nov
Twickenham
England 6
Australia 12

England: Pens – Webb 2 Aus: Try – Daly; Conv – Lynagh; Pens – Lynagh 2
Teams: England: J Webb; S Halliday, W Carling (capt), J Guscott, R Underwood; R Andrew, R Hill; J Leonard, Moore, J Probyn; P Ackford, W Dooley; M Skinner, P Winterbottom, M Teague
Australia: M Roebuck; D Campese, J Little, T Horan, Egerton; M Lynagh, N Farr-Jones (capt); A Daly, P Kearns, E McKenzie, R McCall, J Eales; S Poidevin, W Ofengaue, T Coker.
Ref: D Bevan (Wales).

Total attendance 1991: 1,007,760 ∎

12 Oct
Brive
Romania 17 Fiji 15

13 Oct
Agen
France 19 Canada 13

Qtr FINALS

19 Oct
Murrayfield
Scotland 28
Western Samoa 6
(Scotland: Tries – Jeffrey 2, Stanger; Convs – G Hastings 2; Pens – Hastings 4. W Samoa: Pen – Vaea; DG – Bachop)

19 Oct
Paris
France 10 England 19
(France: Try - Lafond; Pens - Lacroix 2. Eng: Tries – Underwood, Carling; Conv – Webb; Pens – Webb 3)

20 Oct
Lansdowne Road
Ireland 18 Australia 19
(Ireland: Tries - Hamilton, Keyes; Conv - Keyes; Pens - Keyes 3; DG - Keyes. Aus: Tries – Campese 2, Lynagh; Convs – Lynagh 2; Pen – Lynagh)

20 Oct
Lille
New Zealand 29
Canada 13
(NZ: Tries – Timu 2, McCahill, Brooke, Kirwan; Convs - Fox 3; Pen – Fox. Canada: Tries - Tynan, Charron, Conv - Wyatt; Pen - Wyatt)

Semi FINALS

26 Oct
Murrayfield
Scotland 6 England 9
(Scot: Pens - G Hastings 2. Eng: Pens – Webb 2; DG – Andrew)

27 Oct
Lansdowne Road
Australia 16
New Zealand 6
(Aus: Tries – Campese, Horan; Conv – Lynagh; Pens - Lynagh 2. NZ: Pens – Fox 2)

Third Place

30 Oct
Cardiff
NZ 13 Scotland 6

RECORDS IN THE FINALS

Highest score:
New Zealand 74 (v Fiji, 1987)

Most points:
G Fox (NZ), 170; M Lynagh (Aus), 148; G Hastings (Scot), 123

Most tries:
D Campese (Aus), 10; J Kirwan (NZ), 7

Most penalties:
G Fox, 27; M Lynagh, 22; J Webb (Eng), 21; G Hastings, 19

Most points in a match:
D Camberabero (France), 30 (v Zimbabwe 1987) ; G Hastings (Scot), 27, (v Romania, 1987)

John Eales and Tony Daley celebrate Australia's victory over England in the final. Will Carling and his men were out-played on the day

3. Tours

DEREK WYATT says that excessive touring is threatening the game, and he recalls the different atmosphere of rugby tours when he was an England player 20 years ago

THE TROUBLE WITH TOURING

Touring has almost become a disease in the 1990s. Players are not just subjected to arduous league and cup matches but have rigorous commitments to their national sides, coaching weekends, pre-Five Nation international matches, preparations for the Five Nations and the Five Nations. Then, there are your country's own tours and/or a Lions Tour. Remember, Scotland, England and Wales all toured in 1993 despite the Lions tour to New Zealand.

In 1975, when I became a tourist, it was so different. First, I received a phone call from my local newspaper, the East Anglian Times, telling me at the school where I was teaching that I was in the England team to tour Australia. They had just read it on the PA wire. As I was uncapped and had only just been added to the subs bench for the England team in the last game of the Five Nations Championship, this came as a lovely surprise. I had got the nod ahead of the illustrious David Duckham.

"Oh dear," said the headmaster, John Blatchly, "that means you'll be away for the whole of May just when your O and A level classes will need you. I'm not sure we can let you go."

The next day, the letter arrived from Bob Weighill, the Secretary of the RFU, telling me I had been selected and giving me a list of things to do before we were to meet as a squad at Heathrow Airport. Blatchly summoned me to say that, after consultations with housemasters and my head of department, Peter Hill, I could go, provided that the RFU would pay for the temporary teacher who would have to be employed in my absence.

> **"Oh dear," said the headmaster, "that means you will be away for the whole of May just when your O and A level classes will need you. I'm not sure I can let you go"**

I duly wrote to Bob Weighill asking him if the RFU would fund my replacement. The letter I received by return told me that if the RFU paid for my replacement that that would be a breach of amateur regulations as broken time payments could not be made. However, the headmaster was not impressed with this information. Not only was he agreeing to pay my salary, in absentia, but also my replacement. I could understand his annoyance but he agreed I could go. Bless him.

It was my first major tour beyond Europe. I had never been to Australia and my notes from my tour diary tell me that, in my list of 10 countries I most wanted to visit, Australia did not feature. Surprising how wrong can you be at the tender age of 26.....

As a newcomer to the England squad I was an

outsider. I was also the spare wing-threequarter and Alan Morley and Peter Squires were the preferred choices, so I knew I would be lucky to play in more than four of the eight games.

On the plane, I sat in my No.1s, my tour trousers and jacket. Sitting to my right was a delightfully attractive girl, who became more attractive to me as the journey continued, but that's another story. The "senior pros", as they dubbed themselves, stripped quickly

This is madness. It is driving the game into submission

into tracksuits and seat-jumped looking for space so that they could sleep more peacefully on the 17-hour flight. I was definitely one of the tour virgins.

To my left sat an 'old geezer' who could just about squeeeze into his seat. For a while I gave him the cold shoulder. In due course, I had to ask him his name. *"Vivian Jenkins,"* he said. *"Vivian Jenkins"* I said, *"not Vivian Jenkins of the Sunday Times and Rugby World?"*

"Quite so," he said, *"and who the devil are you?"* We had 14 hours left to talk rugby. Talk we did. *"Have you been to Australia?"* I asked.

"Yes, four or five times."
"When did you first go?"
"I think in the early 1950s."
"How did you travel"
"It was marvellous. We went by sea-plane, five or six days it took. It was wonderful." I wish I had had Vivian Jenkins' luck to have gone to Australia by sea-plane.

The story also shows how the times have changed with respect to the amateur regulations. (Just out of interest, whereas we went economy class, the President of the RFU, Ken Chapman, travelled first class when he came out a little later on).

And it illustrates that, whereas just 20 years ago touring was restricted largely to the Lions, now tours are an integral part of any country intent on winning the Rugby World Cup. In the past season, Australia toured America, Canada and France; New Zealand toured England and Scotland; South Africa were in the Argentine; Japan travelled to Wales; a South African Barbarians side also visited the Four Home Unions.

In May and June 1994 England were in South Africa, Scotland in Argentina, Ireland in Australia, France in Canada and New Zealand and Wales were in the Pacific Islands having stopped off in Canada (not forgetting they had also to play some World Cup qualifyers against Portugal and Spain in May).

This is madness. It is driving the game into submission.

Be that as it may, more tours are happening, and with the changes in tow for the Rugby World Cup 1999, most existing fixture lists will need to be torn up. Countries will have to work back from the dates of RWC 99 and then set their international fixtures before they can even start to determine their cup and league dates. What chance?

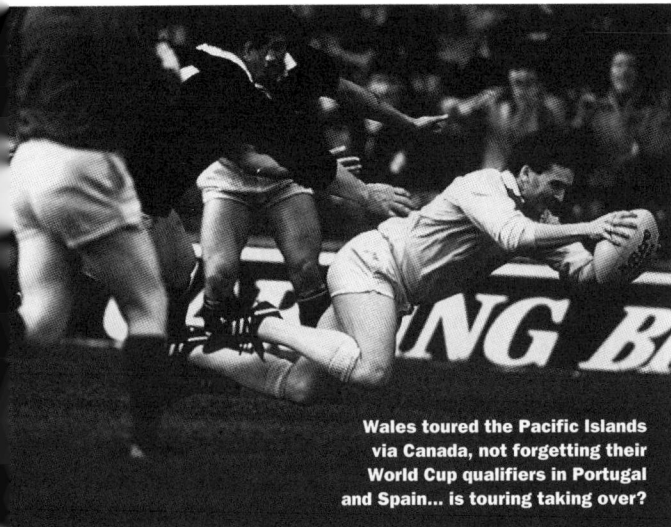

Wales toured the Pacific Islands via Canada, not forgetting their World Cup qualifiers in Portugal and Spain... is touring taking over?

DIARY OF AN ALL-BLACK

Rugby players are chancing their arm by writing about the game too. Eddie Butler and Peter Fitzsimmons are the best of the new bunch. Meanwhile, Matthew Cooper, whose duties included taking the kicks and choosing the music, kept a diary of his All Blacks tour to England and Scotland which we print below

MY LIFE IN CHARGE OF THE TAPE COMMITTEE

18 OCTOBER

Arrive Heathrow

It was straight in, no problems, we all got on well from the start. It's probably even better than last year in that there have been no groups, partly because we're from all over the country. Auckland has been dominant in the past, but not here. Gradually the real characters show their colours: Stuey Forster, he's a top little bloke; Marc Ellis is a pretty humorous sort of guy; Eric Rush, who just loves life, and Zinzan Brooke, a guy who's toured a lot and who relates to everyone.

And of course Fitzy. Sean Fitzpatrick's a true All Black captain. He epitomises what being an All Black is all about. He loves the black jersey, he handles the All Black captaincy pressures brilliantly. He's always looking right through the whole squad and he keeps a special eye on the new boys.

23 OCTOBER

London 12 All Blacks 39
Cooper starts well with six kicks from eight

That was just about a start. We played good, hard, running New Zealand rugby. I was very pleased with my kicking. I missed my first one, but I kept on saying to myself, "You've got to take the responsibility now, Grant Fox

isn't here." I thought that if I could do it here, I could do it anywhere.

There was talk that we wouldn't do the haka, because last year in Australia we did it all the time and the sides just didn't respect it. We thought, "No, we're in the UK and they've already respected our haka". I admit I get hyped up doing it, but teams over here have accepted the challenge. Good. We've had no problems here.

26 OCTOBER

Midlands 6 All Blacks 12
Cooper comes on as a replacement and kicks two match-winning penalties

Those match-winning kicks were something I've always wanted to do. I've seen Foxy do it week in, week out. I was sitting in a cold stand and then all of a sudden I was out there. I was relaxed after Twickers, I allowed the noise to come right off me and luckily I hit my kicks really well.

30 OCTOBER

South West 15 All Blacks 19
Phil de Glanville's injury dominates the headlines

For the first time, we may have gone into a bit of a cruise mode and we were especially disappointed with our discipline. The

Phil de Glanville, none
the worse for wear after
the South West v NZ
game, won his first cap
for England against the
All Blacks during their
tour of the British Isles

The incident with Phil de Glanville was unfortunate. Forget about the rights and wrongs of the whole thing, the management handled it, and made our stance. The really disappointing thing was how long it dragged on

incident with Phil de Glanville was unfortunate. Forget about the rights and the wrongs of the whole thing, the management handled it, and made our stance. The really disappointing thing was how long it dragged on.

2 NOVEMBER

North 21 All Blacks 27

Again, we were doing only enough to win, which was a worry and again we gave away a lot of penalties. It's not an excuse but we might have been penalised for a lot of the things we get away with at home; the interpretations can be a bit different, but that's really up to us to adapt.

Off the pitch, our committees – all part of the formula for a successful tour – were working well. Everyone is on a committee: the Video Committee, the Larks and Perks Committee and the Laundry Committee (that usually goes to the new boys, and whenever it's announced there's always a big laugh. Jeff Wilson and Richard Fromont got it this time).

We've got the Back-Seat Committee, which is the senior pros, basically the top dogs – Ian Jones, Zinzan Brooke and Paul Henderson – they always sit in the back seat of the bus and make the decisions. Fitzy isn't there, though, the captain always sits at the front of the bus.

I'm in charge of the Tape Committee for music on the coach. There always has to be a tape playing and, if there's not, I'll get fined. I got the guys all to buy a tape, they all had to be played right through once and if that tape's no good, the committee have the chance to throw it out on to the motorway. Earle Kirton's was a shocker – something that dated way back to his early days – and it's now in pieces on the M1.

7 NOVEMBER

England A 12 All Blacks 26

Stu Barnes had a good game for England. I like him as a footballer; he reminds me a little bit of Stephen Bachop. He's got that unpredictable side to him and go from halfway, whereas normally we know the scrum or fly-halves will kick it. I've always got on with Barnesy. I ran into a few of those guys – Stu Barnes, Tony Underwood – on the Lions tour. I've met up with them here and they're top blokes. The teams generally get on really well. They enjoy having a brown ale with us as much as we do with them; they're friends, good friends.

10 NOVEMBER

S of Scotland A 5 All Blacks 85
The All Blacks record score in the British Isles

The pace of life in Scotland was a lot slower than England. Coming from Waikato, that was refreshing. The Borders were nice, very similar to a lot of New Zealand, but like everywhere, we just had no time for any sight-seeing. We never even got to see Big Ben.

13 NOVEMBER

Scotland A 9 All Blacks 20

This didn't go too well for us and we were fuming all week because of that. We were hurting because we didn't play well. Stuey Forster had by now established himself in the side. He was lucky, as all of us were, to get that first London game and create that first impression. Unfortunately the early games for Jon Preston, who started as first-choice scrum half, were niggly affairs when he didn't have a lot of chance to show what he can do.

16 NOVEMBER

Scotland Dev't XV 12 All Blacks 31

We played golf up in Edinburgh and honestly it was the coldest day of my life. By the time we got to the eighth or ninth we were feeling warm again, but I think that's because we were numb. Zinzan likes to think he's good, he reads coaching manuals all the time, he's very competitive and if one sprays, he'll go back to the text book. Marc Ellis was interesting. He played one hole using a wood all the way.

The other things we've been up to is 10-pin bowling – I cleaned out Marc Ellis. We've also spent some quality time with the Space Invaders.

20 NOVEMBER

Scotland 15 All Blacks 51
Jeff Wilson scores three tries, Cooper injured

Back home, to be an All Black, it's like a religion. To chuck on the black jersey with the silver fern, the tradition factor hits home. You think of the history, you think of Meads, of Wilson Whineray, Waka Nathan, Ian Kirkpatrick. These were legends to me. As a boy you'd always get up at two o'clock in the morning and watch live games – I'd never miss one – and all of a sudden we were in Murrayfield, thinking of all those people getting up in the middle of the night back home.

The biggest fear we had was that Scotland had never beaten the All Blacks. The whole week was filled with the fear of losing. That, the fear of losing, is an enormous part of All Black rugby. As it happened, we dominated the whole thing. I was disappointed because I'd got injured but I was pleased to get the

Test, especially because my mother and father had flown over for the last three weeks – at least they saw one game.

24 NOVEMBER

Emerging England 19 All Blacks 30

Cold, just freezing. That place Gloucester, I don't think I'll be back in a hurry. The midweekers did well in this Test week, and rallied round brilliantly.

27 NOVEMBER

England 15 All Blacks 9
All Blacks lose, a result described as a national disaster

I was commentating for a New Zealand radio station that day. I was a bit worried from the start: the guys' normal routine was rushed, we got to the ground a bit late, at about 1.15pm when we usually arrive at 12.55pm for a 2pm kick-off. But still, when they ran out on to the field, I thought we'd be strong enough.

The game started quite slowly, a lot of kicking and then the English slowed it down further to suit their game. We had to get a few early points up but after about half an hour it was still 3-0 and I turned to my other commentator and just shook my

England played superbly, all credit to them. Their back-row was incredible, Tim Rodber especially, he epitomises a New Zealand forward. Afterwards I felt empty for myself. I felt for the whole squad. This was tough

Vaiaga Tuigamala wants to run with the ball. Will Carling has other ideas and helps cause a "national disaster"

head. At half-time we said it was looking shaky but, as Kiwis, we thought, no, they'll come right.

Of course, they didn't. We can make no excuses – England played superbly, all credit to them. Their back row was incredible, Tim Rodber especially, he epitomises a New Zealand forward. Afterwards I felt empty for myself. I felt for the whole squad. This was tough. I went straight into the dressing-room afterwards and they were very quiet. It's a very personal time for each member and you've got to leave them on their own to do their own thing.

But then, about 15 minutes after the match, we got in Neil Finn, the lead singer from Crowded House – he's a Kiwi and a legend back home. We knew he was at the ground and he came into the dressing-room and strummed away on the guitar, singing away, all the famous Crowded House songs, just unplugged, it was superb. That lifted the boys immensely, all of a sudden the smiles were back and we realised that OK, that's life, there's going to be a new day tomorrow.

30 NOVEMBER

Combined Services 3 All Blacks 13

The midweekers walked off with an unbeaten record, they played with pride and they helped the rest of us pick up a gear. It's been said we've had enough and want to go. That has surprised me. OK, you get disappointed but we knew it was 13 matches. Also I've talked to a few of the guys and they're all looking forward to the Baa-Baas game, they're still buzzing.

After last Saturday's let down, we want to go out on a high. Over here, everyone is still talking about the game in '73 – I know our boys want to throw it around, so I hope we'll get everyone talking about '93. Then it's back home to reality and normal life. Some of the new guys have really appreciated just what being an All Black is. When I cam back from touring South Africa last year, I noticed how much stronger and more confident I was. I think it'll be like that again. I honestly believe that being an All Black helps you grow ∎

© *Matthew Cooper 1993. This diary appeared in* The Independent *in 1993*

TOURING RESULTS 1993 – '94

JAPAN to WALES 10 Sept – 21 Oct 1993

v Wales A, lost 5-61
Date: 29 Sept
Venue: Llanelli
Referee: D. Matthews (Eng)
Crowd: 3,500
Japan: *Try – H.Kaneshiro*
Wales A: *Tries – P. Arnold 2, A. Davies 2, N. Jenkins 2, S. Quinnell, M. Back & G. Wilkins; Penalties – N. Jenkins; Conversions – A. Davies 2 & N. Jenkins 2.*

Played under floodlights, the Japanese tour kicked off against the wrong opponents – a side containing 11 full internationals... Ian Williams, the former Oxford University Blue and Australian wing three-quarter made his debut for Japan.

v Dunvant, won 24-23
Date: 2 Oct
Venue: Dunvant, near Swansea
Referee: J.Bacigalupo
Crowd: 2,600
Japan: *Tries – M.Fujikake H.Ouchi T.Fujihara; Penalties – T. Maeda; Conversions – T. Maeda 3*
Dunvant: *Tries – D. or P.Morris & W.Lloyd; Penalties – M. Thomas 3; Conversions: M. Thomas 2*

Hirofume Ouchi, the Japan-

ese flanker was sent off. The narrow win, Dunvant scored seven points on the whistle when the game was well won by the Japanese, just about kept the flame of the visitors tour alive.

v East Wales, lost 12-38
Date: 6 Oct
Venue: Abertillery Park
Referee: B. Campsall (RFU)
Crowd: 3,000
Japan: *Tries – T. Faamasino & T. Fujihara Conversion T. Maeda*
East Wales: *Tries – A. Harries 3 (Newport); J.Humphreys 1 (Cardiff) Conversions – I. Evans 3 (Treorchy) Penalties – I. Evans 4*

The Japanese were simply out-classed and their hopes of being able to build a foundation for their forth-coming RWCup 95 qualify-ing matches took a further knock. The game was played in appalling conditions.

v West Wales, won 26-10
Date: 9 Oct
Venue: Narberth
Referee: R. McDowall (Sco)
Crowd: 2,800
Japan: *Tries – M. Kunda, T. Maeda, H. Ouchi & S. Latu; Conversions – Y. Nagatoma 2 & Maeda*

West Wales: *Tries – S. Bar-clay & R. Jones.*

As Tim Glover put it in *The Independent:* "Japan are described as one of the emerging countries, but the trouble is they have been emerging for 60 years with-out ever quite arriving."

v Wales Select XV (from Third & Fourth Division clubs), won 39-10
Date: 12 Oct
Venue: Pontypridd
Referee: S. Lander (Eng)
Crowd: 4,100
Japan: *Tries – T. Fujihara, M. Fujikake, T. Matsuda, Nakamura & I. Williams; Penalties – Y. Nagamoto 2; Conversions – Nagamoto 4*
Wales Select: *Tries – P. Nolan; Drop – M. Dacey; Conversion – M. Tatchell*

The mid-week XV had no trouble cruising to a com-fortable win against oppo-nents short on staying power.

v Wales, lost 5-55
Date: 16 Oct
Venue: Arms Park, Cardiff
Referee: E. Morrison (Eng)
Crowd: 23,500
Japan: *Try – I. Williams*
Wales: *Tries – I. Evans 2, S.*

Gibbs 2, N.Jenkins, R. Moon, E. Lewis, M. Rayer, A. Clement; Conversions – Jenkins 5

CONCLUSION: Japan have simply stood still in their technical development and appreciation of tactics. It is surely time for Shiggy Konno to retire and hand over to a younger man. In sum, the tour was a great disappointment.

TOUR RECORD:
P6 W3 L3 F-A 111-197

AUSTRALIA to USA, CANADA & FRANCE Oct – Nov 1993

v USA Eagles
won 26-22
Date: 3 October
Venue: Riverside, California
Australia: *Tries – I. Tabua, B. Lea, P.Howard & D. Wilson; Conversions – M. Lynagh 3.*
USA: *n/a*
New caps: 5 *USA*

Played in 40°C, water bottles were being passed about the field faster than the ball. Australia did not award caps for this match and very nearly lost. Their coach Bob Dwyer said: "The weather was a great leveller. The team had a handy lead with 10 minutes to go but you can't blame them for falling back a little given the terrible conditions."

v Canada A, won 40-3
Date: 6 October
Venue: Calgary
Australia: *Tries – A. Murdoch 2, B. Lea, G.Morgan, M.Roebuck, D.Smith; Penalties – Roebuck 2; Conversions – Roebuck 2*
Canada: n/a

v Canada, won 43-16
Date: 10 October
Venue: Calgary
Referee: D.Bevan (Wales)

Crowd: 4,000
Australia: *Tries – D. Campese 3, A. Daly, W. Smith, T. Horan; Penalties – M. Lynagh 3; Conversions – Lynagh 2.*
Canada: *Tries – I.Kennedy & D.Jackson; Penalties – J. Graf 2*

David Campese scored his 55th, 56th and 57th tries thus bringing his total to a remarkable 57 in 79 Tests. Michael Lynagh brought his points to 775 in 63 Tests.

CONCLUSION: Canada were without half their team because of the decision by the Canadian RFU not to pay for the travelling expenses for those players in England, France and Japan. This was counter-productive. The absence of the best players affected the audience for television, and the value of the television rights package overseas despite the initial guarantees. The advertising around the game was diminished, so the broadcasters felt cheated; and the game was the loser. These are the facts if life.

The Canadians may not like their best players going overseas, but they're travelling to become better players, to enrich the quality of the Canadian national side, and to help their Rugby World Cup chances in 1995 (after all their pool gives them little prospective of automatically qualifying for 1999). Short termism will never work in rugby and the Canadians must be persuaded to play their best team whatever the cost. They will live to rue this defeat.

v Aquitaine
won 30-15
Date: 16 October
Venue: Dax
Referee: A. Spreadbury (Eng)
Crowd: 10,000
Australia: *Tries – A. Murdoch, J. Little & S. Bowen; Penalties – M. Roebuck 3; Conversions – Roebuck 3*
Aquitaine: *Penalties – S. Prosper 5*

"It's impossible to play enterprising rugby with a piece of chamois disguised as a ball" said Bob Dwyer. Two of the Australian tries included knock-ons missed by the referee and ultimately saved the Aussies' faces.

v South West Regional XV, won 20-19
Date: 21 October
Venue: Agen
Australia: *Tries – T. Horan;
Penalties – M. Lynagh 5*
SW Regional XV: *Tries – Diaz
or T. Bourdet; Penalties P.
Montlaur 4; Conversion – P.
Montlaur*

v Languedoc-Rousillon. won 35-18
Date: 23 October
Venue: Narbonne
Crowd: 10,000
Australia: *Tries – G. Morgan
2, M. Burke & A. Murdoch;
Penalties – M. Lynagh 3;
Conversions Lynagh 3*
Languedoc-Rousillon: *Tries –
P. Laurent & M. Lievremont;
Penalties – J. Lescure 2;
Conversion – Lescure*

Tim Gavin was brutally
kicked in the head and needed 14 stitches. This happened
just seconds from the end of
the game which didn't
become dirty until Languedoc
were well out of contention.

v South-East Regional XV won 24-23
Date: 26 October
Venue: Grenoble

(match statistics unavailable)
v France First Test, lost 13-16
Date: 30 October
Venue: Stade Municipale,
Bordeaux
Referee: David Bishop (NZ)
Crowd: 36,000

Australia: *Try – T, Gavin;
Penalty: M. Lynagh 2; Lynagh*
France: *Try – A.Hueber;
Penalty – T. Lacroix; Drop
goals – A. Penaud & J-L
Sadourny; Conversion – Lacroix*

NEW CAPS
Australia – M. Brial & A.
Murdoch

Australia had all the play and
all the positional advantages,
and they had a Tim Horan
try disallowed, but lost.
France were disciplined and
firm in the tackle and in the
end won a tight game but
the Wallabies will have
kicked themselves for losing.

v Provence-Littoral, lost 15-21
Date: 2 November
Venue: Toulon
Australia: *Penalties – M. Roe-
buck 5.* **P-L:** *n/a*

v FRANCE Second Test, won 24-3
Date: 6 November
Venue: Parc des Princes
Referee: D. Bishop (NZ)
Crowd: 45,000
Australia: *Tries – M. Roebuck
& T. Horan; Penalties – Roe-
buck 4; Conversion – Roebuck*
France: *Penalty – T. Lacroix*

This was a first win for Australia at Parc des Princes. Tac-
tically, the Australians rucked
going forward and laid the ball
back for their back-row all of

whom had storming games.
Roebuck took over the place-
kicking and some of the line
kicking so that Lynagh could
concentrate on moving the
ball wider. In fact, they both
had excellent games and the
two centres, Horan and Little,
tore holes in the French opposition. It wasn't supposed to be
like this – for this was Phillipe
Sella's world record breaking
94th international cap.

v French Barbarians, won 43-26
Date: 11 November
Venue: Clermont-Ferrand
Australia: *Tries – Lea, D.
Campese & Catchpole;
Penalties – M. Roebuck 8;
Conversions J. Little & Roebuck*
French Baa-Baas' *Tries –
Saint-Andre, Dal Maso;
Penalties - D. Charvet 4;
Conversions - Charvet 2*

**CONCLUSION: Australia
won three of their four Tests,
sharing the series with France
which means they have yet to
win a series on French soil.
This will matter little to Bob
Dwyer who has his mind on
the World Cup 1995.**
　　**At the beginning of
November 1993 the world
ranking was still New
Zealand first, Australia second and France third.**

**TOUR RECORD:
P12 W10 L2 F313 A182**

Australia's first win at Parc des Princes: Alain Penaud and Michael Lynagh provided the aerial ballet as Australia danced their way to a convincing 24-3 victory

NEW ZEALAND to ENGLAND & SCOTLAND Oct – Dec 1993

v London & SE Division, won 39-12
Date: 23 Oct
Venue: Twickenham
Referee: P. Thomas
Crowd: 56,400 (record for a divisional match)
NZ: *Tries – S. Bachop 2, J. Wilson 2, M. Berry; Penalties – M. Cooper – 2; Conversions – Cooper 4*
London: *Tries – R. Jenkins & C. Oti; Conversion – R. Andrew*

The All Blacks destroyed the London side by playing open and attractive football, the like of which has not been seen at Twickenham. It was was one of the best exhibitions of rugby ever experienced at headquarters and set the whole country talking. This devastating display seriously exposed London's tactical thinking (despite their 10 caps on view).

v Midlands, won 12-6
Date: 26 Oct
Venue: Leicester
Referee: B. Stirling (Ireland)
Crowd: 16,000 sell-out
NZ: *Penalties – S. Howarth 2, M. Cooper 2 (sub)*
Midlands: *Penalties – J. Steele 2*

An awful game and a total let down for the capacity crowd. New Zealand were strangled by the the Leicester back-row of Richards, Back and Wells. Steele could have settled it with five minutes to go but in the end the All Blacks just got home.

v South-West, won 19-15
Date: 30 Oct
Venue: Redruth
Referee: C. Thomas (Wales)
Crowd: 15,000 sell-out
NZ: *Try – J. Joseph; Penalties – M. Cooper 4; Conversion – Cooper*
SW: Penalties – J. Callard 4; *Drop goal – P. Hull*

Jonathan Callard tipped to be the new full back for England fluffed his lines missing three relatively simple penalties which would have won the match. The match itself was a bruising affair and showed the unseemly side of the Kiwi's game. Phil de Glanville had 15 stitches inserted just below his left eye having been very seriously raked (and quite deliberately so). Again Matt Cooper produced the goods when needed. Grant Fox seems a distant memory. In eight days we have seen the complete face of New Zealand rugby. If they are to deserve their status as the world's number one they must also take on board that their old game is a thing of the past.

v North, won 27-21
Date: 2 Nov
Venue: Anfield, Liverpool, a

first for the soccer stadium
Referee: J. Fleming (Sco)
Crowd: 24,636
NZ: Tries – *M. Ellis 2, E. Rush & N. ; Penalties – J. Wilson; Conversions – J. Wilson*
North: Penalties – Grayson 7

A desperately dull match, riddled with error, which the All Blacks had sewn up after 20 minutes and then gone to sleep. Still, it gave them a clean sweep against the four England Divisions.

v England A, won 26-12
Date: 7 Nov
Venue: Gateshead International Stadium
Referee: R. Megson (Sco)
Crowd: 19,100 sell-out
NZ: *Tries – J. Wilson, J. Timu; Penalties – M. Cooper 3; Drop goal – M. Ellis; Conversions – Cooper 2.*
England A: *Penalties – J. Callard 4*

The All Blacks defence was brilliant and they snaffled out any promising moves. In some ways the A team lost this game giving away too many penalties and two tries, one from a gentle interception by fly-boy Wilson.

v South of Scotland, won 84-5
Date: 10 Nov
Venue: Netherdale, Galashiels
Referee: D.Matthews (Eng)
Crowd: 5,000

NZ: *Tries – Z. Brooke 4, N.Hewitt 2, S.Howarth 2, S.Bachop, J.Mitchell, M.Ellis, J.Preston; Penalties – Howarth 2; Conversions – Howarth 9*
S Scotland: *Try – G.Parker*

Record margin of victory for NZ in the British Isles.

v Scotland A, won 20-9
Date: 13 Nov
Venue: Old Anniesland, Glasgow
Referee: A. Spreadbury (Eng)
Crowd: 8,500
NZ: *Try- M.Ellis; Penalties – M.Cooper 5*
Scotland A: *Penalty – M. Dods; Drop goals – D.Wylie 2*

v Scottish Development XV, won 31-12
Date: 16 Nov
Venue: Myreside
Referee: G. Black (Ire)
Crowd: 5,000
NZ: *Tries – E.Rush, L.Barry, J. Mitchell; Penalties – S.Howarth 4; Conversions – Howarth 2*
Scottish Dev: *Penalties – K.Bray 4*

The mid-week side maintained its unbeaten record

v Scotland. won 51-15
Date: 20 Nov
Venue: Murrayfield
Referee: F. Burger (South Africa)
Crowd: 37,500
NZ: *Tries – J. Wilson 3, M. Ellis 2, Z. Brooke & F. Bunce;*

Penalties – M.Cooper 2; Conversions – Cooper 4 & Wilson
Scotland: *Penalties – G.Hastings 4 & C. Chalmers*
New caps: *J.Wilson, M.Ellis, S.Foster, S.Gordon (NZ); A.MacDonald, I.Jardine (Sco).*

It was an even more comprehesive victory than the score-line suggests. This was an awesome display of attacking rugby with props Fitzpatrick and Brown dummying and side-stepping as though it was par for the course. The All Blacks received a standing ovation from the generous crowd.

v England Emerging Players, won 30-19
Date: 23 Nov
Venue: Kingsholm, Gloucester
Referee: D.Mene (France)
Crowd: 13,000
NZ: *Tries – E.Clarke, S.Howarth, E.Rush; Penalties – Howarth 2; Drop goal – S.Bachop; Conversions – Howarth 3*
England Emerging: *Tries – P.Challinor, D.Sims; Penalties – Challinor 3*

v England, lost 9-15
Date: 27 Nov
Venue: Twickenham
Referee: F. Burger (South Africa)
Crowd: 68,000
NZ: *Penalties – J. Wilson 3*
England: *Penalties – J. Callard 4; Drop goal – R. Andrew*
New caps: *J.Callard &*

K.Brackan (Eng)

The tour was looking triumphant as the All Blacks came back toTwickenham to whip the English. It was not to be. However, England deserved their win. Most observers, including the *Almanack* Editor, had to eat much humble pie and wipe much scrambled egg off their faces, as England produced one of the great displays of the 20th century.

The performance of the whole pack, and the kicking of Callard and Andrew, were outstanding in a game which had the crowd and the watching TV viewers on the edge of their seats. Everyone noted what a great theatre for rugby Twickenham has become with the building of the new stands; and the English fans have never been so emotionally powerful.

Irish touch judge Stephen Hilditch also had a crucial part to play when he ruled (correctly) that All Black John Timu had put a foot in touch before he had "scored" a try.

The game set the agenda for the 1995 World Cup and will change the way rugby will be reported in the tabloids and the broadsheets for the next two years. It is sad to record that television will go on giving us such a dreary picture of the game as the BBC retained the contract.

At the end of the match,

Brian Moore alleged that Sean Fitzpatrick was sledging Victor Obogu during the scrums which was hard to believe given the Maori make-up of his own side; and Will Carling called the All Blacks a four-letter name.

v Combined Services, won 13-3

Date: 30 Nov
Venue: Devonport
Referee: D. Davies (Wales)
NZ: Try – *N. Hewitt;*
Penalties – S. Howarth 2;
Conversion: Howarth
Comb Servs: Penalty –
S. Worrall

A dismal game that the All Blacks eventually managed to win having been 3-0 down at one stage.

v Barbarians, won 26-16

Date: 4 Dec
Venue: National Stadium, Cardiff
Referee: P. Robin (France)
Crowd: 55,000
Sponsor: Scottish Amicable
NZ: Tries –*C. Dowd,*
V. Tuigamala, I.Jones;
Penalties – J. Wilson 2;
Conversions – Wilson 2
Barbarians: Penalties – *E. Elwood 4*

A fast and furious game which had moments of brilliance and inevitably the tourists were too good for

the scratch side.

CONCLUSION: The All Blacks set crowd records wherever they went. Never has there been such enthusiasm to see them nor such media coverage although the television coverage was indifferent.

It was galling that, although there was a full house at Twickenham for the opening fixture against London Counties, *Grandstand* viewers on BBC1 were shown the Toyota World Matchplay golf, which is neither a world championship nor does it attract the best. The schedules should have been cleared so that either the golf or the rugby was on BBC2. Jonathan Martin, Head of Sport, Alan Yentob, Controller of BBC1 and Michael Jackson, Controller of BBC2, missed a trick here.

After the memorable London game, it seemed inevitable that the All Blacks would win all their 13 matches. But, in the next game, the darker side of the All Blacks emerged with the raking of Philip de Glanville. The culprits, allegedly, were Sean Fitzpatrick, the captain, and Jamie Joseph.

Neither were punished and the absurd 12-hour rule instituted by the Four Home Unions Tours Committee (a team must lodge a complaint within 12 hours of the game finishing) could not be invoked

because amazingly no-one from the committee was watching the game on television nor had anyone from the SW Division committee videoed the game at the hotel.

The RFU could have been much tougher but in the end all de Glanville received was a muted apology from the New Zealand management. The SW game witnessed another element – the cynical way in which the All Blacks would rather give penalties away than concede tries. They were lucky that day for, although they won 17-15, Jonathan Callard missed so many kicks at goal.

The tourists meandered through England playing largely scratch sides and winning comfortably, even if some of the scores suggested otherwise. Because, no Test was played before the tourists reached Scotland, there was some danger that the tour was losing its impetus. The first game in Scotland changed that with the largest victory (or defeat) ever recorded when South of Scotland, apparently the strongest divisional side north of the border, was comprehensively beaten 84-5. Ten days later much the same thing happened to the Scots themselves when they lost 51-15

The All Blacks were self-critical about the way they had played the media game in 1991 World Cup, especially in Dublin before the semi-final against Australia. Not much has changed. Despite the presence of a media adviser, they got it wrong again especially against England. They are now, rightly or wrongly, cast as the villains of world rugby. Their management could all do with media training.

That aside, this was a for-midable All Blacks team. Once they have ironed out the captaincy, found a line-out jumper to support Ian Jones and a more creative back row, they will challenge again for honours. Had Timu been used as a running full-back and the wingers been properly utilised, this side could have beaten anybody.

TOUR RECORD:
P13 W12 L1 F386 A156

(F. 42 tries, 31 conversions, 36 penalties and 2 drop goals. A. 5 tries, 1 conversion, 40 penalties and 3 drop goals)

Leading points scorers:
Howarth 81 *(3t 15c 12p)*
Cooper 76 *(11c 18p)*
Wilson 58 *(6t 5c 6p)*
Ellis 33 *(6t 1dg)*

Leading try scorers:
Wilson 6, **Ellis** 6,
Brooke 5, **Hewitt** 4

ENGLAND to SOUTH AFRICA May – June 1994

v Orange Free State, lost 11-22
Date: 18 May
Referee: P. Lombard (Durban)
England: *Try – D. Hopley; Penalties – S. Barnes 2*
OFS: *Tries – C. Badenhorst 2, A. Venter & J. Coetzee; Conversion – D. van Rensburg*

Not the ideal start to the tour by the mid-week team.

v Natal , lost 6-21
Date: 21 May
Referee: M. Franken (Kimberley)
England: Penalties – R. Andrew 2
Natal: Penalties – A. Joubert 4, H. Honiball 3

This was a dreadful game for England which was appallingly refereed. Andrew

missed seven penalty kicks and David Pears' tour ended with injury. Jonathan Callard was called up from the Barbarians tour in Kenya. England looked as if they would rather not be on tour.

v Western Transvaal, won 26-24
Date: 25 May
Referee: N. Heilbron

England: *Tries – T. Underwood 2; Penalties S. Barnes 4; Conversions – Barnes 2*
Western Transvaal: *M. van Greunen & D. Basson; Penalties – Basson 4; Conversion – Basson*

A desperately boring game but one England were grateful to win.

v Transvaal, lost 21-24
Date: 28 May
Referee: I. Rogers
England: *Tries – R. Andrew & R. Underwood; Penalties – Andrew 3; Conversion – Andrew*
Transvaal: *Tries – H. Le Roux & J Louw; Penalties – Van Rensburg; Conversion – Van Rensburg*

Martin Johnson was concussed and ruled out of further play for the mandatory three weeks. Simon Shaw, the Bristol lock, was flown out as his replacement. Will Carling was denied a try by the referee who whistled too early without seeing that a Transvaal defender had failed to make a proper touchdown. A television referee or touch judge would have over-ruled him.

v South Africa A, lost 16-19
Date: 31 May
Referee: S. Neethling (Boland)
England: *Try – D. Hopley;*

Penalties – J. Callard 3; Conversion – Callard
S Africa A: *Tries – C. Scholtz & J. Stransky; Penalties – Stransky 2; Drop goal – Stransky*

Another dreadfully refereed match. Although England deserved to be beaten, they are learning that, in South Africa, winning at all costs is all that matters. You have to feel sorry for the South Africans if this really is the case. Let's hope that, as they are exposed to world values, that the community of modern South Africa will rid itself of this underlying nastiness. Four losses from five games did not augur well for the Tests.

v South Africa, First Test, won 32-15
Date: 4 June
Venue: Loftus Versfeld, Pretoria
Referee: C. Hawke (NZ)
Crowd: 70,000
England: *Tries – B. Clarke, R. Andrew; Penalties – Andrew 5; Drop goal – Andrew; Conversions – Andrew 2*
SA: *Penalties – A. Joubert 5*
New caps: *P. Hull (England); B. Venter, O le Roux & F van Heerden (SA)*

This was a truly remarkable Test with England 20 points up in 16 minutes. This victory turned the tour on its head and several players reputations were saved.

The forwards, especially an inspired Tim Rodber, played superbly and Rob Andrew's 27 points set a new England record, beating Jon Webb's 24.

v Eastern Province, won 31-13
Date: 7 June
Referee: P van Blommestein (Cape Town)
England: *Tries – P. Hull 2, S. Bates; Penalties – J. Callard 2, M. Catt 2; Conversions – Catt 2*
Eastern Province: *Try – A. Fourie; Penalties – B. Kruger 2; Conversion – Kruger*

Sent off:
T. Rodber & S Tremain

Injury list:
Dean Ryan and John Mallett broken hands; Graham Rowntree knocked out cold; Jonathan Callard 25 stitches; Martin Mostert, a broken nose

Another totally imcompetent refereeing performance. Clearly, the game in South Africa has more to do with thuggery than with the spirit of playing the ball. South Africa will win no friends on the international circuit if she continues in this vein. Rodber was let-off (wrongly) with a caution and played in the second Test, when he would have been suspended at home. Given the furore of the President of the RFU's remarks when Phil de

Glanville's face was re-arranged by the All Blacks last October, his silence over Rodber's sending off was deafening. By refusing to step in the RFU lost the high moral ground – perhaps forever.

v South Africa Second Test, lost 9-27

Date: 11 June
Venue: Newlands, Cape Town
Referee: C. Hawke (NZ)
Crowd: 60,000
England: Penalties – *R. Andrew 3*
SA: Tries: *H. le Roux & A. Joubert; Penalties – le Roux 3 & Joubert 2; Conversion – Joubert*

England were blown away almost as comprehensively as the South Africans were in the first Test. Tim Rodber was a ghost of his former self and cannot have been match fit after his mid-week illness; he certainly wasn't mentally

fit. The South Africans were, to use that overworked cliche, awesome. This was their first victory on home soil under a neutral referee. For England, many of whose players were punch-drunk with too much rugby in the last two years, could not peak yet again.

Quote of the Tour:
Louis Luyt, President of SARFU to Ian Beer, President of the RFU: *"You don't believe in professionalism. You are a pure amateur. I believe in amateurism. But I am a true professional."*

CONCLUSION:

This tour showed how far behind world standards the Five Nations Championship is. It also showed England how they must adjust their game if they are to move past the quarter-finals in 1995 when their likely opponents will be South Africa.

This was a tough baptism

for new manager Jack Rowell. Apart from not insisting that Rodber be suspended for one Test, he handled his new responsibilties well. If he is destined to have a running game he must change his half backs, Rob Andrew's brilliant first test performance notwithstanding and especially as Stuart Barnes has announced his retirement. Rowell should also choose a new captain; Carling looks wrong.

TOUR RECORD
P8 W3 L5 F152 A165
(F: 11t, 26p, 1 dg, 8c. A: 13t, 29p, 1dg, 5c)

Tries:
2 – Andrew, Hopley, Hull, T. Underwood,
1 – Bates, Clarke, R. Underwood

Leading scorers:
Andrew 58 *(2t, 13p, 1dg, 3c)*
Barnes 22 *(6p 2c)*
Callard 17 *(5p 1c)*

IRELAND to AUSTRALIA May – June 1994

v Western Australia, won 64-8

Date: 18 May
Referee: A. Cole
Ireland: Tries – *M. Field 2, T. Kingston 2, D. Corkery 2, C. O'Shea, P. Johns, J. Davidson; Penalty – E.Elwood; Conversion – Elwood 8*
W Australia: Try – *J.*

O'Callaghan; Penalty – T. Fearn

Perth is always a lovely place to start a tour in Australia but, as rugby is probably fourth in importance to Rules, League and Soccer, tourists are hardly ever going to be tripped up. Rugby in Perth is not a true reflection

of the game in Australia and this tends to soften up visitors

v New South Wales, lost 18-55

Date: 22 May
Referee:
Ireland: Tries – *J. Bell & N. Francis; Penalties E. Elwood 2; Conversion – Elwood*

NSW: Tries – D. Campese 2, S. Payne 2, R. Tombs 2, M. Brial & R. Waugh; Penalties – T. Wallace; Conversions – Wallace 6

As if the Irish needed any reminding, rugby begins and ends in Sydney for all tourists and they went down to a massive defeat.

v Australian Capital Territories, lost 9-22

Date: 25 May
Referee: B. Kinsey (NSW)
Ireland: Penalties – A. McGowan 3
ACT: Tries – M. O'Connor, J. Swan & D. Grimmond: Penalty – O'Connor; Conversions – O'Connor 2

With their Wednesday side, the Irish suffered another defeat; this tour is shaping up to be as bad as their last visit here.

v Queensland, lost 26-29

Date: 29 May
Ireland: Tries – S. Geoghegan, K. Wood; Penalties – C. O'Shea 3; Drop goal – Elwood; Conversions – Elwood & O'Shea
Queensland: Tries – P. Slattery & D. Herbert; Penalties – M. Lynagh 5; Conversions – Lynagh 2

An injury-time kick deprived the Irish of a draw. The Irish needed to play like this in the Tests to run

Australia close.

v Australia B, lost 9-57

Date: 1 June
Ireland: Penalties – A. McGowan 3
Australia B: Tries – Catchpole 3, Apps, Dalton, Howard, Mandrusiak, Murdoch, Ofahengaue; Penalties – Mandrusiak 2; Conversions Mandrusiak 3

A record loss for the Irish side; good to see Willie Ofengaue playing again. The Irish sent for scrum half Niall Hogan to cover for Alain Roland injured in this match.

v AUSTRALIA First Test lost 13-33

Date: 5 June
Venue: Brisbane
Referee: J. Dume (France)
Crowd: 26,545
Ireland: Try – P. Johns; Penalties – E. Elwood & C. O'Shea; Conversion – Elwood
Australia: Tries – M. Lynagh & I. Tabua, D. Campese, D.Smith & M. Burke; Penalties – Lynagh 2; Conversion – Lynagh

NEW CAPS
Ireland: N. Woods, K. Wood, J. Bell & D. Corkery;
Australia: M. Piti & M. O'Connor

Campese scored his 58th international try – a new world record.

v NSW County, won 20-18

Date: 8 June
Referee: K. O'Halloran (Queensland)
Ireland: Tries – J. Staples; Penalties – A. McGowan 5
NSW County: Tries – M. Sykes, J. Nowlan, S. Rutledge; Penalty – S. Salter

This was a lucky win for the Irish but they were grateful for it. Salter and Eddy missed eight kicks at goal for NSW County. Still a win's a win and this will put the Irish in better mood for the second Test.

v AUSTRALIA Second Test, lost 18-32

Date: 11 June
Venue: Sydney
Referee: J. Dume (France)
Ireland: Tries – P. Clohessy & N. Francis; Penalty – C. O'Shea; Drop goal – O;Shea; Conversion – O'Shea
Australia: Tries – D. Herbert, D. Wilson & I. Tabua; Penalties – M. Lynagh 5; Conversion – Lynagh

NEW CAPS
Ireland: G. Fulcher;
Australia: D. Herbert

Michael Lynagh took his point scoring record to 801 points in a disjointed game. The Australians are expected to win these encounters by a landslide and, as a result, are finding it difficult to motivate themselves at present.

CONCLUSION: The Irish record was woeful; given that they are often hard-pressed to find 15 truly international players it is difficult to know how they will proceed from here.

TOUR RECORD
P8 W2 L6 F157 A236

ITALY to AUSTRALIA May – June 1994

v S Australia, won 60-12
Date: 28 May

v N Territory, won 37-6
Date: 1 June

v Sydney, won 36-26
Date: 8 June

v Queensland XV won 21-19
Date: 11 June

v Queensland County Districts won 57-13
Date: 15 June

v AUSTRALIA, First Test, lost 20-23

Date: 18 June
Venue: Brisbane
Australia: *Tries – M. Burkee; Penalty – T. Wallace 3; Conversions – Wallace*
Italy: *Try – M. Bonomi; Penalties – L. Troiani 5*

v New South Wales County won 30-20
Date: 22 June

v AUSTRALIA, Second Test, lost 7-20
Date: 25 June
Venue: Melbourne
Australia: *Try – D. Campese; Penalties – T. Wallace 5*
Italy: *Try – C. Orlandi; Conversion – L. Troiani*

Played in a rain-storm this game did not live up to the first Test. David Campese scored a try, his 59th, but admitted after the game that he had not grounded it, further evidence of the need for the use of television as an adjudicator.

CONCLUSION: This tour put Italian rugby on the map. Why do they find playing the Five Nations countries so taxing?

TOUR RECORD
P8 W6 L2 F268 A139

WALES to CANADA, FIJI, TONGA & W. SAMOA June 1994

v Canadian Select won 28-19
Date: 8 June
Referee: D. Mews (Alberta)
Wales: *Tries – P. Arnold, A. Clement & D. Manley; Penalties – N. Jenkins 3; Conversions – Jenkins 2*
Canadian Select: *Try – McKinnon; Penalties – Ross 4; Conversion – Ross*

v CANADA, Test, won 33-15
Date: 11 June

Venue: Hamilton
Referee: I. Rodgers (SA)
Wales: *Tries: M. Hall (2), I. Evans – equalling Welsh record of 20 tries with Gareth Edwards and Gerald Davies; Penalties – N. Jenkins 4; Conversions – Jenkins 3*
Canada: *Penalties – G. Rees 5*

Wales put right their defeat in November at the Arms Park with a forward controlled platform which gave their elusive backs much to play with....

Jenkins has now scored 246 points in 20 internationals.

v FIJI, Test, won 23-8
Date: 18 June
Venue: Suva
Referee: E. Skiar (Argentina)
Wales: *Tries – M. Rayner, R. Collins; Penalties – A. Davies 3; Conversions – Davies 2*
Fiji: *Try – J. Veitayaki; Penalty – R. Bogisa*

NEW CAP:
Robin McBryde

Not exactly end to end stuff but another win for the Welsh as they prepare for what is really their only true test on tour, Western Samoa next week.

v TONGA, Test,
won 18-9
Date: 23 June
Venue: Nuku'alofa
Wales: *Penalties – N. Jenkins 6*
Tonga: *Penalties – K. Tu'lpulotu 3*

NEW CAPS:
Gwilym Williams, Paul John,

Ian Buckett & Steve Williams Wales' fifth win on the trot away from home and a record of sorts. Neil Jenkins edged closer to Paul Thorburn's all-time points scoring record.

v WESTERN SAMOA,
Test, lost 9-34
Date: 25 June
Venue: Apia
Referee: B.Leask (Aus)
Crowd: 20,000
Wales: *Penalties – N. Jenkins 3*
WS: *Tries – B. Lima 2, Lam; Penalties – D. Kellett 5; Conversions – Kellett 2*

This was the game the Welsh had to win to justify many things to themselves not least the £250,000 cost of the tour. But once again they found the Western Samoans too strong for them, especially up-front.

Rob Leyshon, the Welsh team doctor, claimed the conditions were dangerous as temepratures topped 100°F; he treated two players for heat exhaustion.

TOUR RECORD
P5 W4 L1 F111 A85

FIJI to NEW ZEALAND May – June 1994

This was a tour set up to re-establish the Fijian team. No Test was played against NZ which gave the six match schedule an air of unreality.

v Bay of Plenty
lost 26-36

v Thames Valley
won 35-16

v NZ Universities
lost 5-11

v Horowhenua
won 42-25

v New Zealand Maoris
lost 13-34

v East Coast
won 62-6

TOUR RECORD
P6 W3 L3 F183 A129

FRANCE to CANADA & NEW ZEALAND June – July 1994

v Canadian XV
won 34-31
Date: 1 June

v CANADA, Test,
lost 16-18
Date: 4 June
Venue: Nepean, Ontario
Referee: M. Rogers (SA)
France: *Try – E. Ntamack; Penalties – T. Lacroix 3*
Canada: *Penalties G. Rees 6*

Sendings off:
Philippe Sella, on the day he won his 99th cap, and Mark Cardinal, the Canadian hooker.

This was Canada's first win against the French.

v Northland won 28-23
Date: 9 June

v North Harbour

lost 23-27
Date: 12 June

v Wairarapa Bush
won 53-9
Date: 15 June

v New Zealand A
won 33-25
Date: 18 June

This was an important match

for the French to win and showed they could peak at the right time.

v Nelson Bay won 46-18
Date: 22 June

Xavier Blond, France's acting captain, was sent off

v NEW ZEALAND, First Test, won 22-8
Date: 26 June
Venue: Christchurch
Referee: D. Bevin (Wales)
France: *Try – P. Benetton; Penalties – T. Lacroix 2; Drop goals – C. Deylaud 2 & J. Sadourny*
NZ: *Try – F. Bunce; Penalty – M.Cooper*

NEW CAPS:
Jonah Lomu, youngest ever player to be capped for NZ at 19 years of age

Historic landmark:
Philippe Sella's 100th cap

France have a habit of upsetting the form book and they

did it again with this comprehensive victory over a XV that simply did not represent the best in New Zealand. Expect selectors heads to roll. France have now beaten both Australia and New Zealand within the space of eight months. Sella's diminishing pace is beginning to find him out, he missed two scoring chances.

v Hawke's Bay lost 25-30
Date: 29 June

France pressed the self-destruct button after leading 25-3. They blamed the referee who gave away 31 penalties four to the French and the rest (27) to Hawke's Bay......

v NEW ZEALAND Second Test, won 23-20
Date: 3 July
Venue: Auckland
Referee: D. Bevan (Wales)
France: *Tries – E. Ntamack &*

J-L Sadourny; Penalties – T. Lacroix 2 & C. Deylaud; Conversions – Lacroix & Deylaud
NZ: *Try – S. Fitzpatrick; Penalties – M. Cooper 5*

New Zealand were leading 20-16 with two minutes to go when a sweeping movement starting in France's own 22metres led to Jean-Luc Sadourny touching down. Christian Deylaud converted and France became the first country to win a series in New Zealand since 1986.

This success will certainly lead to a re-appraisal of the French side who began this tour with a Test loss against Canada. Much credit for their perfromance has been given to the leadership qualities of Jeff Tordo even if he is no longer "le capitaine".

As for New Zealand, John Hart waits in the wings to assume control again as coach.

TOUR RECORD
P10 W7 L3 F303 A209

Top ranking Australia – a lot to live up to in the coming season

World Rankings 1994
(1993 ranking in brackets)

1. Australia (3)
2. England (4)
3. France (2)
4. New Zealand (1)
5. South Africa (5)
6. Western Samoa (7)
7. Wales (9)
8. Canada (10)
9. Ireland (8)
10. Argentina (–)

Rugby World Cup Seeding 1995
(1991 seeding in brackets)

1. Australia (4)
2. England (6)
3. New Zealand (1)
4. Scotland (5)
5. France (2)
6. Ireland (7)
7. Western Samoa (–)
8. Canada (–)
9. South Africa (–)
10. Argentina (–)

OF RED WINE, WARTHOGS – AND RUGBY

The final tour match brought down the curtain on a journey that had travelled full circle. The defeats against Orange Free State and Natal seemed ancient history after that marvellous day in Pretoria. This Saturday the wonderful city of Cape Town offered rather less hospitality on the pitch than at Loftus Versfeld. South Africa matched England's intensity of the first Test and, after some heroic defence, England wilted. Even England's renowned courage could not block all the holes in a dam which South Africa's forward play burst.

A record of three wins and five defeats for England is perceived as failure, yet this does not tell the whole story. England learned much about themselves. That Test win in Pretoria must rank among their finest performances of recent times. Additionally, the tour was a happy one. Manager Jack Rowell should be congratulated for keeping the morale of all 30-plus players high. This was a task beyond the management of the 1993 Lions.

Most importantly, we were offered an opportunity to live in a country that is working so hard to expel old ghosts. We understand that apartheid is now illegal, but in parts of the Free State and Pretoria the culture is ingrained.

On arrival, I confess I expected all Afrikaners to be morally bankrupt. To my great pleasure I discovered that they are not. Cape Town, in particular, taught me that a good Afrikaner is no different to his English, Welsh or Scottish counterpart.

On the day before the final Test I drank wine with an Afrikaner journalist, Louis de Villiers. Intelligent, irreverent and witty, he was great company as I stared at Table Moun-tain and the surf crashed around me. It had been a voyage of discovery and a pleasure.

THURSDAY MAY 12

ONLY TWO days ago I celebrated the election of Nelson Mandela in South Africa House, London. Even as the champagne flowed I wondered how the Embassy staff could be more interested in the England tour than the focus of the day's festivities.

Doubtless four weeks of grillings on the training field lie ahead. The notoriously indolent Nigerian trio will definitely suffer their share of agony, but at least there will be time for the beach. Even as I write at 6.45pm my room-mate, Adedayo Adebayo, has fallen into a blissful slumber.

FRIDAY MAY 13

COMPLETION OF the tour's first serious training session. It is good news for those who enjoy good back play. Les Cusworth's vision of attacking the midfield using subtle running angles is similar to Rowell's view. It is old hat to the Bath backs.

After training, minds turn to more serious matters – the Players Court, perhaps the most enduring symbol of a rugby tour. Our judge is Damian Hopley, he of the theology degree, while Brian Moore is prosecution and I defend any miscreants. Steve Bates, a master at Radley, is the clerk of the court. Sadly the original fines collectors, Leonard and Ojomoh, have been sacked. It was felt that the carpenter from Barking and embezzler from Benin City were not the "right sort of chaps". Their replacements are Dewi Morris and Graham Dawe. Few will argue with our farming friend.

SATURDAY MAY 14

DURBAN IS supercharged for the SuperTen final which decides the strongest province in the Southern Hemisphere. Sadly for the locals, Natal performed in a style that would delight England if they repeat it in seven days.

SUNDAY MAY 15

RUGBY IS BARELY mentioned today, both innovative and sensible. On a tour a purportedly amateur sport becomes professional in all

Back in Durban the tour claims its first victim of illness – me. When I try to curb my drinking I catch a virus. Perhaps I will change my tour strategy and increase my consumption of South African red wine . . .

bar payment. Everybody needs a day off once in a while, including the rugby squad.

We have travelled four hours north from Durban to Hluhluwe Game Reserve, deep in Zulu territory. It seems an inordinate distance for an overnight stop, but the tranquility and colour of the night sky made it worth-while. On the same front the boys on safari saw little other than warthogs. My wife, Lesley, claims to sleep with one.

MONDAY MAY 16

BACK IN DURBAN the tour claims its first victim of illness – me. When I try to curb my drinking I catch a virus. Perhaps I will change

my tour strategy and increase my consumption of South African red wine. It is hard to feel sorry for yourself watching the crashing surf from your room, but it is frustrating.

As others focus on the Orange Free State I ponder my fate. I will attempt to train tomorrow but my tour ebullience is dimmed. At least the doctor's deluxe suite is consolation.

TUESDAY MAY 17

A MIRACLE OCCURS as I am passed fit to play. We travelled to Bloemfontein for the Orange Free State match tomorrow. The liberal loathing of old South Africa is exposed at a reception for those involved in tomorrow's game. Our big eaters did not even make the main course.

WEDNESDAY MAY 18

ANOTHER TOUR, another loss. The South African honeymoon is officially over as our young team fails to come to terms with the loose power and pace of the Free State. Some line-out ball and determined tackling may have proved our salvation. The press are not unduly aggressive, but defeat against Natal on Saturday will test the mettle of us all.

Referees test the composure of even the most experienced tourist. At the post-match function, when Rowell called upon the referee to accept an England tie, we found his mother acting as his replacement. Jack, dead-pan, said "most of us are surprised that he has parents".

THURSDAY MAY 19

LIKE THE BRAINS of a local farmer who accosted me in a drunken stupor last night, our hotel pool stands empty. It does not deter the troops from unwinding in the sun alongside it, after a training session that offered hope.

Despite the traditional post-match drinking wake, the squad train well, committed to righting the poor start. Hopley and Catt are absent through injuries received yesterday; Adebayo sits out the whole session with an ankle injury, at least that was his plan. Fortunately press-ups and other assorted inquisitorial torments should ensure that he will probably be fit to resume running tomorrow.

FRIDAY MAY 20

6.00PM AND THE stars are over the ocean. It has been a long day, the midweek side trained for two long hours under the savage tongue of Rowell. Players received rebukes the likes of which most had never heard. Rowell loves to be bad. The afternoon is spent poolside writing my Monday column for the *Telegraph* and this diary. The squad are getting to wonder whether I am a player or a journalist on tour. Attempting to be both makes it a tiring tour for me. Luckily I am still rooming with Adebayo, who is happy to sleep on my behalf.

SATURDAY MAY 21

DREADFUL DAY. Our so-called Test team are outplayed by Natal. Rowell masked his despair by grinning and wise-cracking all evening but the Bath boys know that this means a temper typhoon is about to blow.

David Pears, always regarded as a racing certainty for an injury, sadly confirmed his vulnerability and will be homeward bound. Doubtless Jon Callard will be recalled to the squad. The odds of 8-1 I took against JC playing in the second Test must be a good bet. The evening is alcoholic. Thankfully the Natalians are rather more modest in victory than the Free State stormtroopers.

SUNDAY MAY 22

THE BEST TRAINING session of the tour.

The 15 who did not play yesterday respond to the awful tour start with an overt display of enthusiasm. Worryingly, many of us were equally enthusiastic about drinking through the day. Rowell has identified a number of players as playboys. In typical fashion those highlighted form a Playboy Club. The basic rule is to drink and act with a degree of panache. The founding members include Damian Hopley, myself and Mike Catt, although the chief socialite is Jack.

MONDAY MAY 23

THAT FAMILIAR hangover feeling rears its head for the first time in training. The Playboy Club decides that it would be sensible to go underground. There is tangible tension on the training pitch.

Off the field the Natal defeat and the predictable press reaction has resulted in the normal tour ill-feeling between players and press. One article suggested that Will Carling may be dropped. It was touching to see the players' support of the captain but it is also incredibly naive to expect the press corps to act as a PR firm.

TUESDAY 24 MAY

A SAD DAY for the tour party as we leave our sunshine base in Durban. If the future generation of South Africans follow in the footsteps of the Natalians we have encountered, the country can expect to smile.

The locals almost queue to inform us that

It was touching to see the players' support of the captain but it is also incredibly naive to expect the press corps to act as a PR firm

any enjoyment will be curtailed throughout the stay in the Transvaal. The Afrikaans dislike of Empire runs deep. An article of mine published yesterday in the *Telegraph* has raised journalistic eyebrows. Tomorrow we play at Potchefstroom, a mere 30 miles from Eugene Terreblanche and friends. I wonder whether the local police will be detailed to protect me alone.

WEDNESDAY MAY 25

A RARE DAY of double delight. The side win against Western Transvaal and a group of schoolboys who invade the pitch carrying a giant flag of the old South Africa are booed by the crowd. As Potchefstroom is considered an AWB stronghold, it is a wildly encouraging sign.

The game itself offered less about which to be enthusiastic. Fear of failure stifles even the most experienced. Hopefully victory will relieve the tension. I receive my first injury – four stitches in the head. The press hope that it is retribution, but it is less sensational, although me receiving an injury from tackling would shock many.

THURSDAY MAY 26

THE FOUR STITCHES rule me out of bench duty for the Transvaal game. This means I travel as part of the nefarious nine to a gala dinner organised by Mr Big himself, Louis Luyt. Luckily my hosts are decent people who pour vast quantities of red wine down my throat. Martin Bayfield's hosts were even more generous. It takes a lot of wine to make a 6'10" man sick.

Our president, Ian Beer, informs me that I have caused the RFU embarrassment with my comments about the Free State. After 20 years of turning the other cheek to apartheid the RFU still feel uncomfortable about opinions. The price we pay for the sport's elitist rule.

FRIDAY MAY 27

CONCERNED ABOUT the relative worthlessness of the rand in Britain, I decide to donate a large amount to the casino around the corner from our hotel in Pretoria. Damian Hopley and Lawrence Dallaglio are also keen on supporting local gambling establishments.

We arrive at 10pm and were informed that the roulette wheel would not spin until the owner returned. The crowds of desparate souls seen in British casinos were limited to three players and two nameless press associ-

> ...I have caused the RFU embarrassment with my comments about the Free State. After 20 years of turning the other cheek to apartheid the RFU still feel uncomfortable about opinions

ates. Despite losing it takes a major effort to keep the place open until 1.30am. The owner, like Pretoria, is a sleepy soul.

SATURDAY MAY 28

TRANSVAAL REMIND us how exciting a game rugby can be. Their play with ball in hand would have some rugby league fans doubting the superiorty of their game. I watch Hennie le Roux, the Transvaal fly half, in envy. It must be marvellous to play with the freedom he is allowed. Everybody wants the ball in hand. There are no negative shouts of "give it leather" from forwards. A third defeat in four games is devastating. We console ourselves, confident that our major allies in the forthcoming Test series will be the South African selectors.

SUNDAY 29 MAY

THE TEAM FOR Tuesday includes no Saturday names. However, a number of players believe one good game could win a recall to the Test side. One good game has been beyond most of us.

A battered squad travel to the famous Sun City entertainment resort. The place is like a set from a Tarzan film with a Caribbean beach thrown in for good measure. Rotund groups of ladies hypnotically spin fruit machines while drinking sherry. If this is not depressing enough, the mock earthquake and volcanic eruption on the "Bridge of Time" caps a day in hell – and I lost again at roulette.

MONDAY MAY 30

TRAINING HAS become fragmented between the perceived midweek and Saturday side. Whereas a Friday session is geared specifically to the next day's game, this session is more general. As a few players believe they are playing for a Test spot it appears unfair to prioritise for one group. Simon Shaw, the young Bristol lock, arrives as replacement for the concussed Martin Johnson. Two weeks of playing and two players' tours are ended.

TUESDAY MAY 31

WE FLY INTO Kimberley for the match with South Africa A. The steward points out the Big Hole from which the country's main

The poor start of the tour is emphasised by the delighted reaction to defeat. The side play with more spirit than during any game so far...

supply of diamonds have been mined. We were informed that it is 800 metres deep, about the same depth of mire that the tour would be in if we lost badly.

The poor start of the tour is emphasised by the delighted reaction to defeat. The side play with more spirit than during any game so far but I am amazed at how little defeat hurts this young side. I tell Rowell that the reason for Bath's decade of dominance is self-evident. At Bath defeat is greeted with full-scale mourning, not a small-scale party.

WEDNESDAY JUNE 1

THE TEAM IS announced for the first Test. Unsurprisingly, I am not delighted. The person with most reason to feel disappointment is Steve Ojomoh, who has been the best player on the tour. The selection is clearly conservative, suggesting a considerable lack of confidence in the Rowell-Cusworth vision.

THURSDAY JUNE 2

THE FIRST OFFICIAL visit to a town-ship. The children of Soshanguve are delightful once they overcome their deep-seated fear of white authority. Natural ability merges with naive enthusiasm and helps create the most enjoyable afternoon of the tour. The biggest blemish is the absence of the Test team, apart from Rory, Jason and Victor. I hope that everyone feels enough human responsibility towards these previously oppressed people to make a visit to the township near Port Elizabeth on Monday. There is more to touring than team meetings, training and matches. Even the photographers were sober for this trip.

FRIDAY JUNE 3

THE LULL BEFORE the storm. The Test side are understandably tense. The mood spreads through the squad and the mood is subdued.

SATURDAY JUNE 4

A HISTORIC DAY. South Africa reveals its new friendly face with old and new flags mixing. Even the normally apolitical players seemed genuinely in awe of Mandela when they meet him before the kick off.

The day is a realised dream for the South African nation, but a nightmare for its rugby team. England produce one of their finest performances and destroy South Africa with precise and powerful play. All the provincial debacles seem forgotten as the night explodes into revelry. Igor, the Arsenal-made photographer, is nearly squashed by Dean Richards, who illustrates magnificent bar-diving technique. Normally those players involved feel neglected and deflated, but such is the magnitude of the whole day that everyone celebrates in style. The majority do not consider sleep an option.

SUNDAY JUNE 5

WE ARRIVE IN Port Elizabeth, Mike Catt's home, sporting dark sunglasses despite the rain falling. Red-eyed and hungover I resent the warm welcome we receive from a local choir. Port Elizabeth itself reminds me of New Zealand. No wonder Catt came to England.

Our Holiday Inn provides no room service before 6.30pm and not even enough shampoo per room for Nigel Redman.

MONDAY JUNE 6

I AM MASSIVELY disappointed to be judged unfit for the Eastern Province match tomorrow. After Saturday's win, tour morale is high and the Tuesday side want to keep momentum going.

The players who are not involved in tomorrow's game visit a local township to coach the enthusiastic masses of wide-eyed children. The occasion is somewhat spoiled by the cold wind and rain. I teach my group

to side-step and swerve, they teach me not to feel sorry for myself. There are worse things in life than groin injuries.

TUESDSAY JUNE 7

THE MIDWEEK side finish their games with an heroic victory against a ferocious 'Grizz' Wyllie-inspired Eastern Province. Injuries to Dean Ryan, Graham Rowntree and an appalling injury to Jon Callard tarnish the reputation of this province. Wyllie's coaching seems synonymous with unacceptable violence.

Rather than publicly condemn him and his team the RFU committee men, freeloading on tour, with the honourable exception of Ian Beer, question the decision to allow Tim Rodber to play the Saturday after being sent off. Christ may advocate turning the other cheek, but when three thugs attack you on the ground it is not easy to be a Christian rugby player. All credit to the team, against the normal abject failure of our committee, excluding 'Beero'.

WEDNESDAY JUNE 8

THE TOUR PARTY move on in high spirits to Cape Town. Leaving the horrors of the Holiday Inn Garden Court for the Cape Sun cheers even the most miserable of tourists. One side of the hotel overlooks the ocean, the other Table Mountain.

In celebration of the tour's revival and our re-emergence into civilisation the Playboy Club is revived. Led spiritedly by the 'Bobby Crush' of the tour, Damian Hopley, myself and a few Wasps join forces with the dangerous photographers to throw a piano party. From Madness to Don McLean the boys howl loudly until Igor breaks the microphone. As Elvis Costello says: "Accidents will happen".

THURSDAY JUNE 9

DESPITE THE recent victories the team

appear tense in training. Many players sweat even more when they see the price of diamonds in a Cape Town jewellers. Anybody who thinks rugby players have no price to pay for touring should think again.

Player resentment towards the committee runs high. There is a righteous sense of indignation over the alleged comments that members were disappointed in the decision to play Rodber. They do not seem as concerned about Callard's 25 gruesome stitches. In the evening we attend a cocktail party which South Africa also attend. A sober affair.

FRIDAY JUNE 10

THE FINAL training session. Despite all the weather warnings, the South African sky is a glorious blue. As I stand on Table Mountain looking down on the beautiful city and its historic township scars I cannot fail to reflect on the success of transformation. There is a sense of pride and purpose. The people have lived through infamy but the majority are not mending fences quickly. I hope they drive apartheid from every citizen's mind as well as the law. God bless Mandela and the new South Africa ■

© *Stuart Barnes 1994. This diary appeared in the* Daily Telegraph, *June 1994*

THE IRFB REPORT 1994-95

How 1993-94 was full of shocks and surprises in the world of international rugby.

By KEITH ROWLANDS

A YEAR OF LIVING EXCITINGLY

In this wonderful game of ours we tend to concentrate on the playing side, and quite rightly so. Rugby Football has always been a players' game. It was invented by the schoolboys at Rugby School and since its inception over 170 years ago it has given a great deal of satisfaction to millions of players all over the world, year after year and generation after generation.

The season has been as exciting as any in recent memory. My beloved Wales started by being humiliated by Canada in their own backyard at the Arms Park, but finished the season as Five Nations Champions. England dismantled the seemingly unstoppable All Blacks, only to be beaten by the admirable Irish, before they upset the odds to win the first Test in South Africa.

Italy beat France for the first time in their history, and nearly downed Australia, the World Champions, on their home territory. France were beaten by Wales in Cardiff and by the Canadians in Vancouver but turned the table on New Zealand in two epic encounters. South Africa silenced their critics with an outstanding performance against England in the second Test, to re-establish their credentials as one of the favourites for the 1995 Rugby World Cup.

The background to this frenetic rugby activity is next year's William Webb Ellis tournament. The eyes and ears of the world will focus on South Africa in 1995 and our game will, once more, be under the spotlight when billions of people will watch this spec-

tacular event via numerous television stations throughout the world.

However, let us not forget that over 100 matches have already been played in the qualifying rounds of the Rugby World Cup. It is difficult to single out any one for particular praise. However, the remarkable achievement of Ivory Coast in eliminating Namibia, Zimbabwe and Morocco to qualify for South Africa must rate as one of the biggest upsets in the game's history.

Tonga, one of the nations invited in 1987, knocked out in 1991 by Western Samoa, bounced back with a vengeance. They prevailed over their oldest opponents Fiji, one of the seeded nations in 1991, in a two-match series.

Uruguay, one of the new nations to enter the World Cup fold, nearly knocked out Argentina, the Americas qualifier; while the brave performances of the US Eagles in the play-offs for the American zone makes one feel sorry that they will be unable to display their newly acquired confidence and expertise in South Africa in 1995.

The list of achievements is long and is giving us in the International Rugby Football Board and those in the Rugby World Cup organisation confidence that the tournament is fulfilling its intended role. Playing and refereeing standards generally throughout the world are going up; the status of the game is growing and our member unions are getting increasingly focused on their development.

But the tournament is not only a launching

pad for players. It is also an administrative testing ground for the emerging and developing nations. Putting together the logistics of a four nations tournament is an administrative nightmare which requires competence, patience, acumen and more than anything else time. Hundreds of officials from countries as far apart as Hungary and Chile, Malaysia and the Netherlands, Tunisian and the USA have been involved in making the 1995 tournament possible. Without them the final stages in South Africa would not take place.

The game between Latvia and Germany in Riga, in the early rounds of the east European zone, is one I particularly treasure. It was Latvia's first ever international and was quite an occasion. However, while on the playing side they were more than adequate, there was, quite naturally, very little knowledge of how to organise a game at this level.

Latvia is one of the new rugby nations to have emerged following the collapse of the Soviet empire and not surprisingly the national ethos is very strong. It was a very emotional occasion, as you would appreciate. The Latvian administrators went to considerable effort to provide the game with the required infrastructure and their efforts paid off. On the day, although seemingly a long way from Twickenham, Riga was bound closely to anything the Five Nations could produce, albeit on a smaller scale.

While the outstanding hospitality and organisation in countries like Italy, Romania, Germany and the Netherlands was not unexpected, the quality of the administrative set-up in Kenya, Morocco, Portugal, Uruguay, Tunisia, Poland and Hungary – to mention just a few – took us all by surprise.

The administration in today's game is taken for granted. The players forget, as we did 30 years ago, that their efforts on the playing field

In those days, both sides believed in the amateur ethos of rugby football

are more than matched by the unswerving activity of club, county, provincial and national administrators. In those days, both sides believed in, and to a large extent respected, the amateur ethos of rugby football.

Nothing has changed and yet everything seems to be different. Today's game, caught between the relentless drive towards professionalism of the elite players in a handful of unions and its Corinthian ethos and traditions, is in a catch-22 situation. The deadlock must be overcome. The game is at a crossroads and I took the opportunity, as my tenure as IRFB Secretary was approaching its end, to present to the Council of the Board a list of the burning issues the game is facing as the century is drawing to a close. This document became known as the "Strategic Plan" for Rugby Football, and I am delighted that the Council has accepted a majority of its recommendations. Amateurism is one of the key issues tackled in it and one hopes that the working party set up on Amateurism will produce an all-encompassing philosophy which will allow the game to sort out the contradictions currently tearing it apart.

In my letter to the members of the IRFB Council I pointed out that today's game is facing many challenges: it has to ask itself many questions and find many answers. A methodology to approach the laws and law changes; the constitution of the international body and the role of regional organisations; the promotion of the game among the youngsters; not to mention the inclusion of the women's game, one of the fastest growing team sports in the world; and the international rugby tours and tournament structure, are just a few of the issues the strategic document has identified. The game is waiting for answers – some of which may come in 1995 ∎

Keith Rowlands is the secretary of the IRFB

IRFB STRUCTURE

Address: 5 College Green, Bristol BS1 5TF, UK.
Tel +44 71 272 290111. Fax: +44 272 250033

Council: Peter Brook and John Jeavons-Fellows (England); Tom Kiernan and Dr Syd Millar (Ireland); Alan Hosie and Fred McLeod (Scotland); Vernon Pugh and Ray Williams (Wales); Dr Roger Vanderfield and Norbert Byrne (Australia); Bernard Lapasset and Marcel Martin (France): R.A. Fisher and John Dowling (New Zealand); Dr Louis Luyt and Prof. F.C. Eloff (South Africa); Carlos Tozzi (Argentina); Alan Sharp (Canada); Maurizio Mondeli (Italy); Shiggy Konno (Japan)

Officers

Chairman: Vernon Pugh (Wales)
Vice-chairman: Marcel Martin (France)
Hon treasurer: Fred McLeod (Scotland)
Secretary: Ray Williams (Wales)

INTERNATIONAL FIXTURES 1994-5

SEPTEMBER 1994
3: Bath v Barbarians
6: French Barbarians v Barbarians
17: ROMANIA V WALES (RWC Europe, play-off)
30: Border v Argentina

OCTOBER 1994
1: ITALY v ROMANIA (RWC Europe, play-off)
4: South Africa A v Argentina
8: SOUTH AFRICA v ARGENTINA, 1st Test
11: Northern Free State v Argentina
12: WALES v ITALY (RWC Europe, play-off)
15: SOUTH AFRICA v ARGENTINA, 2ns Test
22: Cardiff v South Africa
22-29: RWC 95 Asia play-offs, Kuala Lumpur
26: Wales A v South Africa (Newport)
29: Llanelli v South Africa

NOVEMBER 1994
1: Ireland Development XV v Namibia
2: Neath v South Africa
5: IRELAND v NAMIBIA
    Swansea v South Africa
    Oxford University v Romania
8: Cambridge University v Romania
9: Scotland A v South Africa (Melrose)
12: ENGLAND V ROMANIA
    Combined Scottish Districts v South Africa;
    Leinster v Namibia
15: Scottish Selection v South Africa (Aberdeen)
19: SCOTLAND v SOUTH AFRICA
22: Pontypridd v South Africa
23: Cambridge University v Steele-Bodger's XV
26: WALES v SOUTH AFRICA
29: Combined Irish Provinces v South Africa

DECEMBER 1994
3: Barbarians v South Africa (Dublin)
    ITALY V CANADA
6: Oxford University v Cambridge University;
    England Emerging Players v Romania
10: ENGLAND v CANADA
17: FRANCE v CANADA

JANUARY 1995
7: Scotland A v Italy
21: FRANCE v WALES; IRELAND v ENGLAND;
    SCOTLAND v CANADA

FEBRUARY
4: ENGLAND v FRANCE; SCOTLAND v IRELAND
18: WALES v ENGLAND; FRANCE v SCOTLAND
19: England A v Italy

MARCH
4: IRELAND v FRANCE; SCOTLAND v WALES
18: WALES v IRELAND; ENGLAND v SCOTLAND
25-26: Cathay Pacific Sevens, Hong Kong

APRIL
22: SCOTLAND v ROMANIA
23: CANADA v NEW ZEALAND

MAY
6: French Cup Final (Paris);
    Pilkington Cup Final (Twickenham);
    Swalec Cup Final (Cardiff)
13: Middlesex Sevens

25 MAY-24 JUNE
    Third Rugby World Cup, South Africa

INTERNATIONAL TOURS 1994-9

1994
SOUTHERN HEMISPHERE
WORLD CUP 95
Far East play-offs
Africa play-offs

S Africa to New Zealand

NORTHERN HEMISPHERE
WORLD CUP 95
Europe play-offs for seeding
Wales, Italy & Romania

S Africa to Wales, Scotland &
Ireland
Canada to Ireland, England,
France, Italy & Scotland

1995
Third Rugby World Cup, S Africa

SOUTHERN HEMISPHERE
Argentina to Australia

NORTHERN HEMISPHERE
W Samoa to England & Scotland
New Zealand to France

1996
SOUTHERN HEMISPHERE
Scotland to New Zealand
New Zealand to South Africa
S Africa to Argentina

NORTHERN HEMISPHERE
Argentina to England
Australia to Scotland & Ireland

1997
SOUTHERN HEMISPHERE
Early rounds Fourth RWC 1999
Rugby World Cup Sevens, Hong
Kong
France to Australia
S Africa & Argentina to N Zealand
British Lions & Australia to S Africa
England & Australia to Argentina

NORTHERN HEMISPHERE
Early rounds of the Fourth RWC
1999
New Zealand to England & Wales
S Africa to France
England to Italy

1998
SOUTHERN HEMISPHERE
RWC 1999 preliminary matches
England to New Zealand
Ireland to S Africa
France to Argentina
Wales to South Pacific

NORTHERN HEMISPHERE
RWC 1999 preliminary matches
S Africa to Scotland & Ireland
Argentina to France

1999
Fourth Rugby World Cup

1995 *RUGBY ALMANACK XV*

njuries and a lack of real talent have severely depleted the choice this year for The International Almanack's World XV 1994 side. There doesn't appear to be an outstanding full-back or scrum-half in the world at present and no-one has really emerged in the front five to dominate the game match after match.

In the five single positions - 15, 10, 09, 08 and 02 only Michael Lynagh, despite his late injury, Phil Kearns and Dean Richards were obvious choices. At full-back there appears no single player of the calibre of a Blanco or a Gallagher whilst at scrum-half, there is an appalling dearth of ability.

It's not much better elsewhere. Which pair of centres have come close to Tim Horan and Jason Little, both sadly injured in the Queensland v Natal SuperTen final? None. And there must be doubts as to whether Jeremy Guscott is ever going to play again. On the other hand there were one or two players who did emerge during the season: Lee Stensness of New Zealand was a player of great vision as was his compatriot, Marc Ellis (even though he was often preferred at fly-half); so too, were Nigel Davies, (Wales) and Mike Catt (England).

THE TEAM

15 John Timu, New Zealand	01 Nick Popplewell, Ireland
	02 Phil Kearns, Australia
14 John Kirwan, New Zealand	03 Ewan McKenzie, Australia
13 Marc Ellis, New Zealand	
12 Nigel Davies, Wales	04 Ian Jones, New Zealand
11 Nigel Walker, Wales	05 Olivier Roumat, France
	06 Ilie Tabua, Australia
10 Michael Lynagh, Australia	07 Ben Clarke, England
09 Johan Roux, South Africa	08 Dean Richards, England

INTERNATIONAL SEVENS & TENS

Rugby traditionally is a 15-a-side game, but that is being challenged by the growing popularity of Tens and Sevens around the world. An international calendar is needed

SEVENS

Sevens has threatened to take off in the past and in the late 1980s groups of businessmen masquarading as rugby players tried hard to establish a Grand Prix vehicle for them – Monte Carlo, Hong Kong, America and Twickenham – but the plans did not find enough support.

Sevens is on the up again. The second RWC Sevens will take place in Hong Kong in 1997 after the colony has been handed back to China and the 1998 Commonwealth Games in Malaysia will also feature them for the first time. It is not clear whether it is Sevens or Fifteens that will feature as a show sport in the Millennium Olympic Games in Sydney. Meanwhile, without a proper Sevens world calendar, they still languish at the Cinderella end of the sport.

Results are patchy.

28 AUGUST
CIS Insurance Selkirk Sevens at Philiphaugh
Northampton 19 Gala 14 *(third consecutive year that the teams have contested the final)*

Ryden Sevens at Old Anniesland
Glasgow High Kelvinside 41 Selkirk 7
(GHK Holders 1992)

Worthington Welsh Sevens
South Wales Police 24 Pontypridd 14

26 NOV
Dubai International Sevens
FINAL: White Hart Marauders (GB) 19 Queensland 14
PLATE: Crawshay's (Wales) 21 Netherlands 7

25 & 26 MARCH 1994
Cathay Pacific Sevens
QUARTER-FINALS:
Western Samoa 21 President's VII 12
Australia 43 Argentina 0
New Zealand 21 France 12
Fiji 14 South Africa 12

SEMI-FINALS:Australia 20 W Samoa 17 (holders) (aet); New Zealand 28 Fiji 14

FINAL: New Zealand 32 Australia 20

PLATE FINAL: South Korea 26 US Eagles 21
BOWL FINAL: Hong Kong 24 Portugal 12

APRIL 1994
Melrose Sevens
FINAL: Gala 17 Wasps 10

14 MAY 1994
Middlesex Sevens
FINAL: Bath 19 Orrell 12

TENS

The event is strong in the southern hemisphere. But, with Bass having pulled out their sponsorship for the English Tens for 1995, the championship may struggle to survive in the UK. Tens were due to be included in the Kuala Lumpur Commonwealth Games but at the last moment Sevens won the day. The Cobra Tens in Kuala Lumpur are the regarded as the unoffcial world championships and the English invitation side, the Penguin RFC, are the holders ■

WOMEN'S RUGBY

Having founded the Women's Sports Foundation (UK) in my offices in Museum Street, London, in 1985, I have a soft spot for equality of opportunity as it relates to sport in general, and rugby in particular. By DEREK WYATT

GREAT STRIDES AGAINST THE ODDS

Women's Rugby has made massive strides in the past decade against all the odds. Few unions have had an equal access policy or have favoured putting more resources into the women's game rather than their own. Some unions are still struggling to recognise the game; some have adopted a pro-active stance and some women's unions want to develop on their own – which is their right – but progress just might be slower.

Sport is heavily biased towards men despite the fact that women frequently make up more than 50% of the population of a country. There exists no comprehensive data on the representation of women in the media.

In the UK, of the 120 print and photographic journalists who received accreditation in the 1988 Seoul Olympics, only two were women; and, of the 513 members of the Sports Writers' Association, only 24 are women. There are no women sports editors of national newspapers though Annie Briggs is Sports Editor of BBC Ceefax.

A cursory look across the UK also revealed:

	men : women
Sports psychologists	40 : 11
Directors of physiology labs	14 : 2
Physiologists	10 : 5
Biomechanists	1 : 0
Directors of Biomechanic labs	7 : 0

Source: British Association for Sports Sciences 1993

These figures are mirrored within the Olympic movement:

Percentage of male/female athletes and officials at Summer Olympics

	% of competitors Male : Female	% of officials Male : Female
1980	68 : 32	67 : 33
1984	68 : 32	73 : 27
1988	64 : 36	75 : 25
1992	61 : 39	80 : 20

Source: British Olympic Association 1980-1992

Women's Rugby is not yet recognised as an Olympic sport but it is an avenue they might consider as it would give them the funding they so badly need. FIRA is a male-only body. The IOC has given FIRA the authority to go forward with plans to celebrate rugby in the Millennium Games, and this might block the way for women.

1994 SECOND WOMEN'S WORLD CUP

So, the fact that in 1994 there was a second Women's World Cup is some kind of minor miracle. The women's game has grown remarkably quickly from 12 clubs in 1983 to over 180 today. Twenty countries are registered with the Women's International Rugby Advisory Board and we will do our best to give them their own directory in next year's *Almanack*.

The first WWC was held in Wales in 1991 just before the second Rugby World Cup. It lacked funding and sponsorship (the RFU generously helped out) but it was a major success and put the game on the map. At least that is what we thought then. A second World Cup was agreed and was due to be held in The Netherlands in 1994. They pulled out with 90 days to go, blaming a lack of sponsorship and sundry other matters.

Far from being down and out, the women's movement responded with alacrity and within days, a new World Cup was agreed and a new venue, Scotland, was hurriedly put in place.

The result? Without Italy, Spain (who pulled out with 10 days to go; hence the inclusion of the Scottish Students side), the Netherlands, and New Zealand (banned by their union) the second World Cup was not as strong as it could have been. The opening results were very one-sided and only the final showed the potential of the game. England, playing a restricted game, beat the more expansionist Americans and thus gained sweet revenge for their defeat in the 1991 final.

The women's game now needs a major organisational fillip and a global sponsor to help it grow. It's time, too, that some of the major television channels gave it more space.

RESULTS
Pool A
Sweden 5 Japan 10; USA 121 Japan 0:
USA 111 Sweden 0
Pool B
Scotland 51 Russia 0; Scotland 0 England 26;
England 66 Russia 0
Pool C
Scottish Students 0 France 77; France 31 Ireland 0;
Scottish Students 5 Ireland 18
Pool D
Wales 29 Kazakhstan 8; Canada 28 Kazakhastan 0;
Wales 11 Canada 5

QUARTER-FINALS
USA 76 Ireland 0
England 24 Canada 10
France 99 Japan 0
Wales 8 Scotland 0

SEMI-FINALS
USA 56 Wales 15
England 18 France 6

PLAY-OFF FOR THIRD PLACE
France 27 Wales 0

FINAL
England 38 USA 23

SHIELD FINAL
Scotland 11 Canada 5
THIRD PLACE
Ireland 11 Japan 3

1991 WOMEN'S WORLD CUP RESULTS
Pool 1
New Zealand 24 Canada 8; Wales 9 Canada 9;
New Zealand 24 Wales 6
Pool 2
France 62 Japan 0; France 37 Sweden 0;
Sweden 20 Japan 0
Pool 3
USA 7 Netherlands 0; Netherlands 28 USSR 0;
USA 46 USSR 0
Pool 4
England 12 Spain 0; England 25 Italy 9;
Spain 13 Italy 7

SEMI-FINALS
USA 7 New Zealand 0
England 13 France 0

FINAL
USA 19 England 6

Further reading: Women and Sport: Policy and Framework for Action Published by the Sports Council (England) 1993, 16 Upper Woburn Place, London WC1H 0QP

England scrum half, Emma Mitchell feeds the backs during the Women's 1994 World Cup Final. England beat the USA 38-23

INTERNATIONAL DIRECTORY

In the middle of June 1994 following the fiasco of the England tour to South Africa, Peter Bills, Editor *Rugby World,* and Steve Jones, Rugby Correspondent of *The Sunday Times,* both called for the International Rugby Football Board to wake up to their responsibilities and impose its authority on the game, DEREK WYATT writes. We have already commented elsewhere in the *Almanack* on the disastrous effect on the game if the International Olympic Committee awards the organisation of rugby as a show sport in the Millennium Games in Sydney to the Fédération International de Rugby (FIRA). For the IRFB to allow such a situation to arise is a major dereliction of its duty.

We must ponder whether anyone is listening. As we suggested in last year's *Almanack,* the world headquarters should not be sited outside of a major international city unless it is for tax purposes. Bristol is not the centre of anyone's universe and the IRFB should move to London.

In 1993-4, the number of countries affiliated to the IRFB totalled 63. Tahiti, Moldavia and Papua New Guinea were the latest countries to be admitted to membership; somehow, though they no longer exist, Yugoslavia held on to theirs.

Following international rugby is not easy. Persuading secretaries and media officers to part with information has been as difficult as last year and this is reflected again in the different levels of entries in the directory. In every case we have asked the national union to write a comment about how rugby has fared in their country over the past year. Sadly, some never reply, despite frequent reminders.

We still need field reporters out there to help increase our knowledge of the game and if you are interested please write to the Editor. We are particularly in need of correspondents in the US, Japan and the Pacific islands.

ANDORRA

Administration Centre:
Federacio Andorrana de Rugby, Casa de Lesprit del MICG, Baixada Del Moli No 31, Andorra La Vella
Telephone: 33 628 61222 or 22232
Fax: 33 628 64564
President: Francesc Molne
Secretary: Jordi Font
Treasurer: Salvado Braso
Press Officer: Annick Mussolas
Date of origin: 1963
No. of clubs in affiliation: 2
No. of players: 285

A substantial rugby promotional campaign is taking place in schools.

ARABIAN GULF

Administration Centre:
PO 839, Post Code 111, Muscat, Oman

Telephone: 968 616 948
Fax: 968 616 017
President: C A J Malcolm
Secretary: R Hughes
Fixtures Secretary: Martyn Gulliford
Treasurer: Stephen Ducker
Date of origin: 1975
No. of clubs in affiliation: 8 full members, 7 associate members
No. of players: 500 approx

Highlight of the season was the Arabian Gulf RFU entering a team in the World Cup for the first time. Despite losing all their matches (in the preliminary rounds in Kenya) they still managed to score over 20 points in each match, losing the final match to Kenya 23-22.

Three leagues are now operated under the auspices of the AGRFU.

Standard Chartered Bank Gulf 1st XV League:
won by Abu Dhabi RFC
Emirates 2nd XV League: won by Abu Dhabi RFC
Saudi League: won by Riyadh RUFC

Fosters Cup 2nd XV Cup: won by Bahrain RFC

The following tournaments were also held:
Dubai Sevens; Al Ain Sevens; Riyadh XV's; Doha Sevens
Sharjah Tens; Bahrain XV's

ARGENTINA

Administration Centre:
Union Argentina de Rugby
J A Pacheco de Melo 2120
Cod Pos 1126 Capital
Buenos Aires, Argentina
Telephone: 541 805 8544, 7529, 8036
Fax: 541 805 8484
President: Lino Perez
Secretary: Hugo Tucci
Manager: Luis Mario Chaluleu
Treasurer: Constantino Riganti
Coach: Hector Mendez
Asst Coach: Jose Javier Fernandez
Captain: Marcelo Loffreda (San Isidro Club)
Ground name: Ferro Carril Oeste Stadium
Address: Buenos Aires
Spectator capacity: 28,000
Date of origin: 1899
No of clubs in affiliation: 188
No of players: 16,500

By Frankie Deges

In October Argentina won the South American championship – as they have done every year except in 1981 when they withdrew. They scored 18 tries against Brazil with winner Gustavo Jorge getting eight. They defeated Chile, Paraguay and Uruguay when a player from each side was sent off.

South Africa toured for the first time in 1993 and their coach Ian McIntosh complained bitterly about the referee after the Springboks had been beaten by Buenos Aires in the second game.

Next came the "Battle of Tucumin" which was so brutal that it should have been suspended – as early as the third minute. Two players from each side were sent off and the Springboks emerged worthy winners. In the first Test the Pumas could have earned a draw after recovering from 10-26 down, losing 26-29; but the Springboks dominated the second Test, winning 52-23.

The two-Test series against Scotland in 1994 did not enhance the reputations of either side and the Pumas won 16-15 and 19-17. This was sandwiched by Argentina's two final RWC95 qualifiers against the US. For the first, veteran centre Marcelo Loffreda was made captain and the Pumas won 28-22 at Long Beach; in the June return they beat the Eagles 16-11 to clinch their place in the final. Although the Pumas won four Tests in a row, the margins were narrow and their coaches will need to review tactics to make an impact on the World Cup.

AUSTRALIA

Administration Centre:
PO Box 333, Kingsford
NSW 2032, Australia
Telephone: 612 662 1266
Fax: 612 663 4053
President: P L Harry
Chairman: L G Williams
Executive Director: Bruce Hayman (contact)
Secretary: R J Fordham
Women's Rugby Committee Chairman:
J H Scott
Medical Advisory Committee Chairman:
R W Meagher
Australian Referees Selection Committee Chairman:
R G Barnes
Amateurism and Player Welfare Committee Chairman:
R B McGruther OBE
Australian Selectors : P McLean, R S F Dwyer, R McQueen
National Director of Coaching: R J P Marks
Ground names: Sydney Football Ground (50,000);
Ballymore, Brisbane (25,500)
Date of origin: 1949
No of clubs in affiliation: 350
No of players: 11,500

Australia looked ragged and out of sorts when they lost the Bledisloe Cup match to New Zealand at the end of the 1993 season. Rumours of their eclipse were premature and laid to rest in a splendid tour to America, Canada and France in the Autumn. Record crowds came to see them in France, but not for the two Tests – only one of them in Paris. The series was shared 1-1 and it seems ridiculous not to have been a best of three series.

At home Australia made some administrative changes after the sad death of their president, Joe French. With the 1994 season nearly finished as the *Almanack* went to press, Australia had beaten both Ireland and Italy 2-0 and had only the Bledisloe Cup remaining. While the Emerging Wallabies will soon be touring Africa, Australia's approach to next year's World Cup has been relatively low-key. There was still some speculating that Nick Farr-Jones would come out of retirement (again) for 1995. In the meantime, they must hope that Michael Lynagh steers clear of the kind of injury he picked up during the hard-fought series against Italy, because he is their key player.

AUSTRIA

Administration Centre:
Ostereichischer Rugby Verband
A-1190 Wien, Flemminggasse 5/3/6
Telephone: 431 443 130
Fax: 431 443 038

President: Dr Giancarlo Tiziana
Secretary: Christian Schwab
Finance director: Lydia Schmitt
Press officers: Thomas Gabriel,
Thomas Ditriech
Marketing managers: Ben Martens,
Johann Schweiger
Technical admin/coaching: Allan Roche
Schools liaison officer: Colin Campbell
Team manager: William Crisp
Coach: Allan Roche
Head of selectors: Allan Roche
Schools U19 Team manager: Colin Campbell

BELGIUM

Administration Centre:
Brue Timmermans, 1190 – Brussels, Belgium
Telephone: 322 343 3831
Fax: 322 640 9496
Secretary: Daniel Brunet
Date of origin: 1931
Ground name: FBR Ground
Address: Brussels
No. of clubs in affiliation: 59
No. of players: 3400

BERMUDA

Administration Centre:
Bermuda Rugby Union
PO Box 1909, Hamilton HM EX, Bermuda
Telephone: 809 295 0587 (H), 7006 (W)
Fax: 809 292 5962
President: Peter E Borland
Secretary: David Cooke (contact)
Coach: Keiron Peacock
Manager: Patrick McHugh
Captain: Alvin Harvey
Ground Name: National Sports Club
Address: Middle Road, Devonshire Parish, Bermuda
Spectator Capacity: 4,000
Date of Origin: 1962
No. of clubs in affiiliaton: 7
No. of Players: 150

Bermuda played the USA in the RWC 95 preliminaries at home and lost 3-60. in front of 2,500
people, 5% of the population! Bermuda boasts four
clubs and 200 players; the US has over 1000 clubs and
some 20,000 players.

Among the current ideas floating about the future
of rugby in the Carribean is to create a West Indian
side rather like its cricketing counterpart. Currently,
there is a bi-annual championship involving Trinidad,
Guyana and Martinique. Bermuda are the holders having beaten Trinidad & Tobago 78-5, Guyana 28-3 and
Martinique, in the final, also by 28-3.

The fifth Bermuda Classic Tournament took place

in November. This year the ages had been reduced
down from 35 to 33 and for once the All Blacks did
not win (they had won the first four tournaments).
POOL:
England 18 Barbarians 29
New Zealand 15 USA 10
Bermuda 5 New Zealand 45
Barbarians 25 Australia 0
USA 27 Bermuda 12
FIFTH PLACE: Australia 40 Bermuda 20
THIRD PLACE: England 30 USA 10
FINAL: Barbarians 10 New Zealand 5

BULGARIA

Administration Centre:
Bulgarian Rugby Federation, Blvd. "Vasil Levski" 75,
1040 Sofia, Bulgaria
Telephone: 359 2 865329
Fax: 359 2 800520, 879670
Secretary: Gueorgui Marinkin

CANADA

Administration Centre:
Canadian Rugby Union
National Sport and Recreation Centre
1600 Prom. James Naismith Drive
Gloucester, Ontario K1B 5N4, Canada
Telephone: 1 613 748 5657
Fax: 1 613 748 5739
Executive Director: John Billingsley (contact)
Date of Origin: 1929 (reformed 1965)
Ground Name: Burnaby
Address: Vancouver
No. of clubs in affiliation: 220
No. of players: 11,670

CANADIAN FOCUS

By Peter Mc Mullen: To celebrate the growth of rugby,
each issue of the *International Almanack* is featuring a country in close up to provide a clearer picture of how the game
has taken root and progressed worldwide.

1994 CANADIAN RUGBY STATISTICS

Province	SR Men	Women (includes High School girls)	Youth (under 19)	Over 40s	Total
British Columbia	3,500	375	6,700	500	11,075
Alberta	1,700	525	2,000	60	4,285
Saskatchewan	500	450	300	40	1,290
Manitoba	650	350	300	40	1,340
Ontario	3,500	3,900	7,500	400	15,300
Quebec	650	600	50	60	1,660
New Brunswick	500	180	450	50	1,180
Nova Scotia	450	200	175	-	825
Prince Edward Island	40	200	100	-	340
Newfoundland	180	160	350	-	690
TOTALS	**11,670**	**6,940**	**18,225**	**1,150**	**37,985**

CERTIFIED COACHES – 1,600 CERTIFIED OFFICIALS – 375: Total – 39,960

RUGBY FIRST PLAYED: Quebec – 1865; Nova Scotia – 1870; Ontario – 1864; New Brunswick – 1884; Prince Edward Island – 1884; British Columbia (BC) – 1889; Alberta – 1891; Manitoba – 1879; Saskatchewan – 1889; Newfoundland – 1897

MEN'S INTER-PROVINCIAL CHAMPIONSHIPS (SINCE 1982)
1982 – Ontario 21 BC 9 at Edmonton; 1983 – BC 25 Ontario 9 at Victoria; 1984 – BC 16 Ontario 9 at Montreal; 1985 – BC 31 Ontario 11 at Calgary; 1986 – BC 29 Ontario 12 at Toronto; 1987 – BC 27 Ontario 0 at Vancouver; 1988 – BC 22 Ontario 13 at Edmonton; 1989 – BC 55 Ontario 7 at Victoria; 1990 – BC 48 Ontario 9at Ottawa; 1991 – BC 35 Newfoundland 3 at Victoria; 1992 – BC 69 Ontario 13 at Abbotsford; 1993 – BC 38 Ontario 22 at Calgary

CHAMPIONSHIP FACTS
Number held – 31; Winners – British Columbia 27 times and Ontario 4; Number of Appearances – British Columbia 29, Ontario 22, Quebec 4, Alberta and Newfoundland 2 each

INTERNATIONAL MATCHES – SENIOR MEN

1932
Jan 31 v All-Japan, at Osaka, lost 8-9
Feb 11 v All-Japan , Tokyo, lost 5-38

1962
Nov 17 v Barbarians, Gosforth, drawn 3-3
Dec 1 v Wales Under 23, Cardiff, lost 0-8

1966
Sept 17 v British Lions, Toronto, lost 8-19

1967
Sept 30 v England, Vancouver, lost 0-29

1970
Nov 28 v Fiji, Burnaby, lost17-35

1971
Oct 2 v A Wales XV, Cardiff, lost 10-56

1973
June 9 v Wales, Toronto, lost 20-58

1974
October 25 v Tonga, Vancouver, lost 14-40

1976
June 12 v Barbarians, Toronto, lost 4-29

1977
May 21 v USA , Burnaby, lost 17-6
June 4 v England U23, Ottawa, lost 13-26
June 11 v England U23, Toronto, lost 9-29

1978
May 28 v USA, Baltimore, lost 7-12
Sept 30 v France, Calgary, lost 9-24

1979
June 9 v USA, Toronto, won 19-12
Sept 29 v France A, Paris, lost 15-34

1980
May 24 v Wales B, Burnaby, lost 7-24
June 8 v USA, Saranac Lake, won 16-0
Oct 11 v New Zealand, Burnaby, lost 10-43

1981
June 6 v USA, Calgary, won 6-3
Oct 3 v Argentina, Buenos Aires, lost 0-35

1982
April 11 v Japan, Osaka, lost 18-24
April 18 v Japan, Tokyo, lost 6-16
May 29 v England, Burnaby, lost 6-43
June 12 v USA, Albany, drawn 3-3

1983
June 11 v USA, Burnaby, won 15-9
June 25 v Italy, Burnaby, won19-13
July 1 v Italy, Burnaby, lost 9-37
Oct 15 v An England XV, Twickenham, lost 0-27

1984
June 9 v USA, Chicago, lost 13-21
1985
June 15 v Australia, Sydney, lost3-59
June 23 v Australia, Brisbane, lost15-43
Nov16 v USA. Vancouver, won 21-10

1986
June 7 v Japan, Burnaby, lost 21-26
Nov 8 v USA, Tucson, won 27-16

1987
May 10 v USA, Vancouver, won 33-9
May 24 v Tonga, Napier (Rugby World Cup), won 37-4
May 30 v Ireland, Dunedin (RWC), lost 19-46
June 3 v Wales, Invercargill (RWC), 9-40
Nov 14 v USA, Victoria, won 20-12

1988
June 11 v USA, Saranac Lake, lost16-28

1989
Sept 2 v Ireland, Victoria, lost 21-24
Sept 23 v USA, Toronto, won 21-3

1990
March 30 v Argentina, Vancouver, won 15-6
June 9 v USA, Seattle, lost 12-14
June 16 v Argentina, Buenos Aires, won 19-15

1991
May 11 v Japan, Vancouver, won, 49-26
May 25 v Scotland, Saint John, won, 24-19
June 8 v USA, Calgary , won 34-15
Oct 5 v Fiii. Bayonne (RWC), won13-3
Oct 9 v Romania,Toulouse (RWC), won 19-11
Oct13 v France, Agen (RWC), won 13-19
Oct 20 v New Zealand, Lille (RWC Quarter Final), lost 26-13

1992
June 13 v USA, Denver, won 32-9
Oct 17 v England, Wembley, lost 26-13

1993
May 29 v England, Burnaby, won 15-12
June 5 v England, Nepean, lost 19-14
June 19 v USA, Winnipeg, won 20-9
Oct 9 v Australia, Calgary, lost 43-16
Nov 10 v Wales, Cardiff, won 26-24

1994
May 21 v USA, Long Beach, won 15-10
June 4 v France, Nepean, won 18-16
June 11 v Wales, Markham, lost 33-15

1994 CANADIAN RUGBY (continued)

FIXTURES IN 1994-95

Dec 10 v England, Twickenham
Dec 17 v France, venue to be confirmed
Jan 21 v Scotland, Murrayfield
April 22 or 23 v New Zealand, venue to be confirmed

WORLD CUP

May 26 v Europe 3 at Port Elizabeth
May 31 v Australia at Port Elizabeth
June 3 v South Africa at Port Elizabeth

OFFICIALS

Raymond Skett, manager of Canada World Cup Squad in South Africa. Born in New Zealand. Vice-president of Manitoba and vice principal of Winnipeg. Manager of Canada team which defeated Wales and the USA in 1993.

Ian Birtwell, coach. Appointed 1989. and confirmed for 4-year term after 1991 World Cup. He has seen Canada to wins of Argentina (twice) Japan, Scotland, Fiji and Romania (in the World Cup), England and Wales. In 1992 he was British Columbia's coach of the year. Born in England, he is a fisheries scientist who works for the Canada Federal Government. Played for Sedgeley Park, Hampstead, King's College, London, in England and for Merolomas, whom he coached after moving to Canada in the Seventies.

Rod Holloway. Assistant Coach, since 1992. A Vancouver lawyer, he succeeded Birtwell as coach to BC, but has relinquished that post to concentrate on national duties. He had a 14-year playing career with a number of clubs, including University of BC, Meralomas and North Shore.

Ian Stuart, centre and captain. Born 8 October 1961, Victoria BC. First capped at centre against Ireland in 1989. Canada's first choice scrum half in 1987 World Cup, and then reverted to centre. He was made captain against Australia in October 1993 and the following month he was chaired of the field at the National Stadium, Cardiff, after scoring one of Canada's two tries in their 26-24 victory against Wales. Plays for Vancouver Rowing Club.

Leading Cap Winners

31 – Rod Hindson, lock 1973-90
28 – Mark Wyatt, full back, 1982-91
26 – Gareth Rees, Fly half, centre, 26 caps 1986-
24 – Hans de Goede, lock, 1974-87 Spence McTavish, wing, 1986-
23 – Glenn Ennis, No 8, flanker, 23 caps 1986-

WOMEN

1987
Nov 14 v USA, Victoria, lost 22-3

1988
v USA, Saranac Lake, lost 26-10

1989
v USA, at Edmonton, lost 28-3

1991 (first women's World Cup)
April 6 v New Zealand, lost 24-8
April 8 v Wales, drawn 9-9
April 11 v USSR, won 38-0
April 12 v Italy won 6-0
April 13 v Spain, won 19-4

1992
Sept 13 v USA, Blaine, lost 13-12

1993
June 8 v Wales, Brampton, won 20-8
June 10 v England, Ajax, lost 12-8
June 12 v USA, Markham, lost 60-3

1994 (second women's World Cup in Scotland)
April 11 v Wales, lost 11-5
April 15 v Kazastan, won 28-0
April 17 v England, lost 24-10
April 20 v Japan, won 57-0
April 23 v Scotland, lost 11-5

Women's National Championships

1987: Alberta 14 Quebec 4
1988: Alberta 13 Quebec 11
1989: Alberta 8 Manitoba 4
1990: Alberta 16 BC 0
1991: BC 7 alberta 0
1992: Ontario 11 BC 10
1993: Ontario 23 Alberta 8

CHILE

Administration Centre:
Federacion de Rugby de Chile
Av. vicuna Mackenna 44 Santiago, Chile
Telephone: 562 635 27 73
Fax: 562 222 6285
President: Ernesto Sirner Bugueno
Vice President: Pablo icaza Noguera
Secretary: Roberto Guell Charles (contact)
Treasurer: Martin Langford Horn
Directors: Marco Garcita Retamal, Octavio Bertoni Adrove, Erick Rodriguez Araya
Date of origin: 1953
No. of clubs in affiliation: 124
No. of players: 8,000

Chile came unstuck in the RWC 95 South America section, losing to Paraguay 24-25, to Uruguay 6-14 and Argentina 7-70. This came as a rude shock to the Chileans who had always thought of themselves as the natural heirs to the Argentine side.....

CROATIA

Administration Centre:
Croatian Rugby Football Union, Hrvatski Ragbi Savez
TRG Sportova 11
4100 Zagreb, Croatia
Telephone: 38541 339333

Fax: 38541 327111
President: Dr Adalbert Redic
Secretary: Branimir Alaupovic
Team Manager: Darko Miskilin
Coach Head of Selectors: Zdenko Jajcevic
Under 21 Head of Selectors: Niksa Burazin
Int. Commission (Chair): Sinisa Tartaglia
Secretary: Branimir Alaupovic (contact)
No. of clubs in affiliation: 12
No. of players: 1,050
No. of referees: 12
No. of trainers: 32
Current League Club Champions:
Ragbi Club Nada – Split
Current Cup Club Champions:
Ragbi Club Nada – Split
League Club Champions (Region of Nord):
Ragbi-Klub Zagreb
League Club Champions (Region of Dalmatia):
Ragbi Club Nada – Split
Board (Region of Nord):
HRVatski , Ragbi Savez, Odbor Za Regijusjever, TRG Sportova 11 41000 Zagreb
Board (Region of Dalmatia):
HRVatski Ragbi Savez, Odbor za Regiju Dalmacija Kruziceva 11 5800 Split

Not much has changed for poor Croatia but we have at least maintained contact with their national body.

CZECH REPUBLIC

Administration Centre:
Czech Rugby Union, Stadion Strahov, Mezi Stadiony, PO Box 40, 160 17 Praha 6, Czech Republic
Tel/Fax: 42 2 353 292
Ground Name: SK Smichov – Rugby
Address: Podbelohorska, 150 00 Praha 5
Date of origin: 1926
President: Judr Ladislav Procazka
Secretary: Eduard Krutzner (contact)
Finance Director: Jir I Vopalensky
Technical Admin/Coaching: Milan Malovany, Jir I Stuksa
No. of clubs in affiliation: 21
No. of players this represents: 2987
Team Manager: Bruno Kudrna
B XV Team manager: Zdenek Matejka
Under 21 Team manager: Jiri Stastny
Colts Team manager: Jiri Sevcik

Czech rugby was always stronger than Slovak rugby because the game was centred on Prague when it was first introduced in the mid-1920s. The great changes that the country has undergone has reduced the number of clubs to 20. Clearly, much rebuilding is in progress. The editor visited Prague recently and can strongly recommend it to clubs wanting a long weekend in a beautiful city. Rugby is still coming to terms with the workings of the new Czech Republic. Though it is still under the Sports Ministry it does receive nearly the same grants it did when that was under the communist regime.

It is worth remembering that when the national side lost all its matches in one season in the 1960s, that the then sport minister, Antonin Himi, banned them from international competition for three years. It was also that minister who asked the then captain, and now the only fully paid rugby official today, Eduard Krutzner, what quantity of steroids the team needed in order to win.

DENMARK

Administration Centre:
Dansk Rugby Union, Idraettens Hus
Brondby Stadion 20, DK-2605 Brondby, Denmark
Telephone: 45 42 45 55 55
Fax: 45 43 42 01 07
President: Erik Andersen
Secretary: Ms Maibritt (contact)
Manager: Palle Andersen
Coach: Allan Giles
Assistant Coach: Thomas Andersen
Captain: Jan Hilmer Larsen
Date of origin: 1950
No. of clubs in affiliation: 20
No. of players this represents: 1,800

DANISH CHAMPIONS 1994

Seniors	Aarhus Rugby Club
Under 17	Hundested Rugby Club
Under 14	Frederksberg Rugby Club
Under 12	Aalborg Rugby Club

INTERNATIONAL MATCHES IN 1994
v British Army of the Rhine, lost 12-13
v Welsh District, lost 7-12

ENGLAND

Administration Centre:
Rugby Football Union, Twickenham
Middlesex TW1 1DZ, England
Telephone: 44 81 892 8161
Fax: 44 81 892 9816, 744 2940 (Direct)
Secretary: Dudley Wood
Ground name: Twickenham
National stadium owned: Yes
Flood lights: Yes
Wired for radio: Yes
TV Access: Yes
Spectator capacity: 54,500 (at present)
Date of origin: 1871
No. of Clubs in Affiliation: 2,405. Unions and Clubs 72,955, (Schools, County Schools and District Schools in membership of ERFSU)
No. of players: 375,000

In 1993-94 it was clear that the best run Unions were New Zealand and Australia – in the sense of their excellent administrations, their openness and their media awareness. England, who have undergone significant changes, have now joined their ranks. In 1993 England published *The Year of Rugby 1994: the Official Yearbook of the Rugby Football Union*, which by some way was the best publication we have received from any Union. For their AGM in July England produced a glossy 32-page *Annual Report and Financial Statement*. This included a breakdown of gate receipts at Twickenham. These two publications are similar to reports shareholders receive and its just the quality of information which we sought in the first *Almanack*. On the playing field England had a momentous year. They beat the All Blacks; they lost only one Five Nations match – to Ireland; and they came back from the dead in South Africa to win the first Test, though in the end they had to share the series.

Back home the Queen officially opened the East Stand at Twickenham and in May the West Stand came tumbling down. The union has a Bishop Report to come to terms with. When Dudley Wood retires as secretary they must think seriously of replacing him with a chief exect ive officer; and not as is planned with two people – one for the national game and one for the internatonal game (which we interpret as meaning one for the amateur and one for the professional game).

By Captain Tony Hallett. Chairman, Twickenham Ground Committee, June 1994

On a sunlit day in spring 1994, the complete Twickenham East Stand glittered and shone with pride as the the Queen officially opened it. The East, with 25,000 seats, is now wrapped into the North to form a continuous stand with 40,000 all-seated capacity. It meets the highest requirements for spectator safety, for easy access and an exceptionally wide-angled pitch view. It is an awesome cathedral for specatators and players. The atmosphere and decibel count on its first outing surpassed all expectations. In the new stand there are two long bars – Scrum and Lineout at the lower level, complemented by the Young England Rugby Club soft drinks bar. The Corner Flag Café operated from the North East Stand and was an immediate success (7,000 pizzas on its opening day). A shop and more bars at the middle level complete the current facilities on offer to the spectator. The press have a new home designed in concert with the Rugby Writers Club. In the summer of 1995 it is planned to add a brassereie, a new shop and further facilities for the disabled with their own bar and raised panoramic views served by a lift.

In the summeer of 1994 the bulldozers moved in and the first columns of the final phase grew out of the ruins. By late autumn 10,000 spectators will be back in the new lower tier, dressing rooms, medical facilities and match day offices. In the next 18 months there will be added to the West Stand: a fitness centre, England Rugby International Club bar, bars, cafés, shops, and a restaurant. Then Twickenham's capacity crowd of 75,000 will be ready to herald in the millennium.

FIJI

Administration Centre:
Fiji Rugby Union, PO Box 1234, Suva, Fiji
Telephone: 679 302 787
Fax: 679 300 936
Secretary: Tevita Ratuva
Date of origin: 1913
Ground name: National Stadium, Suva
Spectator capacity: 18,000
No. of clubs in affiliation: 600
No. of players: 12,250

It's hard to know where Fijian rugby is going. Deprived of a place in the SuperTens, beaten in the Pacific Islands competition and losing to Tonga in the RWC 95 preliminaries has meant that rugby 15-a-side has been given a wide berth. Fiji succumbed to Wales without any real understanding of how to switch tactics in mid-stream. The problem is island politics and the short-termism of the Union who prefer success in the Hong Kong Sevens to the graft of the senior game. The answer? A new administration. The chances? Nil. In 1992 alone over 60 players represented Fiji. Fiji simply doesn't have 60 international players; it's time to tip compromise over-board.

FRANCE

Administration Centre:
Fédération Française de Rugby

7 Cite d'Antin, 75009 Paris, France
Telephone: 331 4874 8475
Fax: 331 4526 1919
Secretary: Jacques Laurans
Date of origin: 1920
Ground name: Parc de Princes, Paris (49,500)
Stade Municipal, Toulouse (35,000)
No. of clubs in affiliation: 1,782
No. of players: 218,500

By Jonathan Cavender

It has been an unsatisfactory year for the French. Three concerns pervade French thinking – violence on the field, referees (particularly those of other nations) and money. Sella won his 98th cap during a Five Nations Tournament (which saw France winning for the first time at Murrayfield, losing for the first time at Cardiff), and his 100th on the extraordinary summer tour of New Zealand.

French Rugby is always expected by its followers to peak against England. So much was promised but so little delivered. The team turned in a very sterile performance that was roundly criticised and led to changes. Wins against Scotland and Ireland barely compensated. There was a distinct lack of flair and experiment in the backs, a grinding acceptance of the need to scrummage powerfully. There were a few examples of the flashes of brilliance seen over the years, the unique French ability to link forwards and backs in broken play.

For all that the team scored more tries and more points, while converting fewer penalties and conceding fewer tries, than any other. Their points were therefore collected in the style of pure rugby so sought by the impartial spectator, but they still finished midway.

INTERNATIONAL RESULTS
v South Africa drew 20-20; won 18-17.
v Romania, won 51-0.
v Australia, won 16-13; lost 3-24.
v Ireland (home), won 35-15.
v Wales (away), lost 15-24.
v England (home), lost 14-18.
v Scotland (away), won 20-12.
v Canada, lost 16-18.
v New Zealand, won 22-8, won 23-20.

NATIONAL CLUB CHAMPIONSHIP
Losing Quarter Finalists: Narbonne; Toulon; Bourgoin. Losing Semi Finalists: Grenoble; Dax.
FINAL: Toulouse 24 Montferrand 15.

Club rugby mirrored the international scene. The pressure to succeed at any cost mars the games of importance, where teams dare not lose. The passing movement is becoming rarer, the penalty quotient huge. During both phases of the Championship, not helped by poor weather, the spectacle was limited. On the last day, when many places were already assured, there were more tries scored than any other day (42 in eight matches).

In the quarter-finals there were only 5 tries but 86 points kicked. The Agen-Grenoble match summed up what is happening inside French club rugby; Agen ran the ball for all they were worth and scored a spectacular try but the juggernaut of Grenoble kept the pressure on and won by kicks. Their Technical Manager is Jacques Fouroux, lambasted for ruining the national team, and now getting his own back by ruining the national championship. There is constant agonising about this so-called anglicising of the French game. Toulon, the hot favourites, were beaten in the quarter-finals and then severely criticised for lack of pride that had made them run penalties rather than kick them. Already the French press is accepting that open play is only allowed where it does not get in the way of a famous victory.

In general though, the French spectator is more critical of an uninteresting winning team than his Anglo-Saxon counterpart, and games like the Dax-Toulouse semi-final remind everyone what good 15-man rugby is all about.

Politics are never very far away. Power struggles sap the strength. An interview in March explained the continuing absence from the national team of Frank Mesnel by saying that there was a ban on him in high places. In April he was chosen for the tour to Canada and New Zealand. Bans on talented players like Gallion, on talented clubs like Toulouse, have long formed part of the nagging background to what is, after all, a minority sport. The huge strength of the sport itself is based in the South, particularly the South West. Traditions die hard in any country. Violence is an undercurrent. The game is fierce and unforgiving. Passions run high. Fights involving spectators are not rare. In January a 2nd Division game was abandoned before the kick-off as the teams started fighting when the visitors got off the team bus. The referee sensibly decided he had no authority and the gendarmes were called to separate the factions.

League regulations come down hard on suspensions. Racing failed to get through to the Quarter Finals, and Béziers were relegated to Group B, through such transgressions.

But you need the suspensions in the first place. In the du Manoir semi-finals a player punched a touch judge; the sanction was a penalty kick. Higher authority then decided to intervene.

Decisions of referees are always put under the microscope, especially when the national team lose. The refereeing always seems to be average to good when they win. That the French team have been let down in the past by indiscipline is not surprising when you watch a club game. There the referees' role is to let the game flow. The rules are bent to allow free use of the ball. When the players try to follow the same path in an international match, they get penalised and fail to understand.

Just after the last World Cup a local council took out a serious banning order against two referees: David Bishop of New Zealand and Steve Hilditch of Ireland. Their crime was to have officiated at the previous two French defeats at the hands of the English.

The French have long been suspected of paying their players. Whatever form it takes there is no doubt that their players are made to feel more appreciated at every level of the game.

This season the FFR have come close to an acceptance of this. A charter has been drawn up, seen by some to recognise this status quo, by others as the thin end of the professional wedge. Expenses are now put on a formal footing. The Gallic flair for obfuscation through complications comes in to its own in the club regulations which set out several grades of players and their attendant recompense, as agreed with the French Revenue.

Never very high, this official compensation figure is thought by the president of the Federation to be roughly FFr2,000 and apply to 350,000 licensed players. It was hoped that such openness would nip in the bud any gripes about money, to pay or not to pay, but in the event it is likely to increase the rumbling sounds.

And anyway, as any thinking Frenchmen knows, it is the English team who are leading the way to professionalism...

The tour to New Zealand was an outstanding success, with a 2-0 win in the series. (see Tours 1993-94). It was prefaced by a disastrous few days in Canada. There were two problems – no time was given to acclimatise after the stress of the national season and there was a marked underestimation of the Canadian team, whatever public mutterings there were.

The French did not deserve to win; for most of the game they played against 14 men but still could only score one try. The Canadians played a tough uncompromising game, which was simple and effective but showed off their basic ball skills.

France lost 16-18; they showed little panache or determination. The crowd were horribly partisan, to the extent of being boorish; at the end there was the sad sight of the Canadian team mobbing each other, rather than paying any attention to their opponents. It was that sort of game.

Since their 1993 tour to South Africa the French seemed to have shrugged off their tradition of being a poor touring team. Their first few forays in New Zealand suggested otherwise; but in the end the Tricolors emerged triumphant.

GEORGIA

Administration Centre:

Georgia Rugby Union, Ragis Kavshiri, Sportis Departmenti, Tchavtchav azis Garnziri 49a, Tbilisi 62 Republic of Georgia
Telephone: 7 8832 235380, 294763
Fax: 7 8832 294754
Secretary: Zurab Reqviashvili

Georgia has been involved in a civil war centred on its capital Tbilisi and this had great impact on all sporting activity including rugby.

GERMANY

Administration Centre:
Deutscher Rugby Verband, Ferdinand Wilhelm
Fricke Weg 2A, 30169 Hanover, Germany
Telephone: 49 511 14763
Fax: 49 511 1610206
Secretary: Volker Himmer
Date of origin: 1,900
No. of clubs in affiliation: 75
No. of players: 5,800

Germany has the talent to become a major rugby nation but not the means. Once this is addressed she will become the new "Italy" of Europe at least in rugby terms. The side toured Namibia which was once a German protectorate and some of her players are registered in France and New Zealand; but it is coaches and referees that she needs most, if she is to progress. In the early rounds of the RWC 95 she beat Lithuania 31-5 and Latvia 27-5 but in the recent play-offs she lost 6-60 to Romania and 5-67 to Russia.

HONG KONG

Administration Centre:
Hong Kong Rugby Football,
Rooms 2003 & 2004 Sports House,
1 Stadium Path, So Kon Po,
Causeway Bay, Hong Kong
Telephone: 852 504 8311
Fax: 852 576 7237
Secretary: Peter Else
Date of origin: 1953
No. of clubs in affiliation: 10
No. of players: 850

Hong Kong is very much a law under itself. It basks in the sunshine of its own brilliant Sevens but it must now begin to address its future within the Republic of China and start to be missionaries there. Only this year the Chinese launched their first professional soccer league with assistance from IMG. So they are ready to listen, but does Hong Kong care?

HUNGARY

Administration Centre:
Hungary Rugby Federation
Dozsa Gyorgy ut 1-3, H-1143 Budapest
Telephone: 361 251 1222
Fax: 361 251 1297
Secretary: Ria Ispan
Date of origin: 1989
No. of clubs in affiliation: 8
No. of players this represents: 500

Hungary wants to be part of the new world order and is desperate to improve its rugby image and

performance. Here is a country with the right attitude that desperately needs the funding of the Olympic Solidarity movement. Does the IRFB accept it has a wider responsibilty to the game? All it has to do is put a levy of 5% on all gate taking countries' income and the money would be there.

IRELAND

Administration Centre:
Irish Rugby Football Union
62 Lansdowne Road, Ballsbridge, Dublin 4, Eire
Telephone: 353 1 668 4601
Fax: 353 1 660 5640
Secretary: P J O'Donoghue
Date of origin: 1874 and 1879
Ground name: Lansdowne Road
Address: Dublin
National stadium owned: Yes
Floodlights: Yes
Wired for radio: Yes
TV Access: Yes
Spectator capacity: 54,500
No. of players: 12,500

Ireland is doing its very best these days; its very best means treading water while other countries either catch up or steam ahead. They do not appear to have the right coaching infrastructure and desperately need to spend more money on its development squads at every level. Much as they can raise their game for the "big one" this will not be enough in the RWC 95.

They came severely unstuck in their close-season tour to Australia losing both Tests against an Australian side well below par.

ISRAEL

Administration Centre:
Israel Rugby Football Union, PO Box 6062,
Tel Aviv, Israel 61060
Telephone: 972 3 528 0043
Fax: 972 3 560 4080
Secretary: David Kretzmer
Date of origin: 1971
No. of clubs in affiliation: 8
No. of players: 400

Israel play little international rugby. The last game they played before their amazing win against Hungary in the preliminary round of RWC 95 in 1993, which they won 67-8, was in 1989 against Switzerland in France. Hardly surprisingly, they came unstuck in the play-offs losing to Sweden, 10-26, The Netherlands, 0-56, and the Czech Republic, 0-28, in the RWC 95 in October and November, 1993.

They too need money and support. They are also members of FIRA but have had little support from them either.

ITALY

Administration Centre:
Federazione Italiana Rugby
Via L. Franchetti 2, 00194 Rome, Italy
Telephone: 396 368 57309
Fax: 396 323 6059
Secretary: Sandro Di Santo
Date of origin: 1928
Ground name: Fir Stadium
Address: Rome
Spectator capacity: 27,000
No. of clubs in affiliation: 265
No. of players: 15,200

Italian rugby came of age in Australia in the summer of 1994, when they lost 2-0, but narrowly. There have been false dawns before, but the Italians may now have turned the corner. If they beat Wales in Caediff in October we will have a sixth European country of truly World standards.

ITALY RESULTS
Russia 19 Italy 30 (Fira Cup), Moscow
Italy 16 France A 9 (Fira Cup), Treviso
Italy 18 Scotland A 15, Rovigo
Italy 62 Spain 15 (Fira Cup), Palma
Romania 26 Italy 12 (Fira Cup), Bucharest

B MATCHES
Italy B 9 England A 15, Piacenza
Romania B 16 Italy B 17, Bucharest

UNDER-23
Italy 21 France 30, Genoa
Italy 3 France 34, La Spezia

UNDER-21
Italy 33 Scotland 30, San Dona
Italy 6 England 43, Rovigo

UNDER-19
Italy 11 England 12, Piacenza
Italy 22 Romania 6 (Fira Junior)
Italy 18 France 16 (Fira Junior)
Italy 18 South Africa 41 (Fira Junior)

IVORY COAST

Administration Centre:
Fédération Ivoirienne de Rugby
01 BP 2357, Abidjan 01,
Ivory Coast
Telephone: 225 215 588
Fax: 225 431 968
Secretary: Benjamin Dakoury
Date of origin: 1973
No. of clubs in affiliation: 15
No. of players: 2,700

Just as in soccer so in rugby; in soccer the emerging countries have been the Cameroons, then Nigeria, soon it will be the Southern African nations. In rugby it was Namibia and Zimbabwe but these were false dawns to an extent because they relied on ex-colonial personnel. The Ivory Coast is the first African state to make it on its own merits. The RWC 99 must embrace more countries from the underdeveloped world and one way it could achieve this is to hold a senior and a junior world cup simultaneously.

The game is young. Their first official rugby international was against Zimbabwe in 1990! Some of their players play in France which is hardly surprising given the French connections. They play a fluid game – a mix between the French and the Fijians. They beat Tunisia, the pre-match favourites, 19-16, and Morocco 15-3 to qualify for the African play-offs. In Casablanca in June they lost to Morocco 9-17, beat the favourites, Namibia 13-12 and then Zimbabwe 17-10, to qualify for their first ever RWC finals.

JAPAN

Administration Centre:
Japan Rugby Football Union,
2-8-35, Kitya Aoyama 2 Chome,
Minatto-Ku, Tokyo 107 Japan
Telephone: 813 3401 3321
Fax: 813 3401 6610
President: Tochiro Kawagoe
Chairman: Zenzaburo Shirai (contact)
Secretary: Masato Yokoo
Executive Vice President: Shiggy Konno
Treasurer: Nobuyuki Takashime
Administrator: Koji Tokumasu
Date of origin: 1926
Ground name: National Stadium
Spectator capacity: 60,000
No. of clubs in affiliation: 1,650
No. of players: 52,000

INTERNATIONAL RESULTS
v Argentina, lost 27-30
and 20-45 (May 94)

JAPAN U23
v Canada Under 23, won 28-26

TOUR OF WALES
v Wales A, lost 5-61
v Dunvant, won 24-23
v East Wales, lost 12-38
v West Wales, won 26-10
v 3rd and 4th Selects, won 39-10
v Wales, lost 5-55

FIJI TOUR TO JAPAN
v Japanese Universities, won 22-21
v Japan A, won 22-9

v Japan, lost 18-24
v Japan A, won 20-9
v Japan, lost 8-20

Having lived off the reputation of being the only truly "amateur" country left playing in the world, the Japanese clubs broke rank and went "professional" recruiting internationals from Canada, New Zealand, Australia and lesser players from Oxford University. This will cause a further imbalance to its national side and she may now be left behind as the South Koreans, the Malays and the Chinese take to the game.

KENYA

Administration Centre:
Kenya Rugby Football Union, PO Box 48322, Nairobi, Kenya
Telephone: 254 2 223161, 223176
Fax: 254 2 218207
Secretary: Zack Oloo
Date of origin: 1921 (East Africa RU 1953)
Ground name: East African RFC Ground
Address: Nairobi
Spectator capacity: 8,000
Telex: 010 254 2 224022
No of clubs in affiliation: 12
No of players: 1,000

The Africanisation of the game is a critical part of the future of Kenyan rugby and now that the South African and Namibian corridors are open again for rugby contact, theirs should improve. Like everywhere else on this continent, funding and sub-structures are in short supply. Still Kenya battled hard in the RWC 95 preliminaries losing to Zimbabwe, 7-42, and Namibia, 9-60, but beating the Arabian Gulf, 24-23.

KOREA

Administration Centre:
506 Olympic Building,
88 Oryun-Dong
Songpa-Gu, Seoul, Korea
Telephone: 822 420 4244/5
Fax: 822 420 4246
Date of origin: 1945
Ground name: Seoul Rugby Football Stadium
National stadium owned: Yes
Addresss: Seoul, Korea
President: Lee Jae-Hong
Secretary: Kim, Sang Gook (contact)
Press officer: Lee, Joong-Ho
Technical admin/coaching: Shon, Du-Hok

South Korean rugby is at a critical stage. She has emerged to threaten the hegemony of Japan and we must wait until the Far East rounds of the RWC

95 are completed in October 1994 before we quite know where Korean rugby stands.

LATVIA

Administration Centre:
Latvian Rugby Federation, Terbatas Street
LV-1723 Riga, Latvia
Telephone: 371 2 281741
Fax: 371 2 284412
Secretary: Janis Berzins (contact)
Team Manager: Maris Smits
Coach: Uldris Bautris

RUGBY WORLD CUP SEVENS 1993 RESULTS (ALL LOST):
v Fiji 0-42, v Romania 5-22, v South Africa lost 5-47, v Wales 7-36 and v Japan 14-21. (For the Rugby World Cup 1995 tournament she lost to Germany 5-27 and beat Lithuania 7-6 but Germany qualified to go through.)

LITHUANIA

Administration Centre:
2675 Vilnius, Zernaites 6, Lithuania
Telephone: 37 02 635474
Fax: 37 02 661223
Secretary: Alphonsus Grumbinas

LUXEMBOURG

Administration Centre:
Fédération Luxembourgeoise de Rugby FLR
BP 1965, Luxembourg-Gare
Telephone: 352 4301 34420
Fax: 352 4301 32717
Date of origin: 1973
Ground name: Parc des Sports de Cessange
Spectator capacity: 2,000
No. of clubs in affiliation: 3
No. of players: 200
President: Fernand Goldschmitt
Secretary: Bernard Jargeac (contact)
Finance director: Tim Crosby
Press officer: Bernard Jargeac
Marketing manager: Tim Crosby
Ticket office manager: Tim Crosby
Technical Admin/Coaching: C Dodeuil
Schools Liaison Officer: Bernard Jargeac
Groundsman: Service des Sports de la Ville de
Playing Management: Christophe Negre
Team Manager: Michel Lanier
Coach: M Gillis and A Cohen
Head of Selectors: Anthony Savage
Schools U19 Team Manager: Bernard Jargeac

Luxembourg is a member of FIRA and also of the IRFB. It has participated in several FIRA championships and in spite of its size it has had some excellent results, particularly against Andorra, and a sensational match against Georgia in October 1993. Rugby was introduced in to Luxembourg in May 1973 by a group of expatriates working in The Grand Duchy.

Several of the founder members still live there and contribute in one way or another to the sport.

Maladministration by the organisers – not poverty – was allegedly the real reason for Luxembourg's no-show in Andorra for the opening rounds of the World Cup.

MALAYSIA

Administration Centre:
Malaysian Rugby Union
A95 – Jalan Tuankudua, Salak South Garden
57100 Kuala Lumpur, Malaysia
Telephone: 010 603 783 1102, 0800, 0910
Fax: 010 603 781 0469
Secretary: Abdul Jaliil Bin Haji Borhanuddin
No. of clubs in affiliation: 11
No. of players: 750

Malaysia dines out on its Cobra Ten-a-side unofficial world championship which it had hoped would be included in the 1998 Kuala Lumpur Commonwealth Games. Instead, the Games will see the first Commonwealth Sevens competition.

MOLDAVIA

Administration Centre:
Federation Moldovei de Rugby
Str Columns 106, Chisinau, Moldavia
Telephone: 373 2 22 83 19
Fax: 373 2 3444 53
Date of origin: 1956
New member IRFB 1994

MOROCCO

Administration Centre:
Fédération Royale Marocaine de Rugby, Complexe
Sportif Mohamed V, Porte No. 9, Casablanca
Do not send mail direct to Morocco, send to:
Frank Barber OBE, 34 Julian Road, Folkestone,
Kent CT19 5HW, UK. Tel: 44 303 250343
Telephone: 2122 221570
Fax: 2122 267253
Date of origin: 1956
Ground name: Complexe Sportif Mohamed V
Spectator capacity: 6,000
President: Abderrahim Bougja
Transports Touristique:
24 Bld. Felix Houphouet Boigny
Casablanca, Morocco
Finance Director: Houem Abdelaziz
Press Officer: Ken Kadmiri
Marketing Manager: Mansouri Mohamed
Technical Admin/Coaching: Hamdiaber Rahman
Schools Liaison Officer: Gachaoui
Team Managers: Bougja Aziz,

The north of Africa is a fertile land for rugby though it is largely unexplored. Morocco had a great chance to play through to the RWC finals. They beat Tunisia 6-5 and lost to Ivory Coast 3-15 in RWC 95 preliminaries but they qualified for the African play-offs beating Ivory Coast 17-9. They then surprisingly lost 9-21 to Zimbabwe and going into the last game they needed a win to qualify. So did their opponents, Namibia. The result? A draw 16-16; kickers on both sides kicked themselves for ever after as they missed sitters......

NAMIBIA

Administration Centre:
Namibia Rugby Union, PO Box 138,
Windhoek, Namibia
Telephone: 264 61 51775, 51717
Fax: 264 61 51028
Date of origin: 1916
Ground name: Namibia Rugby Stadium
National Stadium Owned: Yes
Floodlights: Yes
Wired for Radio: Yes
TV Access: Yes
Spectator capacity: 11,000
No. of clubs in affiliation: 54
No. of players: 1,745
President: Henning J Snyman (Elected Annually)
Secretary: Mrs C A Smith (contact)
Finance Director: Stoffel Rocher
Press Officer: Keith Allies
Marketing Manager: Gerhard Roux
Ticket Office Manager: Johan de Toit
Hospitality: Jonathan Basson
Technical Admin/Coaching: Gert Fourie
Schools Liaison Officer: Fanie van Zyl
Groundsman: Frans de Wit
Team Manager: H J Snyman
B XV Team Manager: Henry Pretorius
Under 21 Team Manager: Wim Lotter
Schools U19 Team Manager: Fanie van Zyl
Schools U16 Team Manager: Peter Burger

This was the year that Namibia blew it. Perhaps it was over-confidence to begin with because they couldn't have expected to lose to Ivory Coast; but they did, 12-13. This effectviely undermined their chances. What a pity because they had put in an immense amount of work and should have qualified.

She has joined Zimbabwe in the Currie Cup but is not yet a party to the SuperTens which might serve her better. Perhaps for RWC 99 she will concentrate on developing the game amongst its 11 ethnic group.

NETHERLANDS

Administration Centre:
Nederlands Rugby Bond, Brinklaan 74C,
1404-GL Bussum, Netherlands

Date of origin: 1932
Telephone: 31 2159 38087
Fax: 31 2159 18145
President: J Roozeboom
Secretary: L van Schoonhoven (contact)
Team Manager: P vd Deijssel
Coach: J van Altena
Head of Selectors: R Brouwer
Treasurer: W van Houwelingen
Press Officer: H Grader
Museum: L van Schoonhoven
No. of clubs in affiliation: 104
No. of players: 5,000
Ground name: Geementilijk Sportpark
Address: Hilversum
Spectator capacity: 23,000

INTERNATIONAL RESULTS

v Israel, won 56-0
v Sweden, won 31-6
v Czech Republic, won 42-6
v Andorra, won 49-10
v Poland, lost 13-10
v Sweden, won 48-6
v Czech Republic, won 38-9
v Italy, lost 9-36

UNDER 21

v Br Colleges, won 17-0

YOUNG ORANGE

v Czech Republic, lost 5-13
v British Colleges, lost 13-31
v Paraguay, lost 7-18
v Germany, lost 5-19
v Morocco, lost 15-20

LITTLE ORANGE

v Wales under 16, lost 12-24

The Dutch easily qualified for the final rounds of their European zone by beating the Czech Republic 42-6, Israel 56-0 and Sweden 31-6. But though they beat the Czech Republic again by 33-9 they lost heavily to the Italians, 9-63.

NEW ZEALAND

Administration Centre:
New Zealand Rugby Union
PO Box 2172,
Wellington, NZ
Telephone: 644 499 4995
Fax: 644 499 4224
Patron: The Honourable Sir David Beattie, GCMG, GCVO, QSO, QC, LLD
President: M R Barnett
Chief Executive Officer: G R Verry (contact)
Vice Presidents: R T Daws, Don Shuker

Chairman: E J Tonks, CBE
Media Liaison: Ric Salizzo
Appeal Council: C A Blazey CBE, ED, C K Saxton MBE, R C Stuart OBE, R W Thomas CBE, I M H Vodanovich MBE
Ground names: Eden Park, Auckland
Lancaster Park, Christchurch
Athletic Park, Wellington, Dunedin
National stadium owned: Yes
Wired for radio: Yes
TV Access: Yes
Spectator capacity: Eden Park, 58,000;
Lancaster Park, 52,500; Athletic Park, 45,000;
Dunedin, 35,000
Date of origin: 1892
No. of clubs in affiliation: 1,000
No. of players: 182,500
Administration Committee: GW J Atkin,
G Taylor, EJ Tonks CBE
North Zone: RA Fisher, NJ Gray, RA Guy,
CA Meads
Central Zone: DJ Galvin, MD Shannon,
KR Tremain, LF Walsh
South Zone: JA Dowling, TM Gresson, JA Sturgeon MBE, RW Thomas CBE
Maori Representative: M Blackburn
Chairman of Council and Administration Committee:
EJ Tonks CBE
Deputy Chairman of Council and Administration Committee: JA Dowling
Finance Director: Barry Jobson
Marketing Manager: Margot Cory Wright,
Liz Dawson
Technical Admin/Coaching: Lee Smith

By Ray Cairns

As this was written, before the Summer 1994 series against the Springboks, New Zealand's southern hemisphere international season was only a third of the way through. But the unthinkable had already happened, with a 0-2 series loss to France. Coach Laurie Mains and his selection panel (the others were old hand Earle Kirton and newcomer Lyn Colling) were under threat. A legion of experts were ready with their theories.

France won 22-8 at Christchurch, their first win in seven attempts at Lancaster Park, and 23-30 at Eden Park. It had previously won only one Test in New Zealand since tours started in 1961. But the more damning statistic was that this was New Zealand's third successive Test defeat, with the loss to England in November taken into account. This hadn't happened since New Zealand lost Tests three and four in South Africa in 1970, and the opening international of the 1971 series with the Lions.

Even more significantly, New Zealand had not lost consecutive Tests at home since the C team lost both matches — and then the top 30 players were touring South Africa. Go back to 1937, against Philip Nel's Springboks, before the best available All Blacks side, losing two in a row at home.

Sean Fitzpatrick's team was perhaps unlucky against France. Although New Zealand could have lost even more severely at Lancaster Park, they deserved to win handsomely at Eden Park. Such is the expectation in New Zealand of success that a series loss, at home, is unacceptable – even more unacceptable than losses to England (or South Africa)!

The All Blacks have had a chequered 12 months. There was a stuttering series against the Lions to kick things off: a scrambling win, a bit of a thumping, and a convincing victory. There was a relatively easy win over an under-strength Wallabies side; a comfortable enough one against enthusiastic Western Samoa; a demolition job against one of the worst of all Scotland sides; and a miserable loss to England.

The latter will live as a memorable match only to the English because they won. It was otherwise a poor game, and perhaps more to the point, underlined New Zealand's inability to change tactics in mid-match. That places question marks against captain and coach, Fitzpatrick and Mains. When much the same happened at Lancaster Park against the French, the same issues were raised. Fitzpatrick improved his own game dramatically at Eden Park, as did the rest of the forwards.

The spectre of Grant Fox remains to haunt New Zealand. The influence of his kicking – tactical and at goal – is known, but New Zealand's recent leadership problems hint that his greatest influence was in his role as playmaker. Wayne Shelford, in his final comments as a Test captain, acknowledged that Fox was his eyes and ears.

The All Blacks have made many changes in the five-eighths – fly-half and inside-centre to those in the northern hemisphere – since Fox, and even in his final days. By the time of the second Test against France, they were into their fifth different combination in as many matches. Fox himself, Marc Ellis twice, Simon Mannix and Stephen Bachop had taken the infield position; Lee Stensness, Matthew Cooper, Eroni Clarke, then Cooper again were outside them.

The France series showed the major problem was at half-back. Scrum half Stu Forster had a tolerably successful tour of Britain, but passed and kicked appallingly in the first Test against France. He was barely workmanlike in the second match when paired with club and provincial team-mate Bachop.

The selectors have been reluctant to use Graeme Bachop, who was the outstanding half-back of the second World Cup. He lofts the kick from the base of the scrum more tellingly than Forster, and clears the pass more swiftly, although his style is unorthodox. He is quicker than Forster to take quick free kicks, before the opposition has blinked.

The selectors have not been faithful to Jeff Wilson, the wondrously-gifted all-round sportsman who managed to play for New Zealand at both cricket and rugby before he was 20. British audiences saw his aplomb in November.

After a slow start in the season due to injury, Wilson was replaced by a 19-year-old of huge potential, Jonah Lomu. Lomu had opportunities in the two France Tests, but his naivety was starkly obvious. After all, he was being played on the left wing whereas in his last year at school he was a No 8. No wonder there were poor defensive lines and approach, and weak kicking. Lomu should have been allowed to develop in the national championship in New Zealand.

As I write, New Zealand is about to face a three-Test series against the Springboks, a mid-week night Test against Australia to come (see Addendum). There is also a Test against Canada, the only meeting since the last World Cup quarter-finals, as part of the build up to 1995. Between the domestic matches, and before the next season, the NZRFU deliberate on its management and selection teams for 1995. In New Zealand, the buck stops with the coach and only sometimes with the captain and the other selectors. So Mains is under the most pressure. Even a clean sweep against the Springboks and a win at Sydney might not be enough for him to survive.

There is a widespread belief that John Hart is the only alternative coach to Mains. Neither Kirton nor Colling rates a mention in the pub-and club-room gossip. Twice overlooked, Hart reacted badly the first time; but handled his rejection better the second time round, and has since done little to get off-side. Everyone knows it was a disaster to foist Hart on Alex Wyllie for the 1991 World Cup, and he took hevy criticism for taking on the so-called co-coach role. Now he is seen as as saviour.

Hart wouldn't bring many changes to the present team. He might reinstate Graeme Bachop and retain Zinzan Brooke, whose wide-ranging match in the second Test against France was unquestionably the outstanding individual performance of that series. Wilson should play a part somewhere; and probably Stensness would get sensible selection treatment. Matthew Cooper, who started the British tour so promisingly, has not maintained that momentum; he now offers little in midfield and his kicking success rate – five out of 13 in the French Tests – is not good in the Land of Grant Fox. And there is a case for making Mike Brewer captain. If he can command a place in the top side, Brewer might make up for the trauma of twice missing the World Cup because of injuries, and lead New Zealand in South Africa.

NORWAY

Administration Centre:

Norges Rugby Forbund, Idrettens Hus
Hauger Skolevei 1, 1351 Rud Norway
Telephone: 47 22 311628
Fax: 47 22 312900
President: Per S Hodne
Date of origin: 1985
No. of clubs in affiliation: 2
No. of players: 110

PAPUA NEW GUINEA

Administration Centre:
Papua New Guinea RFU,
PO Box 42, 42 Port Moresty,
Papua New Giunea
Telephone: 675 300 5220
Fax: 675 300 5206
Secretary: W J Burgess
New member IRFB 1994

PARAGUAY

Administration Centre:
Herrara 195, Asuncion, Paraguay
Telephone: 595 21 490 100
Fax: 595 21 496 390
President: Geoffrey L Bishop
Vice President: Victor Burt
Date of origin: 1970
Secretary: Pedro J Logan (contact)
Finance Director: Pedro Alsina
Technical Admin/Coaching: Jean-Pierre Juan Chich
(International coach on loan from French Govt). Ricardo
Baez (Adult National Team)
No of clubs in affiliation: 9
No of players: 1,200

There are isolated pockets in the world where rugby is
played and Paraguay is one such country. Its isolated
geographical position makes games difficult to contemplate. It's amazing the game survives at all.

RWC 95 RESULTS
v Chile won 25-24
v Uruguay lost 3-67
v Argentina lost 3-51

POLAND

Administration Centre:
Polish Rugby Union, Marymoncka 34
01-813 Warsaw, Poland
Fax: 482 2 353 587
Secretary: Henryk Kuczko
Date of origin: 1956
Ground name: Polski-Zwiazek
Address: Warsaw
No. of clubs in affiliation: 21
No of players this represents: 3,200

PORTUGAL

Administration Centre:
Federaçcáo Portuguesa de Rugby,
Rue Sociedade Farmaceutica 56-20,
1100 Lisboa, Portugal
Telephone: 351 1 353 5702 or 351 1 315 8577
Fax: 351 1 353 5632

Secretary: Delfim Barreira
Date of origin: 1957
Ground name: Estadio Universitario
Address: Lisbon
Spectator capacity: 12,500
No. of clubs in affiliation: 42
No. of players: 3,500

Portugal became the focus of the British media
because in May she entertained Wales in one of
the European zones. She set some sort of record; she
lost 11-102 but thankfully that record was erased
from the record books a day later.

ROMANIA

Administration Centre:
Federatia Romana De Rugbi,
16 Vasile Conta Street,
Bucharest 1, Romania
Tel/Fax: 401 210 0444
Secretary: Radu Demian
Date of origin: 1913
Ground name: 23 August Stadium,
Address: Bucharest
Spectator capacity: 90,000
No. of clubs in affiliation: 98
No. of players: 20,000

Romania was hardly tested in qualfying for the European play-offs against Italy and Wales for the final
seeding positions for South Africa, beating Germany 60-
6 and Russia 30-0. The fact remains that Romania has
not improved as much as she should have, notwtih-
standing its political problems which are immense. She
needs to beat Italy comprehensively to prove to her critics that her game is back on the road. But will she?

RUSSIA

Administration Centre:
The Rugby Union of Russia,
Luzhnetskaya NAB 8,
119871 Moscow, Russia
Telephone: 7095 2010237
Fax: 7095 2480814
Secretary: Alexander Latyshev
Date of origin: 1966
Ground name: National Stadium
Spectator capacity: 30,000
No. of clubs in affiliation: 148
No. of players: 25,000

Despite a tour to South Africa and Namibia where
they won four matches from their five match itinerary, including a decisive win against Namibia – in all
but name a "President's XV" – the Russians did not
qualify for South Africa, losing in the end 0-30 to
Romania, though they beat Germany 67-5.

Russia has a fine rugby union tradition, but as the country splits there must be some doubt as to whether it will retain its borders by the next World Cup.

SCOTLAND

Administration Centre:
Scottish Rugby Union, Murrayfield,
Edinburgh EH12 5JP, Scotland
Telephone: (44) 31 337 9551
Fax: (44) 31 313 2810
President: G K Smith (Annual appointment)
Secretary: I A L Hogg CA (contact)
Finance director: G A Ireland CA
Director of Rugby: J W Telfer
Date of origin: 1873
Ground name: Murrayfield
Address: Roseburn Street, Edinburgh EH12 5PJ
Wired for radio: Yes
TV Access: Yes
Spectator capacity: 67,500
No. of clubs in affiliation: 276
No. of players: 25,000

Where will Scottish rugby be by the end of the season? Bottom of the Five Nations in 1994 with just one draw, they were beaten in a two-Test series by Argentina, though both scores were close. Their club rugby is in disarray, but, it is to be hoped, only for one more year because changes have been agreed for 1995-96. Their rugby needs a major overhaul and with Jim Telfer in charge it may get it.

SINGAPORE

Administration Centre:
Singapore Rugby Union, 11 Dhoby Ghaut,
12-04 Cathay Building, Singapore 0922
Telephone: 65 33 81266
Fax: 65 33 68987
Secretary: Tay Huai Eng
No of clubs in affiliation: 18
No of players: 800

SOUTH AFRICA

Administration Centre:
South African Rugby Football Union,
PO Box 99, Newlands 7725,
Cape Town, South Africa
Telephone: 2721 685 3038/9
Fax: 2721 685 6771
Secretary: Arrie Oberholzer
Date of origin: 1889
Ground name: Ellis Park,
Address: Johannesburg
Spectator capacity: 95,000
No. of clubs in affiliation: 1,004
No. of players: 78,000

By Quintus van Rooyen

South Africa's hopes of winning the 1995 World Cup tournament as the hosts would be improved if they performed well in the nine Test matches they faced in the latter half of 1994. They started 1994 on a satisfying note by sharing the Test series against England – winning the second Test by 27-9 after losing the first by 15-32.

They were expected to defeat Argentina in the two-match home series in August. As the *Almanack* was going to press, they had lost in the first Test, 14-22, in a tough three-match series against the All Blacks in New Zealand – although they were then confident of coming back. Then, at the end of the year, they were scheduled to have a 14-match tour of Scotland and Wales with Tests against both countries.

For South African rugby 1993-94 was an up and down year. It started badly when the executive president of the Rugby Football Union, Dr Danie Craven, died of a heart attack at the age of 82. Prof Fritz Eloff was the acting president of SARFU until the end of March, when Ebrahim Patel – according to the interim arrangements between the old SA Rugby Board and SARU in 1993 and 1994 – became the executive president for 1993 and acquitted himself well of his task. Although the 1995 World Cup tournament was granted to South Africa there was still doubt whether they would be the hosts because of the uncertain political future, the unrest and the violence in the country.

On the playing field the performances of the national team was not much better than in 1992. Professor John Williams was axed as coach at the end of the1993 season – in retrospect a hasty decision. His replacement, Gerrie Sonnekus, resigned before he had the chance to prove himself.

Ian McIntosh, the former Natal and Zimbabwean coach, was an emergency choice, with Gysie Pienaar surviving as his assistant. McIntosh changed the playing pattern with mixed results. At the end of the 1993 season there was widespread criticism of his controversial pattern with the emphasis on the creating of second, third and fourth phase play, although he has been appointed until after the World Cup.

With Naas Botha announcing his retirement a new national captain had to be found. The choice was Francois Pienaar, the successful Transvaal captain and flanker, who made his debut as captain and as a flanker against the French touring team and captained South Africa in all seven internationals played in 1993.

OFFICIALS FOR 1994
President: Dr L Luyt, P O Box 2050,
Johannesburg, 2000
(0 011-4022960; Fax 011-4027282).
Senior Vice-President: Mr M E George,
P O Box 1243, East London, 5200
(0 0431-43300; H 0401-954114431; Fax: 0431 435848)
Junior Vice-President: Prof J T Claasson, 7

Drommodaris Street, Potchefstroom, 2520 (0 0148-2971130; H 0148-2946017; Fax: 0148-2931076)
Representatives on International Rugby Board: Dr L Luyt, Prof F C Eloff
Representatives on SA Rugby Referees' Societies on the Union: L J Terblanche, 78 Sandown Road, Rondeebosch, 7700 (0 021 6421651; H021-6856771; H 021-6852700)
SA Rugby Football Union: PO Box 99, Newlands, 7725, Mill House, Boundary Road, Newlands 7700 (00216583038; Fax: 6856771)

SPAIN

Administration Centre:
Federacion Española De Rugby,
Calle Ferraz 16-4,
Orcha 28008 Madrid, Spain
Telephone: 341 541 4978, 4988
Fax: 341 559 0986
President: Antonio Moreno
Secretary: Jose M Moreno (contact)
Manager: Jose M Epalza
Treasurer: Jose A Maldonado
Coach: Bryce Bevin
Assistant Coach: Santiago Santos
Captain Jaime Guiterrez
Ground Name: Ciudad Universitaria de Madrid
Address: Avenida Juan de Herrara, s/n
Spectator Capacity: 12,000
Date of origin: 1923
No of clubs in affiliation: 236
No of players: 14,300

INTERNATIONAL RESULTS – SENIORS WORLD CUP CLASSIFICATION
v Wales, lost 0-54
v Portugal, won 35-19

FIRA EUROPEAN CHAMPIONSHIPS
v Morocco, won 48-17
v France, lost 3-49
v Russia, lost 9-16
v Romania, won 11-3
v Italy, lost 62-15

Spain enjoyed 15 minutes of fame when the UK media turned up in force to watch her game against Wales in which she did not disgrace herself, despite the result 0-54. She went on to beat Portugal 35-19. Rugby is part of the culture in Spain and they will improve. They need to be a part of a junior European championship that might embrace the Five Nations A XVs.

SRI LANKA

Administration Centre:
28 Longdon Place, Colombo 07, Sri Lanka
Telephone: 941 580294
Fax: 941 574868
President: Rudra Rajasingham
Vice President: S B Pilapitiya
Chairman: Gamini Fernando
Secretary: Cdr. Harsha Mayadunne (contact)
Finance Director: Uddaka Tennakoon
Press Officer: Cdr H Mayadunne
Administration Secretary: M S Zainudeen
Date of origin: 1879
Ground name: Suga thadasa Stadium
Floodlights: Yes
Spectator capacity: 30,000
Technical admin/coaching: Jeff Matheson
School liason officer: Uddaka Tennakoon
Current league champion: Colombo Hockey & Football Club
No. of clubs affiliated: 45 schools & 30 clubs
No. of players: Approx 4,000
Team manager: Col. J P A Jayawardene

SWEDEN

Administration Centre:
Svenska Rugby Forbundet, Idrottens Hus
S-123 87 Farsta, Sweden
Telephone: 468 605 6524
Fax: 468 605 6525
Secretary: Bo Sundström
Date of origin: 1931
No of clubs in affiliation: 51
No of players: 3,500

Sweden was grouped with Israel, the Netherlands and the Czech Republic in the RWC 95 European play-offs. She beat Israel despite being down at half-time, but lost to the Netherlands and also to the Czech Republic.

RWC 95
v Israel won 26-10
v The Netherlands lost 6-31
v Czech Republic lost 7-34

SWITZERLAND

Administration Centre:
Fédération Suisse de Rugby
Case Postale 94, 1018 Lausanne, Switzerland
Telephone: 41 21 323 4242, 4121 or 648 0723
Fax: 41 21 646 0366
Secretary: Evelyne Oberson
Date of origin: 1971
No. of clubs in affiliation: 25
No. of players: 1,000

As long ago as 1869 rugby was played in Geneva. But the First World War put an end to this promising beginning. The Swiss Federation of Rugby (FSR) was not constituted until 1972 even though a championship existed from 1968. In 1992 rugby in Switzerland took a great step forward when it became part of the national movement of Youth and Sport. This meant that rugby became a recognised sport and was taken very seriously by the Swiss.

Switzerland won through the first round of the 1995 World Cup tournament and then met Portugal, Spain and Belgium, and there, their progress ended.

TAHITI

Administration Centre:
Fédération Tahitienne de Rugby de Polynésie Françcaise, BP 10815 PAEA, Tahiti
Telephone: 689 533655
Fax: 689 531757
President: Philippe Maunier
New member IRFB 1994

TAIWAN

Administration Centre:
Republic of China RFU, No. 10 Pa-Te Road, Section 3, Taipei, Taiwan 105
Telephone: 886 2578 7856
Fax: 886 2578 3602
Secretary: Ching-Chung Lin

THAILAND

Administration Centre:
Thai Rugby Union, Tephasdin Stadium Rama 1 Road, Patumnan, Bangkok 10330
Telephone: 662 215 3839
Fax: 662 214 1712
Secretary: Niyom Sansanakom
Date of origin: 1938
No. of clubs in affiliation: 22
No. of players: 1,600

TONGA

Administration Centre
Tonga Rugby Football Union PO Box 369, Nuku Alofa, Tonga
Telephone: 676 21366
Fax: 676 24260
Secretary: Ha'unga Petelo
Date of origin: 1924
Ground name: Teufaiva Park
Address: Nukn Alofa
Spectator capacity: 15,000
No. of clubs in affiliation: 70
No. of players: 2,457

TRINIDAD AND TOBAGO

Administration Centre:
PO Bag 587, Newton Post Office, Maraval Road

Newtown, Trinidad W1
Telephone: 1809 622 1784
Fax: 1809 625 7868
Date of origin: 1901
President: Hollis Charles
Secretary: Andrew Reece (contact)
Finance Director: Kenneth Lumlok
Press Officer: Gordon Gatt
Technical admin/coaching: David Charles
Head of Selectors: Brian O'Farrell
Team Manager: Grant Taylor
Coach: David Charles
League Club Champions: Caribs RFC
Club Cup Champions: Caribs RFC
No of clubs in affiliation: 12
No of players this represents: 250

TUNISIA

Administration Centre:
Federation Tunisienne De Rugby, Boite Postale 318, El Menz-ah 1004, Tunis, Tunisia
Telephone: 216 1 259 155
Fax: 216 1 347 762
Chairman: Dr Hamada Belkhiria
Secretary: Dr Bouraoui Regaya
Press Officer: Moncef Boulakbeche
Date of origin: 1972
No of clubs in affiliation: 32
No of players: 3,000

INTERNATIONAL RESULTS:
Fira Championship Group A2

v Germany, won 19-6; v Morocco, lost 10-25

v Portugal, won 18-16; v Belgium, drew 16-16

UKRAINE

Administration Centre:
National Rugby Federation of Ukraine 42 Esplanada Street, Kiev 252023, Ukraine
Telephone: 7 44 220 0109
Fax: 7 44 220 1294
Secretary: Volodimir Ukrainskily

UNITED STATES
Administration Centre:
USA Rugby Footbball Union 3595 E Fountain Boulevard M2, L Colorado Springs, Colorado 80910, USA
Telephone: 1 719 637 1022
Fax: 1 719 637 1315
President: Dr Ian Nixon
Vice President: Randy Stainer
Secretary: Jami Jordan
Treasurer: Anne Barry
Director of Administration: Ms Karen Kast (contact)

Date of origin: 1975
No of clubs in affiliation: 1349
No of players: 45,000

1994 RESULTS

National Men's Club Champion: Old Mission Beach Athletic Club.
National Women's Club Champion: Berkeley Rugby Club.
National Men's Collegiate Champion: University of California- Berkeley
Rugby Club, Berkeley , CA.
National Women's Collegiate Champion: United States Air Force Academy
Rugby Club, Colorado Springs CO
National Division 11 Champion: Santa Rosa Rugby Club, Santa Rosa, CA
National High School Champion: Highland Rugby Club, Salt Lake City, UT
National Military Champion: Pensacola Rugby Club, Pensacola FL

MEN'S NATIONAL TEAM RESULTS

v Bermuda, won 60-3
v Canada, lost 10-15
Argentina, lost 22-28

WOMEN'S NATIONAL TEAM RESULTS

v Sweden, won 111-0
v Japan, won 121-0
v Ireland, won 76-0
v Wales, won 56-15
v England, lost 23-38

The Americans are the "nearly team" of world rugby. They have massive potential but the problems they are faced with would be more daunting to lesser sides – size, shortage of funding, the amateur ethos, little school-based rugby...Yet, they ran Australia close, albeit in a heatwave, and narrowly lost both matches to Argentina in the Americas Zone. So, they will not be in South Africa. This is a pity and it was foolish of the seeding committee to allow only one side from the Americas just because Canada had already pre-qualified.

RWC 95

v Bermuda won 60-3
v Argentina lost 22-28
v Argentina lost 11-16

URUGUAY

Administration Centre:
Union De Rugby del Uruguay
Yaguaron 1093, Montevideo, Uruguay
Tel/Fax: 598 2 925519
Secretary: Jorge Villa
Date of origin: 1951
No of clubs in affiliation: 11
No of players: 1,100

Uruguay very nearly pulled off the surprise result in the RWC 95 preliminaries, for in the South American section she beat Paraguay 67-3, Chile 14-6 and at home lost narrowly to Argentina 10-19. Her

Seven-a-side tournament at Punte del Este attracts more and more teams.

WALES

Administration Centre
Welsh Rugby Union,
PO Box 22, Cardiff
CF1 1JL, Wales
Telephone: (44) 222 390 111
Fax: (44) 222 378 472
Date of origin: 1880
Ground name: Cardiff Arms Park
Address: Cardiff
Spectator capacity: 54,000
Telex: 498966
No of clubs in affiliation: 178
No of players: 40,000

ELECTED OFFICERS

President: Sir Tasker Watkins VC GBE PC DL
Chairman: V Pugh QC
Honorary Treasurer: G S Griffiths
Life Members: K M Harris CBE, H Evans
National Representatives: E R Jenkins, V Pugh, L Williams, S Simon, R Williams
Nominees of Affiliated Organisations: M J Davies, D R Johnson, D H Matthews, J D Rees

EXECUTIVE STAFF

Secretary: E H Jones (contact)
Finance Executive: T Jones
Technical Director: J Young OBE
Administration Executive: P Owens

DISTRICT REPRESENTATIVES

District A: A T Vaux, K J Hewitt, P S G Williams
District B: A D Williams, R L Giddings
District C: C Pritchard, G H Williams
District D: R R Jones, D W Rees
District E: B Michael, G Edwards
District F: W L Roderick, C James
District G: S Walters
District H: J Jones
District J: A J Gray
Anglo Welsh Representative: G Evans

HONORARY OFFICERS

Honorary Medical Officer: Dr J E Davies
Surgeon: R Leyshon
Physician: R Evans
Dental Surgeon: Professor G D Stafford
Physiotherapist: T Jones

It is hoped that 1993/94 marked the dawn of the renaissance of Welsh Rugby as a major force on the world stage. From 1 September to 31 May, WRU sponsored teams played 28 fixtures at all levels and won 21 of these matches, scoring 106 tries against 33 tries by their opponents.

The highlight of the season was the Wales team success in the Five Nations Championship. The team played some very exciting rugby during the season and in particular, the victory over Scotland in atrocious weather conditions was gained by playing adventurous rugby. By winning easily against Portugal and Spain, Wales qualified for the Rugby World Cup 1995.

The A Team went through the season without defeat, their season culminating in a storming performance to defeat a strong France A team on a very wet night in Cardiff. The Wales Under 21 team completed an undefeated season with victories over Scotland Under 21, Ireland Under 21 and France Under 21. The team played with great character and some considerable style. A number of players from this side will be seen on the full international field in the near future.

The Welsh Students team played only two matches but were successful in both, beating France and England. The victory over England at Oxford was particularly meritorious because injuries and selection difficulties had severely hampered team preparation.

The new Committee, under the Chairmanship of Vernon Pugh QC, set about reforming the administration of the game in Wales. Their objective was to modernise and streamline the structure but ensuring that the Clubs which constitute the Union were afforded direct means of influencing the policies adopted by their elected representatives.

The most significant decision taken by the Committee was to institute a fully integrated National League for all WRU Clubs from the beginning of the 1994/95 season.

WESTERN SAMOA

Administration Centre:
Western Samoa Rugby Football Union
PO Box 3940, Apia,
Western Samoa
Telephone: 685 22880
Fax: 685 23626 or 685 21407 (R M Barlow)
Secretary: R M Barlow
Date of origin: 1927
Ground name: National Stadium
Address: Apia
Spectator capacity: 12,000
No. of clubs in affiliation: 91
No. of players: 4,400

It is difficult to gauge how good the Western Samoans are. They generally win at home, but they have struggled in the two SuperTen competitions so far and it must be hard for them because even their home games are played in New Zealand. Yet it would be unfair to call them a "flash-in-the-pan" side because they have built on their success from RWC 91. Scotland in 1993 and Wales in 1994 can testify to that.

YUGOSLAVIA

Administration Centre:
Ragi Savez Jugoslavie
Terazije 35, 11000 Beograd
Yugoslavia
Telephone: 38111 339 321
Fax: 38111 143 844
Secretary: Pedrag Obradovic
Date of origin: 1954
No. of clubs in affiliation: 17
No. of players: 2,900

The IRFB must move with the times and ask the Yugoslavian authorities to stand down.

ZIMBABWE

Administration Centre:
PO Box 1129, Zimbabwe, Harare
Telephone: 263 4 702086
Fax: 263 4 721771
Date of origin: 1895
Ground name: Police Ground
Addresss: As above
National Stadium Owned: On long lease
Wired for radio: Yes
TV Access: Yes
Spectator capacity: 10,000
President: Basil Forster-Jones
General Manager: Ian McVey (contact)
Finance Director: Lionel Meltzer
Press officer: John Henderson
Ticket office manager: Mrs Oriel Brown
Hospitality: The Presidents Room
Rugby Headquarters, Police Ground, Harare
Technical admin/coaching: Frank Putterill
Schools Liason Officer: Neil Todd
Team manager and coach: Sid Dawson
Head of selectors: Frank Putterill
Under 21 Team Manager: Rusty Russell
Schools U19 Team manager: Neill Todd

This has been a tough year for Zimbabwe; their future development, like Namibia, depends on being allowed to play in one of the South African cup competitions. They reached the final rounds of the African section RWC 95 beating Morocco, 21-9, but were defeated by Namibia, 20-25, and Ivory Coast, 10-17 ■

4: International

Before the World Cup in 1987 international rugby was dominated by two championships: the Five Nations in the Northern Hemisphere and the Bledisloe Cup in the Southern, linked by the occasional British Lions tour.

By Nicholas Keith

THE FAMOUS 5 AND THE SUPER SOUTHERN 3

The first international was at Raeburn Place, Edinburgh, in March 1871 when Scotland beat England. This was also the year when the Rugby Football Union was founded (in January).

It was four more years before Ireland joined in; the Calcutta Cup for England v Scotland matches was inaugurated in 1877; and Wales first took part in 1881, when they lost to England by seven goals, six tries and a dropped goal (82-0 in modern terms!). The championship became the "Five Nations" in 1910 with the admission of France.

France introduced rugby to the Olympic Games in Paris in 1900 when they won the gold medal; and their first official international was in 1906 when they lost to New Zealand. They won an international for the first time in 1911 – and then proceeded to lose 17 successive matches from 1911 to 1925. This was all before the formation in 1920 of the Fédération de France Rugby (FFR). It was back to the four home nations between 1931 and 1947 when

France were excluded over allegations of professionalism. *Plus ça change!*

Rugby historians and statisticians still refer to the Five Nations, rather grandly, as the "International Championship", as if there were no other competitions between nations worth the name. The early years were sketchy: the championships of 1885 and 1888-89 were incomplete; the International Board was not formed until 1886; and there was no agreement about the value of points until 1890, when it was 1 point for a try, 2 for a conversion and a penalty, 3 for a dropped goal and for a goal from a mark. This was changed from 1891-93 when 1 point was added to each score; from 1893 the value of tries and conversions were swapped; the value of the dropped goal was reduced from 4 to 3 points in 1948; and the value of a try was increased to 4 points in 1971 and to 5 points in 1992.

The paraphernalia of championships, Grand Slams, Triple Crowns and Wooden Spoons sprang up without any formal meetings or agreements between the countries involved. The first championship table was published in *The Times* in 1896. It should be noted that

> The paraphernalia of Championships, Grand Slams, Triple Crowns and Wooden Spoons sprang up without any formal meetings or agreement between the countries involved

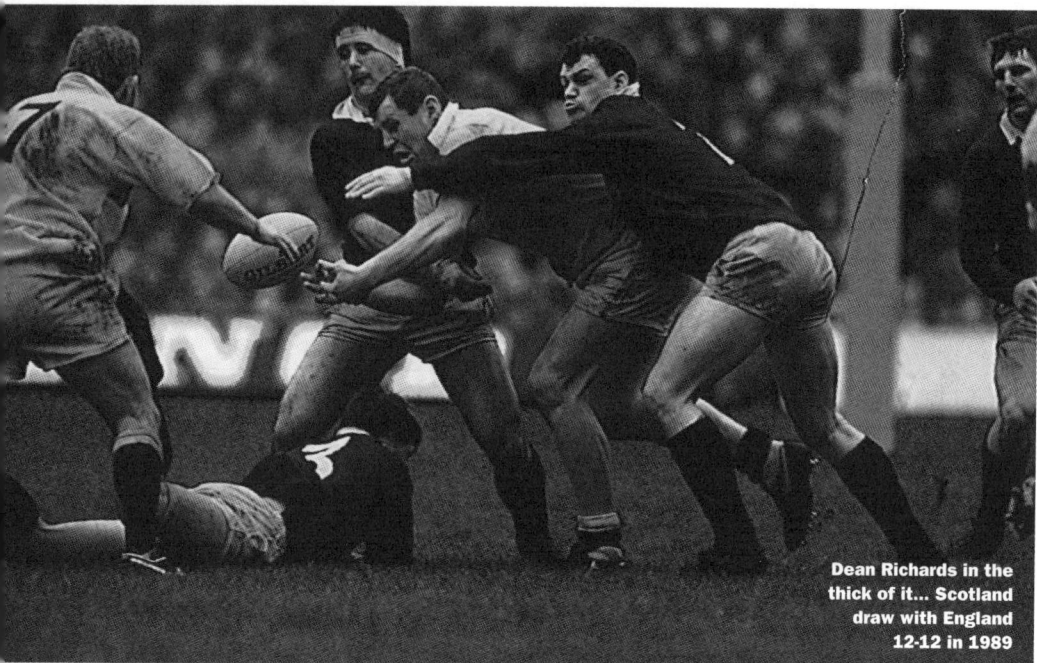

Dean Richards in the thick of it... Scotland draw with England 12-12 in 1989

two of England's Triple Crowns were in the 1880s. And the first of Wales's so-called Grand Slams in 1909-10 was before France had been admitted. The Five Nations Cup was started in 1993 and won outright by Wales on points difference in 1994 although they lost their final match to England at Twickenham. The anomalies keep happening.

Considering the strengths of the northern and southern hemispheres, the more significant international contest may be the Bledisloe Cup between Australia and New Zealand, inaugurated in 1931. Should you suppose that the Australians have attained greatness only recently, they whitewashed the All Blacks 3-0 in 1929, and they won the Bledisloe Cup for the first time in 1934. To date New Zealand have 52 wins to Australia's 17 with 4 drawn.

Although the NZ RFU was not formed until 1892, they had received a Great Britain team in 1888, and undertook their first official tour in 1893, to Australia. The first full international was in 1903 against Australia; they toured Britain in 1905-06, when the term "All Blacks" was supposedly started by the local press, and they lost only to Wales.

The Sydney Rugby Club in Australia is one of the oldest in the world, founded in 1864. The first representative team lost a series 3-1 to Britain in 1899. The Australians were Olympic gold medallists in 1908! But the game was decimated by Rugby League in the early part of this century; and it was organised on a state basis until 1949 when the Australian Rugby Union was formed.

The third member of the "super southern 3" is South Africa. The South African Rugby Board was formed in 1889; the first British tour was in 1891 when the visitors won all their matches and conceded only one try; and the Currie Cup began in 1892 (although there was an inter-provincial competition from 1889). The first overseas tour was in 1906, when they were nicknamed the Springboks; and the first official British Lions tour to South Africa was in 1924. They were elected to the IB two years later ■

INTERNATIONAL RESULTS 1871-1994

1871
Raeburn Place,
Edinburgh
Scotland 1goal 1try
England 1t

1872
The Oval, London
England 2g 2t Scotland 1g

1873
Glasgow
Scotland 0 England 0

1874
The Oval
England 1g Scotland 1t

1875
Raeburn Place
Scotland 0 England 0

1876
The Oval
England 1g 1t Scotland 0

THE CALCUTTA CUP
(FROM 1877)

1877
Raeburn Place,
Edinburgh
Scotland 1g England 0

1878
The Oval
England 0 Scotland 0

1879
Raeburn Place
Scotland 1g England 1g

1880
Whalley Range,
Manchester
England 2g 3t Scotland 1g

1881
Raeburn Place
Scotland 1g 1t England 1g 1t

1882
Whalley Range
England 0 Scotland 2t

1883
Raeburn Place
Scotland 1t England 2t

England v Scotland

1884
Rectory Field,
Blackheath
England 1g Scotland 1t

1886
Raeburn Place
Scotland 0 England 0

1887
Whalley Range
England 1t Scotland 1t

1890
Raeburn Place
Scotland 0 England 1g, 1t

1891
Athletic Ground,
Richmond
England 3pts Scotland 9pts

1892
Raeburn Place
Scotland 0 England 5

1893
Headingley, Leeds
England 0 Scotland 8

1894
Raeburn Place
Scotland 6 England 0

1895
Athletic Ground
England 3 Scotland 6

1896
Old Hampden Park,
Glasgow
Scotland 11 England 0

1897
Fallowfield,
Manchester
England 12 Scotland 3

1898
Powderhall, Edinburgh
Scotland 3 England 3

1899
Rectory Field
England 0 Scotland 5

1900
Inverleith, Edinburgh
Scotland 0 England 0

1901
Rectory Field
England 3 Scotland 18

1902
Inverleith
Scotland 3 England 6

1903
Athletic Ground
England 6 Scotland 10

1904
Inverleith
Scotland 6 England 3

1905
Athletic Ground
England 0 Scotland 8

1906
Inverleith
Scotland 3 England 9

1907
Rectory Field
England 3 Scotland 8

1908
Inverleith
Scotland 16 England 10

1909
Athletic Ground
England 8 Scotland 18

1910
Inverleith
Scotland 5 England 14

1911
Twickenham
England 13 Scotland 8

1912
Inverleith
Scotland 8 England 3

1913
Twickenham
England 3 Scotland 0

1914
Inverleith
Scotland 15 England 16

1920
Twickenham
England 13 Scotland 4

1921
Inverleith
Scotland 0 England 18

1922
Twickenham
England 11 Scotland 5

1923
Inverleith
Scotland 6 England 8

1924
Twickenham
England 19 Scotland 0

1925
Murrayfield,
Edinburgh
Scotland 14 England 11

1926
Twickenham
England 9 Scotland 17

1927
Murrayfield
Scotland 21 England 13

1928
Twickenham
England 6 Scotland 0

1929
Murrayfield
Scotland 12 England 6

1930
Twickenham
England 0 Scotland 0

1931
Murrayfield
Scotland 28 England 19

1932
Twickenham
England 16 Scotland 3

1933
Murrayfield
Scotland 3 England 0

1934
Twickenham
England 6 Scotland 3

1935
Murrayfield
Scotland 10 England 7

1936
Twickenham
England 9 Scotland 8

1937
Murrayfield
Scotland 3 England 6

1938
Twickenham
England 16 Scotland 21

1939
Murrayfield
Scotland 6 England 9

1947
Twickenham
England 24 Scotland 5

1948
Murrayfield
Scotland 6 England 3

1949
Twickenham
England 19 Scotland 3

1950
Murrayfield
Scotland 13 England 11

1951
Twickenham
England 5 Scotland 3

1952
Murrayfield
Scotland 3 England 19

1953
Twickenham
England 26 Scotland 8

1954
Murrayfield
Scotland 3 England 13

1955
Twickenham
England 9 Scotland 6

1956
Murrayfield
Scotland 6 England 11

1957
Twickenham
England 16 Scotland 3

1958
Murrayfield
Scotland 3 England 3

1959
Twickenham
England 3 Scotland 3

1960
Murrayfield
Scotland 12 England 21

1961
Twickenham
England 6 Scotland 0

1962
Murrayfield
Scotland 3 England 3

1963
Twickenham
England 10 Scotland 8

1964
Murrayfield
Scotland 15 England 6

1965
Twickenham
England 3 Scotland 3

1966
Murrayfield
Scotland 6 England 3

1967
Twickenham
England 27 Scotland 14

1968
Murrayfield
Scotland 6 England 8

1969
Twickenham
England 8 Scotland 3

1970
Murrayfield
Scotland 14 England 5

1971
Twickenham
England 15 Scotland 16

1972
Murrayfield
Scotland 23 England 9

1973
Twickenham
England 20 Scotland 13

1974
Murrayfield
Scotland 16 England 14

1975
Twickenham
England 7 Scotland 6

1976
Murrayfield
Scotland 22 England 12

1977
Twickenham
England 26 Scotland 6

1978
Murrayfield
Scotland 0 England 15

1979
Twickenham
England 7 Scotland 7

1980
Murrayfield
Scotland 18 England 30

1981
Twickenham
England 23 Scotland 17

1982
Murrayfield
Scotland 9 England 9

1983
Twickenham
England 12 Scotland 22

1984
Murrayfield
Scotland 18 England 6

1985
Twickenham
England 10 Scotland 7

1986
Murrayfield
Scotland 33 England 6

1987
Twickenham
England 21 Scotland 12

1988
Murrayfield
Scotland 6 England 9

1989
Twickenham
England 12 Scotland 12

1990
Murrayfield
Scotland 13 England 7

1991
Twickenham
England 21 Scotland 12

1992
Murrayfield
Scotland 7 England 25

1993
Twickenham
England 26 Scotland 12

1994
Murrayfield
Scotland 14 England 15

England v Ireland

1875
The Oval, London
England 2g 1t Ireland 0

1876
Dublin
Ireland 0 England 1g 1t

1877
The Oval
England 2g 2t Ireland 0

1878
Lansdowne Road, Dublin
Ireland 0 England 2g 1t

1879
The Oval
England 3g 2t Ireland 0

1880
Dublin
Ireland 1t England 1g 1t

1881
Whalley Range, Manchester
England 2g 2t Ireland 0

Brian McCall hands
off an English tackler
in 1986. England went
on to win 25-20

1882
Lansdowne Road
Ireland 2t England 2t

1883
Whalley Range
England 1g 3t Ireland 1t

1884
Lansdowne Road
Ireland 0 England 1g

1885
Whalley Range
England 2t Ireland 1t

1886
Lansdowne Road
Ireland 0 England 1t

1887
Lansdowne Road
Ireland 2g England 0

1888 & 1889
No matches

1890
**Rectory Field,
Blackheath**
England 3t Ireland 0

1891
Lansdowne Road
Ireland 0 England 9

1892
Whalley Range
England 7 Ireland 0

1893
Lansdowne Road
Ireland 0 England 4

1894
Rectory Field
England 5 Ireland 7

1895
Lansdowne Road
Ireland 3 England 6

1896
**Meanwood Road,
Leeds**
England 4 Ireland 10

1897
Lansdowne Road
Ireland 13 England 9

1898
**Athletic Ground,
Richmond**
England 6 Ireland 9

1899
Lansdowne Road
Ireland 6 England 0

1900
**Athletic Ground,
Richmond**
England 15 Ireland 4

1901
Lansdowne Road
Ireland 10 England 6

1902
**Welford Road,
Leicester**
England 6 Ireland 3

1903
Lansdowne Road
Ireland 6 England 0

1904
Rectory Field
England 19 Ireland 0

1905
Mardyke, Cork
Ireland 17 England 3

1906
Welford Road
England 6 Ireland 16

1907
Lansdowne Road
Ireland 17 England 9

1908
Athletic Ground
England 13 Ireland 3

1909
Lansdowne Road
Ireland 5 England 11

1910
Twickenham
England 0 Ireland 0

1911
Lansdowne Road
Ireland 3 England 0

1912
Twickenham
England 15 Ireland 0

1913
Lansdowne Road
Ireland 4 England 15

1914
Twickenham
England 17 Ireland 12

1920
Lansdowne Road
Ireland 11 England 14

1921
Twickenham
England 15 Ireland 0

1922
Lansdowne Road
Ireland 3 England 12

1923
Welford Road
England 23 Ireland 5

1924
Ravenhill, Belfast
Ireland 3 England 14

1925
Twickenham
England 6 Ireland 6

1926
Lansdowne Road
Ireland 19 England 15

1927
Twickenham
England 8 Ireland 6

1928
Lansdowne Road
Ireland 6 England 7

1929
Twickenham
England 5 Ireland 6

1930
Lansdowne Road
Ireland 4 England 3

1931
Twickenham
England 5 Ireland 6

1932
Lansdowne Road
Ireland 8 England 11

1933
Twickenham
England 17 Ireland 6

1934
Lansdowne Road
Ireland 3 England 13

1935
Twickenham
England 14 Ireland 3

1936
Lansdowne Road
Ireland 6 England 3

1937
Twickenham
England 9 Ireland 8

1938
Lansdowne Road
Ireland 14 England 36

1939
Twickenham
England 0 Ireland 5

1947
Lansdowne Road
Ireland 22 England 0

1948
Twickenham
England 10 Ireland 11

1949
Lansdowne Road
Ireland 14 England 5

1950
Twickenham
England 3 Ireland 0

1951
Lansdowne Road
Ireland 3 England 0

1952
Twickenham
England 3 Ireland 0

1953
Lansdowne Road
Ireland 9 England 9

1954
Twickenham
England 14 Ireland 3

1955
Lansdowne Road
Ireland 6 England 6

1956
Twickenham
England 20 Ireland 0

1957
Lansdowne Road
Ireland 0 England 6

1958
Twickenham
England 6 Ireland 0

1959
Lansdowne Road
Ireland 0 England 3

1960
Twickenham
England 8 Ireland 5

1961
Lansdowne Road
Ireland 11 England 8

1962
Twickenham
England 16 Ireland 0

1963
Lansdowne Road
Ireland 0 England 0

1964
Twickenham
England 5 Ireland 18

1965
Lansdowne Road
Ireland 5 England 0

1966
Twickenham
England 6 Ireland 6

1967
Lansdowne Road
Ireland 3 England 8

1968
Twickenham
England 9 Ireland 9

1969
Lansdowne Road
Ireland 17 England 15

1970
Twickenham
England 9 Ireland 3

1971
Lansdowne Road
Ireland 6 England 9

1972
Twickenham
England 12 Ireland 16

1973
Lansdowne Road
Ireland 18 England 9

1974
Twickenham
England 21 Ireland 26

1975
Lansdowne Road
Ireland 12 England 9

1976
Twickenham
England 12 Ireland 13

1977
Lansdowne Road
Ireland 0 England 4

1978
Twickenham
England 15 Ireland 9

1979
Lansdowne Road
Ireland 12 England 7

1980
Twickenham
England 24 Ireland 9

1981
Lansdowne Road
Ireland 6 England 10

1982
Twickenham
England 15 Ireland 16

1983
Lansdowne Road
Ireland 25 England 15

1984
Twickenham
England 12 Ireland 9

1985
Lansdowne Road
Ireland 13 England 10

1986
Twickenham
England 25 Ireland 20

1987
Lansdowne Road
Ireland 17 England 0

1988
Twickenham
England 35 Ireland 3

1989
Lansdowne Road
Ireland 3 England 16

1990
Twickenham
England 23 Ireland 0

1991
Lansdowne Road
Ireland 7 England 16

1992
Twickenham
England 38 Ireland 9

1993
Lansdowne Road
Ireland 17 England 0

1994
Twickenham
England 12 Ireland 13

OTHER MATCH

The Dublin Millennium
Challenge
23 April 1988
Lansdowne Road
Ireland 10 England 21
Not for the International
Championship

England v Wales

1881
Blackheath, London
England 7g 6t 1dg Wales 0

1882
No match

1883
St Helens, Swansea
Wales 0 England 2g 4t

1884
Cardigan Fields, Leeds
England 1g 2t Wales 1g

1885
St Helens
Wales 1 g 1t England 1g 4t

1886
Rectory Field
England 2t 1gm Wales 1g

1887
Stradey Park, Llanelli
Wales 0 England 0

1888 & 1889
No matches

1890
Crown Flatt, Dewsbury
England 0 Wales 1t

1891
Rodney Park,
Newport
Wales 3 England 7

1892
Rectory Field
England 17 Wales 0

1893
Cardiff Arms Park
Wales 12 England 11

1894
Birkenhead Park
England 24 Wales 3

1895
St Helens
Wales 6 England 14

1896
Rectory Field
England 25 Wales 0

1897
Rodney Parade
Wales 11 England 0

1898
Rectory Field
England 14 Wales 7

1899
St Helens
Wales 29 England 3

1900
Kingsholm, Gloucester
England 3 Wales 13

1901
Cardiff Arms Park
Wales 13 England 0

1902
Rectory Field
England 8 Wales 9

1903
St Helens
Wales 21 England 5

1904
Welford Road, Leicester
England 14 Wales 14

1905
Cardiff Arms Park
Wales 25 England 0

1906
Athletic Ground, Richmond
England 3 Wales 16

1907
St Helens
Wales 22 England 0

1908
Ashton Gate, Bristol
England 18 Wales 28

1909
Cardiff Arms Park
Wales 8 England 0

1910
Twickenham
England 11 Wales 6

1911
St Helens
Wales 15 England 11

1912
Twickenham
England 8 Wales 0

1913
Cardiff Arms Park
Wales 0 England 12

1914
Twickenham
England 10 Wales 9

1920
St Helens
Wales 19 England 5

1921
Twickenham
England 18 Wales 3

1922
Cardiff Arms Park
Wales 28 England 6

1923
Twickenham
England 7 Wales 3

1924
St Helens
Wales 9 England 17

1925
Twickenham
England 12 Wales 6

1926
Cardiff Arms Park
Wales 3 England 3

1927
Twickenham
England 11 Wales 9

1928
St Helens
Wales 8 England 10

1929
Twickenham
England 8 Wales 3

1930
Cardiff Arms Park
Wales 3 England 11

1931
Twickenham
England 11 Wales 11

1932
St Helens
Wales 12 England 5

1933
Twickenham
England 3 Wales 7

1934
Cardiff Arms Park
Wales 0 England 9

1935
Twickenham
England 3 Wales 3

1936
St Helens
Wales 0 England 0

1937
Twickenham
England 4 Wales 3

1938
Cardiff Arms Park
Wales 14 England 8

1939
Twickenham
England 3 Wales 0

1947
Cardiff Arms Park
Wales 6 England 9

1948
Twickenham
England 3 Wales 3

1949
Cardiff Arms Park
Wales 9 England 3

1950
Twickenham
England 5 Wales 11

1951
St Helens
Wales 23 England 5

1952
Twickenham
England 6 Wales 8

1953
Cardiff Arms Park
Wales 3 England 8

1954
Twickenham
England 9 Wales 6

1955
Cardiff Arms Park
Wales 3 England 0

1956
Twickenham
England 3 Wales 8

1957
Cardiff Arms Park
Wales 0 England 3

1958
Twickenham
England 3 Wales 3

1959
Cardiff Arms Park
Wales 5 England 0

1960
Twickenham
England 14 Wales 6

1961
Cardiff Arms Park
Wales 6 England 3

1962
Twickenham
England 0 Wales 0

1963
Cardiff Arms Park
Wales 6 England 13

1964
Twickenham
England 6 Wales 6

1965
Cardiff Arms Park
Wales 14 England 3

1966
Twickenham
England 6 Wales 11

1967
Cardiff Arms Park
Wales 34 England 21

1968
Twickenham
England 11 Wales 11

1969
Cardiff Arms Park
Wales 30 England 9

1970
Twickenham
England 13 Wales 17

1971
Cardiff Arms Park
Wales 22 England 6

1972
Twickenham
England 3 Wales 12

1973
Cardiff Arms Park
Wales 25 England 9

1974
Twickenham
England 16 Wales 12

1975
Cardiff Arms Park
Wales 20 England 4

1976
Twickenham
England 9 Wales 21

1977
Cardiff Arms Park
Wales 14 England 9

1978
Twickenham
England 6 Wales 9

1979
Cardiff Arms Park
Wales 27 England 3

1980
Twickenham
England 9 Wales 8

1981
Cardiff Arms Park
Wales 21 England 19

1982
Twickenham
England 17 Wales 7

1983
Cardiff Arms Park
Wales 13 England 13

1984
Twickenham
England 15 Wales 24

1985
Cardiff Arms Park
England 15 Wales 24

1986
Twickenham
England 21 Wales 18

1987
Cardiff Arms Park
Wales 19 England 12

1988
Twickenham
England 3 Wales 11

1989
Cardiff Arms Park
Wales 12 England 9

1990
Twickenham
England 34 Wales 6

1991
Cardiff Arms Park
Wales 6 England 25

1992
Twickenham
England 24 Wales 0

1993
Cardiff Arms Park
Wales 10 England 9

1994
Twickenham
England 15 Wales 8

Ireland v Scotland

1883
Ormeau, Belfast
Ireland 0 Scotland 1g 1t

1884
Raeburn Place, Edinburgh
Scotland 2g 2t Ireland 1t

1885
Raeburn Place
Scotland 1g 2t Ireland 0

1886
Raeburn Place
Scotland 3g 2t 1dg Ireland 0

1887
Ormeau
Ireland 0 Scotland 1g 2t 1gm

1888
Raeburn Place
Scotland 1g Ireland 0

1889
Ormeau
Ireland 1dg Scotland 0

1890
Raeburn Place
Scotland 1t 1dg Ireland 0

1891
Ballynafeigh, Belfast
Ireland 0 Scotland 14

1892
Raeburn Place
Scotland 2 Ireland 0

1893
Ballynafeigh
Ireland 0 Scotland 0

1894
Lansdowne Road, Dublin
Ireland 5 Scotland 0

1895
Raeburn Place
Scotland 6 Ireland 0

1896
Lansdowne Road
Ireland 0 Scotland 0

1897
Powderhall, Edinburgh
Scotland 8 Ireland 3

1898
Balmoral Showgrounds
Ireland 0 Scotland 8

1899
Inverleith, Edinburgh
Scotland 3 Ireland 9

1900
Lansdowne Road
Ireland 0 Scotland 0

1901
Inverleith
Scotland 9 Ireland 5

1902
Balmoral Showgrounds
Ireland 5 Scotland 0

1903
Inverleith
Scotland 3 Ireland 0

1904
Lansdowne Road
Ireland 3 Scotland 19

1905
Inverleith
Scotland 5 Ireland 11

1906
Lansdowne Road
Ireland 6 Scotland 13

1907
Inverleith
Scotland 15 Ireland 3

1908
Lansdowne Road
Ireland 16 Scotland 11

1909
Inverleith
Scotland 9 Ireland 3

1910
Balmoral Showgrounds
Ireland 0 Scotland 14

1911
Inverleith
Scotland 10 Ireland 16

1912
Lansdowne Road
Ireland 10 Scotland 8

1913
Inverleith
Scotland 29 Ireland 14

1914
Lansdowne Road
Ireland 6 Scotland 0

1920
Inverleith
Scotland 19 Ireland 0

1921
Lansdowne Road
Ireland 9 Scotland 9

1922
Inverleith
Scotland 6 Ireland 3

1923
Lansdowne Road
Ireland 3 Scotland 13

1924
Inverleith
Scotland 13 Ireland 8

1925
Lansdowne Road
Ireland 8 Scotland 14

1926
Murrayfield
Scotland 0 Ireland 3

1927
Lansdowne Road
Ireland 6 Scotland 0

1928
Murrayfield
Scotland 5 Ireland 13

1929
Lansdowne Road
Ireland 7 Scotland 16

1930
Murrayfield
Scotland 11 Ireland 14

1931
Lansdowne Road
Ireland 8 Scotland 5

1932
Murrayfield
Scotland 8 Ireland 20

Gain Jenkins practises his high tackling on Ireland's Rob Saunders, 1992. Ireland were narrowly defeated by the Welsh 16-15

1933
Lansdowne Road
Ireland 6 Scotland 8

1934
Murrayfield
Scotland 16 Ireland 9

1935
Lansdowne Road
Ireland 12 Scotland 5

1936
Murrayfield
Scotland 4 Ireland 10

1937
Lansdowne Road
Ireland 11 Scotland 4

1938
Murrayfield
Scotland 23 Ireland 14

1939
Lansdowne Road
Ireland 12 Scotland 3

1947
Murrayfield
Scotland 0 Ireland 3

1948
Lansdowne Road
Ireland 6 Scotland 0

1949
Murrayfield
Scotland 3 Ireland 13

1950
Lansdowne Road
Ireland 21 Scotland 0

1951
Murrayfield
Scotland 5 Ireland 6

1952
Lansdowne Road
Ireland 12 Scotland 8

1953
Murrayfield
Scotland 8 Ireland 26

1954
Ravenhill, Belfast
Ireland 6 Scotland 0

1955
Murrayfield
Scotland 12 Ireland 3

1956
Lansdowne Road
Ireland 14 Scotland 10

1957
Murrayfield
Scotland 3 Ireland 5

1958
Lansdowne Road
Ireland 12 Scotland 6

1959
Murrayfield
Scotland 3 Ireland 8

1960
Lansdowne Road
Ireland 5 Scotland 6

1961
Murrayfield
Scotland 16 Ireland 8

1962
Lansdowne Road
Ireland 6 Scotland 20

1963
Murrayfield
Scotland 3 Ireland 0

1964
Lansdowne Road
Ireland 3 Scotland 6

1965
Murrayfield
Scotland 6 Ireland 16

1966
Lansdowne Road
Ireland 3 Scotland 11

1967
Murrayfield
Scotland 3 Ireland 5

1968
Lansdowne Road
Ireland 14 Scotland 6

1969
Murrayfield
Scotland 0 Ireland 16

1970
Lansdowne Road
Ireland 16 Scotland 11

1971
Murrayfield
Scotland 5 Ireland 17

1972
No match

1973
Murrayfield
Scotland 19 Ireland 14

1974
Lansdowne Road
Ireland 9 Scotland 6

1975
Murrayfield
Scotland 20 Ireland 13

1976
Lansdowne Road
Ireland 6 Scotland 15

1977
Murrayfield
Scotland 21 Ireland 18

1978
Lansdowne Road
Ireland 12 Scotland 9

1979
Murrayfield
Scotland 11 Ireland 11

1980
Lansdowne Road
Ireland 22 Scotland 15

1981
Murrayfield
Scotland 10 Ireland 9

1982
Lansdowne Road
Ireland 21 Scotland 12

1983
Murrayfield
Scotland 13 Ireland 15

1984
Lansdowne Road
Ireland 9 Scotland 32

1985
Murrayfield
Scotland 15 Ireland 18

1986
Lansdowne Road
Ireland 9 Scotland 10

1987
Murrayfield
Scotland 16 Ireland 12

1988
Lansdowne Road
Ireland 22 Scotland 18

1989
Murrayfield
Scotland 37 Ireland 21

1990
Lansdowne Road
Ireland 10 Scotland 13

1991
Murrayfield
Scotland 28 Ireland 25

1992
Lansdowne Road
Ireland 10 Scotland 18

1993
Murrayfield
Scotland 15 Ireland 3

1994
Lansdowne Road
Ireland 6 Scotland 6

Ireland v Wales

1884
Cardiff Arms Park
Wales 2t 1dg Ireland 0

1885
No matches

1886
No matches

1887
Birkenhead Park
Wales 1t 1dg Ireland 3t

1888
Lansdowne Road
Ireland 1g 1t 1dg Wales 0

1889
St Helens, Swansea
Wales 0 Ireland 2t

1890
Lansdowne Road
Ireland 1g Wales 1g

1891
Stradey Park, Llanelli
Wales 6 Ireland 4

1892
Lansdowne Road
Ireland 9 Wales 0

1893
Stradey Park, Llanelli
Wales 2 Ireland 0

1894
Ballynafeigh, Belfast
Ireland 3 Wales 0

1895
Cardiff Arms Park
Wales 5 Ireland 3

1896
Lansdowne Road
Ireland 3 Wales 4

1898
Limerick
Ireland 3 Wales 11

1899
Cardiff Arms Park
Wales 0 Ireland 3

1900
Balmoral Showground, Belfast
Ireland 0 Wales 3

1901
St Helens
Wales 10 Ireland 9

1902
Lansdowne Road
Ireland 0 Wales 15

1903
Cardiff Arms Park
Wales 18 Ireland 0

1904
Balmoral Showgrounds
Ireland 14 Wales 12

1905
St Helens
Wales 10 Ireland 3

1906
Balmoral Showgrounds
Ireland 11 Wales 6

1907
Cardiff Arms Park
Wales 29 Ireland 0

1908
Balmoral Showgrounds
Ireland 5 Wales 11

1909
St Helens
Wales 18 Ireland 5

1910
Lansdowne Road
Ireland 3 Wales 19

1911
Cardiff Arms Park
Wales 16 Ireland 0

1912
Balmoral Showground
Ireland 12 Wales 5

1913
St Helens,
Wales 16 Ireland 13

1914
Balmoral Showground
Ireland 3 Wales 11

1920
Cardiff Arms Park
Wales 28 Ireland 4

1921
Balmoral Showground
Ireland 0 Wales 6

1922
St Helens
Wales 11 Ireland 5

1923
Lansdowne Road
Ireland 5 Wales 4

1924
Cardiff Arms Park
Wales 10 Ireland 13

1925
Ravenhill, Belfast
Ireland 19 Wales 3

1926
St Helens
Wales 11 Ireland 8

1927
Lansdowne Road
Ireland 19 Wales 9

1928
Cardiff Arms Park
Wales 10 Ireland 13

1929
Ravenhill
Ireland 5 Wales 5

1930
St Helens
Wales 12 Ireland 7

1931
Ravenhill
Ireland 3 Wales 15

1932
Cardiff Arms Park
Wales 10 Ireland 12

1933
Ravenhill
Ireland 10 Wales 5

1934
St Helens
Wales 13 Ireland 0

1935
Ravenhill
Ireland 9 Wales 3

1936
Cardiff Arms Park
Wales 3 Ireland 0

1937
Ravenhill
Ireland 5 Wales 3

1938
St Helens
Wales 11 Ireland 5

1939
Ravenhill
Ireland 0 Wales 7

1947
St Helens
Wales 6 Ireland 0

1948
Ravenhill
Ireland 6 Wales 3

1949
St Helens
Wales 0 Ireland 5

1950
Ravenhill
Ireland 3 Wales 6

1951
Cardiff Arms Park
Wales 3 Ireland 3

1952
Lansdowne Road
Ireland 3 Wales 14

1953
St Helens
Wales 5 Ireland 3

1954
Lansdowne Road
Ireland 9 Wales 12

1955
Cardiff Arms Park
Wales 21 Ireland 3

1956
Lansdowne Road
Ireland 11 Wales 3

1957
Cardiff Arms Park
Wales 6 Ireland 5

1958
Lansdowne Road
Ireland 6 Wales 9

1959
Cardiff Arms Park
Wales 8 Ireland 6

1960
Lansdowne Road
Ireland 9 Wales 10

1961
Cardiff Arms Park
Wales 9 Ireland 0

1962
Lansdowne Road
Ireland 3 Wales 3

1963
Cardiff Arms Park
Wales 6 Ireland 14

1964
Lansdowne Road
Ireland 6 Wales 15

1965
Cardiff Arms Park
Wales 14 Ireland 8

1966
Lansdowne Road
Ireland 9 Wales 6

1967
Cardiff Arms Park
Wales 0 Ireland 3

1968
Lansdowne Road
Ireland 9 Wales 6

1969
Cardiff Arms Park
Wales 24 Ireland 11

1970
Lansdowne Road
Ireland 14 Wales 0

1971
Cardiff Arms Park
Wales 23 Ireland 9

1973
Cardiff Arms Park
Wales 16 Ireland 12

1974
Lansdowne Road
Ireland 9 Wales 9

1975
Cardiff Arms Park
Wales 32 Ireland 4

1976
Lansdowne Road
Ireland 9 Wales 34

1977
Cardiff Arms Park
Wales 25 Ireland 9

1978
Lansdowne Road
Ireland 16 Wales 20

1979
Cardiff Arms Park
Wales 24 Ireland 21

1980
Lansdowne Road
Ireland 21 Wales 7

1981
Cardiff Arms Park
Wales 9 Ireland 8

1982
Lansdowne Road
Ireland 20 Wales 12

1983
Cardiff Arms Park
Wales 23 Ireland 9

1984
Lansdowne Road
Ireland 9 Wales 18

1985
Cardiff Arms Park
Wales 9 Ireland 21

1986
Lansdowne Road
Ireland 12 Wales 19

1987
Cardiff Arms Park
Wales 11 Ireland 15

1988
Lansdowne Road
Ireland 9 Wales 12

1989
Cardiff Arms Park
Wales 13 Ireland 19

1990
Lansdowne Road
Ireland 14 Wales 8

1991
Cardiff Arms Park
Wales 21 Ireland 21

1992
Lansdowne Road
Ireland 15 Wales 16

1993
Cardiff Arms Park
Wales 14 Ireland 19

1994
Lansdowne Road
Ireland 15 Wales 17

Scotland v Wales

1883
Raeburn Place, Edinburgh
Scotland 3g Wales 1g

1884
Rodney Parade, Newport
Wales 0 Scotland 1t 1dg

1885
Hamilton Crescent, Glasgow
Scotland 0 Wales 0

1886
Cardiff Arms Park
Wales 0 Scotland 2g 1t

1887
Raeburn Place
Scotland 4g 8t Wales 0

1888
Rodney Parade
Wales 1t Scotland 0

1889
Raeburn Place
Scotland 2t Wales 0

1890
Cardiff Arms Park
Wales 1t Scotland 1g 2t

1891
Raeburn Place
Scotland 15 Wales 0

1892
St Helens, Swansea
Wales 2 Scotland 7

1893
Raeburn Place
Scotland 0 Wales 9

1894
Rodney Parade
Wales 7 Scotland 0

1895
Raeburn Place
Scotland 5 Wales 4

1896
Cardiff Arms Park
Wales 6 Scotland 0

1899
Inverleith
Scotland 21 Wales 10

1900
St Helens
Wales 12 Scotland 3

1901
Inverleith
Scotland 18 Wales 8

1902
Cardiff Arms Park
Wales 14 Scotland 5

1903
Inverleith
Scotland 6 Wales 0

1904
St Helens
Wales 21 Scotland 3

1905
Inverleith
Scotland 3 Wales 6

1906
Cardiff Arms Park
Wales 9 Scotland 3

1907
Inverleith
Scotland 6 Wales 3

1908
St Helens
Wales 6 Scotland 5

1909
Inverleith
Scotland 3 Wales 5

1910
Cardiff Arms Park
Wales 14 Scotland 0

1911
Inverleith
Scotland 10 Wales 32

1912
St Helens
Wales 21 Scotland 6

1913
Inverleith
Scotland 0 Wales 8

1914
Cardiff Arms Park
Wales 24 Scotland 5

1920
Inverleith
Scotland 9 Wales 5

1921
St Helens
Wales 8 Scotland 14

1922
Inverleith
Scotland 9 Wales 9

1923
Cardiff Arms Park
Wales 8 Scotland 11

1924
Inverleith
Scotland 25 Wales 10

1925
St Helens
Wales 14 Scotland 24

1926
Murrayfield
Scotland 8 Wales 5

1927
Cardiff Arms Park
Wales 0 Scotland 5

1928
Murrayfield
Scotland 0 Wales 13

1929
St Helens
Wales 14 Scotland 7

1930
Murrayfield
Scotland 12 Wales 9

1931
Cardiff Arms Park
Wales 13 Scotland 8

1932
Murrayfield
Scotland 0 Wales 6

1933
St Helens
Wales 3 Scotland 11

1934
Murrayfield
Scotland 6 Wales 13

1935
Cardiff Arms Park
Wales 10 Scotland 6

1936
Murrayfield
Scotland 3 Wales 13

1937
St Helens
Wales 6 Scotland 13

1938
Murrayfield
Scotland 8 Wales 6

1939
Cardiff Arms Park
Wales 11 Scotland 3

1947
Murrayfield
Scotland 8 Wales 2

1948
Cardiff Arms Park
Wales 14 Scotland 0

1949
Murrayfield
Scotland 6 Wales 5

1950
St Helens
Wales 12 Scotland 0

1951
Murrayfield
Scotland 19 Wales 0

1952
Cardiff Arms Park
Wales 11 Scotland 0

1953
Murrayfield
Scotland 0 Wales 12

1954
St Helens, Swansea
Wales 15 Scotland 3

1955
Murrayfield
Scotland 14 Wales 8

1956
Cardiff Arms Park
Wales 9 Scotland 3

1957
Murrayfield
Scotland 9 Wales 6

1958
Cardiff Arms Park
Wales 8 Scotland 3

1959
Murrayfield
Scotland 6 Wales 5

1960
Cardiff Arms Park
Wales 8 Scotland 0

1961
Murrayfield
Scotland 3 Wales 0

1962
Cardiff Arms Park
Wales 3 Scotland 8

1963
Murrayfield
Scotland 0 Wales 6

1964
Cardiff Arms Park
Wales 11 Scotland 3

1965
Murrayfield
Scotland 12 Wales 14

1966
Cardiff Arms Park
Wales 8 Scotland 3

1967
Murrayfield
Scotland 11 Wales 5

1968
Cardiff Arms Park
Wales 5 Scotland 0

1969
Murrayfield
Scotland 3 Wales 17

1970
Cardiff Arms Park
Wales 18 Scotland 9

1971
Murrayfield
Scotland 18 Wales 19

1972
Cardiff Arms Park
Wales 35 Scotland 12

1973
Murrayfield
Scotland 10 Wales 9

1974
Cardiff Arms Park
Wales 6 Scotland 0

1975
Murrayfield
Scotland 12 Wales 10

1976
Cardiff Arms Park
Wales 28 Scotland 6

1977
Murrayfield
Scotland 9 Wales 18

1978
Cardiff Arms Park
Wales 22 Scotland 14

1979
Murrayfield
Scotland 13 Wales 19

1980
Cardiff Arms Park
Wales 17 Scotland 6

1981
Murrayfield
Scotland 15 Wales 6

1982
Cardiff Arms Park
Wales 18 Scotland 34

1983
Murrayfield
Scotland 15 Wales 19

1984
Cardiff Arms Park
Wales 9 Scotland 15

1985
Murrayfield
Scotland 21 Wales 25

1986
Cardiff Arms Park
Wales 22 Scotland 15

1987
Murrayfield
Scotland 21 Wales 14

1988
Cardiff Arms Park
Wales 25 Scotland 20

1989
Murrayfield
Scotland 23 Wales 7

1990
Cardiff Arms Park
Wales 9 Scotland 13

1991
Murrayfield
Scotland 32 Wales 12

1992
Cardiff Arms Park
Wales 15 Scotland 12

1993
Murrayfield
Scotland 20 Wales 0

1994
Cardiff Arms Park
Wales 29 Scotland 6

England v France

1910
Parcs des Princes, Paris
France 3 England 11

1911
Twickenham
England 37 France 0

1912
Parc des Princes
France 8 England 18

1913
Twickenham
England 20 France 0

1914
Stade Colombes
France 13 England 39

1920
Twickenham
England 8 France 3

1921
Stade Colombes
France 6 England 10

1922
Twickenham
England 11 France 11

1923
Stade Colombes
France 3 England 12

1924
Twickenham
England 19 France 7

1925
Stade Colombes
France 11 England 13

1926
Twickenham
England 11 France 0

1927
Stade Colombes
France 3 England 0

1928
Twickenham
England 18 France 8

1929
Stade Colombes
France 6 England 16

1930
Twickenham
England 11 France 5

1931
Stade Colombes
France 14 England 13

1947
Twickenham
England 6 France 3

1948
Stade Colombes
France 15 England 0

1949
Twickenham
England 8 France 3

1950
Stade Colombes
France 6 England 3

1951
Twickenham
England 3 France 11

1952
Stade Colombes
France 3 England 6

1953
Twickenham
England 11 France 0

1954
Stade Colombes
France 11 England 3

1955
Twickenham
England 9 France 16

1956
Stade Colombes
France 14 England 9

1957
Twickenham
England 9 France 5

1958
Stade Colombes
France 0 England 14

1959
Twickenham
England 3 France 3

1960
Stade Colombes
France 3 England 3

1961
Twickenham
England 5 France 5

1962
Stade Colombes
France 13 England 0

1963
Twickenham
England 6 France 5

1964
Stade Colombes
France 3 England 6

1965
Twickenham
England 9 France 6

1966
Stade Colombes
France 13 England 0

1967
Twickenham
England 12 France 16

1968
Stade Colombes
France 14 England 9

1969
Twickenham
England 22 France 8

1970
Stade Colombes
France 35 England 13

1971
Twickenham
England 14 France 14

1972
Stade Colombes
France 37 England 12

1973
Twickenham
England 14 France 6

1974
Parc des Princes
France 12 England 12

1975
Twickenham
England 20 France 27

1976
Parc des Princes
France 30 England 9

1977
Twickenham
England 3 France 4

1978
Parc des Princes
France 15 England 6

1979
Twickenham
England 7 France 6

1980
Parc des Princes
France 13 England 17

1981
Twickenham
England 12 France 16

1982
Parc des Princes
France 15 England 27

1983
Twickenham
England 15 France 19

1984
Parc des Princes
France 32 England 18

1985
Twickenham
England 9 France 9

1986
Parc des Princes
France 29 England 10

1987
Twickenham
England 15 France 19

1988
Parc des Princes
France 10 England 9

1989
Twickenham
England 11 France 0

1990
Parc des Princes
France 7 England 26

1991
Twickenham
England 21 France 19

1992
Parc des Princes
France 13 England 31

1993
Twickenham
England 16 France15

1994
Parc des Princes,
France 14 England 18

Ireland v France

1909
Lansdowne Road, Dublin
Ireland 19 France 8

1910
Parc des Princes, Paris
France 3 Ireland 8

1911
Mardyke, Cork
Ireland 25 France 5

1912
Parc des Princes
France 6 Ireland 11

1913
Mardyke
Ireland 24 France 0

1914
Parc des Princes
France 6 Ireland 8

1920
Lansdowne Road
Ireland 7 France 15

1921
Stade Colombes, Paris
France 20 Ireland 10

1922
Lansdowne Road
Ireland 8 France 3

1923
Stade Colombes
France 14 Ireland 8

1924
Lansdowne Road
Ireland 6 France 0

1925
Stade Colombes
France 3 Ireland 9

1926
Ravenhill
Ireland 11 France 0

1927
Stade Colombes
France 3 Ireland 8

1928
Ravenhill, Belfast
Ireland 12 France 8

1928
Yves du Manor Stadium
France 0 Ireland 6

1930
Ravenhill, Belfast
Ireland 0 France 5

1931
Stade Colombes
France 3 Ireland 0

1937
Lansdowne Road
Ireland 8 France 12

1948
Stade Colombes
France 6 Ireland 13

1949
Lansdowne Road
Ireland 9 France 16

1950
Stade Colombes
France 3 Ireland 3

1951
Lansdowne Road
Ireland 9 France 8

1952
Stade Colombes
France 8 Ireland 11

1953
Ravenhill, Belfast
Ireland 16 France 3

1954
Stade Colombes
France 8 Ireland 0

1955
Lansdowne Road
Ireland 3 France 5

1956
Stade Colombes
France 14 Ireland 8

1957
Lansdowne Road
Ireland 11 France 6

1958
Stade Colombes
France 11 Ireland 6

1959
Lansdowne Road
Ireland 9 France 5

1960
Stade Colombes
France 23 Ireland 6

1961
Lansdowne Road, Dublin
Ireland 3 France 15

1962
Stade Colombes
France 11 Ireland 0

1963
Lansdowne Road
Ireland 5 France 24

1964
Stade Colombes
France 27 Ireland 6

1965
Lansdowne Road
Ireland 3 France 3

1966
Stade Colombes
France 11 Ireland 6

1967
Lansdowne Road
Ireland 6 France 11

1968
Stade Colombes
France 16 Ireland 6

1969
Lansdowne Road
Ireland 17 France 9

1970
Stade Colombes
France 8 Ireland 0

1971
Lansdowne Road
Ireland 9 France 9

1972
Stade Colombes
France 9 Ireland 14

1973
Lansdowne Road
Ireland 6 France 4

1974
Parc des Princes
France 9 Ireland 6

1975
Lansdowne Road
Ireland 25 France 6

1976
Parc des Princes
France 26 Ireland 3

1977
Lansdowne Road
Ireland 6 France 15

1978
Parc des Princes
France 10 Ireland 9

1979
Lansdowne Road
Ireland 9 France 9

1980
Parc des Princes
France 19 Ireland 18

1981
Lansdowne Road
Ireland 13 France 19

1982
Parc des Princes
France 22 Ireland 9

1983
Lansdowne Road
Ireland 22 France 16

1984
Parc des Princes
France 25 Ireland 12

1985
Lansdowne Road
Ireland 15 France 15

1986
Parc des Princes
France 29 Ireland 9

1987
Lansdowne Road
Ireland 13 France 19

1988
Parc des Princes
France 25 Ireland 6

1989
Lansdowne Road
Ireland 21 France 26

1990
Parc des Princes
France 31 Ireland 12

Jean Condom
takes a clean
ball at the line
out, 1987.
France beat
the Irish 19-13

1991
Lansdowne Road
Ireland 13 France 21

1992
Parc des Princes
France 44 Ireland 12

1993
Lansdowne Road
Ireland 6 France 21

1994
Parc des Princes
France 35 Ireland 15

Scotland v France

1910
Inverleith
Scotland 27 France 0

1911
Stade Colombes
France 16 Scotland 15

1912
Inverleith
Scotland 31 France 3

1913
Parc des Princes
France 3 Scotland 21

1920
Parc des Princes
France 0 Scotland 5

1921
Inverleith
Scotland 0 France 3

1922
Stade Colombes
France 3 Scotland 3

1923
Inverleith
Scotland 16 France 3

1924
Stade Pershing, Paris
France 12 Scotland 10

1925
Inverleith
Scotland 25 France 4

1926
Stade Colombes
France 6 Scotland 20

1927
Murrayfield
Scotland 23 France 6

1928
Stade Colombes
France 6 Scotland 15

1929
Murrayfield
Scotland 6 France 3

1930
Stade Colombes
France 7 Scotland 3

1931
Murrayfield
Scotland 6 France 4

1947
Stade Colombes
France 8 Scotland 3

1948
Murrayfield
Scotland 9 France 8

1949
Stade Colombes
France 0 Scotland 8

1950
Murrayfield
Scotland 8 France 5

1951
Stade Colombes
France 14 Scotland 12

1952
Murrayfield
Scotland 11 France 13

1953
Stade Colombes
France 11 Scotland 5

1954
Murrayfield
Scotland 0 France 3

1955
Stade Colombes
France 15 Scotland 0

1956
Murrayfield
Scotland 12 France 0

1957
Stade Colombes
France 0 Scotland 6

1958
Murrayfield
Scotland 11 France 9

1959
Stade Colombes
France 9 Scotland 0

1960
Murrayfield
Scotland 11 France 13

1961
Stade Colombes
France 11 Scotland 0

1962
Murrayfield
Scotland 3 France 11

1963
Stade Colombes
France 6 Scotland 11

1964
Murrayfield
Scotland 10 France 0

1965
Stade Colombes
France 16 Scotland 8

1966
Murrayfield
Scotland 3 France 3

1967
Stade Colombes
France 8 Scotland 9

1968
Murrayfield
Scotland 6 France 8

1969
Stade Colombes
France 3 Scotland 6

1970
Murrayfield
Scotland 9 France 11

1971
Stade Colombes
France 13 Scotland 8

1972
Murrayfield
Scotland 20 France 9

1973
Parc des Princes
France 16 Scotland 13

1974
Murrayfield
Scotland 19 France 6

1975
Parc des Princes
France 10 Scotland 9

1976
Murrayfield
Scotland 6 France 13

1977
Parc des Princes
France 23 Scotland 3

1978
Murrayfield
Scotland 16 France 19

1979
Parc des Princes
France 21 Scotland 17

1980
Murrayfield
Scotland 22 France 14

1981
Parc des Princes
France 16 Scotland 9

1982
Murrayfield
Scotland 16 France 7

1983
Parc des Princes
France 19 Scotland 15

1984
Murrayfield
Scotland 21 France 12

1985
Parc des Princes
France 11 Scotland 3

1986
Murrayfield
Scotland 18 France 17

1987
Parc des Princes
France 28 Scotland 22

1988
Murrayfield
Scotland 23 France 12

1989
Parc des Princes
France 19 Scotland 3

1990
Murrayfield
Scotland 21 France 0

1991
Parc des Princes
France 15 Scotland 9

1992
Murrayfield
Scotland 10 France 20

1993
Parc des Princes
France 11 Scotland 3

1994
Murrayfield
Scotland 12 France 6

Wales v France

1910
St Helens, Swansea
Wales 49 France 14

1911
Parc des Princes, Paris
France 0 Wales 15

1912
Rodney Parade, Newport
Wales 14 France 8

1913
Parc des Princes
France 8 Wales 11

1914
St Helens
Wales 31 France 0

1920
Stades Colombes, Paris
France 5 Wales 6

1921
Cardiff Arms park
Wales 12 France 4

1922
Stade Colombes
France 3 Wales 11

1923
St Helens,
Wales 16 France 8

1924
Stade Colombes
France 6 Wales 10

1925
Cardiff Arms Park
Wales 11 France 5

1926
Stade Colombes
France 5 Wales 7

1927
St Helens
Wales 25 France 7

1928
Stade Colombes
France 8 Wales 3

1929
Cardiff Arms Park
Wales 8 France 3

1930
Stade Colombes
France 0 Wales 11

1931
St Helens
Wales 35 France 3

1947
Stade Colombes
France 0 Wales 3

1948
St Helens
Wales 3 France 11

1949
Stade Colombes
France 22 Wales 13

1950
Cardiff Arms Park
Wales 21 France 0

1951
Stade Colombes
France 8 Wales 3

1952
St Helens
Wales 9 France 5

1953
Stade Colombes
France 3 Wales 6

1954
Cardiff Arms Park
Wales 19 France 13

1955
Stade Colombes
France 11 Wales 16

1956
Cardiff Arms Park
Wales 5 France 3

1957
Stade Colombes
France 13 Wales 19

1958
Cardiff Arms Park
Wales 6 France 16

1959
Stade Colombes
France 11 Wales 3

1960
Cardiff Arms Park
Wales 8 France 16

1961
Stade Colombes
France 8 Wales 6

1962
Cardiff Arms Park
Wales 3 France 0

1963
Stade Colombes
France 5 Wales 3

1964
Cardiff Arms Park
France 11 Wales 11

1966
Cardiff Arms Park
Wales 9 France 8

1967
Stade Colombes
France 20 Wales 14

1968
Cardiff Arms Park
Wales 9 France 14

1969
Stade Colombes
France 8 Wales 8

1970
Cardiff Arms Park
Wales 11 France 6

1971
Stade Colombes
France 5 Wales 9

1972
Cardiff Arms Park
Wales 20 France 6

1973
Parc des Princes
France 12 Wales 3

1974
Cardiff Arms Park
Wales 16 France 16

1975
Parc des Princes
France 10 Wales 25

1976
Cardiff Arms Park
Wales 19 France 13

1977
Parc des Princes
France 16 Wales 9

1978
Cardiff Arms Park
Wales 16 France 7

1979
Parc des Princes
France 14 Wales 13

1980
Cardiff Arms Park
Wales 18 France 9

1981
Parc de Princes
France 19 Wales 15

1982
Cardiff Arms Park
Wales 22 France 12

1983
Parc des Princes
France 16 Wales 9

1984
Cardiff Arms Park
Wales 16 France 21

1985
Parc des Princes
France 14 Wales 3

1986
Cardiff Arms Park
Wales 15 France 23

1987
Parc des Princes
France 16 Wales 9

1988
Cardiff Arms Park
Wales 9 France 10

1989
Parc des Princes
France 31 Wales 12

1990
Cardiff Arms Park
Wales 19 France 29

1991
Parc des Princes
France 36 Wales 3

1992
Cardiff Arms Park
Wales 9 France 12

1993
Parc des Princes
France 26 Wales 10

1994
Cardiff Arms Park
Wales 24 France 15

OTHER MATCHES

1991
Cardiff Arms Park
Wales 9 France 22

Other Internationals

France V Australia

1948
Paris
France 13 Australia 6

1958
Stades Colombes, Paris
France 19 Australia 0

1961
Sydney
Australia 8 France 15

1967
Stade Colombes
France 20 Australia 14

1968
Sydney
Australia 11 France 10

1971
Toulouse
France 11 Australia 13

1972
Sydney
Australia 14 France 14

Brisbane
Australia 15 France 16
France win series, 1-0

1976
Parc des Princes
France 34 Australia 6

1981
Ballymore Oval, Brisbane
Australia 17 France 15

Sydney Cricket Ground
Australia 24 France 14
Australia win series, 2-0

1983
Clermont-Ferrand
France 15 Australia 15

Parc des Princes
France 15 Australia 6
France win series, 1-0

1986
Sydney Cricket Ground
Australia 27 France 14

1989
Meinau Stadium, Strasbourg
France 15 Australia 32

Stade Grimpooris, Lille
France 25 Australia 19
Series tied 1-1

1990
Sydney Football Stadium
Australia 21 France 9

Ballymore Oval
Australia 48 France 31

Sydney Football Stadium
Australia 19 France 28
Australia win series, 2-1

France V New Zealand

1906
Parc des Princes
France 8 New Zealand 38

1925
Stade des Ponts Jumeaux, Toulouse
France 6 New Zealand 30

1954
Stade Colombes
France 3 New Zealand 0

1961
Eden Park, Auckland
New Zealand 13 France 6

Athletic Park, Wellington
New Zealand 15 France 3

Lancaster Park, Christchurch
New Zealand 32 France 3
New Zealand win series, 3-0

1964
Stade Colombes
France 3 New Zealand 12

1967
Stade Colombes
France 15 New Zealand 21

1968
Lancaster Park
New Zealand 12 France 9

Athletic Park
New Zealand 9 France 3

Eden Park
New Zealand 19 France 12
New Zealand win series, 3-0

1973
Parc des Princes
France 13 New Zealand 6

1977
Stadium de Toulouse
France 18 New Zealand 13

Parc des Princes
France 3 New Zealand 15
Series drawn 1-1

1979
Lancaster Park
New Zealand 23 France 9

Eden Park
New Zealand 19 France 24
Series tied 1-1

1981
Stadium de Toulouse
France 9 New Zealand 13

Parc des Princes
France 6 New Zealand 18
New Zealand win series 2-0

1984
Lancaster Park
New Zealand 10 France 9

Eden Park
New Zealand 31 France 18
New Zealand win series 2-0

1986
Lancaster Park
New Zealand 18 France 9

1986
Stadium de Toulouse
France 7 New Zealand 19

Stade Beaujoire, Nantes
France 16 New Zealand 3
Series drawn 1-1

1989
Lancaster Park
New Zealand 25 France 17

Eden Park
New Zealand 34 France 20
New Zealand win series, 2-0

1990
Stade Beaujoire
France 3 New Zealand 24

Parc des Princes
France 12 New Zealand 30
New Zealand win series, 2-0

1994
Christchurch
New Zealand 8 France 22

Auckland
New Zealand 20 France 23
France win series, 2-0

France V South Africa

1913
Bordeaux
France 5 South Africa 38

1952
Stade Colombes, Paris
France 3 South Africa 25

1958
Newlands, Cape Town
South Africa 3 France 3

Ellis Park, Johannesburg
South Africa 5 France 9
South Africa win series, 1-0

1961
Stade Colombes
France 0 South Africa 0

1964
Springs, South Africa
South Africa 6 France 8

1967
Kingsmead, Durban
South Africa 26 France 3

Free State Stadium, Bloemfontein
South Africa 16 France 3

Ellis Park
South Africa 14 France 19
South Africa win series, 2-1

Newlands
South Africa 6 France 6

1968
Bordeaux
France 9 South Africa 12

Stade Colombes
France 11 South Africa 16
South Africa win series, 2-0

1971
Free State Stadium
South Africa 22 France 9

Kings Park, Durban
South Africa 8 France 8
South Africa win series, 1-0

1974
Stadium de Toulouse
France 4 South Africa 13

Parc des Princes, Paris
France 8 South Africa 10

1975
Free State Stadium
South Africa 38 France 25

Loftus Versveld
South Africa 33 France 18
South Africa win series, 2-0

1980
Loftus Versveld, Pretoria
South Africa 37 France 15

1905
Crystal Palace, London
England 0 New Zealand 15

1925
Twickenham
England 11 New Zealand 17

1936
Twickenham
England 13 New Zealand 0

1954
Twickenham
England 0 New Zealand 5

1963
Eden Park, Auckland
New Zealand 21 England 11

Lancaster Park, Christchurch
New Zealand 9 England 6
New Zealand win series, 2-0

1964
Twickenham
England 0 New Zealand 14

1967
Twickenham
England 11 New Zealand 23

1973
Twickenham
England 0 New Zealand 9

Eden Park
New Zealand 10 England 16

1978
Twickenham
England 6 New Zealand 16

1979
Twickenham
England 9 New Zealand 10

1983
Twickenham
England 15 New Zealand 9

1985
Lancaster Park
New Zealand 18 England 13

1985
Athletic Park, Wellington
New Zealand 42 England 15

1905
Inverleith, Edinburgh
Scotland 7 New Zealand 12

1935
Murrayfield, Edinburgh
Scotland 8 New Zealand 18

1954
Murrayfield
Scotland 0 New Zealand 3

1964
Murrayfield
Scotland 0 New Zealand 0

1967
Murrayfield
Scotland 3 New Zealand 14

1972
Murrayfield
Scotland 9 New Zealand 14

1975
Eden Park, Auckland
New Zealand 24 Scotland 0

1978
Murrayfield
Scotland 9 New Zealand 18

1979
Murrayfield
Scotland 6 New Zealand 20

1981
Carisbrook, Dunedin
New Zealand 11 Scotland 4

Eden Park
New Zealand 40 Scotland 15

Eden Park
New Zealand 40 Scotland 15
New Zealand win series, 3-0

1983
Murrayfield
Scotland 25 New Zealand 25

1990
Carisbrook
New Zealand 31 Scotland 16

Eden Park
New Zealand 21 Scotland 18
New Zealand win series, 2-0

1905
Lansdowne Road, Dublin
Ireland 0 New Zealand 15

1924
Lansdowne Road
Ireland 0 New Zealand 6

1935
Lansdowne Road
Ireland 9 New Zealand 17

1954
Lansdowne Road
Ireland 3 New Zealand 14

1963
Lansdowne Road
Ireland 5 New Zealand 6

1973
Lansdowne Road
Ireland 10 New Zealand 10

1974
Lansdowne Road
Ireland 6 New Zealand 15

1976
Athletic Park, Wellington
New Zealand 11 Ireland 3

1978
Lansdowne Road
Ireland 6 New Zealand 10

1989
Lansdowne Road
Ireland 6 New Zealand 23

1992
Carisbrook, Dunedin
New Zealand 24 Ireland 21

Athletic Park
New Zealand 59 Ireland 6
New Zealand win series, 2-0

1905
Cardiff Arms Park
Wales 3 New Zealand 0

1925
St Helens, Swansea
Wales 0 New Zealand 19

Rory Underwood finds Jamie Joseph a bit of a drag during the Lion's third Test against NZ. The Lions won the test convincingly by 30-13, but lost the series 2-1

1935
Cardiff Arms Park
Wales 13 New Zealand 12

1953
Cardiff Arms Park
Wales 13 New Zealand 8

1963
Cardiff Arms Park
Wales 0 New Zealand 6

1967
Cardiff Arms Park
Wales 6 New Zealand 13

1969
**Lancaster Park,
Christchurch**
New Zealand 19 Wales 0

Eden Park, Auckland
New Zealand 33 Wales 12
New Zealand win series, 2-0

1972
Cardiff Arms Park
Wales 16 New Zealand 19

1978
Cardiff Arms Park
Wales 12 New Zealand 13

1980
Cardiff Arms Park
Wales 3 New Zealand 23

1988
Lancaster Park
New Zealand 52 Wales 3

Eden Park
New Zealand 54 Wales 9
New Zealand win series, 2-0

1989
Cardiff Arms Park
Wales 9 New Zealand 34

British Isles (Lions) V
New Zealand

1904
**Athletic Park,
Wellington**
New Zealand 9 Lions 3

1930
Carisbrook, Dunedin
New Zealand 3 Lions 6

**Lancaster Park,
Christchurch**
New Zealand 13 Lions 10

Eden Park, Auckland
New Zealand 15 Lions 10

Athletic Park
New Zealand 22 Lions 8
New Zealand win series, 3-1

1950
Carisbrook
New Zealand 9 Lions 9

Lancaster Park
New Zealand 8 Lions 0

Athletic Park
New Zealand 6 Lions 3

Eden Park
New Zealand 11 Lions 8
New Zealand win series, 3-0

1959
Carisbrook
New Zealand 18 Lions 17

Athletic Park
New Zealand 11 Lions 8

Lancaster Park
New Zealand 22 Lions 8

Eden Park
New Zealand 6 Lions 9
New Zealand win series, 3-1

1966
Carisbrook
New Zealand 20 Lions 3

Athletic Park
New Zealand 16 Lions 12

Lancaster Park
New Zealand 19 Lions 6

Eden Park
New Zealand 24 Lions 11
New Zealand win series, 4-0

1971
Athletic Park
New Zealand 13 Lions 3

Carisbrook
New Zealand 3 Lions 9

Lancaster Park
New Zealand 22 Lions 12

Eden Park
New Zealand 14 Lions 14
British Isles win series, 2-1

1977
Athletic Park
New Zealand 16 Lions 12

Lancaster Park
New Zealand 9 Lions 13

Carisbrook
New Zealand 19 Lions 7

Eden Park
New Zealand 10 Lions 9
New Zealand win series, 3-1

1983
Lancaster Park
New Zealand 16 Lions 12

Athletic Park
New Zealand 9 Lions 0

Carisbrook
New Zealand 15 Lions 8

Eden Park
New Zealand 38 Lions 6
New Zealand win series, 4-0

1993
1st Test, Wellington
New Zealand 18 Lions 20
2nd Test, Wellington
New Zealand 20 Lions 7
3rd Test, Auckland
New Zealand 13 Lions 30
New Zealand won series, 2-1

British Isles (Lions) V
Australia

1930
Sydney Cricket Ground
Australia 6 Lions 5

1950
Brisbane Cricket Ground
Australia 6 Lions 19

Sydney Cricket Ground
Australia 3 Lions 24
British Isles win series, 2-0

1959
**Brisbane Exhibition
Ground**
Australia 6 Lions 17

Sydney Sports Ground
Australia 3 Lions 24
British Isles win series, 2-0

1966
Sydney Cricket Ground
Australia 8 Lions 11

Lang Park, Brisbane
Australia 0 Lions 31
British Isles win series, 2-0

1989
**Sydney Football
Stadium**
Australia 30 Lions 12

Ballymore, Brisbane
Australia 12 Lions 19

1989
**Sydney Football
Stadium**
Australia 18 Lions 19
British Isles win series, 2-1

British Isles (Lions) V
South Africa

1891
**Crusader Ground, Port
Elizabeth**
South Africa 0 Lions 4

Kimberley
South Africa 0 Lions 3

Newand, Cape Town
South Africa 0 Lions 4
British Isles win series, 3-0

1896
Crusader Ground
South Africa 0 Lions 8

Johannesburg
South Africa 8 Lions 17

Kimberley
South Africa 3 Lions 9

Newlands
South Africa 5 Lions 0
British Isles win series, 3-1

1903
Johannesburg
South Africa 10 Lions 10

Kimberley
South Africa 0 Lions 0

Newlands
South Africa 8 Lions 0
South Africa win series, 1-0

1910
Johannesburg
South Africa 14 Lions 10

Crusader Ground
South Africa 3 Lions 8

Newlands
South Africa 21 Lions 5
South Africa win series, 2-1

1924
Kingsmead, Durban
South Africa 7 Lions 3

Johannesburg
South Africa 17 Lions 0

Crusader Ground
South Africa 3 Lions 3

Newlands
South Africa 16 Lions 9
South Africa win series, 3-0

1938
Johannesburg
South Africa 26 Lions 12

Crusader Ground
South Africa 19 Lions 3

Newlands
South Africa 16 Lions 21
South Africa win series, 2-1

1955
Ellis Park,
Johannesburg
South Africa 22 Lions 23

Newlands
South Africa 25 Lions 9

Loftus Versveld,
Pretoria
South Africa 6 Lions 9

Crusader Ground
South Africa 22 Lions 8
Series tied 2-2

1962
Ellis Park
South Africa 3 Lions 3

Durban
South Africa 3 Lions 0

Newlands
South Africa 8 Lions 3

Free State Stadium,
Bloemfontein
South Africa 34 Lions 14
South Africa win series, 3-0

1968
Loftus Versveld
South Africa 25 Lions 20

Boet Erasmu, Port
Elizabeth
South Africa 6 Lions 6

Newlands
South Africa 11 Lions 6

Ellis Park
South Africa 19 Lions 6
South Africa win series, 3-0

1974
Newlands
South Africa 3 Lions 12

Loftus Versveld
South Africa 9 Lions 28

Boet Erasmus
South Africa 9 Lions 26

Ellis Park
South Africa 13 Lions 13
British Isles win series, 3-0

1980
Newlands
South Africa 26 Lions 22

Free State Stadium
South Africa 26 Lions 19

Boet Erasmus
South Africa 12 Lions 10

Loftus Versveld
South Africa 13 Lions 17
South Africa win series, 3-1

England v Australia
1909
Blackheath, London
England 3 Australia 9

1948
Twickenham
England 0 Australia 11

1958
Twickenham
England 9 Australia 6

1963
Sydney Sports Ground
Australia 18 England 9

1967
Twickenham
England 11 Australia 23

1973
Twickenham
England 20 Australia 3

1975
Sydney Cricket Ground
Australia 16 England 9

Ballymore, Brisbane
Australia 30 England 21
Australia win series, 2-0

1976
Twickenham
England 23 Australia 6

1982
Twickenham
England 15 Australia 11

1984
Twickenham
England 3 Australia 19

1988
Ballymore
Australia 22 England 16

Concord Oval, Sydney
Australia 28 England 8
Australia win series, 2-0

1988
Twickenham
England 28 Australia 19

1991
Sydney Football
Stadium
Australia 40 England 15

1991 World Cup final
Twickenham
England 6 Australia 12

Ireland V New Zealand
1947
Lansdowne Road,
Dublin
Ireland 3 Australia 16

1958
Lansdowne Road
Ireland 9 Australia 6

1967
Lansdowne Road
Ireland 15 Australia 8

Sydney Cricket Ground
Australia 5 Ireland 11

1968
Lansdowne Road
Ireland 10 Australia 3

1976
Lansdowne Road
Ireland 10 Australia 20

1979
Ballymore, Brisbane
Australia 12 Ireland 27

Sydney Cricket Ground
Australia 3 Ireland 9
Series tied 1-1

1981
Lansdowne Road
Ireland 12 Australia 16

1984
Lansdowne Road
Ireland 9 Australia 16

1994
Brisbane
Australia 33 Ireland 13

Sydney
Australia 32 Ireland 18
Australia win series, 2-0

Scotland v Australia
1947
Murrayfield,Edinburgh
Scotland 7 Australia 16

1958
Murrayfield
Scotland 12 Australia 8

1966
Murrayfield
Scotland 11 Australia 5

1968
Murrayfield
Scotland 9 Australia 3

1970
Sydney Cricket Ground
Australia 23 Scotland 3

1975
Murrayfield
Scotland 10 Australia 3

1981
Murrayfield
Scotland 24 Australia 15

1982
Ballymore, Brisbane
Australia 7 Scotland 12

Sydney Cricket Ground
Australia 33 Scotland 9

1984
Murrayfield
Scotland 12 Australia 37
Series drawn 1-1

1988
Murrayfield
Scotland 13 Australia 32

1992
Sydney Football Stadium
Australia 27 Scotland 12

Ballymore, Brisbane
Australia 37 Scotland 13
Australia win series, 2-0

Wales v Australia

1908
Cardiff Arms Park
Wales 9 Australia 6

1947
Cardiff Arms Park
Wales 6 Australia 0

1958
Cardiff Arms Park
Wales 9 Australia 3

1966
Cardiff Arms Park
Wales 11 Australia 14

1969
Sydney Cricket Ground
Australia 16 Wales 19

1973
Cardiff Arms Park
Wales 24 Australia 0

1975
Cardiff Arms Park
Wales 24 Australia 3

1978
Ballymore, Brisbane
Australia 18 Wales 8

Sydney Cricket Ground
Australia 19 Wales 17
Australia win series 2-0

1981
Cardiff Arms Park
Wales 18 Australia 13

1984
Cardiff Arms Park
Wales 9 Australia 28

1991
Ballymore
Australia 63 Wales 6

England v South Africa

1906
Crystal Palace
England 3 South Africa 3

1913
Twickenham
England 3 South Africa 9

1932
Twickenham
England 0 South Africa 7

1952
Twickenham
England 3 South Africa 8

1961
Twickenham
England 0 South Africa 5

1969
Twickenham
England 11 South Africa 8

1972
Ellis Park, Johannesburg
South Africa 9 England 18

1984
Boet Erasmus Stadium, Port Elizabeth
South Africa 33 England 15

Ellis Park
South Africa 35 England 9
South Africa win series, 2-0

1994
Pretoria
South Africa 15 England 32

Newlands, Cape Town
South Africa 27 England 9
Series drawn 1-1

Ireland v South Africa

1906
Belfast
Ireland 12 South Africa 15

1912
Lansdowne Road, Dublin
Ireland 0 South Africa 38

1931
Lansdowne Road
Ireland 3 South Africa 8

1951
Lansdowne Road
Ireland 5 South Africa 17

1960
Lansdowne Road
Ireland 3 South Africa 8

1961
Newlands, Capetown
South Africa 24 Ireland 8

1965
Lansdowne Road
Ireland 9 South Africa 6

1970
Lansdowne Road
Ireland 8 South Africa 8

1981
Newlands
South Africa 23 Ireland 15

King's Park, Durban
South Africa 12 Ireland 10
South Africa win series, 2-0

Wales v South Africa

1906
St Helens
Wales 0 South Africa 11

1912
Cardiff Arms Park
Wales 0 South Africa 3

1931
St Helens, Swansea
Wales 3 South Africa 8

1951
Cardiff Arms Park
Wales 3 South Africa 6

1960
Cardiff Arms Park
Wales 0 South Africa 3

1964
King's Park, Durban
South Africa 24 Wales 3

1970
Cardiff Arms Park
Wales 6 South Africa 6

Scotland v South Africa

1906
Hampden Park, Glasgow
Scotland 6 South Africa 0

1912
Inverleith, Edinburgh
Scotland 0 South Africa 16

1932
Murrayfield, Edinburgh
Scotland 3 South Africa 6

1951
Murrayfield
Scotland 0 South Africa 44

1960
Boet Erasmus, Port Elizabeth
South Africa 18 Scotland 10

1961
Murrayfield
Scotland 5 South Africa 12

1965
Murrayfield
Scotland 8 South Africa 5

1969
Murrayfield
Scotland 6 South Africa 3

Australia v South Africa

1933
Newlands, Cape Town
South Africa 17 Australia 3

Durban
South Africa 6 Australia 21

Johannesburg
South Africa 12 Australia 3

Boet Erasmus, Port Elizabeth
South Africa 11 Australia 0

Free State Stadium, Bloemfontein
South Africa 4 Australia 15
South Africa win series 3-2

1927
Sydney Cricket Ground
Australia 5 South Africa 9

Sydney Cricket Ground
Australia 17 South Africa 26
South Africa win series, 2-0

Ian Jones and Gary Whetton of New Zealand celebrate their Bledisloe Cup victory over Australia in 1991. The final score was 6-3

1953
Ellis Park, Johannesburg
South Africa 25 Australia 3

Newlands
South Africa 13 Australia 18

Durban
South Africa 18 Australia 8

Crusader Ground, Port Elizabeth
South Africa 22 Australia 9
South Africa win series, 3-1

1956
Sydney Cricket Ground
Australia 0 South Africa 9

Brisbane
Australia 0 South Africa 9
South Africa win series, 2-0

1961
Ellis Park
South Africa 28 Australia 3

Boet Erasmus
South Africa 23 Australia 11
South Africa win series, 2-0

1963
Loftus Versveld, Pretoria
South Africa 14 Australia 3

Newlands
South Africa 5 Australia 9

Ellis Park
South Africa 9 Australia 11

Boet Erasmus
South Africa 22 Australia 6
Series drawn 2-2

1965
Sydney Cricket Ground
Australia 18 South Africa 11

Lang Park, Brisbane
Australia 12 South Africa 8
Australia win series, 2-0

1969
Ellis Park
South Africa 30 Australia 11

King's Park, Durban
South Africa 16 Australia 9

Newlands
South Africa 11 Australia 3

Free State Stadium
South Africa 19 Australia 8
South Africa win series 4-0

1971
Sydney Cricket Ground
Australia 11 South Africa 19

Brisbane Exhibition Ground
Australia 6 South Africa 14

Sydney Cricket Ground
Australia 6 South Africa 18
South Africa win series 3-0

Australia v New Zealand

1903
Sydney Cricket Ground
Australia 3 New Zealand 22

1905
Tahuna Park, Dunedin
New Zealand 14 Australia 3

1907
Sydney Cricket Ground
Australia 6 New Zealand 26

Woolloongabba, Brisbane
Australia 5 New Zealand 14

Sydney Cricket Ground
Australia 5 New Zealand 5
New Zealand win series, 2-0

1910
Sydney Cricket Ground
Australia 0 New Zealand 6

Sydney Cricket Ground
Australia 11 New Zealand 0

Sydney Cricket Ground
Australia 13 New Zealand 28
New Zealand win series, 2-1

1913
Athletic Park, Wellington
New Zealand 30 Australia 5

Carisbrook, Dunedin
New Zealand 25 Australia 13

Lancaster Park, Christchurch
New Zealand 5 Australia 16
New Zealand win series, 2-1

1914
Sydney Sports Ground
Australia 0 New Zealand 5

Brisbane Cricket Ground
Australia 0 New Zealand 17

Sydney Sports Ground
Australia 7 New Zealand 22
New Zealand win series, 3-0

1929
Sydney Cricket Ground
Australia 9 New Zealand 8

Exhibition Ground, Brisbane
Australia 17 New Zealand 9

Sydney Cricket Ground
Australia 15 New Zealand 13
Australia win series, 3-0

1931
Eden Park, Auckland
New Zealand 20 Australia 13

1933
Sydney Cricket Ground
Australia 22 New Zealand 17

Exhibition Ground
Australia 3 New Zealand 21

Sydney Cricket Ground
Australia 13 New Zealand 21
New Zealand win series, 2-1

1934
Sydney Cricket Ground
Australia 25 New Zealand 11

Sydney Cricket Ground
Australia 3 New Zealand 3
Australia win series, 1-0

1936
Athletic Park
New Zealand 11 Australia 6

Carisbrook
New Zealand 36 Australia 13
New Zealand win series, 2-0

1938
Sydney Cricket Ground
Australia 9 New Zealand 24

Exhibition Ground
Australia 14 New Zealand 20

Sydney Cricket Ground
Australia 6 New Zealand 14
New Zealand win series, 3-0

1946
Carisbrook
New Zealand 31 Australia 8

Eden Park
New Zealand 14 Australia 10
New Zealand win series, 2-0

1947
Exhibition Ground
Australia 5 New Zealand 13

Sydney Cricket Ground
Australia 14 New Zealand 27
New Zealand win series, 2-0

1949
Athletic Park
New Zealand 6 Australia 11

Eden Park
New Zealand 9 Australia 16
Australia win series, 2-0

1951
Sydney Cricket Ground
Australia 0 New Zealand 8

Sydney Cricket Ground
Australia 11 New Zealand 17

Brisbane Cricket Ground
Australia 6 New Zealand 16
New Zealand win series, 3-0

1952
Lancaster Park
New Zealand 9 Australia 14

Athletic Park
New Zealand 15 Australia 8
Series tied 1-1

1955
Athletic Park
New Zealand 16 Australia 8

Carisbrook, Dunedin
New Zealand 8 Australia 0

Eden Park
New Zealand 3 Australia 8
New Zealand win series, 2-1

1957
Sydney Cricket Ground
Australia 11 New Zealand 25

Exhibition Ground
Australia 9 New Zealand 22
New Zealand win series, 2-0

1958
Athletic Ground
New Zealand 25 Australia 3

Lancaster Park
New Zealand 3 Australia 6

Epsom Showgrounds, Auckland
New Zealand 17 Australia 8
New Zealand win series, 2-1

1962
Exhibition Ground
Australia 6 New Zealand 20

Sydney Cricket Ground
Australia 5 New Zealand 14
New Zealand win series, 2-0

1962
Athletic Park
New Zealand 9 Australia 9

Carisbrook
New Zealand 3 Australia 0

Eden Park
New Zealand 16 Australia 8
New Zealand win series, 2-0

1964
Carisbrook
New Zealand 14 Australia 9

Lancaster Park
New Zealand 18 Australia 3

Athletic Park
New Zealand 5 Australia 20
New Zealand win series, 2-1

1967
Athletic Park
New Zealand 29 Australia 9

1968
Sydney Cricket Ground
Australia 11 New Zealand 27

Ballymore Oval, Brisbane
Australia 18 New Zealand 19
New Zealand win series, 2-0

1972
Athletic Park
New Zealand 29 Australia 6

Lancaster Park
New Zealand 30 Australia 17

Eden Park
New Zealand 38 Australia 3
New Zealand win series, 3-0

1974
Sydney Cricket Ground
Australia 6 New Zealand 11

Ballymore Oval
Australia 16 New Zealand 16

Sydney Cricket Ground
Australia 6 New Zealand 16
New Zealand win series, 2-0

1978
Athletic Park
New Zealand 13 Australia 12

Lancaster Park
New Zealand 22 Australia 6
New Zealand win series, 2-0

1978
Eden Park
New Zealand 16 Australia 30

1979
Sydney Cricket Ground
Australia 12 New Zealand 6

1980
Sydney Cricket Ground
Australia 13 New Zealand 9

Ballymore Oval
Australia 9 New Zealand 12

Sydney Cricket Ground
Australia 26 New Zealand 10
Australia win series, 2-1

1982
Lancaster Park
New Zealand 23 Australia 16

Athletic Park
New Zealand 16 Australia 19

Eden Park
New Zealand 33 Australia 18
New Zealand win series, 2-1

1983
Sydney Cricket Ground
Australia 8 New Zealand 18

1984
Sydney Cricket Ground
Australia 16 New Zealand 9

Ballymore Oval
Australia 15 New Zealand 19

Sydney Cricket Ground
Australia 24 New Zealand 25
New Zealand win series, 2-1

1985
Eden Park
New Zealand 10 Australia 9

1986
Athletic Park
New Zealand 12 Australia 13

Carisbrook
New Zealand 13 Australia 12

Eden Park
New Zealand 9 Australia 22
Australia win series, 2-1

1988
Concord Oval, Sydney
Australia 7 New Zealand 32

Ballymore Oval
Australia 19 New Zealand 19

Concord Oval
Australia 9 New Zealand 30
New Zealand win series, 2-0

1990
Lancaster Park
New Zealand 21 Australia 6

Eden Park
New Zealand 27 Australia 17

Athletic Park
New Zealand 9 Australia 21
New Zealand win series, 2-1

1991
Sydney Football Stadium
Australia 21 New Zealand 12

Eden Park
New Zealand 6 Australia 3

1992
Sydney
Australia 16 New Zealand 15

Brisbane
Australia 19 New Zealand 17

Sydney
Australia 23 New Zealand 26
Australia win series, 2-1

1921
Carisbrook, Dunedin
NZ 13 South Africa 5

Eden Park, Auckland
NZ 5 South Africa 9

Athletic Park, Wellington
NZ 0 South Africa 0
Series drawn 1-1

1928
Kingsmead, Durban
South Africa 17 NZ 0

Ellis Park, Johannesburg
South Africa 6 NZ 7

Crusader Ground, Port Elizabeth
South Africa 11 NZ 6
South Africa win series, 2-1

1928
Newlands, Cape Town
South Africa 5 NZ 13

1937
Athletic Park
NZ 13 South Africa 7

Lancaster Park, Chrishchurch
NZ 6 South Africa 13

Eden Park
NZ 6 South Africa 17
South Africa win series, 3-1

1949
Newlands
South Africa 15 NZ 11

Ellis Park
South Africa 12 NZ 6

Kingsmead
South Africa 9 New Zealand 3

Crusader Ground
South Africa 11 NZ 8
South Africa win series, 4-0

1956
Carisbrook
NZ 10 South Africa 6

Athletic Park
NZ 3 South Africa 8

Lancaster Park
NZ 17 South Africa 10

Eden Park
NZ 11 South Africa 5
New Zealand win series, 3-1

1960
Ellis Park
South Africa 13 NZ 0

Newlands
South Africa 3 NZ 11

Free State Stadium, Bloemfontein
South Africa 11 NZ 11

Boet Erasmus Stadium, Port Elizabeth
South Africa 8 NZ 3
South Africa win series, 2-1

1965
Athletic Park
NZ 6 South Africa 3

Carisbrook
NZ 13 South Africa 0

Lancaster Park
NZ 16 South Africa 19

Eden Park
NZ 20 South Africa 3
New Zealand win series, 2-1

1970
Loftus Versveld Stadium, Pretoria
South Africa 17 NZ 6

Newlands
South Africa 8 NZ 9

Boet Erasmus Stadium
South Africa 14 NZ 3

Ellis Park
South Africa 20 NZ 17
South Africa win series, 3-1

1976
King's Park, Durban
South Africa 16 NZ 7

Free State Stadium
South Africa 9 NZ 15

Newlands
South Africa 15 NZ 10

Ellis Park
South Africa 15 NZ 14
South Africa win series, 3-1

1981
Lancaster Park
NZ 14 South Africa 9

Athletic Park
NZ 12 South Africa 24

Eden Park
NZ 25 South Africa 22
New Zealand win series, 2-1 ∎

Old Hamptonians deliver the ball from the line out during the 1994 Pilkington Sheild. The Old Hamptonians went on to lose the match to Malvern, 8-6

5. Divisional Provincial & Clubs

Section compiled by Anna Yallop

Nowhere is the difference between Northern and Southern hemisphere Rugby so marked than in its organisation below international level. In this up-graded section we have tried to show this by examples, in particular, provincial rugby in New Zealand and South Africa

Below international rugby, the game has no fixed centre across the world. In England, the Divisional championship is gaining ground. It sifts talent between the club and the national team. Before the Divisionals there was a poor quality county championship and a number of trial matches. The former has been down-graded in importance and the trials have been terminated.

In Wales, Scotland and Ireland the tradition of final trials goes on. In Scotland and Ireland there have been strongly rooted provincial championships and now the two countries play one another at this level too. In effect the England Divisional set-up is equivalent to both the Irish and Scottish provincial scene.

France do not believe in trials. Instead, through her FIRA roots, they have always been able to arrange international fixtures in October, November and December against the likes of Italy, Romania or Russia. In recent years, too, they had the South Africans and the Australians coming through before Christmas to test the national side. Underneath international rugby, club rugby rules.

Wales and England have wanted to move the Five Nations towards the end of the season but France have always dug their heels in and said clubs would object. How interesting

to note that next year the clubs have agreed to move their championship to accommodate the needs of the French side as it prepares for the RWC 95.

In the Southern Hemisphere, provincial rugby is the rule. In Natal, for instance, the province welcomed 1 million paying spectators through its gates. That's some business. Provincial rugby dominates in New Zealand too.

The SuperTens series was brilliantly conceived and has ignited interest in the game everywhere. Northern Hemisphere countries need something similar so that a world championship can develop at this level.

Australia has two states that have played one another for ages, New South Wales and Queensland. Into this mix has come the Australian Capital Territory (ACT), which beat NSW for the first time in 1994 by 44-28. But, essentially, it is club rugby that dominates in Australia, though few of them ever host incoming tourists.

Club rugby badly needs a world body to help it grow and mature. This may have to start in Europe first. Certainly, the need for a European-based competition is essential if club rugby in the UK, France and Italy isn't to stultify. An outsider looking at rugby, such as the International Olympic Committee, must ponder who is running it ∎

DIVISIONAL & PROVINCIAL RESULTS

A. DIVISIONAL

ENGLAND DIVISIONAL CHAMPIONSHIP

Sponsor: CSI Insurance

North 21 London & SE 22

Date: 16 Oct
Venue: Newcastle Gosforth
Referee: E. Murray (Scotland)
North: Tries – J. Mallinder & M. Fielden; Penalties – P. Grayson; Dropped Goals – Grayson 2; Conversion – Grayson.
London: Tries – T. Underwood, W. Carling, D. Hopley; Penalty: R. Andrew; Conversions – Andrew 2.

London, with 10 internationals and playing the side they hoped would take on the All Blacks in a week's time, just won this tight game with a Hopley try five minutes from time.

South-West 31 Midlands 3

Date: 16 Oct
Venue: Recreation Ground, Bath
Referee: D. Matthews (Liverpool Society)
SW: Tries – A. Lumsden 2, N. Beal, A. Adebayo; Penalties – J. Callard 3; Conversion – J. Callard
Midlands: Penalty – S. Hodgkinson

The holders, the South West, cruised to a comfortable win. Their side included 12 Bath players but only six internationals with Barnes and Guscott injured.

South-West 29 North 16

Date: 23 Dec
Venue: Kingsholm, Gloucester
Referee: D. McHugh (Cork)
SW: Tries – P. Hull, A. Adebayo & S. Ojomoh; Penalties – J. Callard 4; Conversion – Callard
North: Try – J. Mallinder; Penalties – P. Grayson 3; Conversion – Grayson

The SW still missing Barnes, Guscott and Clarke still found the going to their liking, comfortably beating a disappointing North side.

Midlands 14 London & SE 23

Date: 30 Oct
Venue: Welford Road, Leicester
Referee: A. Spreadbury (Bristol)
Midlands: Try – E. Saunders; Penalties – J. Steele 2; Drop goal – F. Packman.
London & SE: Tries – C. Sheasby & D. Ryan; Penalties – R. Andrew 2; Drop goal – Andrew; Conversions – Andrew 2.

This was an irrelevance as a match. The Divisional competition, as so many players were "unavailable", should have been halted this year, given the All Black tour. As Tony Jorden, the London coach, put it with regard to the play-off between London and South West (holders): "It's daft to have a Divisional Championship play-off with two sides considerably below strength."

Midlands 9 North 31

Date: 6 Nov
Venue: Franklin Gardens, Northampton
Referee: E. Morrison (Bristol)
Midlands: Penalties – J. Steele 3
North: Tries – N. Ashurst, J. Sleightholme, K. Simms; Penalties – P. Grayson 2; Conversions – Grayson 2; Dropped goal – Grayson

The battle for the wooden spoon which the North won thanks in part to Grayson's ubiquity.

London & SE 17 South-West 25

Date: 4 Jan
Venue: Twickenham
Referee: G. Simmonds (Wales)
Crowd: 7,000
London: Try – J. Alexander; Penalties – G. Gregory 4
S-W: Try – P. Holford; Penalties –

J. Callard 4; Drop-goals P. Hull & N. Beal; Conversion – Callard

Importantly, many players had the chance to play at Twickenham after the postponement from 1993. But once most of the Bath players pulled out, followed by some illustrious London names, this was very much a second team contest and showed. Sadly, it looks as though the Bath club will now take the rap for this and not be allowed to schedule invitation matches in their fixture list whilst the Divisional Championship is in progress.

Final placings

	P	W	D	L	F	A	P
SW	3	3	0	0	85	36	6
London	3	2	0	1	62	62	4
North	3	1	0	2	68	60	2
Midlands	3	0	0	3	26	85	0

B. PROVINCIAL

IRISH INTER-PROVINCIAL CHAMPIONSHIP 1993

Sponsor: Smithwicks

Connacht 9 Munster 15

Date: 16 Oct
Venue: Sports Ground, Galway
Referee: O. Doyle (Leinster)
Connacht: Penalties – A. White 3
Munster: Tries – R. Wallace & B.Begley; Penalty – Begley; Conversion – Begley

Connacht were a very depleted side (missing four Irish internationals in their back-line) and lost to a mundane Munster side.

Ulster 21 Exiles 3

Date: 16 Oct
Venue: Ravenhill, Belfast
Referee: B. Smith (Munster)
Ulster: Tries – D. Tweed, D. Millar; Penalties – D. Humphreys 3; Conversion – Humphreys

Exiles: Penalty – P. Burke
The Exiles lost their vice-captain and captain in the first 25 minutes and with it a undistinguished match.

Connacht 10 Ulster 39
Date: 23 Oct
Venue: Sports Ground, Galway
Referee: A. Lewis (Munster)
Connacht: Try – G. Curley;
Penalty – E. Elwood;
Conversion – Elwood
Ulster: Tries – A. Blair, C. Wilkinson, D. Humphreys, S. McKinty, McBride; Penalties – M.McCall 2; Conversion – McCall 4

Ulster's 39 points established a new record for points scored on an opponent's ground since the championship was established on a four province basis in 1946.

Exiles 8 Leinster 13
Date: 23 Oct
Venue: Sunbury
Referee: A. Watson
Exiles: Try – J. Etheridge;
Penalty – P. Hopley
Leinster: Try – K.Potts; Penalties – C. O'Shea, A. McGowan; Conversion – McGowan

A match that the Exiles lost – with some woeful kicks at goal – rather than a match that Leinster won, though they were happy to have sneaked a victory.

Exiles 42 Connacht 12
Date: 30 Oct
Venue: Sunbury
Referee: D. Lamont (Leinster)
Exiles: Tries – D. Cleary, M. Keenan, P. Hopley & K. Hickey; Penalties – M. Corcoran 4; Drop goals – N. Malone 2; Conversions – Corcoran 2
Connacht: Penalties – A. White 3; Drop goal – E.Elwood

Munster 21 Leinster 19
Date: 30 Oct
Venue: Musgrave Park, Cork
Referee: S. Hilditch (Ulster)
Munster: Tries – P. Danaher & K. Murphy; Penalties – G. O'Sullivan 3; Conversion – O'Sullivan
Leinster: Try A. McGowan;

Penalties McGowan 3 & C. O'Shea; Conversion – McGowan

A match that Leinster should have won having been 16-3 in the lead at half time.

Ulster 24 Munster 21
Date: 18 Dec
Venue: Ravenhill
Referee: G. Black (Leinster)
Crowd: approx 1200
Ulster: Tries – C.Wilkinson & T. Howe; Penalties – M. McCall 3; Drop goal – D. Humphreys; Conversion – McCall
Munster: Penalties – G.O'Sullivan 7

A draw would have meant Munster taking the championship and, when they were 18-11 up at half time, they must have thought the game was in the bag. But Ulster never gave up, although they gave away an inordinate number of kickable penalty goals which was very nearly their downfall.

Leinster 15 Connacht 11
Date: 18 Dec

Final Table

	P	W	D	L	F	A	Pts
Leinster	4	3	0	1	72	40	6
Ulster	4	3	0	1	84	59	6
Munster	4	3	0	1	91	71	6
Exiles	4	1	0	3	72	80	2
Connacht	4	0	0	4	42	111	0

SCOTTISH INTER-DISTRICT CHAMPIONSHIP 1993
Sponsor: McEwans

Glasgow 28 Edinburgh 6
Date: 23 Oct
Venue: Hillhead/Jordanhill
Referee: W. Calder (Selkirk)
Glasgow: Penalties – D. Barrett 6, Drop goal – Barrett
Edinburgh: Penalties – C. Glasgow; Drop Goal – Glasgow

South 37 North & Midlands 13
Venue: Jed-Forest

FINAL
South 21
Glasgow 14
Date: 30 Oct
Venue: Melrose
Referee: E. Morrison (Bristol)
South: Tries – S. Nichol, C. Chalmers, D. Turnbull; Penalties – G. Parker 2; Drop goal – Chalmers; Conversions – Parker 2
Glasgow: Try – J. Brough; Penalties – Barrett 3

PLAY-OFF THIRD AND FOURTH PLACES
Edinburgh 28
North & Midlands 25
Venue: Melrose

SCOTTISH-IRISH INTER-PROVINCIAL

Glasgow District 22
Munster 17

Leinster 8
Edinburgh District 13

Scottish North Midlands 19
Connacht 20

Ulster 44
South of Scotland 26

Connacht 25
Glasgow District 47

Edinburgh 39 Ulster 13

Munster 6
Scottish North/Midlands 13

South of Scotland 16
Leinster 26

Final table

	P	W	D	L	F	A	Pts
Edinburgh	2	2	0	0	69	42	4
Glasgow	2	2	0	0	52	21	4
Leinster	2	1	0	1	34	29	2
Scot N/M	2	1	0	1	32	26	2
Ulster	2	1	0	1	57	65	2
Connacht	2	1	0	1	45	66	2
Munster	2	0	0	2	23	35	0
South of Scotland	2	0	0	2	42	70	0

PROVINCIAL FOCUS (New Zealand and South Africa)

NATIONAL MUTUAL CHAMPIONSHIP 1993

Since 1992 there has been a round robin format with the top four in the three divisions qualifying for semi-finals and a grand final. After losing the Ranfurly Shield to Waikato, Auckland won the first divison final against Otago. In the second and third divisions Counties and Horrowhenua – who both qualified in third – won the finals, against Bay of Plenty and Wanganui respectively.

FIRST DIVISION

	P	W	D	L	F	A	Pts
Waikato	8	6	0	2	219	106	26
Auckland	8	6	0	2	356	131	25
N Harbour	8	6	0	2	257	161	24
Otago	8	5	1	2	221	141	23
Wellington	8	4	1	3	174	166	20
Canterbury	8	4	0	4	188	235	16
King C'ntry	8	2	0	6	90	317	9
Taranaki	8	2	0	6	175	338	8
Hawke's Bay	8	0	0	8	157	242	3

SEMI FINALS
Otago 36 Waikato 22;
Auckland 43 North Harbour 20.

GRAND FINAL
(at Eden Park, Auckland)
Auckland 27 Otago 18
Auckland: Tries – Tonu'u, Sotutu, Clarke; Penalties – Fox 2; Conversions – Fox 3
Otago; Tries – Kronfield and Latta; Penalties – Wilson 2; Conversions – Wilson

SECOND DIVISON (QUALIFIERS)

	P	W	D	L	F	A	Pts
N Auckland	8	7	0	1	322	162	29
S Canterbury	8	6	0	2	238	138	25
Counties	8	6	0	2	401	135	24
B of Plenty	8	6	0	2	318	189	24

SEMI FINALS
Bay of Plenty 41
North Auckland 26;
Counties 33 South Canterbury 18.

GRAND FINAL
Counties 38 Bay of Plenty 10.

DOMINANCE OF FOUR PROVINCIAL UNIONS

Four provincial Unions – Auckland, North Harbour, Otago and Waikato – have dominated New Zealand rugby, writes Ray Cairns. There the prime focus is in provincial or regional teams. This is in line with most of the rest of the southern hemisphere, certainly Australia and South Africa. And, in the last two years four unions have established themselves as the elite of New Zealand rugby in the annual battle for the twin prizes of the national championships and the Ranfurly Shield. They are Auckland, North Harbour, Waikato and Otago.

The first three are all from the greater Auckland region, by far the largest area of New Zealand's population and wealth. Auckland spent the best part of a decade as the premier rugby province in New Zealand, certainly the best unit that country had seen and probably the best regional rugby side of all time.

Things are levelling out a bit. In New Zealand rugby, there is the championship and the Ranfurly Shield (a challenge trophy, contested in a one-off match generally at the holder's home ground). Waikato won the national championship in 1992, demolishing Otago in the final, and the Ranfurly Shield in 1993. However, Auckland, which yielded the shield after a record tenure, won the championship final against Otago.

North Harbour is the over-the-harbour part of Auckland, which only seceded in 1985, and has become the greatest pretender of the provincial scene in New Zealand. But it has not been an achiever until this year, when it beat all its New Zealand fellow-contenders, and, but for a missed penalty goal from in front at Bris-bane, would have been tackling Natal for the SuperTen title.

As the 1995 issue of the *Almanack* went to print, North Harbour were nudging Auckland for the top spot in New Zealand, pressed hard by the ageing Waikato team. The pride of the South Island, Otago, just keeps falling at the last hurdle and, although a beaten finalist the last two years, has to rank fourth.

New Zealand's oldest two unions, Canterbury and Wellington, are next in the pecking order, and both are working hard to improve their rankings. Wellington are coached by 1987 World Cup-winning captain David Kirk, while Canterbury are guided by 1976-79 All Blacks lock, Vance Stewart. It is hard to separate them, but based on their 1993 game, and their early-season 1994 meeting, Canterbury would appear to be just a shade ahead.

Two largely rural-based unions are next in line, and the other survivors of the 1993 championships. King Country is the spiritual home of Colin Meads and has amazed the nation as it clings to premier ranking without any starts. It has, however, enormous commitment and guts.

The other is Taranaki, the conqueror of many a touring team. It is an isolated outpost which produced Graham Mourie, and still has Kieran Crowley in its back division. With the relegation of Hawkes Bay – despite its wins over the 1993 Lions, and the French in 1994. King Country and Taranaki have been joined by Counties. This is essentially south Auckland, underlining the dominance of the area. There is a bit of a merry-go-round of the class players: All Blacks lock Mark Cooksley has left Counties for Waikato, a stronger union though in the same division; Ian Jones shifted south from his beloved Northland to North Harbour. And the raids by rugby league and by

Japan continue unabated.

Although New Zealand rugby has a mystique and a standing all of its own, it does not have the economy and the commercial backing to withstand these sorts of challenges. New Zealand rugby, internationally, is now under siege, but its domestic competition remains the strongest and most competitive in the world.

The 27 provincial unions are divided into three nine-team divisons, based on ability and performance, for championship competition. A typical first division club in New Zealand might play 20 first-class matches in a season. Each plays eight matches in the national championship – four home, four away – and for the last couple of seasons, there have been semi-finals (involving the top four in each case) and a final. There's automatic promotion-relegation in each case.

Unions complement their programmes with another dozen or so matches: against touring sides, against other overseas sides and local matches. Queensland and New South Wales and sometimes Fiji are fairly regular visitors and South African provinces are starting to join in. The so-called "friendlies" are against neighbouring unions or those with which they have long ties, matches against unions in lower divisions.

First division unions are required to play a couple of third division sides and a couple from the second division, as part of the flag-waving exercise. It's become of particular significance in recent years with rural recession in New Zealand, and the increasing concentration of the best players in only a handful of areas. There are some walloping scores: a couple of years ago, Canterbury beat West Coast 128-0 – and that was before tries became worth five points – and last season Auckland had a 139-5 win against North Otago. The minnows don't seem to mind, as long as they have the privilege of playing against the best, but it underlines how the gap between top and bottom is widening.

A part from the provinces there are also hundreds of clubs in New Zealand and they are still firmly regarded as the grass roots of rugby. These clubs compete in league competitions – virtually all matches are competitive, and count for championship points – against teams of comparable age, weight or ability and at all levels.

Boys (and girls these days) start from as young as five, more usually seven or eight, in strictly development rugby: only 10-a-side for a start, half-size pitches, no full tackling but more "touch", no pushing in scrums, no line-outs, and coaches on the field helping them learn the game.

They progress towards "normal" rugby rules as they get older. Both clubs and schools field sides in competitions; all have their champions from around 12. And in various grades, up to the senior level, representative teams are picked for the 27 provincial unions which constitute the New Zealand Rugby Union.

So Canterbury, for example, has feeder clubs like Christchurch, Marist and University, and most of the rest with names of suburbs or areas. The comparison in Europe is, say, with the local, junior clubs whose players aspire to play for the big clubs – Cardiff, Bath, Gloucester, Northampton, Agen etc...

FIRST DIVISION UNIONS

AUCKLAND RFU

Founded: 1883
1993 placing: First
Ground: Eden Park, Reimers Avenue, Auckland 3
Address: P O Box 56-152, Auckland 3
President: Bob Graham
Chairman: Rob Fisher
Executive Director: Murray Wright
Colours: Blue/white hooped jerseys, socks; white shorts
Selector/Coach: Graham Henry (Assistant: John Graham)
Record score: 139 v North Otago 1993
Record points scorer: G Fox 2746

Most appearances: Hallard ("Snow") White
Most tries: Terry Wright 112

A uckland is consistently one of New Zealand's premier unions and has the strongest population base, including a number of South Pacific islands races. For an outstanding season in 1902, Auckland was first awarded the Ranfurly Shield, which became a challenge trophy in 1904, and in the period 1985-93 had 61 successful defences, more than twice the old record. Auckland has also produced the greatest number of All Blacks.

CANTERBURY RFU

Founded: 1879
1993 placing: Sixth
Ground: Lancaster Park, Stevens St, Christchurch
Address: P O Box 755, Christchurch
President & Chairman: Craig Sullivan
Executive officer: Warren Barberel
Colours: Scarlet/black diminishing hooped jerseys/socks; black shorts
Selector/Coach: Vance Stewart (Assistant: Brian McLean)
Record score: 128 v West Coast 1992
Record points scorer: R Deans 1641
Most appearances: Fergie McCormick 222
Most tries: Ross Smith 93

T he largest South Island union and most successful, is also the oldest union in New Zeland and produced the first New Zealand captain (William Millton). Though it did not win the Ranfurly Shield until 1927, had a near-record tenure of 23 defences 1953-56, and a record-equalling 25 1982-85. Has the best record of New Zealand unions against touring international sides and the only major sides it has not beaten are France and Wales, which it has never played. Only Auckland has had more All Blacks.

HAWKE'S BAY RFU

Founded: 1884

1993 placing: Ninth, relegated
Ground: McLean Park, Napier
Address: P O Box 201, Napier
President: Norris Durham
President: Tom Mulligan
Executive officer: Bob Mitchell
Colours: Black/white hooped jerseys and socks; black shorts
Selector/Coach: Graeme Taylor
Record score: 88
v Poverty Bay 1993
Record points scorer: Ian Bishop 631
Most appearances: Neil Thimbleby 158
Most tries: Bert Grenside 74

An original member of the NZRFU, Hawke's Bay was the most powerful force in New Zealand in the 1920s, when it had a long Ranfurly Shield reign and produced many of the great players in the 1924 'invincibles', but has since had erratic successes with population fluctuations. Again produced an outstanding team late in the 1960s, and while it has dropped out of the first division, strong administrative leadership in recent years hint at renewed successes.

KINGS COUNTRY RFU

Founded: 1922
1993 placing: Seventh
Ground: Taumaranui Domain
Address: P O Box 123, Otorohanga
President: Dave McEwan
Chairman: Colin Meads
Secretary: Ross Alleman
Colours: Maroon jersey with gold trim, maroons socks, gold shorts;
Selector/Coach: John Sisley
Record score: 99
v East Coast 1992
Record points scorer: Hutana Coffin 752
Most appearances: Colin Meads 139
Most tries: Murray Kidd 46

Situated in the centre of the North Island, south of Waikato, with no large centre, but a variety of small rural towns which variously stage matches, such as Otorohanga, Taumaranui, Te Kuiti and Turangi and more recently Taupo. New Zealand Prime Minister Jim Bolger might come from Te Kuiti, but far and away its most famous son is Colin Meads – to many Colin Meads IS King Country. Many felt King Country would not handle its unexpected promotion to the first division, but it has flourished.

OTAGO RFU

Founded: 1881
1993 placing: Fourth, beaten finalist
Ground: Carisbrook, Burns Street, Dunedin
Address: P O Box 691, Dunedin
President: Bill Townsend
Chairman: John Spicer
Executive Director: John Hornbrook
Colours: Dark blue jersey and shorts; dark blue socks with gold bands
Selector/Coach: Gordon Hunter
Record score: 91
v East Coast 1986
Record points scorer: Greg Cooper 1506
Most appearances: Richard Knight 170
Most tries: John Timu 62

About all that has changed in Otago is the shorts, from black to white and now the present dark blue. It has long been a major force in New Zealand with its famed hard-rucking forwards – usually from a rural base – but in the last decade has become more a team of imports with hardly any locally-produced players. That brought a national championship victory finally in 1991. But a major source of concern for Otago is that it has not held the Ranfurly Shield since 1957. It has produced well over 100 All Blacks, and the Otago University club has had more All Blacks from its ranks than any other club in New Zealand.

TARANKI RFU

Founded: 1889
1993 placing: Eighth
Ground: Rugby Park, New Plymouth
Address: P O Box 5004, West-own, New Plymouth
President: Bill Batchelor
Chairman: Neil McLean
Secretary: Mrs Sue Mitchell
Colours: Amber/black hoops; black shorts; amber/black hooped socks
Selector/Coach: John Luckin
Record score: 97
v East Coast 1983
Record points scorer: Kieran Crowley 1651
Most appearances: Ian Eliason 222
Most tries: Kieran Crowley 61

An outpost union located on the big western 'bump' of the North Island, Taranaki has a sometimes undeserved reputation for turning on wet weather, especially for international touring sides. The main centre is the city of New Plymouth, but there are many handy-sized towns like Stratford, Hawera, Inglewood and Eltham. The province is dominated by extinct volcano Mount Egmont. Taranaki has enjoyed three periods of Ranfurly Shield success: 1913-14, 1957-59, then 1963-65; and has produced nearly 70 All Blacks, including great captain Graham Mourie; but has struggled for its first division existence.

WAIKATO RFU

Founded: 1887
1993 placing: First, beaten semi-finalist
Ground: Rugby Park, Hamilton
Address: P O Box 9507, Hamilton North
President: Keith Davis
Chairman: Stan Hickford
Secretary: Don Shergold
Selector/Coach: Kevin Greene
Colours: Red/yellow/black hooped jerseys and socks, white shorts
Record score: 81
v East Coast 1980
Record points scorer: Matthew Cooper 738
Most appearances: John Boe 136
Most tries: Bruce Smith 70

Situated in a rich dairy-farming area with a major population base in the city of Hamilton, it is traditionally one of the top half-dozen unions in playing strength, but had a shaky start; it was reformed in 1892, 1903 and 1909 (as South Auckland) and only officially became Waikato in 1921. It held the Ranfurly Shield sporadically in the early 1950s, again in 1966, and then early in the 1980s, before ending Auckland's record-breaking reign in 1993.

In its history Waikato has produced nearly 30 All Blacks, the greatest name among them that of champion goal-kicker Don Clarke; indeed, the five brothers Clarke all played for Waikato in one match against Thames Valley.

WELLINGTON RFU

Founded: 1879
1993 placing: Fifth
Ground: 354 Lambton Quay, Wellington 1
Address: P O Box 177, Wellington
President: Peter Osborne
Chairman: David Gray
Secretary: Ray Rowsell
Colours: Black jersey/socks with gold trim; white shorts
Selector/Coach: David Kirk
Record score: 100 v Horowhenua 1988
Record points scorer: Allan Hewson 909
Most appearances: Graham Williams 174
Most tries: Bernie Fraser 105

Formed just after Canterbury, Wellington has long been one of the major forces in New Zealand rugby and is also the seat of the national administration.

Its strength is reflected in 13 different tenures of the Ranfurly Shield; and it was the third winner of the national championship. Wellington's headquarters are the city of the same name, but it has two other cities, Lower Hutt and Upper Hutt, within its boundaries. Only Auckland and Canterbury have produced more All Blacks, while windy Wellington itself has one of the most maligned international grounds in the world.

SOUTH AFRICA (1993-4) by Quintas van Rooyen

One of the big problems in South Africa is "provincialism", which has had a negative effect on the national team since their return to the international scene in 1992. In the years of international isolation in the eighties, the Currie Cup competition ensured that South African rugby stayed strong; it was a substitute for international competition. Unfortunately the provincial unions virtually became "national" unions on their own while the rugby fan learned to support province, rather than country.

This provincial influence has also had a detrimental effect on club rugby. A decade or two ago club rugby was very important in South Africa and most of the provincial teams played at the most 15 matches during the season. But in the last two years many of the provincial teams played some 30 games in a season and so the standard of club rugby in the different provincial unions has deteriorated. In the past clubs had provincial and national players available for the majority of their matches. This year the national and provincial players were only able to play two or three matches for their clubs.

In 1981, Northern Transvaal, the strongest provincial union since World War Two, played a record 19 matches. Last year the number of matches played by Northern Transvaal had increased to 31.

The SA Barbarians – the "Rest of SA" – undertook an unbeaten tour of eight matches to the UK. Unfortunately the home teams in most of the matches were not at full strength because the tour took place at the same time as that of the All Blacks.

South African teams also took part in the first Super Ten competition, sponsored by Topsport, against the top provincial teams of New Zealand and Australia as well as the national team of Western Samoa. Transvaal, Natal and Northern Transvaal represented South Africa;

and Transvaal were crowned the first champions when they defeated New Zealand's star-studded Auckland team by 20-17 in the final at Ellis Park. Natal contested the 1994 final, but lost to Queensland.

Transvaal, coached by Kitch Christie and the ex-Springbok, Ray Mordt, were the outstanding team in 1993 in South Africa. They also defeated Natal in the Bankfin Currie Cup final as well as in the Lion Cup final. It was the first time since 1972 that Transvaal had won the Currie Cup. In the M-Net night series they drew 12-12 with Northern Transvaal in the final.

South Africa's leading point scorers for season 1993 were: Gavin Johnson 331 (Transvaal), Chris Maree 309 (Northern Transvaal), and Joel Stransky 255 (Natal). Leading try scorers were Cabous van der Westhuizen 29 in 27 games (Natal), Joost van der Westhuizen 28 in 28 games (Northern Transvaal) and Jamie Small 22 in 27 (Natal).

BOLAND

Founded: 1939
Telegraphic Address: Boland Wellington
Tel/Fax: 02211-34823
Colours: Black and old gold jersey; black shorts
President: Dr G N van Wyk, 14 Flamek Street, Malmesbury 7300 (O 0224 22951; H 0224 24096)
Manager: P A Bergh, P O Box 127, Wellington 7655 (Boland Stadium, Fontein Street, Wellington) (7655 O 02211 32317; H 02211 34602)

BORDER

Founded: 1891
Telegraphic Address: Chaser East London
Tel/Fax: 0431 434636
Colours: Chocolate brown and white jersey; white shorts
President: M E George, P O Box 1243, East London 5200 (0 0431 433007; H 0401 9541431; Fax

0431 435848)
General Manager: S R Laubscher,
P O Box 75, East London 5200
(15 Mayflower Terrace, East London 5241 0 0431 23852; H 0431
471880)

EASTERN PROVINCE
Founded: 1888
Telegraphic Address: Scrummage,
Port Elizabeth.
Tel/Fax: 041 522295
Colours: Red and black jersey;
black shorts
President: T Jennings, 17 Bilbury
Avenue, Linkside, Port
Elizabeth 6001 (0 041 551325;
H/Fax: 0411 33749)
Manager: H J Wessels, P O Box
13111, Humewood, Port
Elizabeth 6013 (Boet Erasmus
Stadium, 36 La Roche Drive,
Humewood, Port Elizabeth 6001
(0 041 561278; H 041 533221).

FREE STATE
Founded: 1895
Telegraphic address: Forward
Bloemfontein
Tel/Fax: 051 473581
Colours: White and orange jersey;
black pants
President: H Verster, P O Box
2319, Bloemfontein 9300
(0 051 4012138; H 051 221631;
Fax 051 474388)
General Manager: A J J Bates, P O
Box 15, Bloemfontein 9300
(Rugby Office, X20599,
Bloemfontein 9300
(0 051 4076101; 051 233660)

GRIQUALAND WEST
Founded: 1886
Tel/Fax: 0531 28773
Colours: Peacock blue and white
jersey; black shorts
President: A T Markgraaff,
P O Box 1, Kimberley, 8300
(9 9531 27713; 0531 28300;
Fax 0531 2716)
Manager: F J Blomerus, P O Box
805, Kimberley 8300 (Hoffepark
Rugby Stadium, Kimberley 8301
(0 0531 28773; H 0531 21074))
Administrative Office: Mrs G

Goodall (Hoffepark Rugby Stadium, as above)

NATAL
Founded: 1890
Telegraphic Address: Rugger Durban
Fax: 031 233230
Colours: Black and white jersey;
whie shorts
President: K Parkinson, P O Box
307, Durban 4000 (0 031 236368;
H 031 842464; Fax 031
233230/842464)
General Manager: B van Zyl, P O
Box 307, Durban 4000 (The Stadium, Kings Park, Waler Gilbert
Road, Durban 4001
(0 031 236366; H 031 294701)

NORTH EASTERN TRANSVAAL
Founded: 1947
Telegraphic Address: Duggie
Springs
Tel/Fax: 011 7409090
Colours: Scarlet and white jersey;
white pants
President: P M du Rand, P O
Box 525, Springs 1560 (O 011
8153010; H 011 563410;
Fax 011 7409090)
Manager: Mrs Lu Pretorius, P O
Box 27, Brakpan 1540 (Bosman
Stadium, Albercorn Avenue,
Brakpan 1540)
(O 011 7409037/8;
H 011 8498764)

NORTH EASTERN CAPE
Founded: 1903
Telegraphic Address: Nefru
Cradock
Tel/Fax: 0481 45443
Colours: Old gold and black jersey; black shorts
President: M J Bekker, Private
Bag x01, Graaff-Reinet, 6280
(O 0491 22283; H 0491 22584)
Manager: A Botha, P O Box 294,
Cradock 5880 (O 0481-4543;
H 0481 711463)

NORTHERN TRANSVAAL
Founded: 1936
Telgraphic Address: Rugby Pretoria

Tel/Fax: 012 3439436
Colours: Light blue jersey;
navy shorts
President: J H P Sortentein, P O
Box 195 Pretoria 0001 (O 012
33285847; H 0112 456678; Fax
012 33256628
General Manager: C C J van
Vuuren, Loftus Versfeld, Kirkness
Street, Sunnyside, Pretoria 0002
(O 012 3444011; H 012 3336733)

SOUTH WESTERN DISTRICTS
Founded: 1899
Telegraphic Address: Suidelikes
Mossel Bay
Tel/fax: 0444 951931
Colours: Green and white jersey;
white pants
President: J G Visser, P O Box
35, Mossel Bay 6500
(H 00444-4959)
Secretary: S D Terblanche, P O
Box 1502, Mossel Bay 6500 (11
Winburg Avenue, Hertenbos
6520 (O/H/Fax 0444 951931)

TRANSVAAL
Founded: 1889
Telegraphic Address: Scrum
Siemend.
Tel/Fax: 011 4027913
Colours: Red and white jersey;
black shorts
President: Dr L Luyt, P O Box
2050, Johannesburg 2000 (0 011
4022960. Susan Kruger 011
7263860; Fax 011 4027282
General Manager: J Prinsloo, P O
Box 2050, Johannesburg 2000
(Ellispark Stadium, c/o 44 Staib and
Curry Street, Doornfontein 2094
(011 4022960; H 011 7925364))

WESTERN PROVINCE
Founded: 1883
Colours: Royal blue and white
jersey; black shorts
President: R Masson, 51 Nederburgh Street, Wetgemaed, 7530
(0 021 9473353; H 021 9132466;
Fax: 021 9473670
Executive Director: Dawie
Schoonraad, P O Box 66, Newlands 7724 (11 Boundary Road,

Newlands 7700 (0 021 6894921; H 021 612211))

WESTERN TRANSVAAL

Founded: 1920
Telegraphic Address: Westrug Potchefstroom
Tel/Fax: 0148 2931076
Colours: Green and red jersey; white pants
President: Prof J T Classen, 7 Drommedaris Street, Potchefstroom 2520 (O 0148 2971130; H 0148 2946017; Fax 0148 2931076
Secretary: Ms R Goosen, P O Box 442, Potchefstroom 2520 (O 0148 92975304/5; H 0148 2976290)

C. CLUBS

ARGENTINA

By Frankie Deges

It was the start of the first ever National Club Championship in 1993-94. This involved the top six sides in Buenos Aires and the champions of the different provincial tournaments. San Isidro Club (SIC), who had won the Buenos Aires tournament, beat Tucuman in the final 27-19. This match was played without the many international players as they were playing the bi-annual South American Championship – which also doubled as World Cup qualifying tournament. To cap a superb season, San Isidro Club won the Sevens Tournament.

ASOCIACION ALUMNI

Founded: 1951
Ground: Tortuguitas Buenos Aires Province
Capacity: 1,500
Telephone: 010 54 1 320 91664
President: Raul Nuvoa
Secretary: Porfilio Carreras
Telephone: 010 54 1 416984
Administrator: Alberto Cafoncelli
Telephone: 010 54 1 342 2557
Manager: Jose Maria Rolandi

Coach: Alberto Del Sel
Captain: Normando Ferrari
Colours: White jersey with red lines, hoops
Teams: 3 seniors but 21 in total
Argentine Champions; 1989, 1990, 1991 & 1992. Internations: Gonzalo Camardon, Sebastian Salvat and Luis Criscuulu.

AUSTRALIA

By John Gates

Leading League placings midseason, up to 4 July 1994

SYDNEY

	P	W	D	L	F	A	Pts
Randwick	15	13	0	2	679	270	26
Warringah	15	13	0	2	527	247	26
Gordon	15	11	0	3	547	247	22
Eastwood	15	10	0	5	325	311	20
Sydney Uni	15	8	0	7	325	311	16

QUEENSLAND

	P	W	D	L	F	A	Pts
Souths	13	10	2	1	404	149	43
GPS	13	9	4	0	347	233	37
Sunnybank	13	7	0	5	323	211	35
Brothers	13	8	1	4	208	218	35
University	13	8	0	5	308	255	32

BROTHERS OLDBOYS RUGBY CLUB INC

Founded: 1905
President: Pat Oswald
Ground: The Jack Ross Oval Crosby Park, Crosby Road, Albion, Brisbane, Queensland
Telephone: 010 61 7 262 4166
Fax: 010 61 7 262 4462
Bar: 010 61 7 262 4166
Floodlights: 2 Pitches
Spectator Capacity: 5,000 – 6,000
Public Transport: Bus and Rail
Wheelchair Access: Yes
Parking: 500
Clubhouse Facilities: 5 bars, board room, conference facilities, 2 restaurants, gym, squash court
Colours: Blue and white butcher's stripe
Nickname: Brothers
No. of Teams: 5 Senior
Training Nights: Tuesday,

Wednesday and Thursday
Wired for radio: Yes
TV Access: Yes
Chief Executive: John Hamilton
Secretaries: Grant Dearlove, Vince Thompson
Treasurer: Ron Ure, Don Jowett
Press Officer: Jim Grant
Coach: Paul McLean MBE, Mark McBain
1st XV Manager: Peter Hoare
Captain: Tim Dodson
Sponsor: Castlemaine XXXX
Financial Turnover 1992-1993: A$1,000,000
International Players: Rod McCall, John Eales, Matt Ryan, IllieTabua, Duncan Hannay (U 21)
Tours Overseas: 1992 New Zealand
Touring Sides Hosted: Argentina Provincial Team, numerous UK and NZ teams throughout year, Australian Army.

EASTERN SUBURBS

Founded: 1900
President: Micheal Rowles
Ground: Woolahra Oval O'Sullivan Rd, Bellevue Hill, Sydney, Australia
Telephone: 010 61 2 327 2565
Bar: 010 61 2 327 2565
Fax: 010 61 2 328 1974
Colours: Red, white and blue
Nickname: Tricolours
Number of Teams: 18
Training nights: Monday, Tuesday and Thursday
Chief Executive: John McKay
Secretary: Robert Wilson
Treasurer: Brendan Taylor
Press Officer: Peter Shipway
Coach: Russell Fairfax
1st XV Manager: Austin Chapman
Captain: Michael Brial
Sponsor: Yalumba Wines
Financial Turnover: 1993-1994 A$750,000
League Position: 7th
International: Tim Gavin, Michael Brial (Wallabies)
Tours overseas: Hawaii International Tournament, Singapore 7's
Touring Sides Hosted: Various Japanese, Transvaal, Eastern Province S.A.

The club's overall performance was mediocre, and on the Club Championship table completed the season in seventh place – a very disappointing result.

However, the 1993 season was certainly not all doom and gloom, and upon reflection there were many positive aspects:

● A very creditable performance, on short notice, to reach the quarter finals of the international Singapore Sevens Tournament in February;

● Two emphatic first grade victories over Randwick, on both occasions when the 1992 premiers were at full strength;

● The consistent and outstanding form displayed by giant Western Australian representative second-rower John Welborn was justly rewarded at seasons end by his inclusion in the NWS State Squad;

● The emergence of former Easts Colts John Isaac and Troy Jaques as future representative players at senior level; Representative honours for Sam Payne and Andrew Heath (NSW) and Wallaby Tours to Ireland/Wales and North America/France for Tim Gavin and Michael Brial (with Steve Goddard attending as gear steward);

● Many exhilarating displays by Colts A team to finish as minor premiers. A composite Colts Team subsequently travelled to Hawaii in October and participated with distinction in winning the Hawaii International Tournament under the guidence of co-coaches John Blondin and Chris Hickman;

● The continuing growth of the Easts Juniors – from one team in 1989 to the seven teams fielded in 1993 – and the ongoing improvements in the standard of play in the juniors;

● Numerous courageous efforts by our 3rd, 4th and 5th grade teams in battling through to reach the semi-finals. Their strong 1993 performances augur well for the depth of our playing strength in the future;

● The general spirit of good fellowship and camaraderie which is obvious among the playing members of the club at all levels.

Taken in balance, the clubs dis-appointing football results in the 1993 season, give reason for genuine optimism.

EASTWOOD

President: William Papworth
Ground: T G Millner Field
146 Vimiera Road, Eastwood, Sydney
Telephone: 010 61 2 868 4222
Fax: 010 61 2 868 5756
Bar: 010 61 2 868 4222
Colours: White with royal blue hoops
Chief Executive: William Papworth
Secretary: Michael Chapman
Coach: Matthew Williams

GORDON RUGBY CLUB

Founded: 1936
President: John Kable
Ground: Chatswood Oval Cnr Albert Ave and Orchard St, Chatswood NSW, PO Box 1396
Telephone: 010 61 2 419 4186
Bar: 010 61 2 412 1092
Fax: 010 61 2 411 3504
Floodlights: Yes
Spectator Capacity: 10,000
Transport: Bus and Rail
Wheelchair Access: Yes
Parking: Surrounding streets
Hospitality Suites: One
Clubhouse Facilities: Bar and lounge
Colours: Navy, black, green and yellow tartan
Nickname: Highlanders
No. of Teams: Senior 6, Colts 5
Training Nights: Monday, Tuesday, Wednesday and Thursday
TV Access: Yes
Chief Executive: Christopher Hawkins
Secretary: Margaret Clark
Treasurer: Ian Tuckwell
Coach: Christopher Hawkins
1st XV Manager: Chris Dagg
Captain: Mark Hartill
International Players: Mark Hartill, Tim Wallace, Tony Dempsey, Alastair Murdoch
Tours Overseas: 1994 Tour to USA
Hosted Tours: Kobe Steel Japan
Sponsor: Peerless Rugby, Andersen Consulting, Mandarin Club/Global

League Positions: Premiers 1993 (1st, 3rd, 4th XVs)
Cup Position: Club Champions in 1993

MANLY

President: Ian MacDonald
Ground: Manly Oval
Sydney Road, Manly
Telephone: 010 61 2 977 6425
Fax: 010 61 2 977 4908
Colours: Royal blue with red hoops
Chief Executive: Ian MacDonald
Secretary: Ron Hughes
Coach: Geoff Mould
Coach: Bruce Malouf

NORTHS

Founded: 1897
President: Russ Wallach(Wallaby 1962)
Ground: Nth Sydney Oval Cnr Miller and Falcon Streets, North Sydney
Admin Adress: 80 Christie St, St Loenards, NSW 2065
Telephone: 61 2 906 6400
Fax: 61 2 906 6196
Bar: 61 2 906 6400
Floodlights: Yes, suitable for TV
Spectator Capacity: 15,000-20,000
Public Transport: Bus routes, Nth Sydney Stn; cabs plentiful
Wheelchair Access: Yes
Parking: street parking
Clubhouse Facilities: Most modern and stylish rugby club in Sydney
Nickname: Norths/Pirates
Training Nights: Tuesday and Thursday
Colours: Red and Black horizontal hoops
Wired for radio: Yes
TV Access: Yes
Chief Executive: Russ Tulloch
Secretary: Tony Hearne
Treasurer: Don Felton
Press Officer: John Hanrahan
Almanack correspondent: John Gates 010 612 954 1624 (H) 010 612 350 8248(B)
Coach: Peter Randall
Captain: Arnie Berkeley
Sponsor: Coca Cola
Financial Turnover: A$1,560,000

International Players: Richard Tombs, Sam Domoni, Danny Maieva, David Sio
Tours Overseas: North American tour won all four games
League Position:

1st Grade	5th
2nd Grade	1st
3rd Grade	4th
4th Grade	2nd
5th Grade	5th
6th Grade	6th
Colts	
1st Grade	5th
2nd Grade	1st
3rd Grade	1st
4th Grade	5th

Cup: 3rd Sydney Club Championships, 1993
(Norths takes in the whole of the lower North Shore up to Gordon/Chatswood, across to Manly in the East and as far west as about Lane Cove).

After a fare measure of success last season there was an influx of overseas and local players, and we are running seven grades in the seniors. Historically, six and seven teams have been the social sides, but this year they are all young, keen, fit and of a fairly high standard. That is also happening at some of the other clubs too, so it speaks highly of the growing standard of Sydney's Club Football.

During the off season, the club sold and moved from its club house of 40 years to bigger and more modern premises in St. Leonards, which was previously the old "729" club (a former media club for television people, which went broke in early 1993). As a result we have the most modern and stylish rugby club in Sydney. Its only disadvantage is that it is away from the ground itself but this doesn't seem to be bothering anyone so far. Norski's Nitespot is the disco which we run every Saturday night, during the season and is fast becoming the most popular place on the North Shore. Players from a number of other clubs are regularly spotted there every week.

Sponsors include Coca Cola and Tooheys/Hahn (brewers).

We do not own our own ground, but use the council-owned North Sydney Oval. It is one of the prettiest settings for rugby you can find anywhere and generally considered one of the best playing surfaces of any ground in Australia. We share it with the North Sydney Rugby League club ("The Bears").

RANDWICK

Founded: 1885
President: Peter Court
Ground: Coogee Oval, Brook St, Coogee
Telephone: 010 61 2 665 5447
Fax: 010 61 2 665 7017
Floodlights: 1 Pitch
Spectator Capacity: 10,000
Public Transport: Bus
Wheelchair Access: Yes
Parking: Yes
Hospitality Suites: Two
Clubhouse Facilities: 5 bars, restaurant, Function rooms, snooker
Colours: Myrtle green
Nickname: Galloping Greens
No. of Teams: 12
Training Nights: Tuesday and Thursday
Bar: Randwick district RUFC 104 Brook St, Coogee,
Telephone: 010 61 2 665 5447
Press Box: 010 61 2 315 7182
Wired for radio: Yes
TV Access: Yes
Chief Executive: W Eric Turner, M Litt., FRSA, JP,
Telephone: 010 61 2 299 1268, 010 61 2 665 6539
Secretary: Eric Turner
Telephone: 010 61 2 389 5383
Treasurer: Douglas E Henry
Coach: John Maxwell
1st XV Manager: Leslie F Barlow, William G Hope
Captain: Tim Kava
Rugby Development Officer: Micheal Jorgenson
Sponsors: Tooheys, Collex, Toyota, Holiday Inn

SYDNEY UNIVERSITY

President: Geoff Caban
Ground: University Oval No 1 Sydney University Sports Union,
HK Ward Gymnasium, University of Sydney, 2006
Telephone: 010 61 2 660 3877
Fax: 010 61 2 660 6165
Colours: Blue with gold hoops
Secretary: Martin Hyde
Bar: Sir Bruce Williams Pavilion, Sydney University
Coach: Dick Laffan

WESTERN SUBURBS

President: Geoffrey Harper
Ground: Concord Oval, Loftus St Concord
Telephone: 010 61 2 744 8686
Fax: 010 61 2 745 2644
Colours: Black and white hoops
Bar: Western Suburbs DRUFC 28A George St Burwood
Secretary: Dennis Woods
Coach: Ian Patterson

WARRINGAH

President: Ron Curry
Ground: Pittwater Rugby Park, Walsh St, Narrabeen
Telephone: 010 61 2 913 3843
Bar: Warringah Rugby Club Walsh St, Narrabeen
Secretary: John Hefferman 010 61 2 560 4444
Coach: Robin Sawtell

CANADA

By Colin Brown

There are well organised and committed clubs across the country from Newfoundland to British Columbia. However, distances are huge – approximately 2,500 miles from Vancouver to Toronto, roughly the same as from London to Amman. The weather differences are huge, and so seasons vary between the provinces.

Any analysis of Canadian rugby must narrow down the target. In reality the only cross-Canada competition is the annual National Championship, played between the provinces, in October. This is the end of the season for most of the country, who play in the spring and summer, but the beginning for

British Columbia, who play from September to May.

This Championship gives the primary indication of where the strength in Canadian rugby lies. BC has won it every year except for 1982. Ontario won that year and have been the beaten finalists every other year, except for 1991 when Newfoundland performed the duties. The national team is the other indicator. Often, all 15 players are from BC although there are currently two or three from Ontario.

EAST

Although, overall, Ontario rugby is not as strong as BC, there are several good clubs. Ottawa Irish have been the strongest club for many years with consistent pressure from Balmy Beach in Toronto. More recently York Yeomen have been in the running, and in 1993/4 they beat Balmy Beach for the Toronto City championship, and then beat Ottawa Irish to win the Ontario championship. Most other clubs are a step down from this top three:

1. Otttawa Irish
2. Balmy Beach
3. York Yeomen

PRAIRIES (MIDDLE)

Rugby in the prairie provinces – Alberta, Manitoba and Saskatchewan – largely lags behind the rest of Canada. Alberta has the strongest clubs, with Calgary Irish being the leading club over the last few years. In Edmonton, the Druids and the Clansmen have been at the forefront. Consensus is that Calgary Irish are consistent enough to play at a similar level to the Ontario clubs and with the middle to the bottom of the BC clubs.

WEST

There are three primary indicators of the clubs strength in British Columbia. The three major unions Vancouver, Vancouver Islands, and the Frazer Valley, all play a league season.

PLAY-OFFS

In April, the top four teams in each league play off for a Union championship – 1st vs 4th, 2nd vs 3rd, and then a final.

The three Union champions then play off for a provincial championship. The Valley team has never won that championship, so the three primary indicators could be (l) The BC Provincial Championship, (2) The Island Champion, and (3) The Vancouver Champion.

With three out of five wins in five years and four out of 10, the UBC Old Boys have clearly been the most successful club in the past 10 years. James Bay Athletic Association with three in 10 have been second in the past five years with the Meraloma Club from Vancouver also in the list, by virtue of their record over 10 years.

The standings, then should be:

1. UBC Old Boys
2. James Bay
3. Meralomas

Honorable mentions to the Vancouver Rowing Club and Cowichan, who won on the Island this year. The Rowing Club has had some league successes in the past couple of years but has been unable to withstand the rigours of championship play. This is largely because they have had only one representative player in their team, which has made their league side very settled. UBCOB and Meralomas have had six and four respectively. This means they play some league games with inferior sides, but have the talent for the big cup games. Credit should also be given to the Burnaby Rugby Club, who have won the valley championship for the past two years but have been unable to get past the semi finals.

CANADIAN TOP 10

Amalgamating the Eastern clubs with the Western clubs is difficult but it was done with the Provincial results as a guide, supported by discussions with players who have played in both leagues, such as John Hutchinson (who won both an Ontario championship with York and a BC championship with the

UBC Old Boys in 1993/4) The best Ontario clubs would come into the middle of the table in BC.

In 1991, Barbarians Denver, the US champions, were beaten by the Canadian champions, the UBC Old Boys. The Old Boys are now arguably the top club side in North America. Based then upon the review of East, West, and Prairie clubs, this would be the top 10 club list:

1. UBC Old Boys
2. James Bay Athletic Association
3. Meralomas
4. Rowing Club RFC
5. Cowichan RFC
6. Burnaby Lake RFC
7. Ottawa Irish RFC
8. Balmy Beach RFC
9. York Yeomen RFC
10. Calgary Irish RFC

UNIVERSITY OF BRITISH COLUMBIA OLD BOYS

Founded: 1974
President: David Smart
Ground: Jericho Park Discovery St, Vancouver BC
Tel: 0101 604 224 2131
Fax: 0101 604 443 7336
Spectator Capacity: 2,000
Public Transport: Bus 4th Avenue UBC
Wheelchair Access: Yes
Parking: Yes
Clubhouse Facilities: 2 bars, dining room
Colours: Red, white and blue
Change of Colours: White
Nickname: Ravens
No. of Teams: 5
Training Nights: Tuesday and Thursday
Chief Executive: David Smart
Secretary: Mike Mallette
Treasurer: Darcy Krohman
Press Officer: Colin Brown
1st XV Coach: Rob Greig
Captain: Colin McKenzie
Sponsor: Labatts
League Position: Vancouver Champion
Cup Position: BC Provincial Champion
International Players: Eddie Evans, Dan Jackart, Norm Hadley, Colin McKenzie, John

Graf, Scott Stewart, Pat Palmer, John Hutchinson

The success of the UBC Old Boys has been to integrate new players with "stars", so that as the representative players retire, a new group of players has followed on behind.

The first "Ravens" were a group of national players who left the University of BC together. They included Spence McTavish, Barry Legh, Ro Hindson, Jack Shaw, Garth Hendrickson and Leigh Hillier. In the early mid-eighties, they were joined by a new group of internationals, including Doug Tate, Rob Greig, Preston Wiley, Andrew Bibby, Rob Strang, John Robertson and Paul Monohan. Towards the end of the eighties, the team that has dominated the early nineties started to emerge, and Eddie Evans. Dan Jackart, Norm Hadley, John Graf and Pat Palmer joined some of the prior group. After some of the team left to play overseas (Evans in Japan and Hadley to Wasps) even newer international stars, Colin McKenzie, Scott Stewart and John Hutchinson, have produced yet another winning side, with another Miller Cup win, and a BC provincial championship in 1993/94!

It is this procession of top players that has generated the interest and led to the constant renewal of the team. Added interest is provided by a commitment to seven-a-sides in the summer months. The Old Boys have been in the Can-Am final for the last seven years and won five, including the last three. This helps foster a year-round commitment to the club.

In addition, all the other club sides: 2nd, and Junior, have won championships recently with the 3rd XV winning the league and cup double for their division in 1993/94. This results in outstanding club camaraderie.

JAMES BAY ATHLETIC ASSOCIATION (JBAA)

President: Gary Johnston

Ground: MacDonald Park, Victoria, BC
Tel: 0101 604 388 7441
Spectator Capacity: 750
Public Transport: Bus
Wheelchair Access: Yes
Parking: 200
Clubhouse Facilities: Yes
Colours: Navy blue and white
Change of Colours: White and navy blue
Nickname: Bays
No. of Teams: 3 teams
Training Nights: Tuesday and Thursday
Chief Executive: Gary Johnston
Secretary: Barry Robbins
Treasurer: Rod MacDonald
Press Officer: Courtney Walls
Captain: Tom Woods
League Position 1994: 2nd
Cup: Runner-up to Cowichan in League play off
International Players: Chris Whittaker, Mark Cardinal, Terry Moew, Ian Gordon, Bob Ross

The "Bays" have been at the forefront of BC and Canadian rugby for many years. Their purple patch was from 1973-1980, when they won seven provincial championships in a row! They are best known for a hard driving forward style of play. Their most famous player is probably Hans di Goede – Canada's cauliflower-eared captain in the 1987 World Cup.

CALGARY CANADIAN IRISH ATHLETIC CLUB

President: Peter Finnegan
Secretary: Dave Hill
Treasurer: Murray Phimester
International Players: Julian Loveday

MERALOMA RFC

President: Mark des Harnais
Ground: Connaught Park 10th Avenue and Vine Street
Tel: 0101 604 733 4366
Fax: 0101 604 688 1841
Spectator Capacity: 2,000
Public Transport: 12th Avenue bus
Wheelchair Access: Yes

Parking: Yes
Clubhouse Facilities: Bar, kitchen
Colours: Orange and black
Nickname: Lomas
No. of Teams: 6
Training Nights: Tuesday and Thursday
Chief Executive: Mark des Harnais
Captain: Bruce Breen
League Position: 1st
Cup: Lost in Final
International Players: Jeff Knauer, Chris Tynan, Mark Williams, Ron Toews, Courtney Smith

The Lomas are the largest club in Vancouver, with beautiful grounds and a fine old clubhouse. They are part of a sporting organisation which includes men and ladies' baseball, soccer, cricket and others. The Meralomas are also one of the oldest of the Vancouver clubs.

BALMY BEACH

President: Malcolm Clayton
Ground: Beach Park, Coxwell and Lakeshore Toronto
Tel: 0101 416 266 1343
Clubhouse Facilities: Bar
Colours: Blue and gold
Chief Executive: Malcolm Clayton
Secretary: Heather Ambrose
1st XV Coach: Bruce Gage

BURNABY LAKE RFC

President: Randy Johal
Ground: Burnaby Lake Sports Complex 3760 Sporling Ave (foot of Sprott and Sporling) Burnaby BC V5B 4X5
Tel: 0101 604 293 2837
Fax: 0101 604 294 5654
Spectator Capacity: Open field
Public Transport: Yes
Wheelchair Access: Yes
Parking: Yes
Clubhouse Facilities: Yes, including banquet hall
Colours: Navy blue
Change of Colours: White
No. of Teams: 6
Training Nights: Tuesday and Thursday
Chief Executive: Randy Johal 0101 604 662 2322
Secretary: Tony Griffin

0101 604 294 4771
Treasurer: Stewart Colbourne
0101 604 294 7195
Captain: Jeffery Lorz
1st XV Coach: Pat Anderson
League Position: Frazer Valley 1st
Division Champions 1992-1993
Cup: Semi-finalists
International Players: Mike James

This is now the title of the newly amalgamated Burnaby and Tro-jan rugby clubs. With Burnaby's fine last two years, winning the Fraser Valley Championship, and the Tro-jans' historical strength, this should be a bigger, stronger club. They will play at the Burnaby Lake Sports Complex, one of the finest in BC. Their newly capped (USA 1994) player, 20-year-old Mike James, is outstanding in a good young team.

YORK YEOMEN RFC

President: David Berio
Tel: 705 435 2853
Fax: 416 494 6435
Spectator Capacity: Open Ground
Wheelchair Access: Yes
Parking: Yes
Clubhouse Facilities: Club bar and spectator's bar
Colours: Red and white hoops and red shorts
Nickname: Yeomen
No. of Teams: 3 Senior sides, Under-19 and 17, and 2 women's sides
Training Nights: Tuesday and Thursday
1st XV Coach: Bruce Smith
Captain: Scott Swizzer
League Position: Won title in 1993
Cup: Won Cup Final against Ottawa Irish (32-12)
International Players: John Hutchinson

Whilst one of the most success-ful won-lost records (13-1) in the last 10 years of rugby in Ontario senior rugby, the area champions in 1993 were the Yeomen who have been building a successful club for the past few years. Described by a player as "bridesmaids" in the past, they beat Ottawa Irish to become the brides this year!

OTTAWA IRISH RFC

President: Robert Orange
Ground: Twin Elm Park
Tel: 0101 613 838 2029
Clubhouse Facilities: Bar
Colours: Green and gold hoops
Nickname: Irish
Secretary: Stuart Robinson
1st XV Coach: Lee Powell
League Position: Winners
Cup: Runner-up
International Players: Al Charron

VANCOUVER ROWING CLUB

Founded: 1908
Chairman: Mark Collister
Ground: Brockton Oval
Stanley Park, Vancouver
Telephone: 0101 604 687-3400
Fax: 0101 604 687 6812
Spectator Capacity: 3,000
Wheelchair Access: Yes
Parking: Yes
Clubhouse Facilities: Yes
Colours: Red and white hoops
Nickname: Rowers
No. of Teams: 7
Training Nights: Tuesday and Thursday
Chief Executive: Mark Collister
Secretary: Stephanie Foote
Treasurer: David Sullings
Coach: Ian Humphreys
1st XV Manager: Brian Martin
Captain: Ian Cooper
League: Second
International Players: Ian Stuart, Andrew Wilson, Ian Cooper, Richard Brice, Alen Phillips

The Rowers had another good season. Their first team came second in the league, but did not progress further in the play-offs. The second team, however, were successful in becoming the provin-cial champions in their division.

ENGLAND

For most of the season there were only two teams in either the league or the cup to watch – Bath and Leicester. They were considerably better than the

rest. The league games were, in the main, desperately poor to watch. Players seemed frozen by the big occasions. Let us hope this is a pass-ing phase.

Like the Welsh, the clubs suffer from playing home and away. For 1995-96, the leagues should be reduced again, this time to eight clubs, who would play on eight consecutive weeks beginning on the first week in October. December would be left to Divisional matches and in January a new league cup could be introduced to run alongside the Pilkington Cup. This would give the best clubs the chance to extend their frontiers into Europe.

COURAGE NATIONAL LEAGUE
FINAL TABLES: LEAGUE 1

	P	W	D	L	F	A	Pts
Bath	18	17	0	1	431	181	34
Leicester	18	14	0	4	425	210	28
Wasps	18	10	1	7	362	340	21
Bristol	18	9	0	9	331	276	18
Harlequins	18	8	0	10	333	287	16
Orrell	18	8	0	10	327	302	16
Gloucester	18	6	2	10	247	356	14
London Irish	18	4	0	14	217	391	8
Newcastle	18	2	1	15	190	483	5
Gosforth							

Champions: Bath
Relegated: London Irish, Newcastle and Gosforth

LEAGUE 2

	P	W	D	L	F	A	Pts
Sale	18	13	2	3	438	160	28
W Hartlepool	18	13	2	3	369	271	28
Saracens	18	11	1	6	299	238	23
Wakefield	18	8	3	7	347	240	19
Moseley	18	9	1	8	266	220	19
Nottingham	18	8	1	9	254	326	17
Waterloo	18	6	2	10	231	346	14
L Scottish	18	6	0	12	232	325	12
Rugby	18	5	1	12	186	302	11
Otley	18	4	1	13	235	449	9

Promoted: Sale and West Hartlepool
Relegated: Rugby and Otley

LEAGUE 3

	P	W	D	L	F	A	Pts
Coventry	18	14	0	4	406	259	28
Fylde	18	13	0	5	339	219	26
Bedford	18	12	0	6	332	219	24
Blackheath	18	11	0	7	305	222	22
Rosslyn Pk	18	10	1	7	372	240	21
Exeter	18	9	1	8	308	271	19

Richmond	18	9	0	9	337	300	18
Morley	18	6	0	12	245	334	12
Havant	18	3	0	15	203	432	6
Redruth	18	2	0	16	178	488	4

Promoted: Coventry and Fylde
Relegated: Havant and Redruth

BATH F C

Founded: 1865
President: L A Hughes
Ground: Recreation Ground, Bath
Telephone: (44) 225 425192
Fax: (44) 225 3253
Public Transport: Not required, once in Bath
Spectator Capacity: 9,000
Wheelchair access: Yes from Pulteney St entrance
Parking: Restricted
Public Transport: 82A Bus
Hospitality Suites: 22 in new Teachers Stand
Colours: Blue, white and black
Change of Colours: White shirt with blue and black hoop
No. of Teams: Senior 3, Junior 6
Training Nights: Senior Monday & Wednesday;
Youth Tuesday; Junior Thursday
Wired for Radio: Yes
TV Access: TV Commentators' space, TV cameras vantage roof
Chief Executive: G W Hancock
Secretary: Major J W Quinn
Press Officer: K Johnstone
10 St Michaels Court, Monkton Combe, Bath BA2 7HA
Telephone: (44) 225 723 579
Coach: B Ashton
Captain: Jon Hall
Team Managers: J Allen, B Shaw
Sponsor: South West Electricty Board, (SWEB)
League: Courage Div 1 winners
Cup: Pilkington winners
Sevens: Middlesex 7's winners
Tours Hosted: South African Barbarians, Toulouse
Tours overseas: Barbados

Even by Bath's standards this was a very special season, especially as it was probably the hardest ever in terms of commitment for the players. The home and away league system, plus the divisional and international calls at all levels, proved a great demand on players' time and fitness. It was to the great credit of all the squad, the trainers and coaches and the medical teams, that the players took the Courage League title, the Pilkington Cup and, the icing on the cake, the Middlesex 7's as well.

There have been a few famous "farewells" over the season with Gareth Chilcott and Richard Hill hanging up their boots but not lost to the club in other important ways. Jack Rowell left the stage at Bath having seen the club transformed over the years to become the "Ace of Clubs", and now to take England through to the next World Cup. Success is confined not only to the 1st XV – all the players in all the teams the club runs, plus all the back-up staff in whatever capacity, can look back on the 93-94 season with great pride. A new feature on "the Rec" next season could well be a Bath Emerging Players XV, the brainchild of Gareth Chilcott and Richard Hill, who, in looking towards the next generation of Bath players, have already had a trial run of their embryo team, with great success.

Punters arriving at the Rec from now on can witness, arising from the South End, the new and exciting Teacher's Stand due to be completed in time for the opening league match against Bristol in early September. The fundraising efforts have been enormous and with all the hospitality suites now taken or spoken for, the enterprise has been one of the biggest events in the club's history. The planning decision not to allow a supermarket to be built at Lambridge means loss of expected revenue from that venture, which would at least have gone into facility improvements on the Rec, including the playing surface. So new ways will have to be found to raise the necessary capital. With new faces expected at the Bath Club next season to enhance those already there, the new Teacher's Stand in operation, and three titles to defend, there is already a buzz of excitement and anticipation about.

TEACHER'S STAND

By Peter Downie

Bath are undoubtedly the leading side in the Northern Hemisphere, and they have embarked upon creating the facilities to go with that phenomenal record. Now £1.3 million of funding have been committed to the Teacher's Stand to be finished for the 94/95 season. The Teacher's Stand – behind the rugby posts at the Sports Centre end – was conceived three years ago when the attempts to get planning permission for the re-building of the West Stand and close off the stadium on the east side were rejected by the City Council.

Planning permission was obtained in the autumn of 1991, but in spite of its success the club hadn't the money to build the stand due to a sizeable overdraft. Its main benefactor was taken over by a large multinational and had withdrawn.

The initial design envisaged standing for 900 or seating for 400, plus 1,200 Hospitality Boxes. John Monahan, FRICS, a former Bath and Cambridge University player, had managed the refurbishment of the famous Theatre Royal in Bath, and was given the task of trying to move the project forward.

John Monahan proposed a feasibility study. This entailed visits to more than a dozen sporting venues, from Arsenal in football, Surrey in cricket, to the leading rugby clubs to seek out ideas as to how their facilities have been developed. Football and cricket received considerable funding from their governing bodies, but even so had to find the sort of funds we were looking for from other sources.

In the final reckoning the club's record and playing ability looked as though it could be harnessed to create the interest for the stand to be financed without resources to borrowing.

The plan was to chop the £1.54 million into component parts,

Bath captain, John Hall, lifts the trophy as his side win the Courage League Championship

retaining a reasonable amount of elasticity as each area might fall short of the projected amount allocated. While the RFU and the local city and sports councils had initially been regarded as potential benefactors only two organisations proved to be realistic – The Foundation for Sports and Arts and Sportsmatch. The former set up by the pools companies with income of about £1 million per week, but receiving applications in excess of 10 times that. The latter, as the name suggests, would entertain applications for pound for pound funding.

Thanks to considerable help from Bath MP, Don Foster, and local councillors and officers, a grant £100,000 was recieved from FSA. We had applied for just under £500,000 so our elasticity was immediately stretched!

That strategy was similarly pursued on the boxes and debentures by using a mix of variable lengths of tenure. The boxes, which have room for 10 to be entertained luxuriously with balcony seating are licensed for one, three, five, seven or 10 years, with prices ranging from £10,000 to £78,400. The debentures are for 10-, 6-. or 4 – year duration with discounts from the list prices of £1,000, £750 and £600 for groups of two or more to encourage families.

General funding has revolved around an inaugural game to open the stand, while the RFU have granted TV rights. Finding a space in the fixture list is not easy, but it is hoped the best from the Southern Hemisphere will play at the Rec to determine the "Best this side of the Antarctic".

The final and most conclusive contribution to the funding has been Hiram Walker, the spirits side of Allied Lyons whose HQ is in Bristol. Their leading whisky brand "Teachers" has given the stand and the end its name for a period of six years.

BEDFORD RUFC

Founded: 1886
President: G B Wiley
Ground: Goldington Road, Bedford
Telephone: (44) 234 347980 (office), (44) 234 354619 (club), (44) 234 347511 (steward)
Floodlights: Yes
Spectator Capacity: 6,000
Wired for radio: Yes
TV Access: Yes
Public Transport: BR about 2,000m from ground, bus outside
Wheelchair Access: Yes
Parking: 300 spaces, but invariably full an hour before kick-off
Clubhouse Facilities: Public and members bar, social club
Hospitality Suites: Yes
Colours: Oxford & Cambridge blue hoops
No. of Teams: Four senior, U21, colts and minis
Training Nights: Monday and Thursday
Chairman: Ian Bullerwell
Secretary: Tony Mills , (44) 234 364351
Treasurer: A Knight
Asst sec & membership sec: P Smith, (44) 234 851455
Fixture sec: J R Saunders, (44) 234 822328
Press: H Travis, (44) 234 213808
Coach: Mike Rafter, (44) 275 870370 (B)
Position in league: 3rd in Division 2

There were high hopes of an immediate return to Division 2, especially after the league season started in mid-October. A home defeat by Richmond in mid-December followed by three away losses at Blackheath, Coventry and Fylde in January brought the club down to earth. In the next seven games the only defeat was at Morley. There was a memorable win against Richmond from 5-20 down. And in the last match Bedford were level on points with Fylde with both clubs facing away fixtures with the latter ahead on goal difference. Bedford lost at Exeter and Fylde came from behind to beat Morley. On a successful close season tour of British Columbia Bedford won all four matches. The squad is young and keen and the club are looking for-

ward to 1994-95 with a certain amount of renewed optimism.

BRISTOL F C

Founded: 1888
President: Arthur Holmes
Ground: Memorial Ground, Filton Avenue, Horfield, Bristol BS7 OAQ
Telephone: (44) 272 514134, (44) 272 514448
Ticket Line: (44) 272 514134
Fax: (44) 272 514226
Rugby Call Line: 0891 660 226 (Premium rates apply)
Floodlights: Yes – suitable for TV
Spectator Capacity: 9,000
Wired for radio: Yes
TV Access: Yes
Public Transport: Bristol City Line
Wheelchair Access: Yes
Parking: 320 spaces
Clubhouse Facilities: Public and members bar, social club
Hospitality Suites: Numerous suites – packages available contact hospitality manager Robert Laurance: 0272 514134
Fax: 0272 514 226
Colours: Blue and white
Change of Colours: Yellow, slate grey and white
No. of Teams: 1st XV, & United, colts and minis
Training Nights: Monday and Wednesday
Chief Executive: B W Redwood
Secretary: T W Jones
Treasurer: J Lewis: Brian Hanlon
Press Officer: D G Tyler
Captain: Derek Eves
Sponsor: Higgs and Hill Homes Ltd
League Position: Courage League One – 4th
Cup : Pilkington Cup – Knocked out at Round 5
Honours: Worthington Tens Champions
Senior Players: Derek Eves – England Emerging Players Captain; Paul Hull – England tour to South Africa 1994; Kieran Bracken – England International; Simon Shaw – England tour to South Africa 1994; Andy Blackmore– England A; Alan Sharp – Scottish International; Mark Denney – England Colts Captain

Last season the *Almanack* said of Bristol: – "Look out because they will be back with a vengeance". Well, they might not have won the league or the cup but they have certainly improved by leaps and bounds. They finished the Courage League in fourth place – their highest ever position – and with a young side the season was seen as a foundation for the coming campaign.

Club captain Derek Eves will be in his fifth season at the helm and predicts greater things will be seen this season. In the Pilkington Cup they were knocked out by the eventual Cup winners Bath at the Fifth Round stage. Bristol won the Worthington Tens at Kingsholm in May beating Gloucester in front of their home crowd in the final.

International honours finally came the way of the Bristol players: – scrum half Kieran Bracken making a memorable debut against the All Blacks at Twickenham; loosehead prop Alan Sharp finally breaking into the Scottish senior side; Paul Hull drafted into the England touring party to South Africa and gaining his first International caps in the two Tests; lock Simon Shaw flown out to South Africa to strengthen the squad; Andy Blackmore again in the England A sides; Derek Eves captained the "England Emerging Players" side that included scrum half Rob Kitchin who has now left Bristol for Harlequins; and a new prospect being centre Mark Denney – the England Colts Captain.

GLOUCESTER RFC

Founded: 1873
President: M V Hughes
Ground: Kingsholm, Kingsholm Road, Gloucester GLI 3AX
Telephone: (44) 452 520901
Ticket Line: (44) 452 381087
Floodlights: Yes
Spectator Capacity: 12,000
Wheelchair Access: Yes
Parking: Yes
Clubhouse Facilities: Lounge, bar, restaurant
Hospitality Suites: Yes
Colours: Cherry and white
Change of Colours: Black and white

Nickname: Elver Eaters, No. of
Teams: 2 Seniors, Under-21's and Colts
Training Nights: Monday and Thursday
TV Access: Yes
Chief Executive: Alan Brinn
Secretary: A D Wadley, Byeways, Belmont Avenue, Hucclecote, Gloucester
Treasurer: A D Wadley
Administrative Officer: Geraldine Peake
Press Officer: Peter Ford, Rovermead, Sandhurst Lane, Gloucester
Coach: Viv Wooley
!st XV Manager: B Corless
Captain: Andrew Deacon
Sponsor: Worthington
League: second bottom
Cup: Knocked out in fifth round
International Players: Ian Smith, Peter Jones
Tours Overseas: Italy
Touring Sides Hosted: Transvaal, Portugese President's XV
Special Awards: National Ten-a-side tournament semi finalists 1994

The average Gloucester supporter in 1993/4 was likely to be a manic depressive with a weak heart. Periods of gloom following abject surrender to sides which could and should have been beaten, in both League and Cup, alternated with wild elation at performances of genuine quality, as when Harlequins were defeated in a game which only yielded four penalties in the entire match. The mood swings weren't helped by a series of injuries to influential players – Ashley Johnson, Simon Morris, Andy Deacon, John Howker, for example – at the worst possible points in the season. The resignation in mid term due to ill health by long-serving chairman, Peter Ford, was a blow as well.

And yet there were many good things for the discerning supporter. Barrie Corless, in his first season as Director of Rugby, began to make his presence felt. Colts, Under-21 and United sides all had excellent seasons. Ian Smith, Peter Jones, Dave Sims, Paul Holford, Richard West and Andy Deacon all received representative honours,

and a whole clutch of young players started to make their mark. All this, plus a new coach and a new captain, have produced a mood of optimism for 1994/5. Don't write Gloucester off yet! .

HARLEQUINS F C

Founded: 1866
President: D K Brooks
Grounds: Stoop Memorial Ground, Twickenham and Craneford Way, Twickenham, TW27SQ
Telephone: (44) 81 892 0822
Fax: (44) 81 744 2764
Floodlight: Yes
Spectator Capacity: 8,500
Public Transport: BR Twickenham
Wheelchair Access: Yes
Parking: Yes
Clubhouse Facilities: 3 Bars and sponsors room, 4 changing rooms and weights room
Hospitality Suites: Yes
Colours: Light blue, magenta, chocolate, french grey, light green and black
Nickname: Quins
No. of Teams: Senior 2, Junior 2
Training Nights: Monday and Thursday
TV Access: Yes
Chief Executive: R F Looker (Chairman)
Secretary: G R Morey
Treasurer: G C Anderson
Press Officer: Gad Seward, 152 Woodseer St, London E1 5HQ
Telephone: (44) 71 377 1151
1st XV Manager: J L B Salmon
Captain: Brian Moore
Sponsor: Flowers Original
League Position: 6th
Cup: Semi-finalists
International Players: Jason Leonard, Brian Moore, Will Carling, Troy Coker
Tours Overseas: South Africa M Nite Series.

The Harlequins is a club which doesn't quite know where it is going. They've paid allegedly as much as £15,000 to have Bob Templeton as a part-time coach and appointed (though he has subsequently resigned in the close season)

Jamie Salmon their first full-time manager; yet by their own standards they had a poor season. In the Cup, their one consolation of a sort was the game against Bath in the semi-final, which was one of the best ever seen in the competition.

Plans are in hand to build a £2 million stand for 5,000 spectators to be ready for the start of the 1995-96 season.

LEICESTER F C

Founded: 1880
President: J T Thomas
Ground: Aylestone Road, Leicester LE2 7LF
Telephone: (44) 533 541 607
Fax: (44) 533 854 766
Ticket Line: (44) 891 884 558
Floodlights: Yes
Spectator Capacity: 13,833
Public Transport: Leicester Railway Station
Wheelchair Access: Viewing area 13
Clubhouse Facilities: Two large bars, upstairs bar with food available before and after the game
Hospitality Suites: Two
Colours: Scarlet, green, white hoop
Change of Colours: Scarlet shirt, green and white band
Nickname: Tigers
No. of Teams: Senior 3, Under 21 and Youth
Training Nights: Monday and Thursday
Wired for Radio: Yes
TV Access: Yes
Secretary: J A Allen, c/o Leicester Football Club Aylestone Rd, Leicester LE 7LF
Telephone: (44) 533 858407 (H) (44) 533 471234 (W)
Treasurer: A P Power c/o Club
Press Officer: J A Allen
Coach: I R Smith
Captain: D Richards
Sponsor: Carlsberg Tetley
League: 2nd
Cup: Beaten Finalists
International Players: Dean Richards, Rory Underwood, Tony Underwood, Martin Johnson, Neal Black, Niall Malone
Tours Overseas: Australia, Fiji, New Zealand, Zimbabwe, Canada, South Africa

Touring sides hosted: South African Barbarians

Leicester finished as runners-up to Bath in both the league and the cup – in the latter, they let themselves down. It seemed as though they were playing too much within themselves.

They will start work on a £2 million, 3,000 seat stand and a £400,000 club-house extension next April and hope to complete work by October 1995. The stand will include 24 hospitality boxes, restaurant and bar facilities will increase ground capacity to 17,000 and is the first step of an £8 million 10-year plan to turn Welford Road into a 20,000 capacity stadium.

LONDON IRISH R F C

Founded: 1898
President: Dr H C Condon
Ground: The Avenue, Sunbury on Thames, Middlesex TW16 5EQ
Telephone: (44) 932 783034
Fax: (44) 932 784462
Bar: (44) 932 784462
Club Rugby Line: 0891 664494
Floodlights: Yes
Spectator Capacity: 7,000
Public Transport: Sunbury on Thames, BR
Wheelchair Access: Yes
Parking: 300 spaces
Hospitality Suites: Function room
Colours: Green and white
Change of Colours: Green
Nickname: The Irish
No. of Teams: Senior 12, Underage 18
Wired for Radio: Yes
TV Access: Custom built TV gantry
Chief Executive: Pat Barragry
Secretary: Kieran McCarthy
Treasurer: P Griffith
Press Officer: Michael A Flatley
Coach: H Reid
!st XV Manager: P Hughes
Captain: Paul Collins
League Position: Relegated to Div 2
International Players:
Tours Overseas: Canada

The 1993/1994 season proved to be a frustrating experience for the Irish. Looking to consolidate

their position in the Courage First Division, injuries and loss of key players cost them dearly. Six matches were lost in the last five minutes. However, London Irish has a strong base on which to re-build. The Second XV, U21s and U19s all had impressive seasons and in the Junior Section the club won every county championship from U8 through to U17. The club is confident that their relegation is only a hiccup in their determination to remain a top ranking club.

LONDON SCOTTISH F C

Founded: 1878
President: A C W Boyle
Ground: Richmond Athletic Ground, Richmond, Surrey TW9 2SS
Telephone: (44) 81 332 2473
Fax: (44) 81 332 6775
Bar: (44) 81 940 0397
Floodlights: Training pitches
Spectator Capacity: 6,200
Public Transport: BR/Tube Richmond
Wheelchair Access: Yes
Parking: 200 spaces
Hospitality Suites: One
Clubhouse Facilities: Two bars, lunch rooms, club and shop
Colours: Blue
Change of Colours: White
Nickname: Scots
No. of Teams: Senior 9, Youth 2, Mini 7
Training Nights: Tuesday and Thursday
Wired for Radio: Yes
TV Access: Yes
Secretary: J J Smith, c/o Ground
Telephone: (44) 784 459643 (H) (44) 81 332 2473 (W)
Treasurer: Bruce Galloway
Press Officer: J J Smith, c/o Ground
!st XV Manager: to be announced
Captain: Paul Burnell
Sponsor: Famous Grouse
League Position: 8th Div Two
Cup: Knocked out Round 4
International Players: A Burnell, D Cronin, Iain Morrison

This has been another wretched year for the Scots who just avoided the drop from the second to the third division on the last day of the league season. It is difficult to judge how the Scots are going to go forward given the general paucity of talent at their disposal.

MOSELEY F C

Founded: 1873
President: D A E Evans
Ground: The Reddings, Reddings Rd, Moseley, Birmingham BL13 8LW
Telephone: (44) 21 449 2149
Fax: (44) 21 442 4147
Ticket Line: (44) 21 449 2149
Press Box: (44) 21 449 2149
Bar: (44) 21 449 2149
Floodlights: Yes
Spectator Capacity: 9,999
Public Transport: No 50 bus.
Wheelchair Access: Yes
Parking: 200 Cars
Hospitality Suites: 10 Boxes
Clubhouse Facilities: Two members bars, public bar, two players bars, club shop
Colours: Red and black
Change of Colours: White with red and black
Nickname: Mose
No. of Teams: Senior 3, Youth 3, Minis & Juniors 10
Training Nights: Tuesday and Thursday
Wired for Radio: Yes
TV Access: Yes
Chief Executive: Alex Keay
Secretary: Peter Veitch, H E Reddings, Reddings Road, Moseley, Birmingham BL13 8LW
Treasurer: Roger Bryant
Press Officer: Alex Keay
Coach: Derek Nutt, Alex Keay
!st XV Manager: Norman Wainwright
Captain: Peter Shillingford
Sponsor: Carlsberg Tetley
League Position: 5th Division Two
Cup: Quarter-Finals
International Players: Mike Teague (British Lions), Mark Chudleigh (England Colts), Mark Linnet (England) Simon Hodgkinson (England)

For their second successive season, Moseley were left with the feeling of what might have been. The club must have wished the season started in January, as their post-Christmas form reflected championship material in the making. In the end a fifth place in the league and an outstanding quarter-final performance against Leicester ending in a narrow 12-6 defeat, reflected a creditable season and the promise of greater things to come.

There are many exciting young talents in: Garry Becconsall (England U21's); Earl Anderson, Nathan Webber, Robin Poll, Matt Whiteley, Matt Birch (All Midland U21's) and Justin Redrup (Wales U21's); Jan Bonney (England U21's); and Charlie Mulraine (England Schools); Mark Chudleigh (England Colts); Dean Ball (Midlands B) allied to the experienced and venerable talents of England Internationals Mark Linnett and Simon Hodgkinson, and Divisional players Steve Lloyd, Peter Shillingford and Richard Moon. They all give Moseley a firm base on which to continue their redevelopment programme.

Alex Keay Director of Rugby, has had his contract extended for a further three years and adds, "The club have a fine tradition but have been somewhat shaken up by the demands of National League rugby. By building a broad base at youth level, and attracting and keeping quality players, the club are well placed to challenge the top echelons of the game.

"Attitudes have had to change on and off the field – strategic planning has given the club a vision and opportunity for the future. We have a good squad, and definite plans to improve facilities and resources at the Reddings. With the continued playing improvement and commitment to creating a centre of excellence we can provide a platform for the club and players to re-establish their place in the 1st Division and ultimately place themselves in the elite top four. We have still got a long way to go, but everyone is positive in the way forward and the challenges ahead. Consistency on and off the field will only enhance that challenge."

NEWCASTLE GOSFORTH RFC

Founded: 1877
President: C Morgan
Ground: Kingston Park Brunton Road, Kenton Bank, Foot, Newcastle upon Tyne NE13 8AF
Telephone: (44) 91 214 0422, (44) 91 271 4429
Fax: (44) 91 214 0488
Floodlights: Full playing & training lights
Spectator Capacity: 10,000
Public Transport: 400 metres, metro Tyne and Wear and bus; one mile airport
Wheelchair Access: Yes
Parking: 400 spaces
Hospitality Suites: 3
Colours: Black, green, white hoops
Change of colours: Black
No. of Teams: 7
TV Access: Yes
Secretary: G McMurchie
Treasurer: David Hall
Press Officer: K Hyland
Coach: A G B Old
!st XV Manager: K Hyiand
Captain: N Frankland
Sponsor: Reed Print and Design, and Scottish and Newcastle Breweries
League Position: 10th in 1st Division
Cup: Winners Northumberland Senior Cup

They struggled throughout the season to come to terms with the standards of the top division which they were playing in for the first time and it was no real surprise that they were relegated.

Alan Old, the former England fly-half, has recently been appointed manager and it will be interesting to see one of the more intelligent members of his profession cope with the responsibilities. Newcastle Gosforth badly need to return to the top flight.

NORTHAMPTON FC

Founded: 1880
President: R B Taylor

Ground: Franklins Gardens, Weedon Road, Northampton NN5 5BG
Telephone: (44) 604 751 543 (44) 751 755 149
Fax: (44) 604 750061
Floodlights: Main pitch
Spectator Capacity: 8,500
Public Transport: Rail 5 mins, bus depot 10 mins
Wheelchair Access: Yes
Parking: Approx 500 spaces
Hospitality Suites: 8 Boxes sponsorship suites
Colours: Black, green, gold
Nickname: Saints
No. of Teams: 4
Wired for Radio: No
TV Access: Purpose built gantry
Chief Executive: M Holmes
Secretary: R Horward
Treasurer: J A Cooper
Press Officer: B Barron
Captain: Tim Rodber
!st XV Manager: D Hurlston and B Ingram
Sponsor: Carlsberg Brewery
League Position: 5th in 1st Division
Cup: Knocked out in 4th Round
Tours Hosted: S A Barbarians
International Players: M Bayfield, I Hunter, T Rodber, P Walton, R McNaughton

Northampton had, by their recent standard,s a poor season. They lost their two controlling influences – on-the-field Wayne Shelford went off to finish his career in Italy; and off-the-field, Barrie Corless moved to Gloucester. These changes seemed to throw the club and they were well below par.

Over the past five years, Northampton have made huge strides to come to terms with the modern game. Many of their innovations are now being copied by the likes of Bath, Leicester and Harlequins. They will need to win something shortly if they are not going to be tagged as the "nearly" club.

NOTTINGHAM RFC

Founded: 1877
President: John Drapkin
Ground: Ireland Avenue, Dovecote Lane, Beeston,

Nottingham NG9 1JD
Telephone: (44)602 254238 (44) 602 224920
Spectator Capacity: 5,000
Public Transport: Railway Stn 2 mins walk
Wheelchair Access: Yes
Parking: Yes
Hospitality Suites: Four plus club house suite
Clubhouse Facilities: Bar, lounge, dining room, 3 squash courts
Colours: Green & White hoops
Change of Colours: Gold
Nickname: Green and whites
No. of Teams: Senior 2, U21, U19
Training Nights: Monday and Thursday
Wired for Radio: Yes
TV Access: Yes
Chief Executive: Alan Bragg
Secretary: Gordon Wallis
Treasurer: To be announced
Press Officer: A Starr
Coach: Peter Stone
!st XV Manager: Neil Hannah
Captain: Chris Gray
Sponsor: To be announced
League Position: 6th in 2nd Division

Nottingham's 1993-1994 season can be summed up in one word – survival! After a disastrous start to the season, by the end of November the First XV had played eight, won zero, drawn one and lost seven and were rooted to the foot of National Division 2. However, on 6 December the team won for the first time in the League and from then on won eight out of 10 league games, finishing sixth in National League 2 – a near miraculous reversal of fortune. The change of fortune on the field coincided with a major reshuffle off the field and the administration is now working hard to return the Club to its rightful position – in National League 1.

ORRELL RUFC

Founded: 1927
President: Bill Huxley
Ground: Edgehall Road, Orrell WN5 8TL
Telephone: (44) 695 623193
Spectator Capacity: 9,999

Hospitality Suites: 3
Clubhouse Facilities: Members lounge, clubroom, restaurant, medical room, shop, President's lounge
Colours: Amber and black
Change of Colours: Red
Nickname: Little Ommers
No. of Teams: Senior 4, Junior 6
Training Nights: Monday, Tuesday & Thursday
Chief Executive: Ron Pimblett
Secretary: John Arrowsmith 1 Fisher Drive, Orrell, Wigan, WN5 8QX
Telephone: (44) 942 216879
Coach: Bill Lyon
Captain: Stephen Taberner

Whither Orrell in 1994? Whither Orrell in 1995? This wonderful club is under threat. It has coped brilliantly with being a "lay-by" on the M6 for 20 years but it is finding the pace hotting up. Unfortunately, the small supply of local talent is being tempted elsewhere. This makes it doubly difficult for Orrell. But they are a gutsy club and they will come through this barren patch.

RUGBY FC

Founded: 1873
President: John Llewellyn
Ground: Webb Ellis Road , Off Bilton Road, Rugby
Telephone: (44) 788 542252
Floodlights: Yes
Spectator: 4,200
Wheelchair Access: Yes
Parking: Restricted
Clubhouse Facilities: Extensive, including sports injury clinic and disabled toilet facilities
Hospitality Suites: Three
Colours: Orange, black & white
Change of Colours: Red & white
Training Nights: Tueday and Thursday
Wired for radio: Yes
TV Access: Yes
Secretary: Ivan Cawood
Coach: Steve Hotton
1st XV Manager: Guy Steele Bodger
Captain: Mark Pennell
Sponsor: Rugby Portland Cement
League Position: Relegated to 3rd Division

Cup: Knocked out in 4th Round
International Players: Mark Rennell (England A), Trevor Bevan (England B), Mark Mapletoft (U21)

The drop from Div 1 to Div 2 has very severe financial implications but not so much from Div 2 to Div 3. In July, the old Rugby FC was dissolved with debts of £500,000 and a new club was being organised.

SALE FC

Founded: 1861
President: A Gibson
Ground: Heywood Road Brooklands, Sale, Cheshire
Telephone: (44) 61 973 6348
Tel/Fax: (44) 061 969 4124
Floodlight: Yes
Spectator Capacity: 4,160
Wheelchair Access: Yes
Clubhouse Facilities: 2 bars, large function room and 3 committee rooms
Colours: Royal blue, white hoops
Change of Colours: Red & white irregular hoops
No. of Teams: 5 Senior, 1 women's senior
Training Nights: Tuesday and Thursday
TV Access: Yes
Chairman: A Castre
Secretary: Laura Murrell
Treasurer: Doug Barden
Press Officer: Christine Kenrick
Coach: Paul Turner
Captain: Mike Kenrick
Director of Rugby: Brian Wilkinson
League Position: Champions 2nd Division
Cup Position: Beaten by Harlequins in quarter-finals
Internationals: Paul Turner
Miscellaneous: Phil Jee scored his 100th point for the club. Simon Verbick was second highest try scorer in the country.

It is an indication of Sale's performance last season that they had the best points for and the best defensive record of any team in the five Courage Divisions. On their way to becoming Second Division Champions they broke two

Courage records in the same game – the best points difference (88-9 v Otley) and most tries scored (Simon Verbick: 5). The season got off to a flying start with wins against London Scottish, Saracens and Waterloo. Defeats by Otley and Moseley and points dropped in the draw against Wakefield were the hiccups of the first half of the league season but it ended on a high with a convincing defeat of league leaders West Hartlepool. The second half saw only one defeat, again at the hands of bogey side Moseley but Sale maintained their position in the table behind leaders West Hartlepool. However, a surprise defeat for West Hartlepool with one game to go, put Sale on top for the first time and the last match of the season became the Championship decider. A draw would clinch the title and that's what they got, to be confirmed as Division Two Champions.

SARACENS FC

Founded: 1876
President: John Heggadon
Ground: Bramley Road Sports Ground, Chaseside, Southgate, London N14 4AB
Telephone: (44) 81 449 3770 (44) 81 449 8662
Fax: (44) 81 449 9101
Floodlights: Training Pitches
Spectator Capacity: 3,000
Public Transport: Cockfosters Tube
Wheelchair Access: Yes
Parking: 200 spaces
Hospitality Suites: No
Clubhouse Facilities: Bar and tea bar
Colours: Black, red star and crescent
Change of colours: Black, red & white hoops
Nickname: Sarries
No. of Teams: Senior 7, Junior 11
Training Nights: Monday to Friday
Wired for Radio: Yes
TV Access: Yes
Chief Executive: Bruce Claridge
Secretary: Barney Richards, 36 Stone Hall Road, Winchmore Hill, London N21 1LP
Telephone: (44) 81 360 4061 (H), (44)81 372 7788 (W)
Treasurer: Chris Sneath

Press Officer: Bill Edwards 15 Braemar Court, 119 Cockfosters Road
Coach: John Davies Mark Evans
1st XV Manager: Bim Downes
Captain: Brian Davies
International Player: John Buckton

Relegation and then an exodus of several of their best players were bitter pills for Saracens to swallow, but they bounced back and so easily could have gained promotion at the first attempt.

It took time for the side to gel and we then saw a new and impressive back row emerge. Anthony Diprose became the latest No 8 to roll off the Saracens production line, winning caps at England A, Emerging England and Under-21 levels and won the Young Player of the Year Award. Alongside him were blind side John Green, who arrived from Bridgend, and Richard Hill, from Salisbury whose pace won many plaudits including a place in the England U21 side. Another to play a key role and win a place in the Emerging England squad was full back Andy Tunningley.

Saracens were narrowly defeated at home by both West Harlepool and Sale and there was a similar result away to West. Those matches could so easily have gone Saracens way and then promotion would have been theirs.

With all personnel staying for next season, plus the return of centre Dan Dooley from London Irish, and several outstanding youngsters, prospects can only be good for Saracens in season 1994-1995.

WAKEFIELD FC

Founded: 1901
President: John Waind
Ground: College Grove Sports Club, Eastmoor Road, Wakefield, West Yorks WF1 3RR
Telephone: (44) 924 372038
Floodlight: Yes
Spectator Capacity: 4,000
Clubhouse Facilities: Lounge, bar, catering, separate sponsors room
Colours: Black & gold quarters

Change of Colours: Gold with black hoop, or red.
No. of Teams: 4 Senior, 1 Junior
Training Nights: Monday and Thursday
Chairman: Nigel Foster
Secretary: Jim Coulson
Press Officer: Jim Coulson
Coach: Jim Kilfoyle
1st XV Manager: Andy Gomersal
Captain: Mike Jackson
League Position: 4th Div 2
Cup: Yorkshire Cup winners '93/'94
International Players: Mike Harrison, Dave Scully
Touring Sides Hosted: Griqueland West, South Africa

Satisfactory year. At one time they were in a position where they could have gone far but suffered close defeats. However they finished a very respectable 4th. Bogged down by sides more forward dominated than themselves they were unable to show flair in their back line. Plans for this year included a tour to Canada in August as a springboard for next season so that new players get a chance to gel with the existing side before the start of the gruelling league matches.

WASPS FC

Founded: 1867
President: W Treadwell
Ground: Repton Avenue, Sudbury, Nr Wembley, Middlesex HAO 3DW
Telephone: (44) 81 902 4220
Fax: (44) 81 900 2659
Press Box: (44) 81 902 4220
Bar: (44) 81 902 4220
Floodlights: 2 Main pitches & training
TV Access: Yes
Spectator Capacity: 5,000
Public Transport: Piccadilly Line, Sudbury Town
Wheelchair Access: Yes
Parking: About 500 spaces
Hospitality Suites: Yes main suite & 5 others
Hospitality Suites: One
Clubhouse Facilities: Bars, restaurant, changing, medical.
Colours: Black, Gold wasp on left breast
Change of Colours: Black and gold stripes
No. of Teams: 12
Training Nights: Tuesday, Wednesday and Thursday
Chief Executive: Sir Patrick Lowrey
Secretary: Ivor Mountlake, c/o Wasps FC, Repton Ave, Sudbury, Middlesex
Treasurer: Malcom Evans
Press Officer: John Gasson, The Manor, Willington, Bedfordshire MK44 3PX
Coach: Rob Smith
Captain: Dean Ryan
League Position: 3rd Div 1
Cup: Knocked out 4th round
International Players: Rob Andrew, Jeff Probyn, Chris Oti, Dean Ryan, Fran Clough, Huw Davies, Rob Lokowski, Steve Bates, Damien Hopley, Lawrence Dallaglio
Tours Overseas: France

Wasps flattered to deceive last season. This is a club with huge resources but like Northampton needs to put some silverware in the cupboard soon.

WATERLOO FC

Founded: 1882
President: C R Brennend
Ground: Blundell Sands, The Pavilion, St Anthonys Road, Blundell Sands, Liverpool
Fax: (44) 51 924 0900
Telephone: (44) 51 924 4552
Spectator Capacity: 8,900
Wheelchair Access: Yes
Clubhouse Facilities: 2 bars, a gym and a dining room
Hospitality Suites: 2
Colours: Myrtle and scarlet with white hoops
Change of Colours: Green
No. of Teams: 4 Senior, U21 & U18
Chairman: R L Wilson
Secretary: Keith Alderson
Press Officer: A Cove
Coach: Mike Briers
Captain: Peter Buckton
League Position: 7th Div 2
Cup: Knocked out in 4th round
Touring Sides Hosted: Buffalo USA, Blaina

Special Awards: Lancashire Cup Winners

After last season's promise the team suffered a terrible run of injuries which put paid to promotion ambitions early in the season.The strength of the squad reflected their ability and where many would have succumbed to relegation Waterloo, the club were able to maintain their league Div 2 position and will hopefully, this season's injuries permitting, be able to challenge for the top flight.

WEST HARTLEPOOL FC

Founded: 1881
President: Nev Brown
Ground: Brierton Lane, Hartlepool, Cleveland TS25 5DR
Telephone: (44) 429 272640
Office: (44) 429 233149
Spectator Capacity: 6,100
Clubhouse Facilities: 2 committee rooms, a lounge and lounge bar
Hospitality Suites: 2
Colours: Green, red, white hoop shirts, white shorts and green socks
Change of Colours: Red shirts
No. of Teams: 4 Senior, U21, 7 Juniors, plus Minis
Training Nights: Tuesday & Thursday
Chairman: Bob Bateman
Secretary: Tony Savage
Press Officer: Jon-Jo Dixon Barker
Coach: Dave Stubbs
Captain: John Stabler

West Hartlepool are back in the big time once again having suffered the ignominy of relegation a year ago. They are fiercely ambitious and have begun a heavy recruitment drive in Scotland which should pay dividends.

FRANCE

By Jonathan Cavender

There is no great art to selecting the Top 20 clubs in France – the difficulty lies in placing them in the right order.

The leagues are well drawn, to create as fair and rigorous a test as possible during the season.

1. The top 32 teams play in four pools of eight; they play each other home and away, 14 matches;

2. The top four in each Pool go in to a sort of Super league, playing home and away in groups of four. The top two in each of these groups go in to the Quarter Final knock-out phase;

3. The bottom four in each pool go into a League called the Moga Cup, fighting for survival. In each of the four leagues of four, the bottom team will be relegated, the next to bottom go in to play-offs with the 2nd placed teams in Group B. In 1993 four teams were promoted to Group A; in 1994 two of those were sent back where they came from, the other two were in the play-offs.

The top 16 are therefore beyond dispute; taking a flyer on the next four places, the top 20 in alphabetical order are:

AGEN

President: Guy Basquet
Stadium: Armandie, rue Pierre de Coubertin, 47000
Capacity: 12,000
Telephone: 53.98.12.64
Floodlights: Yes
Coach: Charly Nieucel and Jean Louis Bernes
Captain: Philippe Sella
Record: Champions: 1930, 1945, 1962,1965, 1966, 1976, 1982, 1988
1994 - Phase 1: Top of Pool 3
Phase 2: 2nd in Group 2;
Quarter finalists

AUCH

President: Jacques Lestrade
Stadium: Patrice-Boucas, ave des Pyrenees, 32000 Auch
Capacity: 6,500
Telephone: 62.05.06.96
Floodlights: No
Coach: Jacques Brunel
Captain: Stephane Graou
1994 - Phase 1: 2nd in Pool 2
Phase 2: 4th in Group 2

BAYONNE

Stadium: Municipal des Sports, 64100 Bayonne
Capacity: 25,000
Telephone: 59.63.93.96
Floodlights: Yes
Coach: Jean-Louis Luneau and Michel Bafcop
Captain: Jean-Michel Gonzales
Record: Champions 1913,1934 and 1943
1994 - Phase 1: 4th in Pool 1
Phase 2: 3rd in Group 2

BEGLES

President: Alain Moga and Michel Moga
Stadium: Stade Andre-Moga, complexe Delphin-Loche, 33130 Begles
Capacity: 11,000
Telephone: 56.85.94.01
Floodlights: Yes
Coach: Christian Lanta and Francis Lartigue
Captain: Andre Berthozat
Record: Champions 1969, 1991
1994 - Phase 1: Top of Pool 1
Phase 2: 3rd in Group 1

BIARRITZ

President:Serge Blanco
Stadium: Municipal d'Aguilera, rue Cino del Duca, 64200 Biarritz
Capacity: 15,000
Telephone: 59.23.93.42
Floodlights: Yes
Coach: Robert Bernos and Alain Marot
Captain: Jean Condom
Record: Champions 1936, 1939
1994 - Phase 1: 2nd in Pool 3
Phase 2: 4th in Group 3

BOURGOIN

President:Daniel Garnier
Stadium: Pierre-Rajon, ave Professeur Tixier, 38300 Bourgoin-Jallieu
Capacity: 6,000
Telephone: 74.28.01.00
Floodlights: Yes
Coach: Michel Couturas and Bernard Ferre

Captain: Marc Cecillon
1994 - Phase 1: 3rd in Pool 3
Phase 2: 2nd in Group 4

BRIVE

President: Jean-Jacques Gourdy
Stadium: Parc Municipal des Sports, 19105 Brive
Capacity: 15,000
Telephone: 55.74.20.14
Floodlights: Yes
Coach: Jean-Michel Daures
Captain: J Boher
1994 - Phase 1: 5th in Pool 1
Phase 2: 2nd in Moga Groupe 1

CASTRES

President: Pierree-Yves Revol
Stadium: Pierre-Antoine, rue des Bisseous, 81100 Castres
Capacity: 8,000
Telephone: 63.35.32.96
Floodlights: No
Coach: Alain Gaillard and Jacques Cauquil
Captain: Frances Rui
Record: Champions 1949, 1950 and 1993
1994 - Phase 1: 2nd in Pool 1
Phase 2: 4th in Group 4

COLOMIERS

President: Michel Bendichou
Stadium: Stade Selery, allee de Briere, 31700 Colomiers
Capacity: 7,000
Telephone: 61.78.92.11
Floodlights: No
Coach: Christian Deleris and Jean-Claude Skrela
Captain: Fabien Galthie
1994 - Phase 1: 3rd in Pool 4
Phase 2: 4th in Pool 1

DAX

President: Jena-Pierre Bastiat
Stadium: Parc Municipal des Sports, bd P-Lasaosa, 40100 Dax
Capacity: 18,000
Telephone: 58.74.14.02
Floodlights: Yes
Coach: Francois Gachet. Jacques Ibanez, Alain Benoit

Captain: Olivier Roumat
1994 - Phase 1: 4th in Pool 2
    Phase 2: 1st in Group 4
    Semi-finalists

GRENOBLE

President: Seraphin Rinaldi
Stadium: Lesdiguieres, 126 Cours de la Liberation, 38100 Grenoble
Capacity: 15,000
Telephone: 76.44.09.63
Floodlights: Yes
Coach: Michel Ringeval
Captain: Herve Chaffardon
Record: Champions 1954
1994 - Phase 1: 3rd in Pool 2
    Phase 2: 1st in Group 3
    Semi finalist

MONTFERRAND (ALSO KNOWN AS CLERMONT FERRAND)

President: Robert Lefrancois
Stadium: Marcel-Michelin, rue de Catarous, 63021 Clermont-Ferrand
Capacity: 13,000
Telephone: 73.24.87.01
Floodlights: Yes
Coach: Patrick Boucheix and Bertrand Rioux
Captain: Jean-Marc Lhermet
1994 - Phase 1: 3rd in Pool 1
    Phase 2: 3rd in Group 3
    Finalists

NARBONNE

President: Andre Marateuch and Francois Sangalli
Stadium: Parc des Sports, av De-Coubertin, 11105 Narbonne
Capacity: 15,000
Telephone: 68.41.76.93
Floodlights: Yes
Coach: A Paco and J Delmas
Captain: Henri Sanz
Record: Champions 1936 and 1979
1994 - Phase 1: 4th in Pool 3
    Phase 2: 2nd in Group 1
    Quarter finalists

NICE

President: Gabriel Degeorges
Stadium: du Ray, av Gravier, 018100 Nice
Capacity: 22,000

Telephone: 93.72.06.06
Floodlights: Yes
Coach: Eric Buchet and Vincent Romulus
Captain: Jean-Francois Tordo
1994 - Phase 1: 7th in Pool 2
    Phase 2: 1st in Moga
    Group 2

NIMES

President: Louis Gagniere
Stadium: Nicolas-Kaufman, le Mas de Ville, 3000 Nimes
Capacity: 5,000
Telephone: 66.29.24.97
Floodlights: Yes
Coach: Marc Andrieu and Michel Berard
Captain: Chritsophe Barriere
1994 - Phase 1: 5th in Pool 3
    Phase 2: 1st in Moga
    Group 3

PERPIGNAN

President: Jacky Rodor
Stadium: Stade Aime-Girard, 66000 Perpignan
Capacity: 10,000
Telephone: 68.61.18.18
Floodlights: Yes
Coach: Paul Foussat and Jean-Louis Arcour
Captain: Alain Macabiau
Record: Champions 1914, 1921, 1925, 1938, 1944, 1955
1994 - Phase 1: 1st in Pool 4
    Phase 2: 3rd in Group 4

RACING

President: Jean Pierre labro
Stadium: Yves-du-Manoir, 12 rue Francois-Fabert, 92700 Colombes
Capacity: 40,000
Telephone: 45..67.55.86
Floodlights: Yes
Coach: J-L Ribot and Eric Blanc
Captain: Xavier Blond
Record: Champions 1892, 1900, 1902, 1959, 1990
1994 - Phase 1: 2nd in Pool 4
    Phase 2: 2nd in Group 3

SBUC (STADE BORDELAISE UNIVERSITE CLUB)

President: Bernard Junca
Stadium: rue Ferdinand-de-

Lesseps, 33110 Le Bouscat
Capacity: 7,000
Telephone: 56.57.45.45.
Floodlights: Yes
Coach: Jean Trillo, Bernard Laporte
Captain: Roland Lafon
Record: Champions 1899, 1904, 1905, 1906, 1907, 1909, 1911
1994 - Phase 1: 5th in Pool 4
    Phase 2: 2nd in Moga
    Group 4

TOULON

President: Patrick Rouard
Stadium: Felix-Mayol, 83000 Toulon
Capacity: 18,000
Telephone: Yes
Floodlights: 94.46.20.31
Coach: Jean-Claude Ballatore and Alain Carbonel
Captain: Leon Loppy
Record: Champions 1961, 1987 and 1992
1994 - Phase 1: 4th in Pool 4
    Phase 2: 1st in Group 2
    Quarter-finalists

TOULOUSE

President: Rene Bouscatel and jacques fabre
Stadium: Les Sept-Deniers, 114 rue des Troenes, 31200 Toulouse
Capacity: 12,000
Telephone: 61.57.05.05
Floodlights: Yes
Coach: G Noves and S Lairle
Captain: Albert Cigagna
Record: Champions 1912, 1922, 1923, 1924, 1926, 1927, 1947, 1985, 1986, 1989
1994 - Phase 1: Top of Pool 2
    Phase 2: Top of Group 1
    Champions

CHAMPIONSHIP IN 1994
Champions: Toulouse
Runners up: Montferrand

The final between Toulouse and Montferrand was a feast of rugby although there were only two tries. Both sides ran at will and showed a desire to entertain after a drab season. Toulouse won by 22-16 because they had the experience when the chips were down. Losing quarter-finalists: Agen, Toulon, Bougoin, and Narbonne. Losing semi-finalists: Grenoble and Dax. In the *du Manoir*, Montferrand were once again the bridesmaid, losing to Perpignan. The team were without some of their stars a week after the championship final and could not scale the heights.

Relegated from Group A: Béziers, Lyon, Mont de Marson, Lourdes.

Promoted: Tyrosse, Chateaurenard, Mandelieu, St-Paul-les-Dax.

PROFESSIONALISM

There has been an attempt to recognise the pressure on players and clubs, to acknowledge that there is money involved, and to limit payments to an acceptable proportion of a club's budget. The top 16 clubs have signed an agreement to limit expense payments to any one player to FFr160,000 a year (approximately £15,000).

The period of *mutations*, when players can change clubs, is limited to three weeks. Through a system of *licences rouges*, Test players who change clubs could be made to play in the second XV of their new club for up to a year. One club president calculated that during this three-week period he made 2,000 phone calls and drove 5,000km in search of new players.

FIXTURES

The dates have been fixed for the 1994-95 season. The *du Manoir* starts in August and has its final on 14 May. The top 32 start their championship campaign on 4 September; phase 2 is from 29 January to 2 April; the quarter-finals are on 16 April; the semis a week later; and the final on 8 May (earlier than usual because of RWC 95).

IRELAND

Irish rugby is now comprehensively "leagued" with every club in the four ICL divisions.

The first division was increased from nine to 11 teams with clubs playing one another once. There has been increasing interest by the public and the media in the leagues but the standard is still variable. Wanderers, having been promoted from the second division, did not alas last and were then relegated along with Greystones who fell apart in the latter half of the season. Once again Cork Constitution were the runners-up.

INSURANCE CORPORATION LEAGUE TABLES
(as at March 18th, 1994)

FIRST DIVISION

	P	W	D	L	F	A	pts
Garryowen	10	18	0	2	172	108	16
Cork Con	10	7	0	3	201	123	14
Blackrock	10	7	0	3	137	99	14
Dungannon	10	5	0	5	181	130	10
Lansdowne	10	5	0	5	162	167	10
St. Mary's	10	5	0	5	157	163	10
Y Munster	10	5	0	5	102	149	10
Shannon	10	4	0	6	107	104	8
Old Wesley	10	4	0	6	114	138	8
Greystones	10	4	0	6	97	156	8
Wanderers	10	1	0	9	141	243	2

Champions: Garryowen
Relegated: Wanderers & Greystones
Top Scorers: 104 – K Megarry *(Dungannon)*; 103 – G O'Sullivan *(Cork Constitution)*; 93 – K Smith *(Garryowen)*; 90 – C O'Shea *(Lansdowne)*; 87 – A McGowan *(Blackrock)*; 72 – A O'Halloran *(Young Munster)*; 65 – A Daly *(Wanderers)*; N Barry *(St. Marys)*; 63 – N Farren *(Old Wesley)*; 61 – G Harvey *(Greystones)*
Tries: 5 – D O'Dowd *(Cork Con)*; 4 – R Wallace *(Garryowen)*; N Murray *(Cork Con)*; B Glennon *(Lansdowne)*; 3 – N Woods *(Blackrock)*; C O'Shea *(Lansdowne)*; A Foley *(Shannon)*; R Carey *(Dungannon)*

SECOND DIVISION

	P	W	D	L	F	A	Pts
Instonians	10	18	0	2	205	100	16
Sunday's Well	10	8	0	2	184	118	16
Ballymena	10	7	0	3	214	125	14
Old Belvedere	10	7	0	3	141	125	14
Bangor	10	5	0	5	122	189	10
Terenure	10	4	1	5	149	112	9
Malone	10	4	1	5	125	141	9
Old Crescent	10	4	0	6	173	150	8
Dolphin	10	4	0	6	139	144	8
Galwegians	10	3	0	7	113	124	6
Ballina	10	0	0	10	72	309	0

Promoted: Instonians and Sunday's Well
Relegated: Bellina & Galwegians
Top Scores: 111 – D McAleese *(Ballymena)*; 94 – S Laing *(Instonians)*; 88 – B Begley *(Old Crescent)*: 76 – B Murphy *(Old Belvedere)*; 76 – R Daly *(Sunday's Wells)*; 71 – D Lynagh *(Terenure)*
Tries: 6 – D Smyth *(Ballymena)*; 3 – A Matchett, W Pollock *(Ballymena)*, G Maxwell *(Bangor)*, J Clarke *(Dolphin)*, W Norse *(OB)*, A Reddan, B Begley, E O'Sullivan *(OC)*, P Walsh *(Terenure)*, G McCausland *(Instonians)*, R Daly *(SW)*

BALLYMENA

Founded: 1887
President: Wilie John Macbride
Ground: Eaton Park, 209 Race View Road, Ballymena BT42 4HV
Telephone: 010 353 266 656 746 010 353 266 653 903
Floodlights: Three training pitches
Spectator Capacity: 3,000
Public Transport: Station two miles
Wheelchair Access: Yes
Parking: Yes
Hospitality Suites: Miller/McBride Room
Clubhouse Facilities: Bars, dance hall, dining room, games room, snooker, squash, table, tennis, bowls and darts
Colours: Black and white
Change of Colours: Red jerseys
Nickname: Braidmen
No. of Teams: Senior 6, Youth 4 and Mini rugby
Training Nights: Tuesday and Thursday
Chief Executive: Dr H Simpson
Secretary: Guy McCullough 2 Harberton Park Circular Road, Ballymena BT43 6NF
Telephone: 010 353 266 49 764
Treasurer: T I Simpson
Press Officer: Gil McCollough
Coach: M Crabbe
1st XV Manager: R Cole
Sponsor: Clerical Medical Investment

League Position: 3rd in Div 2
Still in the second division having been relegated last year, Ballymena finished third, two points behind Sunday's Well and Instonians, both of whom were promoted.

BLACKROCK COLLEGE

Founded: 1882
President: Barry O'Keeffe
Ground: Somerset, Stradbrook Road, Blackrock, Co Dublin
Telephone: 010 353 280 5967
Ticket Line: 010 353 280 2295
Floodlights: Training pitches
Spectator Capacity: 5,000
Public Transport: Bus and rail half a mile
Wheelchair Access: Yes
Parking: 250 spaces
Hospitality Suites: One
Clubhouse Facilities: 3 bars, function room
Colours: Royal blue and white stripes
Change of Colours: Red and navy
Nickname: Rocks
No. of Teams: 11
Training Nights: Tuesday and Thursday
Wired for radio: Yes
TV Access: Yes
Secretary: Gerry Power
22 Dundela Avenue,
Sandy Cove, co Dublin
Telephone: 010 353 280 6046
Treasurer: Seamus Taaffe
Press Officer: Gerry Power
Coach: Eddie O'Sullivan
!st XV Manager: Jimmy Smith
Sponsor: 1st National Building Society
League Position: 3rd Div 1
International Players: Neil Francis, A Rolland

They consolidated their position in Division One finishing a very respectable third (on goal difference) only two points from winners Garryowen.

CORK CONSTITUTION

Founded: 1892
President: Cork Constitution
Ground: Temple Hill
Ballin Temple, Cork

Telephone: 010 353 21 292 563
Floodlights: Training Pitches
Spectator Capacity: 7,000
Public Transport: Bus near gate
Wheelchair Access: Yes
Parking: Yes
Hospitality Suites: Yes
Clubhouse Facilities: Bar and lounge
Colours: Black, blue and white
Change of colours: White, black and blue
No. of Teams: Senior 6, Junior 10
Training Nights: Tuesday and Thursday
Wired for radio: Yes
TV Access: Yes
Secretary: John Hyland,
Auburn, St Francis Avenue,
Off College Road, Cork
Telephone: 010 353 21 341 727 (H);
010 353 21 277 116 (W)
Treasurer: Jom Murphy
Press Officer: Michael Keys
Coach: Walton Morrissey
1st XV Manager: Walton Morrisey
Captain: Len Dineen
League Position: Runners-up Div 1
Cup: Semi-finalists
International players: Michael Bradley, Philip Soden, Brian Walsh, Gabriel Fulsher, David Corkney

In four seasons of league competition, the 1993-94 runners-up Cork Constitution have now finished second twice and won in the inaugural year. Last season they also won the Cork Charity Cup. Five of their players went to Australia with the Irish national squad; but, of the 30-man squad, only five are from Cork. Second two years in succession must make them to ponder what they have to do to lift the championship.

DUNGANNON

Founded: 1873
President: Arthur Hamilton
Ground: Stevenson Park, Dungannon
Floodlights: Yes
Spectator Capacity: 4,500
Public Transport: Bus one mile
Wheelchair Access: Yes
Parking: 400 spaces
Hospitality Suites: One

Clubhouse Facilities: 2 bars, squash, tennis courts
Colours: Blue and white hoops
Change of colours: White
No. of Teams: Senior 5
Training Nights: Monday and Wednesday
Ground: 010 355 8687 23601
Secretary: Derek Clements
14 Springfield Lane,
Dungannon BT70 1QX
Telephone: Dungannon 22549
Treasurer: F S McManus
Press Officer: Don Attridge
1st XV Manager: Ken Armstrong
Captain: Hugh McCaughey
Sponsor: First Trust Bank
League Position: 4th Div 1
Cup Position: Winners Ulster Cup

The only Ulster side in the premier division, Dungannon improved from sixth in 1992-93 to fourth in 1993-4 and must be the outsider's for the championship title this season.

GARRYOWEN FC

Founded: 1884
President: John Fahey
Ground: Dooradoyle, Limerick
Telephone: 010 351 61 227 672
Press Box: 010 353 61 227 672
Bar: 010 353 61 227 672
Floodlights: Yes
Spectator Capacity: 11,000
Public Transport: Bus half a mile
Wheelchair Access: Yes
Parking: 50 spaces
Colours: Navy blue, yellow, white
No. of Teams: Senior 1, Junior 2, Under Age 5
Wired for Radio: Yes
TV Access: Yes
Chief Executive: Frank Hogan
Secretary: Ger Clarke
17 Athlunkard Avenue,
Shannon Banks, Corbally,
Limerick
Tel: Limerick 304091 Ext 278
Treasurer: Tony O' Shea
Press Officer: Gerry O'Mahoney
Coach: Andy Leslie
1st XV Manager: Daniel Hayes
Captain: Paul Hogan
Sponsor: Volkswagen-Audi
League Position: Winners of the League Div 1

Fortunately for their supporters, Garryowen returned to the top of the tree winning the championships again as they did in 1991-92. Last year's performance, which saw them languish one off the bottom, has been well and truly forgotten.

GREYSTONES

Founded: 1937
President: Paul O'Brien
Ground: Dr Hickey Park Delgany Road, Greystones
Telephone: 010 353 287 4640
Bar: 010 353 287 4814
Floodlights: Yes
Spectator Capacity: 5,000
Public Transport: Bus and train
Wheelchair Access: Yes
Parking: Yes
Hospitality Suites: Adapted clubhouse facilities
Clubhouse Facilities: Full
Colours: Green and white stripes
Change of Colours: Solid green
Nickname: Stones
No. of Teams: Senior 10, Youth 16
Training Nights: Monday to Thursday
TV Access: Yes
Chief Executive: Joe Devine
Secretary: Tommy Nolan
Treasurer: Noel Geraghty
Press Officer: Richard Roche, Rosciar, Killin Carrig Road, Greystones, Co. Wicklow
Telephone: 010 353 287 4572 (H); 010 353 681 455 (W)
Fax: 010 353 681 477
Coach: Pierce Power
1st XV Manager: Denzil Jones
Captain: Michael Carney
League Position: 10th Div 1, relegated to Div 2 for next season
Cup: Final Leinster Cup

This was a season best forgotten; the side that finished fourth two seasons ago was relegated this time round. They will be back.

LANSDOWNE

Founded: 1872
President: Johnnie Mitchell
Ground: Lansdowne Road, Dublin 4
Telephone: 010 353 668 9300,

010 353 668 9292
Bar: 010 353 668 9300
Floodlights: Yes
Spectator Capacity: 40,000
Public Transport: Rapid Rail
Wheelchair Access: Yes
Parking: Limited
Clubhouse Facilities: 2 full bars and kitchen
Colours: Red, yellow, black hoops
No. of Teams: 1st XV 10, U19, Junior 8, plus mini rugby
Training Nights: Tuesday and Thursday
Wired for Radio: Yes
TV Access: Yes
Secretary: Frank Thompson 18 Merlyn Park, Ballsbridge, Dublin 4
Telephone: 010 353 269 2398 (H)
Treasurer: Joe Leddin
Press Officer: Aidan McNally, 60 Beechpark Drive, Dublin 18
Telephone: 010 353 289 6386 (H)
Coach: Paul Clinch
1st XV Manager: Frank Forrest
Captain: Fergus Aherne
Sponsor: Eagle Star
League Position: 5th Div 1

Lansdowne finished level on 10 points with the likes of Dungannon, St Mary's and Young Munster but on goal difference were placed fifth. This was most encouraging in their first season in the first division. Perhaps Eric Elwood can lead them to the top this year.

ST MARY'S COLLEGE, DUBLIN

Founded: 1900
President: Paul Sheeran
Ground: Templeville Road
Address: Templeogue, Dublin 6
Telephone: 010 353 900 4440
Floodlights: Yes
Spectator Capacity: 9,000
Public Transport: Bus outside ground
Wheelchair Access: Yes
Parking: Yes
Hospitality Suites: Yes
Clubhouse Facilities: Bars and lounge
Colours: Royal blue with white star
No. of Teams: Senior 8, Under-19 1
Training Nights: Tuesday and Thursday

Wired for radio: Yes
TV Access: Yes
Secretary: John Pyne 16 Glendown Lawn, Templeogue, Dublin 6W
Telephone: 010 849 2677
Treasurer: Arthur Costello
Press Officer: David Moloney 51 Leopardstown Park, Blackrock, Co Dublin
Telephone: 010 353 283 1861(H); 010 353 283 1861(W)
Fax: 010 353 283 4481
Coach: Eddie Wigglesworth
1st XV Manager: Jim Curran
Captain: Kevin Devlin
Sponsor: Holsten Pils
League Position: 6th Div 1

St Mary's lost their way and finished sixth with five wins and five losses.

WANDERERS

Founded: 1870
President: Kevin McGowan
Ground: Play at Lansdowne and Merrion Road, Dublin 4
Telephone: 010 353 269 5272 (Merrion Road), 010 353 668 9275 (Lansdowne Road)
Floodlights: Training Pitches
Spectator Capacity: 55,000
Public Transport: At Lansdowne
Wheelchair Access: Yes
Parking: Yes
Hospitality Suites: At Lansdowne
Clubhouse Facilities: Bar and dining facilities
Colours: Blue, black and white
Change of Colours: Red
No. of Teams: Senior 8
Training Nights: Tuesday to Thursday
Wired for radio: Yes
TV Access: Yes
Secretary: Joseph McDermot 67 Wyatville Park, Louglinstown, Co Dublin
Telephone: 010 280 5633
Treasurer: Tony Wyse
Press Officer: Sam Simmington
Coach: Ian Burns
1st XV Manager: Paul Kendrick
Captain: Jamsie O'Riordan

One of the three clubs promoted from the second division last year, they never fully adjusted to the quality of the premier league and were relegated back to the second division.

YOUNG MUNSTER RFC

Founded: 1895
President: Michael Murray
Ground: Tom Clifford Park, Greenfields, Rosbrien, Derryknockane, Rosbrien
Telephone: 010 353 61 228 433, 010 353 61 301 163
Bar: 010 353 61 228 433
Floodlights: Training Pitches
Spectator Capacity: 10,000
Public Transport: Rail 800 metres
Wheelchair Access: Yes
Parking: 200 spaces
Clubhouse Facilities: 2 Bars
Colours: Black and amber
Nickname: The Wasps
No. of Teams: Senior 4
Training Nights: Tuesday and Thursday
Secretary: Maurice Quinn Mill Road, Limerick
Telephone: 010 353 61 229 069 (H); 010 353 61 301 163 (W)
Treasurer: John Cowhey
Press Officer: Maurice Quinn
Coach: Tony Grant
1st XV Manager: Michael Foley
Captain: Mark Fitzgerald
Sponsor: Bus Eireann
League Position: 7th Div 1
Cup: Finalists Munster Cup

Champions in 1992-3, Young Munster struggled to maintain their form this last season and finished a disappointing seventh though they were level on points with St Mary's, Lansdowne, and Dungannon.

ITALY

By Andrea Passarini

In the last season the first division of the Italian Championship had 12 teams and the second 16 teams. After the end of the regular season eight teams go through to play-offs; the first seven

in the first division were Milan, L'Aquila, Benetton, Simod Petraca, MDP Roma, Panto San Dona and Amatori Catania, plus the winner of the second division, Bologna.

The final in Padua created a surprise because Milan, considered the top club, were defeated by L'Aquila. Milan have several international players and they include the Cuttitta twins, Massimo, Marcello, Properzi and Giovanelli, the Italian captain; plus the Wallabies', Tim Gavin and Jason Little.

Each team plays on a home and away basis except in the final. The best player in the finals were probably the South Africans Danie Gerber and Wim Wisser who played for L'Aquila. Their full-back Ghizzoni is now 39 and the most capped Italian player, having appeared in 60 internationals. Other L'Aquila stalwarts include Troiani and Pietrosanti with emerging players such as Castellani, Alfonsetti and Ciaone.

L'Aquila, who had not won the championship since 1982, beat Benetton Treviso in the semi-final. Treviso, who had played in every final since 1988, included Michael Lynagh, the Australian captain, and Rob Penney, captain of Canterbury, as well as eight Italian internationals.

In the other semi-final MPD Roma included New Zealanders Wayne Shelford and Lawrence Little. The club has signed Gardner from Rovigo and the Argentine-born Pertile, who has seven caps, in their effort to win the title in 1994-95.

In April in Padua there was an invitation match in memory of Cameron Oliver – a South African killed in a car crash in 1993 – with many international visitors such as Gavin Hastings, Sean Linneen, Nass Botha and Brendan Mullin. Oliver was a South African killed in a car crash in 1993.

**RESULTS
SEMI-FINALS
Milan beat MDP Roma 35-16 and 40-13; L'Aquila beat Benetton Treviso 15-12 in a play-off (they won the first match 33-24 and lost the return 16-53);**

**FINAL
L'Aquila 23 Milan 14**

AMATORI CATANIA

Founded: 1963
Colours: White and pink
Address: Amatori Catania, V.le Ruggero di Lauria 2, 95100 Catamoa
Tel: + 95 371342
Fax: +95 441566
Ground address: Campo Comunale, S Maria Goretti, Villaggio S M Goretti, Catania Tel: +95 7231050/345707
President: Silvestro Stazzone
Director of Sport: Benito Paolone
Secretary: Guiseppe Paladino
Public Relations: Paolo Boccaccio
Doctor Roberto Di Stafano
Physiotherapist: Franco D'Amore

L'AQUILA

Founded: 1936
Colours: Black and green
Address: L'Aquila Rugby, s.s. 17 Ovest, Loc. Centi Colella, 67100 L'Aquila
Tel: 0862 317350
Fax: 0862 317400
Ground address: Stadio Comunale, Tommaso Fattori, V le della Croce Rossa, L'Aquila
Tel: 0862 645305
Honours: Champions 1967, 1969, 1981, 1982
Cup Winners: 1973, 1981
President: Ettore Pietrosanti (0862 419267)
Vice President: Raffaele Gallucci
Secretary: Stefania Bianchi
Treasurer: Luciano Cococcetta
Technical Director: Pino Lusi
First Team Coach: Massimo Mascioletti (0862 412473)
Doctor: Pasquale Valentini
Physiotherapist: Vittorio Manso

BENETTON TREVISO

Founded: 1932
Colours: White, blue, green
Address: Benetton Rugby Treviso, via di Nascimben, 1/b, Treviso
Tel: 0422 324242/324238
Fax: 0422 403340
Ground address: Stadio Comu-

nale, di Monigo, Via Olimpia
Tel: 0422 324242/430362
Honours: Champions: 1956, 1978, 1983, 1989, 1992
Cup Winners: 1970
Runners-Up: 1982, 1983, 1984, 1990, 1992
President: Arrigo Manavello (0422 549291)
Vice President: Amerino Zatta (0422 383115)
General Manager: F Gaetaniello (0422 405852)
Secretary: Roberto Trevisiol
Public Relations: P Pregnolato (0422 547606)
Team Manager: Franco Pavan
First Team Captain: Wayne Smith
Coordinator, Juniors: Giovanni Bugno
Physiotherapist: Arturo Cenedese, Roberto Pontello, Paola Franzan
Sponsor: Benetton SpA

LLOYD ITALICO ROVIGO
Founded: 1935
Colours: Red and blue
Address: Lloyd Italico Rugby Rovigo, Viale Alfieri, 46 Rovigo
Tel/fax: +425 30850
Ground address: Stadio Comunale, M. Battaglini, V le Alfieri, 46 Rovigo Tel: +425 308050
President: Enrico Suriani
Secretary: Antonio Zurma
General Director: Danilo Ortolani (+425 30593)
Director of Sport: Raffaello Salvan (+425 91406)
Public Relations: Sebastiano Sferrazzo (+425 35910)
First Team Coach: Grant Andrews (Australia)
Doctor: Bruno Piva
Physitherapist: Loris Randi, Pietro Milan, Fabio Osti
Sponsor: Lloyd Italico Assicuraioni SpA

MDP ROMA
Founded: 1930
Colours: White, black and green
Address: MDP Rugby Roma, c/o Alessandro Missori, Piazza Dei Re di Roma, 3
Tel/Fax: 06 777590
Ground address: Stadio "Tre

Fontane", Via delle Tre Fontane, Roma, Tel: 06/5921 8401
Honours: Champions: 1935, 1937, 1948, 1949
Runners-Up: 1937, 1949, 1977 and 1988
President: Renato Speziali (06 33610764)
Vice President: Alessandro Missori and Gianni Romagnoli
General Manager: Alessandro Missori (06 777590)
Secretary: Armando Crescimbeni
Technical Director: Marco Gabrielli (0337 790530)
Public Relations: Massimiliano Mosetti (0336 749448)
First Team Coach: Wayne Shelford
Doctor: Stefano Marzani, Attilio Rota
Physiotherapist: Alberto Celli
Sponsor: MDP Magaaines

MILAN
Founded: 1927
Colours: White, red and black
Address: Residenza Portici 8, Milano 2, 20090 Segrate
Tel: 02 21022211
Fax: 02 21022933
Ground address: Campo Comunale, "M. Giuriati", Via Pasca Tel: 02 70600358 – 70602642
Honours: Champions: 1929 – 1934, 1936, 1938 –1943, 1946, 1991 and 1993
Runners-Up: 1952, 1955, 1958, 1963, 1987
President: Sandro Manzani (02 75331694)
Secretary: Fiorella Confalonieri
Public Relations: Andrea Buongiovanni (02 21022045) Ugo Allevi
Team Manager: Roberto Fulgoni
First Team Captain: Franco Carnovali (02 93502538)
Coach: Gino Bortolami
Doctor: Filippo Bottiglia, Giordano Geremia, Emilio Radaelli
Physiotherapist: Sergio Carenzio, Antonio Sulis

OSAMA A S RUGBY MIRANO
Founded: 1957
Colours: White and black
Address: Osama Rugby Mirano, c/o Mason Impianti, Via Galilei, 11, Mirano

Tel: +41 430072
Fax: +41 431628
Ground address: Campo Comunale, Via Matteotti 51, Mirano
Tel: +41 5700339
President: Sandro Jani (+41 432630)
Secretary: Guiseppe Mason
Director of Sport: Bianni Callegari
Tel: + 41 431755
Public Relations: Martino Salviato
First Team Coach: Francesco Dotto: +422 260998
Doctor: Guiseppe Boato
Physiotherapist: Fabrizio Zamegno
Sponsor: Osama Scrittura SpA Via 1 Maggio, 11 – Mombretto di Medigliana

PANTO SAN DONA
Founded 1959
Colours: White and blue; yellow and red
Address: Panto Rugby San Dona, Via Unita d'Italia, 8, S Dona di Piave
Tel: 0421 560666
Fax: 0421 331283
Ground address: Campo Comunale, Via Unita d'Italia, 8, S Dona di Piave Tel: 0421 560644
Honours: Runners-Up: 1988
President: Romolo Pacifici (0421 41166)
Secretary: Gaetano Gresti
Public Relations: Luibino Zecchinel (0421 52297)
First Team Coach: Corrado Trame (0421 52645)
Doctor: Claudio Cereser
Physiotherapist: Pietro Guerrato, Giusy Vinciprova
Sponsor: Panto SpA

SIMOD PETRARCA RUGBY
Founded: 1947
Colours: White and blue
Address: Simod Petrarca Rugby, Via Gozzano, 64, 35125 Padova
Tel: +49 8802473-76
Fax: +49 8804160
Ground Address: StadioComunale, Plebiscito, Via del Blebiscito, Pdova Tel: +49 605613
Honours: Italian Champions: 1970-74, 1977, 1980, 1984, 1987
Runners-Up: 1962, 1968, 1976

and 1978
President: Francesco Valier
Secretary Roberto Schiavon
First Team Coach: Pasquale Presutti
Doctor: Roberto Ragazzi
Physiotherapist: Antonio Gregori and Enrico Montagna
Sponsor: Simod SpA,

JAPAN

Japanese club rugby is the best supported in the world. Companies run their own teams and seem over the past few years to have broken away from Konno-ism.

KOBE

Founded: 1928
President: Sokichi Kametaka
Ground: Nadahama Ground, Kobe
3-18 Wakinohamacho 1 Chome, Chuo-Ku, Kobe 651
Telephone: 010 81 78 841 0001, 010 81 78 261 5143
Fax: 001 81 78 261 5155
Floodlights: Full playing floodlights
Public Transport: Hanahin Mikaga Stn (10 mins)
Wheelchair Access: Ground only
Parking: 50 spaces
Clubhouse Facilities: Bar and function room
Colours: Red jerseys, white shorts
Change of colours: Sky blue with yellow stripe, white shorts
Nickname: The Steelers
No. of Teams: Senior 2
Training Nights: Monday, Tuesday and Wednesday
Chief Executive: M Fukuzawa
Secretary: Y Fujiaski
Treasurer: Y Fujiaski
Press Officer: A Ayashiro
Coach: I Onishi
Sponsor: Kobe Steel Ltd
League Position: No 1
Cup Position: No 1
International Players: M Hagimoto (1 Cap), T Hyashi (38), A Oyagi (30), S Hirao (32), T Hosokawa (10), M Horikoshi (15), H Kato (2), A Komura (1),

I Williams (16 Australia)
Tours Overseas: UK, USA, Australia (2), Singapore, Malaysia (2)
Touring Sides Hosted: Canada, Oxford University, Cambridge University, All Brisbane, Allied Steel, Kew Occasionals

SCOTLAND

Scotland is still missing competitive rugby at club and provincial level. Their top clubs need to become part of a UK league. The SRU has decided to introduce a four premier division of eight clubs and seven junior leagues of 10 clubs from 1995-96. This season therefore is going to bring home a few truths to some of Scotland's more famous clubs.

McEwans 70/- League Championships 1993-94
Division One

	P	W	D	L	F	A	Pts
Melrose	13	12	0	1	410	192	24
Gala	12	9	0	3	274	214	18
Edinburgh A	13	8	1	4	265	183	17
Heriots FP	12	7	0	5	230	224	14
Watsonians	13	7	0	6	276	337	14
Stirling C	12	6	1	5	227	163	13
Hawick	12	6	1	5	218	178	13
Jed Forest	13	6	0	7	231	199	12
Curried	12	6	0	6	230	285	12
S Melmille	13	5	1	7	157	190	11
Boroughmuir	12	5	0	7	214	228	10
W of Scotland	13	4	1	8	235	279	9
Kelso	13	4	0	9	175	296	8
Selkirk	13	0	1	12	138	312	1

Division Two

	P	W	D	L	F	A	Pts
Glasgow HK	13	13	0	0	440	115	26
Dundee HSFP	12	11	0	1	395	80	22
Kirkaldy	13	10	0	3	277	150	20
Edinburgh W	13	8	0	5	214	251	16
Musselburgh	13	7	0	6	204	185	14
Peebles	13	6	0	7	206	219	12
Glasgow Acad	13	5	1	7	237	276	11
Wigtonshire	13	5	0	8	172	241	10
Haddington	12	5	0	7	146	220	10
Grangemouth	13	4	1	8	201	293	9
Biggar	13	3	2	8	203	240	8
Preston Lodge	13	4	0	9	158	291	8
Clarkston	13	4	0	9	158	357	8
Ayr	13	3	0	10	168	261	6

Division Three (Top 6)

	P	W	D	L	F	A	Pts
Gordonians	13	10	1	2	263	123	21
Corstophine	13	10	0	3	237	161	20
Kilmarnock	13	9	1	3	277	129	19
Hillhead	13	9	0	4	223	109	18
Hutch Aloys	13	8	0	5	216	159	16
Langholm	12	7	0	5	224	124	14

BOROUGHMUIR

Founded: 1939
President: Arthur T Ross
Ground: Meggetland, Colington Road, Edinburgh EH14 1AS
Floodlights: Yes
Spectator Capacity: 3,000
Public Transport: Bus outside ground
Wheelchair Access: Yes
Parking: 120 spaces
Hospitality Suites: 2
Clubhouse Facilities: Bar and lounge
Colours: Emerald green and blue squares
Change of Colours: Emerald green and blue stripes
Nickname: Muir
No. of Teams: Senior 5, Youth 1, Mini 5
Training Nights: Tuesday and Thursday
Wired for Radio: Yes
TV Access: Yes
Secretary: Ronald W Smith, Eastfield, 12 Barony Terrace, Edinburgh EH12 8RE
Treasurer: Alan Digence, John Mackay
Press Officer: Ronald W Smith
Coach: Bruce Hay, Gary Callender
1st XV Manager: Andy McBain
Captain: Murry Walker
Sponsor: Garden, Haig, Stirling and Burnet Solicitors

EDINBURGH ACADEMICALS

Founded: 1857
President: Charles Jackson
Ground: Raeburn Place
Address: Stockbridge, Edinburgh, EH4 1HQ
Telephone: (44) 31 343 1708
Bar: (44) 31 332 1070
Floodlights: Yes
Spectator Capacity: 5,000

Public Transport: Outside Ground
Wheelchair Access: To ground
Parking: Street Parking
Hospitality Suites: One
Clubhouse Facilities: 2 bars, 2 squash courts
Colours: Sky blue and white hooped shirt; white shorts; dark blue socks with white tops
Change of Colours: Dark blue
Nickname: Accies
No. of Teams: Senior 6
Training Nights: Tuesday and Thursday
TV Access: Yes
Secretary: Ken Lauder
15 Primrose Bank Road,
Edinburgh EH5 3JJ
Telephone: (44) 31 667 2708
(44) 31 551 5451
Treasurer: Sandy MacRae
Press Officer: Magnus Moodie
Coach: Hugh Campbell
1st XV Manager: Paul di Rollo
Captain: David McIvor
Sponsor: Glenmorangie
League Position: 3rd Div 1
International Players: David McIvor, Martin Scott, Rob Wainwright

GALA

Founded: 1875
President: J M Maitland
Ground: Netherdale,
Nether Road,
Galashiels TD1 3HE
Telephone: (44) 896 755145
Fax: (44) 896 755 145
Spectator Capacity: 9,999
Public Transport: Local bus route
Wheelchair Access: Yes
Parking: Large public car park adjacent to ground
Clubhouse Facilities: Members lounge, Centenary lounge Hospitality suites: Two
Colours: Maroon and white
Change of Colours: White jersey; maroon socks
Nickname: "Maroons"
No. of Teams: 1
Training Nights: Tuesday and Thursday
TV Access: Yes
Secretary: A M Pattullo
40 Kenilworth Avenue,
Galashiels TD1 2DB

Treasurer: A L K Brown
Coach: P W Dods
Captain: M Dodds
Sponsor: Keyline Builders Merchant
International Players: Three current Internationals
League: 2nd Div 1
Sevens: The club won the Gala, Melrose, Jedforest and Currie Sevens

The Club had a successful season, finishing second in the Division 1 League. Tehy had a very successful sevens series, winning their own tournament: Gala, Melrose, Blue Riband of Sevens – the trophy being presented by HRH The Princess Royal – the Jed-Forest centenary sevens and also Currie RFC tournament. Michael Dods is the club's 41st cap, and there were three players on tour to Argentina.

GHK (GLASGOW HIGH/KELVINSIDE)

Founded: 1884
President: James Currie
Ground: Old Anniesland,
Crow Road, Glasgow
Telephone: (44) 41 959 1154
Floodlights: Training pitches
Spectator Capacity: 5,500
Public Transport: Bus and train one mile
Wheelchair Access: Yes
Parking: 300 spaces
Hospitality Suites: Yes
Clubhouse Facilities: Bar and lounge
Colours: White green and dark blue hoops
Change of Colours: Navy
No. of Teams: Senior 5, Youth 1
Training Nights: Tuesday and Thursday
Wired for radio: Yes
TV Access: Yes
Secretary: Kenneth Fettes
Treasurer: Richard Eadie
Press Officer: Stan Butler
Coach: Brian Gilbert
1st XV Manager: As above
Captain: To be announced
Sponsor: Burns Stewart
International Players: Alan Watt, Shade Munro

League Position: 1st Div 1
Cup: Quarter-finalists Alloa Cup Season 1993-1994; Voted McEwan's Team of the Year.
All games: P-30, W-28, D-1, L-1, F-936, A-321. Gained promotion from Div 2 of the National Leagues by winning the Division.
League games: P-13, W-13, L-0, F-440, A-116, Pts 26

Apart from their successful league programme, they had wins over opposition from England, Aspatria (H) 61-12; from Ireland, Instonians (A) 19-13; and Wales, a notable win against Newport (A) 17-13.

HAWICK

Founded: 1873
President: T F E Grierson
Ground: Mansfield Park,
Mansfiled Road, Hawick
Telephone: (44) 450 374291,
(44) 450 370687
Floodlights: Yes
Spectator Capacity: 10,000
Public Transport: Hawick
Wheelchair Access: Yes
Parking: Yes
Hospitality Suites: One
Clubhouse Facilities: 2 bars
Colours: Green
Change of Colours: Green and white
Nickname: Greens
No. of Teams: Senior 1, Youth 4
Training Nights: Tuesday and Thursday
Wired for Radio: Yes
TV Access: Yes
Secretary: John Thornburn,
12 Daykins Drive,
Hawick TD9 8PF
Telephone: (44) 450 78808 (H),
(44) 450 72773 (W)
Treasurer: R G Elliot
66 Princes Street, Hawick
Telephone: (44) 450 28808
Coach: R W Murray
1st XV Manager: C B Hegarty
Captain: J A Hay
Sponsor: Pringle of Scotland
Touring Sides Hosted: 93/94 Rosario (Argentina) 7-a-side Randwick (Aus)
International Players: Tony Stanger, Greig Oliver, Derek Turnbull

Last season saw Hawick (proud winners on 10 previous occasions) finish in mid-table again. As is the case nowadays, a lack of a consistent goal-kicker did not help their league position. In fact, the Greens managed to have a 2-0 try count against champions, Melrose, only to lose by poor goal-kicking.

There are a few youngsters in the team last season who, if they adapt themselves, could be the backbone of the club for a good number of seasons, as well as add to the 52 international players Hawick have produced over the years (not a bad ratio for a town with a population of 16,000). They are Cammy Murray (centre), Kevin Reid (scrum half), Ian Elliot (second row), John Graham (wing forward), Colin Turnbull (fly half) and Keith Scott (prop). The latter, incidentally, benefited greatly from playing a season at the Poneke Club in Wellington, New Zealand. Along with experienced international players Tony Stanger, Greig Oliver, Derek Turnbull, Jim Hay (Scotland B), and Brian Renwick (South of Scotland), the club can hope for a better season in 1994/95.

The club held the 100th playing of their Sevens in April. Fortunate to be sponsored by the knitwear giants, Pringle of Scotland, the tournament proved to be a great success. Eventual winners were a Pringle President's 7 (comprising mainly London Scottish players and captained by British Lion Andy Nicol) who beat Randwick (Australia) in a thrilling final. Two composite sides who did themselves no favours for the future were South African Barbarians and Irish Wolfhounds who both called off two weeks prior to the tournament. However, Hawick were fortunate with their replacement clubs, Wakefield and Bristol, in that they are both fine exponents of the abbreviated game.

A disappointment for the club was that when Scotland's squad for the forthcoming tour to Argentina was announced there would be no players from Hawick. This is the first time this has ever happened to the club.

GEORGE HERIOT'S SCHOOL FP RC

Founded: 1890
President: Tony Hogarth
Ground: Goldenacre, Bangholm Terrace, Edinburgh EH3 5QN
Telephone: (44) 31 592 4097
Bar: (44) 31 552 5925
Floodlights: Training Pitches
Spectator Capacity: 4,000
Public Transport: Outside ground
Wheelchair Access: Yes
Parking: Street only
Hospitality Suites: Adapt clubhouse
Clubhouse Facilities: 'Best in Scotland' – 2 bars, lounge
Colours: Blue and white horizontal stripes
Change of Colours: Navy blue
No. of Teams: Senior 5
Training Nights: Tuesday and Thursday
Wired for Radio: Yes, own gear
TV Access: Yes
Secretary: Colin McAllum 20 Blin Kbonny Crescent, Edinburgh EH4 3NB
Treasurer: Douglas Hall
Captain: Stuart Paul
League Position: 5th Div 1
International Players: Ken Milne, Andrew MacDonald
Season 1993/1994: 1ST XV
P23 W16 L7 D0 F574 A423
Tours Overseas: Canada

The season started well for the first team with a victory at home against Lansdowne. Given a rescheduling of national championship fixtures this was the only game the team had prior to their first league fixture against Kelso at Poynder Park. Unfortunately the game was lost 12-18. However the following week saw a return to winning ways with a 24-13 win against Stewart's Melville FP. Thereafter, the team progressed undefeated to the turn of the year when they were second in the table.

This early part of the season contained some sound performances by the team. Notably, the game against Gala was a tightly fought contest with a fine display

of 15 man rugby from both teams. So good a display, that the BBC production who were televising the event were prompted to say that it was the best Scottish club game they had covered for some considerable time. Another interesting game against Currie at Malleny Park in mid December (21-9) saw captain Mike Allingham receive a serious leg injury which rendered him unfit to play for the rest of the season.

In all the first XV had to field no less than 45 players in league encounters as a result of injuries, and it was against this background that the team met Melrose in January. It was not to be Heriot's day, losing the game 19-37, and thereafter the team lost their remaining two games. Overall a satisfactory season with some notable individual displays. Our two current full internationalists Kenny Milne and Andy MacDonald were dominant upfront, whereas the most consistent backs were Andy McRobbie and Henry Murray.

Once again the club provided handsomely players for representative duties. Kenny Milne garnered further caps and was also bestowed the honour of being vice captain for the national side. Andy MacDonald received his first cap.

JED-FOREST

Founded: 1884
President: Lawrence Armstrong
Ground: Riverside Park, Jedburgh
Telephone: (44) 835 862855
Press Box: (44) 835 862232
Bar: (44) 835 862855
Floodlights: Yes
Spectator Capacity: 10,000
Public Transport: 3 km
Wheelchair Access: Yes
Parking: Yes
Hospitality Suites: Adapted
Clubhouse Facilities: Bar and function suite
Colours: Royal blue
Change of colours: Royal blue and white quarters
Nickname: Royal Blues of Jethart
No. of Teams: Senior 4, Youth 2, Mini 5

Training Nights: Tuesday and Thursday
Wired for Radio: Yes
TV Access: Yes
Secretary: J H Waldie, Hynhurst, Honeyfield Road, Jedburgh TD8 6JN
Treasurer: Hugh White
Press Officer: D A Lightbody
Coach: Donald Miller
Captain: Neil McIlroy
League Position: 7th Div 1
International Players: Gary Armstrong
Most Capped Player: Roy Laidlaw

KELSO

Founded: 1876
President: C E B Stewart
Ground: Poynder Park, Poynder Place, Bowmont Street, Kelso, Scotland
Telephone: (44) 573 224 300
Bar: (44) 573 223 773
Floodlights: Yes
Spectator Capacity: 4,000
Public Transport: Bus 400m
Wheelchair Access: Yes
Parking: 300 spaces
Clubhouse Facilities: Lounge, bar
Colours: Black and white
Change of Colours: Red and white
Nickname: The Black and Whites
No. of Teams: Senior 4, Youth 1, Midi 3, Mini 1
Training Nights: Tuesday and Thursday
TV Access: Yes
Secretary: Norman T Anderson, Carraig-Thura, 27 Springwood Bank, Kelso TD5 8BA
Telephone: (44) 573 225 076
Treasurer: D W Smith
Coach: Eric Paxton
Captain: Stewart Bennet
League Position: 13th Div 1

Kelso finished second to last in N L Division 1 so they will be playing in Division 2 in the 1994/95 season. The experienced back row worked hard for survival but scoring tries was a problem.

The Under-18 side has won district league four years in succession and their yougsters are now becoming established in the Senior side. The former President of the club G

K Smith will be President of the Scottish Rugby Union in 94/95.

MELROSE

Founded: 1877
President: Tom McLeish
Ground: The Greenyards, Melrose, Roxburghshire, TD6 9SA
Telephone: (44) 89 682 2993
Fax: (44) 0896 822993
Press Box: (44) 89 682 3413; (44) 89 682 3414
Bar: (44) 89 682 2559
Spectator Capacity: 16,000
Public Transport: Bus Melrose, train Edinburgh/Berwick
Wheelchair Access: Yes
Parking: Adjacent to ground
Hospitality Suites: Two
Clubhouse Facilities: Four bars, catering, function suite
Colours: Yellow and black
Change of Colours: Black
Nickname: The Rose
No. of Teams: Senior 4, Youth 8
Fax: (44) 89 682 2993
Wired for Radio: Yes
TV Access: Yes
Secretary: Stuart Henderson The Greenyards, Melrose TD6 9SA
Tel: (44) 89 682 2069 (H), (44) 89 682 2993 (W)
Treasurer: Hugh Pollock and Alan Smith
Press Officer: Stuart Henderson
Coach: Rob Moffat
1st XV Manager: Rob Moffat
Captain: Craig Chalmers
International Players: Craig Chalmers, Graham Shiel, Doddie Weir, Carl Hogg, Bryan Redpath
League Position: 1st Div 1
Touring Sides Hosted: Manly (Sydney), Villager (Cape Town)
Tours overseas: South Africa
Special Awards: Rugby World Team of the Month, March 1994

Melrose continued their successful run in Scottish Rugby by clinching their fourth McEwans National League title in five years and retaining the Border League title for the fifth year in succession. During the season they only lost one game, the first League game of the season to neighbouring Gala by one point, but from then on proved

unbeatable, clinching the title with a 74-10 win over Currie. In the Scotland v New Zealand game at Murrayfield in November, five players represented Scotland, a club record.

The Bells Melrose Sevens in April, played in the worst conditions in memory, were watched by a very good crowd of over 12,000 despite the counter attractions of live television coverage. Overseas visitors Manly (Sydney) and Villager (Cape Town) were clearly affected by the conditions and the tournament was won by Gala, who defeated Wasps in a close final. HRH the Princess Royal attended the Sevens and presented the cup and medals.

The club's director of Coaching, Jim Telfer, stepped down at the end of the season as he has been appointed Scotland's Director of Rugby. Telfer, who has guided the club through their most successful period, will be replaced by his assistant Rob Moffat.

During August 1994 the club were undertaking a four match tour of South Africa, playing against the leading club sides in Durban and Cape Town during their visit.

WATSONIANS

Founded: 1875
President: R D Buchanan
Ground: Myreside, Myreside Road, Edinburgh EH10 5DB
Telephone: (44) 31 447 5200
Fax: (44) 31 447 5200
Bar: (44) 31 447 5200
Floodlights: Training pitches
Spectator Capacity: 6,000
Public Transport: Nº 38 LRT Bus
Wheelchair Access: Yes
Parking: Yes
Hospitality Suites: Yes
Clubhouse Facilities: Bars, function room, squash courts
Colours: Maroon and white hooped
Change of Colours: Maroon
Nickname: Sonians
No. of Teams: Senior 6
Training Nights: Tuesday and Thursday
Wired for radio: Yes
TV Access: Yes
Secretary: M R Crerar, 6 St Colme Street,

Edinburgh EH3 6AD
Telephone: (44) 31 225 4681 (B)
Treasurer: R A Davie
Press Officer: A P Nimmo
Coach: P Galacher and A Ker
1st XV Manager: P Hogarth
Captain: J D MacDonald
Sponsor: Henderson Boyd Jackson, Solicitors

Played in the Old Belvedere International Sevens in Dublin. There was a special Centenary match v Newport RFC to restart Welsh tours – but sadly Sonians did not win.

UNITED STATES

OLD BLUES
Founded: 1972
President: James "Bo" Meyersieck
Ground: Raimondi Field, 20th Street, Campbell, Oakland
Telephone: 0101 510 848 9986
Fax: 0101 510 603 1109
Spectator Capacity: 3,000
Public Transport: 2 Blocks, AC Transit
Wheelchair Access: Yes
Parking: 200-300 spaces
Colours: Royal blue and Gold
Nickname: Blues
No. of Teams: 1st, 2nd, 3rd and 4th division
Training Nights: Tuesday and Thursday
Ticket Line: Sather Gate Travel, Oakland, CA
Chief Executive: Bo Meyersieck
Secretary: Mike Conn
Treasurer: Steve Goldenberg
Press Officer: Don James
Coach: Tim O'Brian
1st XV Manager: Ramon Samaniego
Captain: Rich Pearson
Sponsor: Holsten Premium Bier
International Players: Don James, Tim Peterson, Tom Billups, Chris O'Brien, Wayn Chai, Steve Hiatt, Gary Hein
Tours Overseas: Malaysia, Hong Kong, Hawai
Special Awards: USA National Club Champions: 1979, 1980,

1981, 1982, 1983, 1986, 1987 and 1992

OLD MISSION ATHLETIC CLUB
Founded: 1954 (Club), 1966 (Rugby)
President: Charles Millenbah
Ground: Robb Field, Mission Bay Park, 525 Bacon St, San Diego
Telephone: 0101 619 531 1563
Spectator Capacity: 2,000
Public Transport: San Diego Transit 2 Blocks
Wheelchair Access: Yes
Parking: Limited
Clubhouse Facilities: Trophy rooms, meeting rooms only
Colours: White, navy blue hoops
Change of Colours: Navy blue with white hoops
Nickname: Ombac
No. of Teams: 4
Training Nights: Tuesday and Thursday
Chief Executive: Pat Boyle 9575 Poole St, La Jolla, Calif 92037
Telephone: 0101 619 557 5013, 0101 619 453 2030
Fax: 0101 619 557 5539
Treasurer: Klaus Mendenhall
Coach: Bing Dawson
1st XV Manager: Micheal Rollis
Captain: Chris Lip

WALES

We have argued elsewhere that rugby must be publicly accountable. Nowhere is this truer than in club rugby where rumour and counter-rumour about payments and counter-payments, or at least under-the-table-payments, abound.

In June, the Inland Revenue confirmed that its Bristol office was investigating the allegations that Swansea and at least six other Welsh sides have concealed payments and benefits to players. A number of players were interviewed in dusk raids in May and questioned about what they had

received from clubs. Tax officials queried the gate money at Pontypool as a result of aerial photographs they took to examine the size of the crowd. Watch this space.

Keith Rowlands, Secretary of the IRFB, has asked the Welsh Rugby Union to investigate comments made by Emyr Lewis, the Llanelli flanker, about some of his public comments concerning the level of money in the game

It would be all so much easier if the clubs were honest in the first place and made their accounts public. If they don't, then the Treasury will move the necessary legislation so to do.

Meanwhile, on-the-field the Heineken League suffers from a dearth of quality. The clubs would be better served playing one game against each club and freeing up the fixture list to play in a UK and a European club championship.

HEINEKEN FINAL LEAGUE TABLES
DIVISION 1

	P	W	D	L	F	A	Pts
Swansea	22	20	0	2	459	264	40
Neath	22	17	2	3	581	286	36
Pontypridd	22	17	1	4	571	299	35
Cardiff	22	15	2	5	668	240	32
Llanelli	22	13	1	8	461	366	27
Bridgend	22	10	1	11	466	434	21
Newport	22	8	2	12	362	472	18
Newbridge	22	7	1	14	367	440	15
Pontypool	22	7	0	15	312	626	14
Dunvant	22	6	1	15	288	464	13
Aberavon	22	6	1	15	242	464	13
Cross Keys	22	0	0	22	239	751	0

Champions: Swansea
Relegated: Aberavon & Cross Keys

DIVISION 2

	P	W	D	L	F	A	Pts
Treorchy	22	20	1	1	425	200	41
Abertillery	22	15	1	6	473	242	31
Maesteg	22	13	1	8	376	259	27
SW Police	22	12	0	10	367	333	24
Tenby U	22	10	0	12	308	366	20
Llanharan	22	9	2	11	259	349	20
Narberth	22	10	0	12	273	294	20
Penarth	22	9	0	13	291	372	18
Ebbw Vale	22	8	2	12	279	321	18
Llandovery	22	8	1	13	269	370	17

Mountain A	22	8	0	14 275	333	16
Glam Wan	22	6	0	16 262	418	12

Promoted: Treorchy and Abertillery
Relegated: Mountain Ash & Glamorgan Wanderers

BRIDGEND

Founded: 1878
President: Bernard M Davies
Ground: Brewery Field, Tondu Road, Bridgend, Mid Glamorgan
Telephone: (44) 656 659032, (44) 656 652707
Floodlights: Yes
Spectator Capacity: 11,000
Public Transport: Bus within half mile
Wheelchair Access: To field only
Parking: Yes
Clubhouse Facilities: 4 Bars, plus catering
Colours: Blue and white stripes
Change of Colours: Gold
No. of Teams: Senior 1, Youth 1
Training Nights: Monday and Thursday
Wired for radio: Yes
TV Access: Yes
Chief Executive: Steve Fenwick
Secretary: David Lock
Treasurer: To be announced
Coach: Clive Norling, Gerald Williams, Keri Townley
Captain: Robert Howley
Sponsor: Riverside Air Conditioning
League Position: 6th Div 1
Cup: Quarter-finalists
International Players: Glen Webb, David Bryant

Full time chief executive now and a new constitution took effect from 4 June, when a new streamlined 7-man management team took over. With a very young side Bridgend are optimistic, but short of a major ball winner. Hopeful of good season 1994/95.

CARDIFF

Founded: 1876
Ground: Cardiff Arms Park Westgate Street, Cardiff
Telephone: (44) 222 383546
Fax: (44) 222 345390

Bar: (44) 222 220082
Floodlights: Yes
Spectator Capacity: 14,000
Public Transport: Rail and bus station 400m
Wheelchair Access: Yes
Parking: Large NCP car parks next to ground
Hospitality Suites: Yes, each end of the ground 26 and 11 suites respectively
Clubhouse Facilities: Bars
Colours: Cambridge blue and black
Change of Colours: Red
No. of Teams: 4
Wired for radio: Yes
TV Access: Yes
Chief Executive: A Heffell, J P
Secretary: J D Nelson, Cardiff Arms Park, Cardiff CF1 1JA
Coach: Alex Evans
Captain: Mike Hall
League Position: 4th in 1st Division of Heineken League
Cup: Winners WRU, SWALEC Cup Final

Cardiff had an up-side down sort of season but redeemed with a fine and unexpected victory against Llanelli in the Swalec Cup Final winning by 15-8 in front of a capacity crowd of 52,000. For loyal Cardiff supporters it has been a long wait, seven years, for a return to winning ways. Now, they must hope this will be converted in improving their league position this season.

LLANELLI

Founded: 1872
President: Alun Bowen Thomas
Ground: Stradey Park, Llanelli, Dyfed
Telephone: (44) 554 774060
Fax: (44) 554 778385
Bar: (44) 554 772310
Floodlights: Yes
Spectator Capacity: 13,500
Public Transport: Bus
Wheelchair Access: Yes
Parking: 800 spaces
Hospitality Suites: Three
Clubhouse Facilities: 500
Colours: Scarlet
Change of Colours: Navy blue and white

Nickname: The Scarlets
No. of Teams: 1st team, U-21s and Colts
Training Nights: Tuesday and Thursday
Wired for radio: Yes
TV Access: Yes
Chief Executive: J D W MacLean
Secretary: Ken Parfitt
Treasurer: Mevrig Jones
Press Officer: Gareth Hughes
Coach: Allan Lewis, Jeremy Cooper
Captain: Rupert Moon
Sponsor: Crown Buckley, Harp
League Position: Heineken League 1st
Cup: Winners Wales Challenge Cup
International Players: Ieuan Evans, Tony Copsey, Emyr Lewis, Ricky Evans, Hugh William James, Ian Jones, Lynn Jones, Andrew Lamerton, Rupert Moon, Mark Perego, Wayne Proctor, Scott Quinnell, Neil Boobyer
Special Awards: Participated in Singapore 7s

From the double of last season, Llanelli came down with a bang, finishing in mid-table in the league and runners-up to Cardiff in the Cup. They could muster 14 internationals and frequently did but something was missing in their general play this season – their spark all too frequently failed to ignite. No doubt they'll be back.

NEATH

Founded: 1871
President: Martin Thomas
Ground: The Courage Gnoll
Address: Gnoll Park Road Neath, West Glamorgan
Telephone: (44) 639 636547
Bar: (44) 639 644420
Floodlights: Yes
Spectator Capacity: 8,000
Public Transport: Bus outside ground
Wheelchair Access: Yes
Parking: Nearby
Hospitality Suites: Under consideration
Clubhouse Facilities: Bars, lounge
Colours: Black with white

maltese cross
Change of Colours: Red
Nickname: The Mourners
No. of Teams: 1
Training Nights: Monday and Thursday
Wired for radio: Yes
TV Access: Yes
Chief Executive: Norman Rees
Secretary: A Benjamin OBE
Hon Sec Neath RFC,
24 The Pines, Brynamlwg Parc,
Penscynor, Neath,
West Glam. A10 8AL
Tel: 0639 642172
Treasurer: John Prichard
Press Officer: Rod Rees
Captain: Gareth Llewellyn
Sponsor: Reebok
League Position: 2nd Div 1
Cup: Quarter-Finalists in SWALEC Cup
International Players: Gareth Llewellyn and John Davies
Rugby Director: Brian Thomas

They will probably always be an unfashionable side but that hasn't stopped them being successful. Second in the league was just reward for this young side.

NEWBRIDGE

Founded: 1888
Ground: Welfare Ground
Bridge Street, Newbridge, Gwent
Telephone: (44) 495 243247
Bar: (44) 495 243247
Floodlights: Yes
Spectator Capacity: 8,000
Public Transport: Bus outside the ground
Wheelchair Access: Yes
Parking: Limited
Hospitality Suites: 1
Clubhouse Facilities: Bar, lounge
Colours: Blue and black hoops
Change of Colours: Red, yellow, black V
Nickname: The Bridge
No. of Teams: Senior 1, Junior 6
Training Nights: Tuesday and Thursday
Wired for Radio: Yes
TV Access: Yes
Chief Executive: Howard Roberts
Secretary: B Wellington

11 Treowen Road, Newbridge, Gwent NP1 4DL
Treasurer: Martin Hiscott
Press Officer: Paul Morgan
Coach: Robert Beale, David Hussey, John Hall-Moore
League Position: 10th
Cup Position: Lost 6th Round
Touring Sides Hosted: Pretoria University
Special Awards: Whitbread 7's Winners
Club Call: 0898 88 4508

Newbridge are playing in the danger zone of Welsh rugby. They finished just off the bottom two points clear of Aberavon who were relegated. Three new coaches – Robert Beale, David Hussey and John Hall Moore – were given the task of building a team from a squad with 15 new signings.

The return of Steve Fealey at scrum half made a big difference, as did Ken Waters at hooker. Andrew Gibbs won a place in the Welsh squad and an A cap and flanker Peter Crane had an outstanding season. Alan Lucas, Steve Reed and Wayne Taylor shone among the backs. Between mid December and early March Newbridge lost only to Bath and ran in a Heineken record of six tries, beating Llanelli 37-20.

Also in March, the club entertained Canada A on their short tour of th UK and lost only 8-9; and they returned home unbeaten from a post-season tour to Ontario. Perfomances on tour by Mike Sage, Jeremy Lloyd, Marcus Lawford and Anthony Wilkshire augur well for the future; and In 1994-95 Newbridge are looking to establish a mid-table postion and make an impact on the top five in the league

NEWPORT RUGBY CLUB

Founded: 1875
President: Martin Hazell
Ground: Rodney Parade
Address: Newport Athletic Club, Rodney Parade, Newport, Gwent NP9 0UU
Telephone: (44) 633 258193
Bar: (44) 633 267410

Fax: (44) 633 220687
Floodlights: Yes
Spectator Capacity: 18,500
Public Transport: Newport transport bus station
Wheelchair Access: Yes
Parking: 200 spaces
Colours: Black and Amber
Change of Colours: Blue with white/green V
Nickname: Black and ambers
No. of Teams: Senior 2, Junior 4, Youth 1
Training Nights: Tuesday and Thursday
Wired for radio: Yes
TV Access: Yes
Secretary: Campbell Black, 7 Kensinton Grove, Newport, Gwent NP9 8GJ
Treasurer: Campbell Black
Press Officer: Campbell Black and David Watkins
Coach: Roger Powell and Paul Evans
1st XV Team Manager: David Watkins
Captain: Richard Goodey
Sponsor: Carlsberg Tetley
League: 7th Heineken League Div 1
International Players: Wales U-21 (unbeaten) – D Hughes, G Wyatt

Newport are slowly coming back to their rightful place in the top echelon of Welsh rugby. In spite of the high standards of the club in the 1970s and 1980s, the well- known amateur status of the club meant that Newport were slow to come to terms with the present day requirements of a first class rugby club. However, under the leadership of team manager David Watkins, they are well on their way to becoming competitive again. Unfortunately, with the advent of League football, the Newport club has no regular fixtures against English opposition.

PONTYPOOL

Founded: 1868
President: Paul Rich
Ground: Pontypool Park
Address: Pontypool, Gwent
Administrative address: Elm House, Pontypool, Gwent
Telephone: (44) 495 763492,

(44) 495 762524
Ticket: 0495 75552
Number of Teams: 7
Colours: Black, white and
red hoops
Change of colours: Navy blue
Nickname: Pooler
Training Nights: Monday and
Thursday
Wheelchair Access: Yes
Wired for Radio: Yes
TV Access: Yes
Secretary: Tony Simmons
Coach: Bob Windsor
Captain: Mark King
1st XV Manager: Ivor Taylor

PONTYPRIDD

Founded: 1874
President: S A Simon
Ground: Sardis Road Ground,
Pwllgwaun, Pontypridd
Telephone: (44) 433 405006
Press Box: (44) 433 407170
Bar: (44) 443 407087
Floodlights: Yes
Spectator Capacity: 10,280
Public transport: Train, bus
half mile
Wheelchair Access: Yes
Parking: Yes
Clubhouse Facilities: 4 bars
Colours: Black and white hoops
Change of colours: White and
black hoops
Nickname: Ponty
No. of Teams: 3
Training Nights: Tuesday and
Thursday
Wired for radio: Yes
TV Access: Yes
Secretary: C G P Thomas
26 Brair Way, Tonteg CF38 1NR
Telephone: (44) 443 204931
Treasurer: P Hendy
40 Mound Road, Pontypridd
Press Officer: C G P Thomas
Coach: Dennis John
Captain: Nigel Bezani
Sponsor: Just Rentals, South Wales
League Position: Third
International Players: Neil Jenkins

Pontypridd have never been
accepted as one of the elite clubs
in Wales but all that has done has
spurred them on. Last season they
were the surprise team in the league.

SWANSEA

Founded: 1873
President: D P Price
Ground: St Helens Ground,
Swansea, West Glamorgan
Floodlights: Yes
Spectator Capacity: 14,000
Public Transport: Bus
Wheelchair Access: Yes
Parking: Yes
League position: Winners

Swansea had a better season all
round reaching a level of consistency unmatched in the league
which they ended up winning.

A TRILOGY OF NON-CONFORMISTS

OXFORD UNIVERSITY

President: Dr A B Tayler, MA (St
Catherine's)
Treasurer: M J Cambell-Lamer-
ton, OBE, MA (Balliol)
Captain: David Henderson
Rugby Union Representative: P M
Johnson, MA (Mansfield)
Fixture Secretary: J C H Anelay
MA (New College)
Administrator: B E Morgan,
MBE, DPhys Ed
Director of Coaching: L R Evans,
DPhys Ed
Admin and Ground: Iffley Road,
Oxford
Telephone: (44) 865 241064
Fax: (44) 865 793406

CAMBRIDGE UNIVERSITY

President: J T Dingle, PhD
(Hughes Hall)
Treasure: B R Mitchell, PhD
(Trinity)
Captain: Nigel Richardson (St
Edmunds)
Assistant Treasurer: Alastair
Meadows (St Edmunds)
Fixture Secretary: F D Clough
PhD (Magdalene),
Rugby Union Representative: M D
Bailey, PhD (Gonville and Caius)
Administrator: C J Taylor,
MA(Corpus Christi)

Administration and Ground:
CURFC, Grange Road,
Cambridge
Telephone: (44) 223 338502
or (44) 223 870215
Fax: (44) 223 355301

112TH VARSITY MATCH
(for the Bowring Bowl)
Oxford 20 Cambridge 9
Date: 7 Dec 1993
Venue: Twickenham
Referee: W D Bevan (Wales)
Crowd: 66,000 (record for Varsity
Match and for the biggest crowd
for a club match)
Sponsor: Bowring's

Oxford: Try – S. du Toit;
Penalties – G. Rees 3;
Drop goals – Rees & L. Boyle
Cambridge: Try – A Boyd; Drop
goals – A Kennedy

Oxford: R. Wintle, L. Boyle, E.
Rayner, T. Watson, G. Rees, B.
Fennell, D. Henderson, C. Clark,
N. Martin & A. Aitken
Cambridge: A. Dalwood, A.
Arentson, A. Palfrey, A. Boyd, A.
Kennedy, C. Tynan, T. Hughes, R.
Bramley, W. Roy, P. Irons, N.
Richardson & A. Meadows. Subs: C.
Thompson & J. Duckworth

COLLEGES REPRESENTED
Oxford: Keble 9, University 1, Oriel
1, St Edmund Hall 1, Christchurch
1, St Catherine's 1, St Anne's 1
Cambridge: Hughes Hall 5, St
Edmund's 6, Corpus Christi 1, Jesus
1, St Johns 1, Trinity 1, Fitzwilliam
1, Downing 1

UNDER-GRADUATES
& POST-GRADUATES
Oxford: 4 – 11;
Cambridge: 6 – 11

STATES SCHOOLS & INDE-
PENDENT SCHOOLS
Oxford: 3 – 12;
Cambridge: 7 – 10

Oxford needed to win to prevent
three-in-a-row from Cam-
bridge and on the day were the better team by some way. Cambridge
were unbelievably naive in several

areas, including up-front which has been their greatest strength. One commentator thought this to be the worst Cambridge side ever, but it was fear of failure that got to them in the end, not a characteristic with which they are associated.

There were rare moments for the record crowd to enjoy and this prompted many rugby journalists to wonder why this fixture is worth its current status.

OTHER RESULTS
2ND XV FIXTURE
Oxford University Greyhounds 20 Cambridge University LX Club 23, at Iffley Road (2 Dec)

Oxford University U21 10 Cambridge University U21 12, at The Stoop Memorial Ground (7 Dec)

MATCH RECORDS
Record since 1871:
112 matches: Oxford 48, Cambridge 51, draws 13.
Highest score: Oxford 35, at Queen's Club 1909.
Highest winning margin: Oxford 32, at Queen's Club 1909.
Most tries: Oxford 9, in 1909, and Cambridge 9, at Twickenham, 1925.
Most points: Alastair Hignell, Cambridge,19 at Twickenham in 1975.
Most tries: Ronnie Poulton (later Poulton-Palmer), 5 at Queen's Club in 1909.
Most penalties: Nigel Quinnen, Oxford in 1974; Alastair Hignell, Cambridge, 5 in 1975.
Most dropped goals: Andy Johnson, Oxford 2, in 1986

PENGUIN RFC
Founded: 1959
President: Air-Commodore R H G Weighill, CBE DFC
Treasurer: J R Morgan
Press Officer: Tony Jarman
Ground: An International Invitation touring side
Colours: Black, white and yellow
Committee: Chairman and Team Secretary Tony Mason, 26 Collington Lane, West Bexhill-on-Sea, East Sussex TN39 3TA
Tel/Fax: (44) 424 844785

Hon Secretary: Alan Wright 8 St James's Place, London SW1A1PD
Telephone: (44)71 493 4121
Fax: (44) 71 408 1872
Special awards: 1994 Cobra Trophy winners 17th Malaysian RU Cobra International Tens Tournament

By Tony Jarman

The 1993/94 season always promised to be heavily influenced by the congestion of the domestic calendar; 18 home and away fixtures for all Courage League clubs, and International Selections, etc. And so it proved. At the beginning of the season the club had commitments to two domestic fixtures against Oxford and Cambridge Universities, an overseas tour to Malaysia and Singapore, and Sevens and Tens tournaments in Italy, Limerick, Dubai, and Kuala Lumpur.

On 22 and 23 May the club returned to Sicily to participate in the Italian Rugby Union International Sevens Tournament where they had lost to Fiji in the finals of 1991. A strong selection, with players from three of the Home Unions as well as SOuth Africa and New Zealand, led by Harlequins Sevens expert Chris Sheasby won all their matches. In the final they defeated the Italian National Seven by 31 – 14. Squad: Chris Sheasby *(Harlequins)*, Mark Thomas *(Rosslyn Park)*, Chad Lion-Cachet *(Oxford University)*, Phil Pask *(Northampton)*, Marty Steffert *(Northampton)*, Nick Knowles *(Northampton)*, Gary Parker *(Melrose)*, Everton Dqvis *(Harlequins)*, Andy Purves *(Melrose)*, Spencer Bromley *(Rugby)*.

At very short notice the invitation to participate in the Dubai Sevens was fulfilled. With little time for preparation, the team lost in the round robins and then in the early rounds of the plate comopetition went down to the ultimate winners, Holland.

The domestic season started with a match against Oxford University at Iffley Road. It was a delight to renew aquaintance with the Varsity but three weeks before their

Twickenham appearance they were too strong for the Penguins line-up which had been depleted by the Courage League calls of the senior clubs. Oxford won 52-14.

On 23 February the annual fixture against Cambridge University took place at Grange Road. Although the University team recorded a rare victory over the Penguins by 30-18 the scoreline might have been closer had not three of the Club's players been delayed until 30 minutes into the first half by a fire on the London to Cambridge railway line! This fixture holds a very special place in the Club's fixture list.

The annual tour was in August to Malaysia and Singapore, sponsored by Cathay Pacific Airways. As usual a good blend of youth and experience, with the emphasis on young emerging players contributed to an excellent trip. Led once again by Peter Cook (Nottingham) they won all six matches in theitinerary including those against the national sides of Malaysia and Singapore. A truly international selection included players from Australia, NZ, Ireland, Scotland, Wales and England.

In January Penguins defended the Malaysian Cobra Tens title which they won at the first attempt the previous year. Seven of the original squad of 13 were unable to travel due to international and league commitments. Nevertheless some exccellent last minute subsitutions were highly effective. Faced with playing Western Samoa in the final, after a tough encounter with most of the Japanese National Side in Kobe Steel, they finally ran out winners 21-17. It was a fine side, led from the front by Craig Brown.

The club would like to record their appreciation to the squad: Spencer Bromley *(Rugby)* Steward Burns *(Blackheath)* Crawford Henderson *(London Scottish)* John Kerr *(Watsonians)* Jason Keyter *(Harlequins)* Andrew Metcalf *(Wakefield)* Gareth Rees *(Oxford University)* Fanie du Toit *(Oxford University)* Bruce Donald *(Northampton)* Les Jackson *(Wasps)* Phil Pask *(Northampton)* Mark Sowerby *(Wakefield)* ∎

From left to right: Fanie du Toit, Crawford Henderson, Tony Mason, Zain Yusoff (Chairman – Cobra Tens Committee and John Kerr, pictured celebrating at the Cobra Tens winner's dinner. Below: "Keep Kuala Lumpur clean". The winning team and their trophy

Punchy headlines in our Newsbites section are totally outclassed by the anonymous Cambridge University player. Such a good picture that we just had to use it again no matter how bad the caption may be...

6. Review

Over the past year, the Almanack has gathered as much press material as was possible. Here is our selection of the Rugby Year 1993-1994, as recorded in the newspapers.

NEWSBITES September 1993–June 94

September 1993

1 Sept
Steve Bale, The Independent

The Scots yesterday exploded their reputation as dour defenders of the old ways when they became the first home country to acquire a sponsor for their national team and at the same time ensured that the Famous Grouse diverted a decent sum straight into the players' kitty. (£60,000 p.a.)........

The company will put more than £1 million into Scottish rugby over four years.....

2 Sept
Steve Bale, The Independent

.....*Meanwhile the Australian RFU has no qualms about putting on a gala dinner which raises nearly £250,000 for its players.*

3 Sept
Robert Armstrong, The Guardian

....Rugby administrators, who are mostly in the 50-to-70 age bracket, also appear to believe that good club players will tamely consent to a greatly increased workload without payment while England stars boost their bank balances with official blessing.

Twickenham clings to the absurd fiction that Courage will pay leading players for "promotional activities" when the rest of the world knows they would not receive a penny if they did not play rugby for England.

5 Sept
Reuters

The official in charge of developing rugby in black areas in South Africa has resigned his post and accused rugby authorities of failing to support development programmes . Ngconde Balfour, the national director of development of the South African Rugby Football Union, quit because club rugby in black townships was: "dying and nobody seems to be doing anything about it". He said established unions in the white-dominated sport cared little about unifying with blacks or sharing training facilities. The established unions pretended to support development in order to secure support for internation-al tours by the national side, Balfour said. Ebrahim Patel, the executive president of the SARFU, rejected Balfour's accusations, saying the union was seriously committed to "promote rugby throughout the country".

10 Sept
Hit Squad announced, The Independent

Ian Beer, the new President of the RFU, said:
"All clubs are being asked to sign a statement of compli-ance that there are no illegal payments. It is being pointed out to clubs that if they raise the stakes in inducing players to join them they cannot use money to improve their facilities. If you induce players to join your club you are spending money that could maintain your stand. If a club pays more and more to players it will not stay in business.

13 Sept
John Mason & Richard Spencer,
Daily Telegraph

An England Rugby Union player banned for life 60 years ago for alleged contacts with rugby league has been granted an unprecedented posthumous pardon after a long campaign to clear his name.... (Tom) Brown played 172 times for Bristol from 1926, and won his first cap against Scotland in Eng-land's 1927-28 Grand Slam winning side. He represented his country another eight times before the ban was imposed....Tom, who was then in the motor trade, had no intention of playing league. He and three Bristol colleagues were discussing a motor agency agreement. A newspaper linked it to rugby league...... In his letter to Brown's widow, Betty, Dudley Wood, the RFU Secretary, said: " There is no stigma whatsoever attached to your late husband for his action, and his character is clear."…. Brown, who went on to run a pub in Ulverston, died in May 1961 at the age of 53.

16 Sept
Press Association

RFU announces £750,000 three-year sponsorship of County and Divisional matches.
Agent: APA

Dick Best, Rugby World

It has to be faced by those charged with making the ultimate decision that to risk serious injury even to a solitary rugby fan would be one too many. When you here every night the latest toll of killings and murders it makes you think. I do not see how the organisers in South Africa can guarantee that by 1995, in as little as 21 months time, the tournament will be staged without trouble.

19 Sept
Eddie Butler, The Observer

Rugby on the vast majority of winter Saturdays unfolds on cabbage patch grounds, surrounded by grotty little shed stands. The Five Nations may be La Scala, but league rugby is the village hall the morning after The Young Farmers' Toga Party......

22 Sept
Steve Bale, The Independent

Even the South Africans themselves are beginning to believe they could lose the 1995 World Cup. International disquiet at the violence in the country, as well as the failure of its rugby administrators to come to grips with drugs and violence, yesterday prompted one of the directors of Rugby World Cup (Nic Labuschagne) to speculate that the tournament be moved elsewhere.

24 Sept
Peter Jackson, Daily Mail

Rugby Union is embroiled in a new crisis over professionalism after the reinstatement of another Australian international from rugby league. The case of Brett Papworth threatens far wider repercussions than an immediate protest led by English members of the International Board who meet in London next month. Legal advisers (Tim Jones, a Swansea solicitor) representing former Welsh international Stuart Evans are to serve a writ against the board for restraint of trade.....

October 1993

Paul Fitzpatrick & David Plummer, The Guardian

The departure of the Swansea and Lions flanker Richard Webster to Salford could herald another exodus of Welsh international players to rugby league. That is the warning voiced by Webster's club and international colleague Scott Gibbs, who last month turned down an offer from St Helen's reported to be worth £300,000......

Webster yesterday signed a contract reportedly worth £150,000 over five years, the first Welsh international to turn professional for nearly three years. Twelve leading Welsh players had joined rugby league clubs in the previous 26 months.

2 Oct
Derek Wyatt, Financial Times

Jack Rowell is the managing "dictator" of Bath rugby club. The charismatic coach from Hartlepool in northeast England has created a centre of excellence that is the envy of the world.......

3 Oct
Kevin Mitchell, The Observer

Dr John Crane, the Arsenal and England team doctor, estimates 18% of the injuries he sees at Highbury are the result of violent play. The figure for rugby union has been found to be 30%. These are statistics that (Edward) Grayson says society should find unacceptable. And, if sport can't clean up its own act, there are plenty of lawyers willing to take on the job.

Eddie Butler, The Observer

In New Zealand in the summer more people watched the three-match Kiwis-Kangaroos rugby league series on television than tuned in for the three All Blacks-Lions Tests.....

Now that rugby union is no longer amateur the best solution would be to allow free passage between the two codes and allow the players to decide for us which is the better. We could run a sort of defection's league table. It certainly wouldn't be one way traffic. Some of the northern lads would be pleasantly surprised at the going rate for win bonuses elsewhere.

Norman Harris, The Observer

Believe or not, the hallowed turf of Twickenham recently hosted an experimental game in which the touch judges were in radio contact with the referee, and, in which they flagged, soccer-style, for off-side.

Mick Cleary, The Observer

The call came a few weeks ago. The Australians were in town and did he fancy a game? Of course he did. He was the captain of Canada and the opposition were the world champions. Daft question really. Norm Hadley was ready to go. Just one little thing, Norm, before you put the phone down. Would you mind paying your own air fare? During the next few minutes of, shall we say, lively discussion, the telephone satellite only just avoided being yanked out of orbit. The putative flight was transatlantic for the match in Calgary next Saturday.........

Barrie Fairhall, The Independent on Sunday

If Neil Back has no future with England, then heaven help English rugby.
(Leicester 38 Wasps 6 – Courage League Division 1)

Stephen Evans, The Independent on Sunday

But relations were not so cordial on the field. Both packs eventually squared up to each other in a brawl of flailing arms, which ended with the Japanese flanker, Hirofume Ouchi being sent off. Everybody else had confined their violence to fists; he had used the boot.
(Dunvant 24 Japan 25 – Japanese tour of Wales)

5 Oct
David Plummer, The Guardian

Geoff Cooke has called for the Five Nations Championship to be restructured. The England manager believes the competition has become too "incestuous" and should be expanded to become the top division of a wider European Championship......

.....,"That would give us the chance to involve the likes of Romania and Italy, countries that I feel are denied the opportunity to develop under the existing format. With international travel now so much easier, I would also bring in the Canadians for the same reasons."

6 Oct
New Zealand News UK

Auckland, with All Black winger Va'aiga Tuigamala unable to displace Waisake Sotutu on the left wing and All Black reject John Kirwan retaining his usual right wing position, played with determination and spark in a six try to three victory which was as decisive as suggested.
(Auckland 43 North Harbour 20 NZ Provincial semi-final play-off)

Robert Cole, The Independent

Denis Evans was last night dismissed from his £48,000-a-year post as secretary of the Welsh Rugby Union. The general committee, after hearing the findings of a three-man internal disciplinary panel, decided to end Evans' contract on the grounds of grave misconduct.

Steve Bale, The Independent

The 1995 World Cup will proceed as planned in South Africa, the organisers declared for the umpteenth time yesterday – even though the prospect of a move elsewhere is now stronger than ever as concern grows about the political situation in the Republic and the role of the South African Rugby Football Union's chief negotiator. (Louis Luyt).....RWC expects to gain £12 million or more in major sponsorships to add to the £18 million in broadcasting deals already settled. The World Cup will need every penny it can get if insurance cover for the tournament turns out to be as prohibitive as some fear.......

7 Oct
Bill Leith, The Independent

Demotion comes at an embarrassing moment for (Doddy) Weir who is tomorrow due to collect a sponsored car from a Galashiels garage. Now, unless there is an improvement in his form Weir, a farmer, may be pitchforked back behind the wheel of the modest vehicle in which he rolled up for this year's World Sevens in Edinburgh. Then, by way of a hint to potential sponsors, he had etched the following message on the door panel of his farm truck: "Doddie's Car – presented by his Dad."

Donald Trelford, Daily Telegraph

I won't spoil the reader's fun by naming their five best players of the year, except to say that I'm pleased to see they include a vertically challenged fair-headed flanker who is rapidly becoming the David Gower of rugby.
(The International Rugby Almanack, 1994)

Robert Cole, The Independent

.......But the 57-year old (Denis) Evans, who played once for Wales on the wing in 1960, last night claimed: "I simply went about my job as chief executive" and said he had done nothing dishonest. He claims that the vast majority of the 18 allegations made against him by the WRU disciplinary sub-committee were "not proven" and that he did not know why he had been sacked.

In the end, the sub-committee decided he had been guilty of claiming for a taxi trip around Los Angeles, worth less than £50, during a 10-hour stop-over on his return from a working trip to New Zealand; erroneously claiming 22 miles on expenses; claiming £1,500 World Cup expenses to which he was not entitled (which was later refunded); using a janitor as a chauffeur while on a drink drive charge without proper authority, and incurring £1,900 in overtime expenditure as a result; excessive use of taxis, and contacting his personal assistant while on paid leave of absence.

"It may seem large figures to some people," Evans said "but when you look at the overall position within the Union in terms of finance it is a very small amount. Irrespective of that, I believe I was entitled to make decisions without running to the committee to ask for permission to do this, that and the other."

Evans will decide over the weekend whether to fight his dismissal through the courts.

9 Oct
Sixth Column, The Guardian

The scale of Denis Evans' misconduct as Welsh RU secretary is revealed in the auditors' report: in three years he claimed £7,865.42 from petty cash, but failed to provide receipts for £1,435.95. While banned from driving Evans, who was sacked on Tuesday, seconded the janitor and a member of the grounds staff to act as a chauffeur, an arrangement which cost the WRU £1,950 in overtime payments. He also claimed £3,299 in taxi fares, £2,077.50 of which related to trips from home to the office and "could not ....have been ratified by the relevant committee". Then there was the World Cup: Evans presented bills for a whopping £3,159.01. This much has been proved.

What has not been discovered is who sold the 25 tickets from the Secretary's pool for the Wales v Scotland game in 1992. Or where the money went. Perhaps World in Action should investigate.

Peter Corrigan, Independent on Sunday

A South Wales multi-millionaire who once played hooker for Cardiff RFC wants to put £500,000 into the club and spend two years organising its finances to include a trust fund for players. Peter Thomas played for the club in the 1960s and has since amassed a fortune based on the pie firm he founded with his brother Stan, another Cardiff fanatic.

Paul Ackford, Daily Telegraph

(Dean) Richards took another tack: "The season is tougher than ever. All the travelling and consulting diaries. Something's got to give, either the players or the amateur regulations."

Rugby is demanding too much of its stars without giving enough in return. Now where have we heard that before?

12 Oct
Alan Watkins, The Independent

I do not think the idea of an Anglo-Welsh league is feasible. What is possible is an Anglo-Welsh knock-out cup of eight clubs, the top four from each country. Why are waiting?

13 Oct
Ian Malin, The Guardian

Orrell's chairman of rugby, Des Seabrook is angry that the club's slender playing resources may be further depleted by the departure of England B's loose-head prop Martin Hynes to Wasps..."These clubs are like vultures on perches. We are hoping our problems with Martin can be resolved because we can ill afford to lose him."

15 Oct
Dr Valerie Goldberg's letter to The Times

.....It might be helpful to have an extra touch judge patrolling each try-line to adjudicate on this point (ie referee's being unsighted when forwards fall over the line)

17 Oct
Clem Thomas, The Independent on Sunday

As Shiggy Konno, the Japanese rugby supremo has often bemoaned, Japan are an emerging side who have never emerged.
(Wales 55 Japan 5)

18 Oct
News story, Daily Telegraph

Inspector Paul Ackford the former British Lions, England and Harlequins lock, is to resign today as manager of England's Emerging Players' squad because of a conflict of interests following a change of career.

Ackford, 35, who is stationed at New Scotland Yard, is leaving the Metropolitan Police after 10 years to become Rugby Football correspondent of the Sunday Telegraph *in succession to John Reason, who is retiring at the end of the year.*

19 Oct
Steve Bale, The Independent

"It's one of the great things about All Blacks teams," Fitzpatrick said yesterday. "We have the fear of losing which creates a pressure to perform and win. If we can manage that pressure the right way, it goes a long way to produce the results." Here are the statistics of 88 years of All Blacks' touring the British Isles: played 222, won 200, drawn 9. lost 13. Beatable? Yes. About to be beaten? Hardly.

Robert Armstrong, The Guardian

When the All Blacks gave a press conference at their Surrey hotel Bob Weighill, the home unions' representative, insisted on the removal of all Steinlager adverts on the grounds that the home unions are the official hosts... A Steinlager representative agreed that the home unions were within their rights to insist on the removal of promotional material.

21 Oct
Mick Cleary, The Guardian

"Some say that I'm jealous of his (Carling's) money," said Jeff Probyn. "Not true. I don't like the fact that his privileged position gives him a head start on the rest of us, but I'd do the same in his shoes.

"What annoys me is that he doesn't have to work for his place. He struggled in New Zealand with the Lions yet came off the plane and straight into the England side. It should not happen like that.

"I think Will's loss of form in the first place was caused by his protected status. Selection should not be about personalities. It should be about performance".

Exactly. Pick the man in form, whoever it might be. Enough of this talk about planning everything for the future. Rugby matches have never been played in crystal balls.

23 Oct
David Hands, The Times

Responsibility for rugby union's World Cup was deftly batted back over the net yesterday when the IRFB executive council concluded its interim meeting in London. The board, the game's controlling body, announced that Rugby World Cup Ltd (RWC) now had "discretion" to draw up contingency plans if South Africa appeared untenable as a venue for the 1995 tournament......

The IRFB has also recognised the benefits to many of its 61 members of formal links with the Olympic movement. It is to apply for non-participating membership of the International Olympic Committee in the hope that funds will become available to countries who desperately need them.

Roughly half the countries who belong to the IRFB are also members of their respective national Olympic committees and would be entitled to aid if rugby's governing body received Olympic recognition......

24 Oct
Chris Rea, Independent on Sunday

It is probably no exaggeration to say that in the first half-hour of the match, the All Blacks' wings – Jeff Wilson, who scored two tries, and Va'aiga Tuigamala – handled the ball more often than many of their predecessors have done on entire tours......
(London Division 12 New Zealand 39)

25 Oct
Frank Keating, The Guardian

The record crowd was stunned by such a show but not half as dazed as the London side – full of household names – must have been long before the finish. The drubbing and scattering of reputations was administered by players with no match practice for over a month and only four full days after a 30 hour flight through a 12-hour time difference.
(London Division v New Zealand)

27 Oct
Steve Bale, The Independent

Every preconception we had about *these* All Blacks' based on the performance of *those* All Blacks against London on Saturday, was shattered by a disarray into which they were thrown by the unconsidered Midlands at Welford Road yesterday.
(Midlands 6 New Zealand 12)

31 Oct
Chris Rea, Independent on Sunday

If the All Blacks are seriously concerned about the number of penalties they are conceding, they showed little sign of it as they merrily gave away a stream of kickable chances.
(South West 15 New Zealand 19)

Clem Thomas, Independent on Sunday

The Australians, who have never won a campaign in France, will rue the day that, after carrying out the prevailing popular phrase in the Wallaby camp, "Working at the coalface", to win what should have been the overwhelming possession, they disavowed their second slogan, "Putting in hard yards", as three tries went begging.
(France 16 Australia 13)

Barrie Fairall, Independent on Sunday

The toast is to absent friends. Last week at Gloucester there were no reported sightings of an England selector when the South-West played the North and the same applied at Welford Road in Leicester yesterday.

Which makes a mockery of what Geoff Cooke was saying at the start of the Divisional Championship. "Divisional rugby has proved itself to be very important to us," the England manager had said. But not that important, judging by the continuing absenteeism here.
(Midlands 14 London 23)

November 1993

1 Nov
Harry Pincott, The Scotsman

The beleaguered Edinburgh selectors met yesterday to draft a XV to play Auckland at Meggetland on 9 November......They managed to pip a hungry North & Midlands in the funereal atmosphere prevailing at the Greenyards on Saturday, when the crowd at the 12.30pm outset might just have topped the three figure mark.....
(Edinburgh 28 North & Midlands 25)

2 Nov
Steve Bale, The Independent

Under the tour agreement, a player allegedly guilty of foul play undetected by the referee or his touch judges, can be formally cited by the opposing management or union within 12 hours of the end of the match. This falls outside the requisite period because de Glanville was confirmed in his view only when he saw a recording outside that limit.

3 Nov
Steve Bale, The Independent

The video evidence shows the boots of Sean Fitzpatrick and Ian Jones in contact with de Glanville's head; he believes it was no accident. However, Neil Gray, the New Zealand manager, has apologised in a telephone call to de Glanville and Fitzpatrick has done the same to Ian Beer, the RFU president.....

Geoff Cooke, the England manager, added his views of the incident last night. "I don't believe the players involved were doing it to clear the ball and I always find it difficult to believe you don't know when you are treading on someone's face," he said.......

Robert Armstrong & David Irvine, The Guardian

(Dudley) Wood said that New Zealand had expressed sincere regret. "We registered a very stiff protest to the New Zealand management," he added. "We have done what we set out to do. I have spoken to de Glanville senior: to say that he is happy with the situation would be an exaggeration but he does accept it."

David Plummer, The Guardian

Vernon Pugh, the Welsh Rugby Union's chairman, has said that a league featuring the top clubs in England and Wales may begin within two years.

5 Nov
Steve Bale, The Independent

"There are so many similarities to a golf swing but I wouldn't say my golf is very good. Your kicking foot is a bit like a three-iron. It's a mental thing as well: you have to be absolutely confident and see the ball going between the posts before you kick it. If you have negative thoughts, you won't kick well."
(Matthew Cooper explains the art of goal-kicking)

6 Nov
L'Equipe magazine cover

Phillipe Sella fete sa 94e selection, record du monde, contre l'Australie au Parc des princes. Ca merite bien une victoire!

David Hands, The Times

Jeremy Guscott paused for reflection: "When you are tackled by him (Phillipe Sella), it's like being hit by a telephone box full of men swung on the end of a crane jib." Guscott, seldom short of a word or two, is only one of many admirers of the man who, today, will become the most capped player in world rugby – Phillipe Sella.

7 Nov
Norman Harris, The Observer

A dossier which the Special Investigations branch of the Inland Revenue has been given by the all-party group of Rugby League MPs, and which they are due to discuss with the MPs early in the new year.

The dossier gives details of alleged payments to

rugby union players – payments, says the group's secretary David Hinchcliffe, "that I have personal knowledge of and which I can prove". He says names could be named in the House. "We could do it without being sued, and may well do it, but that's not the way."

and

Yesterday's South Wales Echo reported that the WRU's former commercial manager Jonathan Price had threatened to expose illicit payments to players and to administrators. The paper said that demands from the former manager for payments totalling £45,000 had been described as "blackmail" in a report by WRU chairman Vernon Pugh to his committee, following a meeting with Price.

Andrew Baker, The Independent on Sunday
The possibility has to be considered that the RFU's advisers, duty-bound to deliver the best possible deal, may suggest that England go the same way as France and negotiate their own exclusive television contract.

10 Nov
Mike Averis, The Guardian
England are on course for a confrontation with Wales and Ireland over plans to increase Twickenham's share of next year's new three-year contract to televise the Five Nations Championship. Sources close to the Welsh Rugby Union believe the championship itself could be under threat.

Martin Johnson, The Independent
Since their high-class performance in the opening match, the All Blacks have been as entertaining as a wet Sunday in Invercargill, but only, they say, because the English, with their accent on static, set-piece rugby, would fill most of the positions in a World Boring XV.

11 Nov
Robert Armstrong, The Guardian
Canada snatched a sensational victory over Wales with a last-minute try by their giant lock, Al Charron, here last night. In a graveyard atmosphere and with the scores tied 24-24 the Canadian fly-half Gareth Rees kicked the conversion that sealed Wales's fate on a night when their best endeavours failed to produce a single try.
(Wales 24 Canada 26 Canadas first win in Cardiff)

Martin Johnson, The Independent
Borders rugby parochialism manifests itself in arranging so many weekends of seven-a-side tournaments that it cuts down the number of meaningful 15-a-side matches and leaves no room for a Scottish Cup competition. Scottish rugby is starving, so what do they do? Do away with the main course and bring round the brandy and cigars.

Two Scottish players, Craig Chalmers and Ivan Tukalo, have already warned of a player drain to England.....

Derek Wyatt, Financial Times
Llanelli has provoked the Welsh and English rugby

unions to open discussions for an Anglo-Welsh league. This would be the saviour of club rugby in Wales. It would not offer the big English clubs sufficient incentives, nor enough fixtures of merit. England must look to the continent of Europe as well. It is a European Cup, including French and Italian clubs with the English and Welsh, that is required.

14 Nov
Clem Thomas & Chris Rea, The Independent on Sunday
A secret meeting last week between eight first class rugby clubs – four from England and four from Wales – may lead to the formation of an Anglo-Welsh league, thus throwing the structure of domestic rugby into chaos. The clubs represented at the meeting, held last Tuesday evening in Tewkesbury, were Cardiff, Llanelli, Neath and Swansea from Wales and Bath, Leicester, Harlequins and Wasps from England.
(The English clubs had all let Twickenham know of the meeting)

Ian Burrell & Richard Palmer, The Sunday Times
Tax inspectors are being urged by MPs to raid the headquarters of the Rugby Football Union (RFU) at Twickenham after receiving details of illicit payments of what is supposed to be an amateur game.......

David Watkins, a former Welsh rugby international, told how one international player recently faxed his demands to Newport rugby club. "He said he would be prepared to come to south Wales for a job and a corporate package worth £50,000..."

19 Nov
Dick Best, The Guardian
They (the All Blacks) have their structure, the provincial system and, judging by their performance of the players in this tour party, it seems to be providing them with an endless supply of hard, fast and uncompromising forwards with marvellous handling skills.

20 Nov
The Economist
The decade of May 1 1983 to May 1 1993 saw 223 Test matches among the nine major countries, or about 22 a year. There were 142 in the north and 81 in the south.....

England's winning rate against majors was 33% in the 1970s and 44.5% in the 1980s; it is 72% in the 1990s to date. The corresponding percentages for Australia are similar: 32.4%, 51% and 72.4%. While these two were rising in tandem, Wales (72.8%,45%,21.4%) and Ireland (42.6%,32.3%, 20.5%) were declining sharply. New Zealand (76.2% in the 1990s), France (54.7%) and Scotland (50%) have been stable.......

25 Nov
David Hands, The Times
Who are the teachers now? Not too many of the passes made by the All Blacks may find their way into textbooks but they work:

overarm, overhead, through the legs it does not really matter how the ball finds its way to the man in space so long as it does.....

27 Nov
Matthew Engel, The Guardian

This week Stephen Jones, rugby union correspondent of the Sunday Times became the fifth winner of the William Hill Sportsbook of the year, the sporting Booker, for his work Endless Winter.....

It is no insult to Jones, though, to say that it is not likely to be regarded hence as an all-time sporting classic........How could it be? Jones has written a journalist's book, of its time and place. Nor is it an insult to him to say that the judges regarded 1993 as a rather dispiriting year for sports publishing.

Ian Malin, The Guardian
The North and East stand development is reckoned to have cost £46 million. It is a far cry from the £5562 12s 6d the RFU committee man Billy Williams paid for a 10 1/4 (quarter) acre site in 1907.

Derek Wyatt, Financial Times

Dudley Wood is a big lad. He needs to be. As Secretary of the Rugby Football Union, he sits on a throne whose power and wealth has swelled in the seven years that he has occupied it. Since 1986, the Rugby Union's business has grown from £5 million to nearer £45 million; the staff from 50 to more than a 100. It owned the Twickenham ground, an assortment of allotments, better known as car parks, and 26 houses nearby, now it has a rebuilt stadium and a second ground complete with hotel in Wolverhampton. You have to pinch yourself to remember that all this has happened while the economy has been in reverse.....

28 Nov
The day after England v New Zealand;
Clem Thomas, The Independent on Sunday

Spurred on by their partisan supporters, the England pack did not flag nor fail, and were all blood, toils, tears and sweat. Even if the Commonwealth and New Zealand last another 1,000 years, then men will say this was one of England's finest hours.
(England 15 New Zealand 9)

29 Nov
Day Two of Fleet Street's Love Affair with Rugby; The Daily Telegraph's Sport Section cover:

England Have Last Dance

The Times:
Carling says best is yet to come

The Guardian
England status rises in All Black Eyes

The Independent
Carling's giants join history men & Fitzpatrick refutes

accusation of racism

30 Nov
David Plummer, The Guardian

The All Blacks last night announced that their flanker Jamie Joseph would be disciplined for stamping on Kyran Bracken's ankle in the opening minutes of the Test against England.

David Frost, The Guardian
Oxonians have joked about the number of players who in recent years have been reading land economy at Cambridge – there are nine in the side announced yesterday – but Cambridge men can now begin wondering about the flush of Blues issuing from Keble, which used to be famous for students of divinity. Keble provides eight of the team for 7 December.

Steve Bale, The Independent
Bad news for the University match: next year the attendance will plummet to 60,000 while the Rugby Football Union is engaged in the rebuilding of Twickenham's West Stand. Only 60,000? Twenty years ago it was half that number.

December 1993

1 Dec
James Carey, Southern Cross

But for the All Blacks to lose when they were on the brink of a glorious unbeaten tour, has left all of New Zealand dumb. "Death by their own hands," screamed The Dominion newspaper in Wellington, "The All Blacks were as flat as warm beer".

Former All Black co-coach and selector John Hart criticised the selection of the inexperienced Marc Ellis at five eighth and blasted Jamie Joseph and other players who gave away crucial penalties.

Judy Free, Southern Cross
"There is far too much high-intensity rugby for them to get excited. It is becoming harder and harder for them to get motivated," (Laurie) Mains said. The coach was not offering that as an excuse for defeat by England, but making an observation about the demands that have been placed on his Test players this year.

...Liam Barry wasn't saying he was hurt, and devastated, by the All Black rugby team management's shock decision to overlook him for Mike Brewer.

The strange move was seen as a vote of no confidence by the management on the players like Barry, Blair Larsen and John Mitchell – all overlooked to replace flanker Paul Henderson on the bench for Saturday's Test against England.

Ian Malin, The Guardian
As expected the Rugby Football Union has approved plans for a new three-tier stand to mirror the East Stand unveiled last

Saturday. The cost is expected to be £25.5 million and the demolition of the old will begin after the Sevens on 14 May

5 Dec
Clem Thomas, The Independent on Sunday

As the bidding for the television rights to rugby's Five Nations' Championship intensifies, an emergency meeting has been convened in Cardiff this weekend by representatives of Wales, Scotland and Ireland in a united attempt to counter England's demand to pocket a bigger slice of TV revenue.

Barrie Fairall, The Independent on Sunday

Rugby lost a prop and panto gained a star performer when the four square Gareth Chilcott finally signed off for Bath at The Stoop yesterday, on his way to play the Brokers Man in Cinderella. He could not have put it better, either. "I'm moving from one field of entertainment into another." And, what better way to go than on a winning note?
(Bath 14 Harlequins 12 in the Courage League Division one)

Chris Rea, The Independent on Sunday

But the selectors' preference for Ellis over Bachop as Test fly-half made no sense. Bachop had given a near flawless display in the opening match against London and throughout, showed a greater appreciation of what was required in that position than Ellis, who ran like a whippet but also kicked like one...

Editorial, Independent on Sunday

Indeed, Varsity sport is more popular than it has been for years. Average attendances at the Varsity Match in the early Nineties have been almost double what they were in the Eighties, while the television audience for the event has doubled (to 1.2 million) in the past five years....
.....To denigrate the Varsity Match would be akin to denigrating Christmas.....

Colin Welland, The Observer

Never have I seen such a humourless, brutal, ruthless lot, and no amount of post-match bonhomie will eradicate the memory of their gamesmanship, cynicism and thug-like behaviour, which, if it happened in the street, would make them firm favourites for the short, sharp shock......Make no bones about it, an apt metaphor, there were really evil elements in that All Black side.

Will Carling, The Mail on Sunday

They will be remembered mostly as a dirty side. Some of their play has been beyond the conventions we obey and they have damaged rugby's image. This tour was a great showcase for the game, but how many mothers will now be saying 'I don't want my son to play rugby?'

6 Dec
Robert Armstrong, The Guardian

Fitzpatrick's frustration was intensified because he believes he has not received a fair press. On Saturday he insisted the raking of Phil de Glanville was an acci-

dent and the alleged racial abuse of Victor Obogu never took place. Certainly it was hard to detect a single Kiwi boot out of place in their finale, though once again the All Blacks gave away more penalties than the 55,000 crowd would have liked.

.....their wins over London, the North, South of Scotland and the Barbarians were far more enjoyable than the average Five Nations match. Their try count of 42 to 5 in 13 games reflects a positive attitude.

7 Dec
Oxford v Cambridge
Frank Keating, The Guardian

Oxbridge standards may be derided in some quarters but England's World Sevens-winning side last spring contained three Old Blues, the London XV this season included seven and it is likely nine or 10 Blues will contest this year's Five Nations Championship. That is quite a representation – with one or two more to emerge today.

Reuters

In Dunedin yesterday their (New Zealand) coach Laurie Mains made his first public response to British criticisms of his player's over vigorous tactics. "Generally, the people in Britain were very good to us, they hosted us well," he said. "The only problems were with a few of the gutter press, and with one or two silly players opening their mouths a bit much."

Ian Malin, The Guardian

Spectators in an almost full Twickenham were disappointed if they expected a Corinthian feast of running rugby after the sombre show of the All Blacks, but this fixture is a bit of an oddity. Part open warfare, part Rotarian outing, it is also the pinnacle of many of its layers' careers. The disappointment on Cambridge faces was all too evident as they left the field.
(Oxford 20 Cambridge 8 in the 112th Varsity Match)

9 Dec
Stuart Barnes, The Daily Telegraph

The entire debate concerning the direction of rugby has seemed to concentrate on whether players play too many games. The clubs need it, the players want it, and the supporters love it, yet if the refuse to understand the pressures away from the pitch, our game will inevitably lead in one direction – backwards. What a tragedy it would be if the English game was to fall on the sword of its own success.

13 Dec
Chris Jones, London Evening Standard

The use of the boot and head butt by rugby's violent minority is continuing to scar the game and while the number found guilty of this kind of thuggery is small, the result is a badly-tarnished image for the game as a whole.

England	1990-91	1991-92	1992-3
Players sent off	1657	1716	1743
Striking an opponent	848	731	769

Use of the boot	404	452	478
Head-butting	n/a	143	125

Statistics compiled by David Spyer, President of the London Society of Referees for the RFU

14 Dec
Robert Armstrong, The Guardian

Plans to create an Anglo-Welsh league were rejected yesterday by the Rugby Football Union. John Jeavons-Fellows, chairman of the RFU sub-committee, said such a venture, irrespective of whether it adopted a league or knock-out format, was "not on the agenda" for the foreseeable future.

15 Dec
David Plummer, The Guardian

(Alan) Davies has been under mounting pressure since the home defeat by Canada last month. He said this week that the Welsh nation was expecting success this season, starting with victory over Scotland in Cardiff on 15 January, but it would "take years to get Wales back on the international map".........

16 Dec
Stephen Moss, The Guardian

A video nasty is circulating in the West Country. It is said to contain singularly gruesome scenes: biting, gouging of the eyes, testicles being agonisingly squeezed. X-certificate stuff you might think; questions in the House; sermons about the depravity of modern society. It's not Death Wish VI, though. It's a recording of a rugby match.

17 Dec
Dick Best, The Guardian

Rugby League had a real problem with violence not so long ago. I felt the game was on a downward spiral, virtually resembling "rollerball". They have cleaned up their act and have shown what can be achieved with thought and direction. I am not for one moment suggesting that there are now 13 angels in a rugby league team but there are 13 players who know that acts of brutal violence will be dealt with harshly.

Robert Armstrong, The Guardian

Neil Gray, the New Zealand manager, yesterday became the first casualty of the All Blacks' recent Test defeat by England at Twickenham. He was sacked from his honorary post at a New Zealand RFU council meeting in Wellington. No replacement has yet been named.

Peter Thorburn, a widely respected national selector, was also dismissed by the council which voted in the former All Black Lin Colling to fill the panel vacancy. Laurie Mains kept his job as New Zealand coach but he was criticised by council members for calling Mike Brewer into the squad for the final week of their British tour.

(Colin Meads, capped 55 times for the All Blacks, was named as the new manager)

27 Dec
David Hadfield, The Independent

Wigan revealed one of the game's worst-kept secrets with the announcement at yesterday's match that they have signed Va'aiga Tuigamala, the All Black wing, on a four-year deal....

29 Dec
Headline, The Daily Telegraph
Harris beats points record in thrashing of Barbarians
(Leicester 51 Barbarians 14; Jez Harris, the Leicester fly-half scored 26 points)

30 Dec
Robert Armstrong, The Guardian

Rugby has seen more changes in the past seven years than in the previous 70, but a fresh set of worries lies ahead as the English game gets swept along in the accelerating process of worldwide change. Violence, money and ultra-conservative tactics are without doubt the truly corrosive factors threatening the game.

January 1994

1 Jan
Alan Bleasdale, The Guardian

I was happy until 11 and then I had a very unhappy time. It was fairly strict, depending on which teachers you had. They played rugby and until I went there I hadn't even seen a rugby ball. During my first game this huge 11-year old lad came running towards me so I tripped him up – it was the only way I knew of stopping him. The PE teacher punched me in the face and the lad went on to play for England. We had to wear uniforms but we were treated like second class citizens by the local kids who called us scallywags because we were from Liverpool and we called them woolly-backs. I would have preferred a more liberal environment.

(Bleasdale, one of England's leading playwrights, talking about his school days at Wade Deacon Grammar School, Widnes)

3 Jan
Robert Armstrong, The Guardian

The greatest obstacle barring England's path to a third Grand Slam in four years will almost be there own domestic league and cup programme.

8 Jan
David Hands, The Times

Denis Evans, who was dismissed as secretary of the Welsh Rugby Union (WRU) in October for "grave misconduct" is to seek compensation for the loss of his £48,000 a year post.

9 Jan
Richard Williams,
The Independent on Sunday

"That's the most heartbreaking thing I've heard in rugby for

years," said Cliff Morgan, another of the heroic figures of Welsh rugby, when I told him that the school at Gwendraeth no longer had a regular 1st XV.

"I can't believe it. Gwendraeth Grammar School. Once upon a time, just the sound of it was like a bell ringing across Welsh rugby."

(Gwendraeth Grammar School fostered Carwyn James, Barry John, Gareth Davies and Jonathan Davies)

11 Jan
Michael Herd, Evening Standard

Regrettably,..........the BBC's television coverage remains banal......it is feeble, puerile, platitudinous, conventional, vapid and emasculated. Put another way, it needs balls. Someone, somewhere has to jolt it out of what has been described as its oligarchic cosiness. ....when All Black Jamie Joseph notoriously stamped all over England's Kyren Bracken, (Nigel) Starmer-Smith could only comment "Well, that begs the question."

14 Jan
Headline: SRU rebukes doctor over Chalmers' injection
Bill Leith, The Independent

The SRU said they deplored allegations in a Scottish Sunday newspaper that Chalmers had been put under pressure to take the field against the All Blacks, and added, "Mr Chalmers was receiving an agreed course of treatment".

Headline, The Guardian

Green movement fears Sella afield
(Preview France v Ireland)

16 Jan
Geoffrey Nicholson,
The Independent on Sunday

...But France, the European champions, were simply biding their time before they could put some space between themselves and the Irish. In the final quarter, they exploded out of their frustration, and the crowd, in which there were unusually large gaps, gave them a heroic ovation with drums and pipes.
(France 35 Ireland 15)

Clem Thomas, The Independent on Sunday

Wales finally emerged from their slough of despond yesterday by scoring three tries of remarkable quality given the impossible conditions.....Behind the respective scrums, Wales moved the ball beautifully and Neil Jenkins at fly-half had his best match in the national colours.
(Wales 29 Scotland 6)

20 Jan
David Plummer, The Guardian

The Wales hooker Garin Jenkins has been reported to South Wales Police by an Edinburgh solicitor for his actions in last Saturday's 29-6 win over Scotland.

Magnus Moodie, a 31-year-old social-player with Edinburgh Academicals who watched the game on television, requests in a letter to the Chief Constable that an incident

early in the match be investigated.

23 Jan
Chris Rea, The Independent on Sunday

If ever the day comes when the Five Nations tournament ceases to meet the rigorous challenges and demands of the world game, then the domestic international season will go to the wall just as it did in football.

25 Jan
John Huxley, The Guardian

"Dewi (Morris) was asked whether he wanted to turn professional but declined the invitation," said McKight. "He has charted his future within rugby union and his ambition is to play for England in the enxt World Cup in two years' time."
(Dewi Morris, the Orrell and England scrum half turned down a two year contract with Queensland Crushers)

28 Jan
Dick Best, The Guardian

Pressure on players seems to be the main topic of conversation these days....What will this mean to the future of the game? Certainly, a top-flight player's career will become shorter. To put it bluntly, he will have a limited shelf-life. His sell-by date will almost certainly be around 30 years of age, and it is highly unlikely that he will still be playing at 35.

30 Jan
Chris Rea, The Independent on Sunday

...The Scots have a ruinously cumbersome national league embracing more than 90 clubs, a district championship which falls woefully short of bridging club and international rugby and, in order to help balance the books of a few Border clubs, they have surrendered April to the frivolous irrelevance of Sevens.

31 Jan
Robert Armstrong, The Guardian

The tantalising saga of Neil Back's prospects of winning an England cap came to an end yesterday with his selection for next Saturday's Calcutta Cup match against Scotland at Murrayfield.

February 1993

5 Feb
Derek Wyatt, Financial Times

England supporters expect a win at Murrayfield this afternoon. They will not be too bothered by the score so long as it is a win. A loss would be too frightening to contemplate.
(Scotland 14 England 15 with the last kick of the game which was already well into overtime)

7 Feb
Colin Adamson, London Evening Standard

The England International rugby union team can expect to cash in on a £380,000 sponsorship windfall this season as big business rushes to capitlaise on one of the fastest appreciating marketing commodities in British sport.

Players who declare earnings which contravene the game's laws will not be "shopped" by the Inland Revenue. Rugby union, like soccer, is being investigated by a Solihull-based tax squad. The England players' pool, said to be worth £300,000 a year, and accounts at all levels are understood to have been opened for

13 Feb
Clem Thomas, The Independent on Sunday
It is proposed that each country's director of referees will meet in Sydney later this year for the very first time. These (ruck law) problems will be high on the agenda, but the most pressing issue will be the question of the recruitment of referees. New Zeaalnd are 2,000 short of their requirement, South Africa are lacking 1,500 and Wales have a shortfall of 300. Given the demands of the job this is hardly surprising.

March 1994

9 March
SA Times
Rugby star Naas Botha has taken his name off the National Party's candidate list for the April elections...

"Although I have not at this time chosen politics as a career, I do take a keen interest in politics and will be sure to support and help the National party in the forthcoming elections."

12 March
Robert Armstrong, The Guardian
Talk with the Bath forwards about Jack Rowell and a picture emerges of a ruthless taskmaster who would send shivers of apprehension through a crack SAS unit. No one dares use the word humiliation but there is no doubt that Rowell often adopts extreme pschological tactics to motivate his players: goading, criticising, insulting and embarrassing them into producing their best.

13 March
Eddie Butler, The Observer
To mention tries to Carling and Co is like shouting 'Bravo MacBeth' at the RSC.

Steve Jones, The Sunday Times
When Cooke's managership ends next week, when he becomes merely another dispassionate observer seeking the sporting thrill and maybe a try or two, he will discover how the dispassionate felt in Paris – bored stiff. And it will only get worse. The deep pit dug by the disastrous new laws into which rugby has almost disappeared, is half dug. Rugby history shows emphatically that defensive systems always outpace attacking systems as the game develops. Consider what will happen when defences really get the new laws worked out. For try, read dodo.

16 March
Robert Armstrong, The Guardian
Neil Jenkins must be sick to death of hearing that the Wales fly-half factory shut down long ago, but he is too polite to say so.

17 March
David Plummer, The Guardian
The close-knit Scottish rugby community has drawn on some remarkable family dynasties, but none quite like the Hastings brothers who will each win a 50th cap against France at Murrayfield on Saturday.

21 March
Ian Malin, The Guardian
Murrayfield's new stadium will be completed by the time South Africa visit. Once the West Stand is finished it will look magnificent, but the ground may stand as a monument to former glories rather than a home for new heroes if the Scotland team is not quickly underpinned.
(Scotland 12 France 20)

Robert Armstrong, The Guardian
England can look forward to their summer tour of South Africa with renewed buoyancy after a bucannering performance against Wales that left no doubts as to who are the real top dogs in European rugby.
(England 15 Wales 8. Wales won the Five Nations Cup)

April 1994

13 April
NZ News UK
The veteran editors of New Zealand rugby's equivalent of Wisden, Rod Chester and Neville McMillan, have been scathing in their criticism of last year's All Blacks management in its handling of the Mike Brewer and Jamie Joseph issues.

18 April
Bill Leith, The Independent
Early in the second half, a left hook by the Canadian captain, Stephanie White, on Gill Burns went unnoticed by the touch-judge but prompted an England coach to declare: "This is going to explode".
(England 24 Canada 0 in the Women's World Championships to qualify for the semi-finals)

20 April
Jan de Koning, SA Times
ANC executive member Steve Tshwete made a passionate plea for South Africa to be retained as the host nation for the 1995 Rugby Union World Cup.

Steve Bale & Dave Hadfield,
The Independent
After three false starts, Scott Gibbs, the Wales and British

Isles rugby union centre, switched codes yesterday, signing for St Helens, and provoking instant outrage at his old club Swansea, who had worked hard to prevent his departure.

22 April
Dick Best, The Guardian
Of the 31 players at the session, only half could complete the full battery of tests, owing to one injury or another. Two, Mike Catt and Matt Poole limped away injured. The medical back-up team was staggered how many players needed surgery but were putting it off until June.

May 1994

4 May
SA Times
New South Wales rugby officials launched a scathing attack on the credibility of the SuperTen tournbament after the Warratahs countered a second half come-back by Auckland to beat the New Zealanders 22-19....

NSW refused to play in Durban, despite safety guarantees, because of the state of emergency in Natal.

5 May
Michael Herd, Evening Standard
Not long ago I pointed out that BBC2's Rugby Special was feeble, puerile, platitudinous, vapid and emasculated. Put it another way, it needed balls.

It transpires that the Rugby Union have similar views as a result of which next season's programmes will be produced for the BBC by an independent company.

That company has not yet been chosen and, naturally, neither has the front man. Presumably however, the company will be looking for someone with more potency and passion than Nigel Starmer-Smith.

9 May
Robert Armstrong, The Guardian
Bath scaled another peak with their eighth Twickenham success since 1984 but rugby union took a sharp nosedive with the most mediocre cup final in recent memory. This stodgy, bad-tempered contest made an embarrassing contrast with the thrilling fluency and self-discipline in the rugby league final at Wembley last week.
(Bath 21 Leicester 9 , Pilkington Cup Final)

11 May
David Hands, The Times
Two days after the inauguration of South Africa's first black president, the rugby union players of England will step into a country on the brink of the unknown.

16 May
Headline: Rowell issues post-Natal warning
Robert Armstrong, The Guardian
Having just seen Queensland's world class players make heavy weather of beating Natal in the SuperTen final, Jack

Rowell warned his players not to drop their commitment levels or they would kiss goodbye to a World Cup berth.

20 May
Ian Malin, The Guardian
New Zealand players will be asked to sign contracts to concentrate minds on next year's World Cup.....the contract will promise them regualr income from promotional work.

24 May
Steve Bale, The Independent
As a voyage of discovery, England's tour to South Africa is already sailing periously close to the rocks and the dicsoveries are being made as much about the England team as by them. Geoff Cooke knew everything there was to know about his players; Jack Rowell still knows all too little.

June 1994

4 June
Headline: "Taxmen swoop on seven prominent Welsh clubs". David Plummer and Mike Adair, The Guardian
The recent disclosure that Moseley are being investigated by a special task force of tax inspectors was followed yesterday by an Inland Revenue confirmation that Swansea and at least six other leading Welsh clubs are also under investigation.....

When Ponytpool were asked to supply a gate figure for a certain game, the tax officials produced an aerial blow-up photograph, divided into squares, and said that they had counted a far larger number there that day.....

The Inland Revenue deny acting on media information but must have noted a statement by Lawrence O'Brien, who last week said he had resigned as coach of the Cardiff club St Peter's because of the increasing influence of money.

Frank Keating, The Guardian
...Noticeably missing from the clinic was the England captain and perceived totem, Will Carling, who cried off with a "queasy stomach". That was a thoughtless boob from a man meant to be a PR whizz.

Carling and the other 14 players who missed the township trip missed something that would have been valuable for the rest of their lives. What were they doing instead? Lying gormless and comatose on their beds reading Wilbur Smith and obsessively tweaking their muscle-bound limbs.

6 June
Peter Jackson, Daily Mail
When he shook hand with the colossal English No 6, President Nelson Mandela looked up and told him: "It is an honour to have you in our country."

"Sir," came the reply, "it is an honour for me to meet you. This is a day I shall never forget." With

that, Tim Rodber was off and running into the game of his life...By destroying the Springboks as never before on their own territory, England's galvanised team turned a losing tour into a monumental statment of their World Cup ambition. There can never have been an opening 15 minutes like it in rugby history.
(South Africa 15 England 32)

Headline: All Blacks alarm over Japanese 'poaching'. The Independent

The Sunday Star (NZ) quoted the chairman of the New Zealand Rugby Football Union, Eddie Tonks, as saying he knew of attempts to recruit more New Zealanders in addition to the All Black No 8, Zinzan Brooke, who has reportedly been offered a lucrative four-year contract in Japan. "I'm aware that there is at least one other All Black plus another leading New Zealand player who have received offers.

7 June
Headline: "Money claims may spark SA pay probe". Robert Armstrong, The Guardian

England players have reacted strongly to reports of illegal payments to South African players by seeking a meeting with RFU officials before Saturday's second Test to improve their financial arrangements.

9 June
Headline: "English turn blind eye and kick fair play in the face", John Mason, Daily Telegraph

Table mountain was shrouded in grey, wispy cloud when England's rugby players and officials flew into Cape Town from Port Elizabeth after lunch yesterday. So were English principles of fair play.

Never again can the Rugby Football Union's pious declaration about foul play and the subsequent punishment of individuals be treated seriously. The abdication of responsibilty on Tuesday for events in Port Elizabeth – in which England players took full part – was complete.

England, unless there is a dramatic change of heart, intend that Tim Rodber, the acting captain on Tuesday, should play against South Africa at Newlands on Saturday despite having been sent off. Arming themselves with the favourable verdict of a disciplinary tribunal, England's managment, supported by Ian Beer, the RFU president, consider the matter closed.

Rodber, an Army officer, is penitent, wholeheartedly regretting that, having been punched twice, he jumped to his feet and lashed out in a great flurry of blows. He deserved, he says, to be sent off. The referee was right. So far, so good. The nature of Rodber's offence, no matter the incompetence of the refereeing, required an instant ban – voluntarily, if as they did, a disciplinary committee decided that dismissal was sufficient.

What, I wonder does, Jonathan Callard think about it? Callard, England's full back, was raked not once but twice on the ground. Two horrific cuts, one stretching from one side of his head to within a centimeter of his right eye, required a total of 25 stitches.

The guilty Eastern Province player was penalised: a midfield kick to touch and the throw-in. The opt-out was ludicrous.

Time for England to make the strongest protest to their hosts.

But no. England's own house was not in apple-pie order. Further Rodber, who was advised four years ago by Roger Uttley, the then coach, to cool a fiery temper, is required on Saturday for the series-deciding match.

The high moral strictures about All Black attitudes – de Glanville facial injuries, Bracken trampled – last autumn have been, as a matter of hypocritical expediency, set aside. The mocking laughter that will accompany any holier-than-thou edict from the Rugby Football Union in future will be an acute embarrassment. Deserved, too.

10 June
Paul Ackford, Daily Telegraph

...Tuesday's match against Eastern Province was a disgrace, containing a series of brawls, stampings and personal vendettas but it did serve one purpose. England felt that they were more sinned agaisnt that sinning and it gave them another reason to do well against the Springboks in the second Test on Saturday.

Rugby on tour is a completely different animal. Away for the civilising influences of friends and family, it is easy to slip into an unreal world where the only concerns are training, travelling and winning. Life loses its sense of proportion......Two things have pulled this tour together – a positive reaction to media criticism and the violence on Tuesday. As the midweek side retired to the privacy of the dressing room to lick their wounds, they encountered the rest of the England squad and a standing ovation. It was not an endorsement of the violence, just an appreciation that the 'dirt-trackers' (as the mid-week side are known) had not capitualted in the face of adversity.

12 June
Headline: Revenge of the furies
Stephen Jones, Sunday Times

South Africa went about their business with an incredible, glazed-eye intensity. They drew the series and the country celebrated mightily their first home victory since their return to the international fold. England had the consolation that there is not a team in the world who could have beaten South Africa yesterday.
(South Africa 27 England 9)

Chris Rea, The Independent on Sunday

Dr Louis Luyt's outrage over the punishment of Tim Rodber is like flamenco dancing in a condemned building. Occupation of the moral high ground can be a lonely business as the Rugby Football Union has itself discovered in the past few days.

13 June
Headline: Evening Standard

£30,000 to play rugby: England stars approached by South Africans.

John Mason, Daily Telegraph

...Which, for goodness sake is the real England? The 32-15 winners in Pretoria two Saturdays ago, or the

27-9 losers in Cape Town this weekend...Deep deep down there is an uncomfortable feeling that the true colours might have been on display in Cape Town, this awe-inspirng city of water and mountian, green and gold...This week it was back to the humdrum bread and buter of the drab Five Nations...the spark was not there. Neither was the coordination nor, ultimately, any authority. South Africa were convincingly the better team, hungry, sharp and very nervous until the points finally began to flow in the second half.

14 June
John Drayton, Daily Mail
Stuart Barnes returned from England's controversial rugby tour of South Africa yesterday and announced his shock retiremnt. He said last night: "I've just had enough. The (groin) injury was getting on top of me."

15 June
Steve Bale, The Independent
The seminal moment for Stuart Barnes came when he and other England players were coaching the township kids of Zwide outside Port Elizabeth. Out of fitness and out of favour, he saw precisely how important his groin strain was; not at all, compared with the deprivation of those children.

A few hundred yards from the Dan Qeqe Stadium was a shanty town, a mangle of rotting corrugated iron set in a sea of mud. No hot shower to go home to. For Barnes, who has spent much of his adulthood fighting apartheid, rugby was suddenly the last thing worth worrying about.

Robert Armstrong, The Guardian
England's most senior official (Ian Beer, President) yesterday set the country on collision course with the rugby playing world when he accused the International Board of being spineless and called two of its senior members spineless.

22 June
Headline: MPs debate rugby 'apartheid'
Nick Townsend, Daily Mail
The Palace of Westminster has echoed to rhetoric concerning many kinds of discrimination. Generally, they tend to be of a sexual or racial nature, or touch on class. Rarely can it have borne witness to the intolerance of a sporting institution. Yet that is the position the Rugby Football Union finds itself , as one of the sport's longest-running conflicts becomes embroiled in the legislation process.

Next year rugby league celebrates its centenary. It would like to do so by announcing that those who have graced it as a professional would subsequently be entitled to don a union jersey. At present "blatant discrimination" against that desire exists. David Hinchcliffe, the Labour MP for Wakefield who yesterday introduced a Private Member's Bill to that effect in the House of Commons, declared that 1995 would be "a very appropriate time to end this nonsense once and for all".

The Bill has no chance of becoming law but the belief of Hinchcliffe – a former rugby league player who was prevented from playing union – is that its publication can generate such support that legislation could appear on the statute books next year. The case of his supporters (cross-party and both Houses) is quite simple: that "sporting apartheid" has no place in modern society and that, anyway, the union men are hypocrites, having failed to counter "shama-teurism" in their own ranks.

Headline: "Lewis on the South Sea mat"
David Plummer, Guardian
When Emyr Lewis returns home from the South Seas this week, he will be questioned by the Welsh Rugby Union and his club, Llanelli, about remarks he made on a Welsh-language television programme. The Wales flanker hinted that he had received financial offers to tempt him away from Llanelli, whom he also criticised for their financial difficulties and for the style of play they adopted last season.

Keith Rowlands, the secretry of the International Rugby Board, heard about the programme and asked the WRU to investigate Lewis's comments about money. The Treorchy international Luc Evans, who was also interviewed in the programme, claimed that no club in Wales could descirbe itself as pruely amateur.

The margin (34-9) flattered Westrn Samoa...but the demands of this tour – coming after a full domestic season – finally caught up with Wales. They wilted in the intense heat...

27 June
Headline: "Wales angry at dangerous conditions". David Roberts, Daily Telegraph
Rob Leyshon, the Welsh team doctor, has claimed that conditions for the final tour match agaisnt Western Samoa in Apia were dangerous, with temperatures topping 100°F. Leyshon treated two players for heat exhaustion after Wales's 34-9 defeat.

"The symptoms displayed by Rupert Moon were similar to those suffered by Tommy Simpson, the British cyclist, shortly before he died years ago," said Lyshon. "Rupert was vomiting and was finding it difficult to catch breath. The conditions in Apia were extraordinary, and were perhaps dangerous."

23 June
Headline: "Quins' Salmon to join Sky Sports". John Mason, Daily Telegraph
Jamie Salmon, the Harlequins general manager, is to join Sky Sports television in August as a rugby union presenter and interviewer. Last March, Sky Sports signed a £7 million three-year contract, beginning in September to screen live matches in England, Scotland and Ireland. Sky will also transmit three eekly programmes as part of the Rugby Package – Beind the goalposts, an hour-long show including analysiys, interviews and weekend highlights; World of Rugby Union, half an hour of highlights from around the world, and Grass Roots Rugby, a 30-minute slot for the junior game ∎

RUGBY PUBLISHING

RUGBY PUBLISHING continues to thrive world-wide. More books have been published over the past two years and, with the 1995 World Cup imminent, we can expect a bumper crop next year! Prices are rising well ahead of inflation with most hardbacks priced at £15.99 or £16.99.

Rugby publishing in New Zealand has always thrived. Rugby is the nearest thing to religion on both islands and there would appear to be an insatiable appetite for them. Australian publishing houses must have been irritated that their best players and coaches were being snapped up by their counterparts in New Zealand. But, as the sport grabs more and more media space there, one or two Australian publishers are beginning to put their toe in the water. One is the impressive Allen & Unwin outfit in Sydney, another is Longman Cheshire in Melbourne.

In the UK, Mainstream in Edinburgh continue to dominate the scene. They can expect some competition from Roddy Bloomfield, who moved from Stanley Paul to Headline; and of course Rod Dymott, of Cassell. Rob Andrew, the England fly-half, attracted some unfavourable comment in *The Guardian* for his decision to sack his writer. This would not have seemed so much as a surprise, except the writer in question, Peter Bills, approached him with the idea and wrote the selling synopsis which at one point had two publishers salivating with bids of over £30,000. Andrew has a squeaky clean image but he sullied it with his unprofessional behaviour. Maybe the book will suffer too.

Stephen Jones, the rugby correspondent of the London *Sunday Times,* won the William Hill Sports Book of the Year with his acclaimed *Endless Winter* ■

The *International Rugby Almanack* 1995 Publishing Awards

Publisher of the Year
International & UK: Mainstream, Edinburgh

Book of the Year
They Ran With The Ball: How Rugby Football Began in Australia by Thomas V. Hickie (Longman Cheshire)

Previous Winners 1994
International Publisher: Moa Beckett
UK Publisher: Mainstream
Book of 1994: *The Great Number Tens* by Frank Keating (Partridge)

BOOK REVIEWS

The *International Rugby Almanack* 1995 Book of the Year

They Ran With The Ball: How Rugby Football Began in Australia by **Thomas V. Hickie**
Price: **UK £19.99.**
Publisher: **Longman Cheshire, Melbourne.**
ISBN: **0582910625**

Australia doesn't have a long nor strong rugby literature. It's beginning to change and this book is definitely a classic and fully deserves our award. We congratulate both the Thomas V. Hickie, its author, and Longman Cheshire, its publisher.

Think Rugby: A Guide to Purposeful Team Play by Jim Greenwood. Price: UK £12.99. Publisher: A&C Black, London. ISBN: 0713637811

An up-date of one of the two best books on rugby (*Tactical and Attacking Rugby* by Izaak van Heerden being the other)

Will Carling: the Authorised Biography by David Norrie. Price: UK £16.99. Publisher: Headline, London. ISBN: 074720902

The country divided about who was the real Carling and Peter Bills' book ambushed the "official" story which grieved the subject if not the author. Fleet Street also divided between those writers who supported David Norrie a sports correspondent of The News of the World and those who didn't. The reviews therefore made quite interesting reading.

The book itself is bland, giving a one dimensional view of Will Carling which couldn't have been in his interests nor those of his publishers seeking recompense for the investment they had laid out.

312pp; cheap paper; no colour photos; black and white photos not integral; over-priced; did the publishers lose their nerve?

Rugby Annual 1993 23rd Edition (in association with Radio Sport New Zealand) by Bob Howitt Price: UK £17.95. Publisher: Moa Beckett, Auckland ISBN: 1869580443

This edition was delayed to coincide with the start of the 1994 season in New Zealand so that it could include the All Blacks tour to England. Old fashioned design – three columns on a page – and little acknowledgement to how magazines are re-defining this area.

Content needs a major re-think. 160pp; dull

Nick Farr-Jones: the Authorised Biography by Peter Fitzsimons. Price: UK £14.99. Publisher: Random House, Sydney. ISBN: 0091827582

This is without doubt the best "biography" to have been written for some time; to be fair the subject matter helps but Peter Fitzsimons asks all the right questions and portrays his man sensitively and compassionately.

Farr-Jones will go far and if like David Kirk he takes to politics it will be no great surprise. He has been a giant for the game.

286pp; cheap paper; good colour, indifferent black and white photos; errata note enclosed ; well priced.

Inga: the Winger by Bob Howitt. Price: NZ $39.95. Publisher: rugby press, Auckland. ISBN: 0908630433

Once the rumours about Inga began to circulate that Wigan were interested in him, it was inevitable that his "autobiography" would be advanced. So, in a sense because this book finishes before Inga's tour with the All Blacks to England late last year and obviously before he then signed for Wigan, it is incomplete.

The publishers would have been better withholding it for a year, especially as Inga appeared at Wembley for Wigan in the Rugby League Challenge Cup Final. Inga is a committed Christian and this shines through this book. As a back-drop to Tongan rugby and the plight of the Pacific islanders this is a most interesting read.

208 pp; outstanding quality for print, paper and photographic reproduction; helped by Pepsi Co sponsorship; dreadful cover

---

Rugby Union Sports Skills by Gill Lloyd & David Jefferis. Price: UK £8.50. Publisher: Wayland, Hove ISBN 0750207000

Aimed at schoolchildren, it has plenty of colour and appeals immediately.

32pp; over-priced.

The Great Number Tens by Frank Keating. Price: UK £16.99. Publisher: Partridge, London. ISBN: 1852251921

This was reviewed in *The International Almanack* 1994 as the publishers sent us an early proof copy to read.
272pp; good use of photos; weighty tome; slightly over-priced?

The Scottish Rugby Book '94 **Edited by Ian McLauchlan. Price: UK £12.99. Publisher: Mainstream, Edinburgh. ISBN: 1851585788**

Slightly thin, the essays could be more substantial and the results section is too long! **160pp; colour throughout thanks to the generous sponsorship of The Royal Bank of Scotland; quality finished book.**

Endless Winter **by Stephen Jones. Price: UK £14.99 Publisher: Mainstream, Edinburgh. ISBN: 1851585613**

Unkindly branded as Endless Writing, Stephen Jones' book deserves all the accolades it received last year. It's a tour de force and takes no prisoners. Congratulations. **288pp, colour and black and white; beautiful production; best price; no index**

Rothmans Rugby Union Yearbook 1993-94 22nd Year **Edited by Stephen Jones. Price: £14.99 Publisher: Headline, London. ISBN: 0747278911**

There is no question that in the northern hemisphere this book is the best of its type. It suffers from a dull production design and a slowness of results – no Lions tours; Barbarian tour write-up being stale; no Summer tours or results – but it is the market leader. **448pp; excellent value; paperback; no colour; photos act as a filler.**

Welsh Brewers Ltd Rugby Annual for Wales 1993-94 25th Edition. **Editor: Arwyn Owen Price: UK £4.95. Publisher: Welsh Brewers, Cardiff**

This is a minor classic of its type. Full of sharp editorial comment and plenty of informa-tion about the totality of the game in Wales. **136pp; the photo quality suffers despite the paper; a gem**

The Save & Prosper Rugby Union's Who Who 1993/94 **by Alex Spink. Price: UK £9.99 Publisher: HarperCollins. ISBN: 000218527X**

This book just gets better and better. This edition included players from Australia, New Zealand and South Africa and still retailed at £9.99 so presumably there is a healthy financial input from the sponsors. **464pp; photos of every current international player; stacks of stats.; a bible for journalists and rugby groupies.**

Straight from The Hart **by Paul Thomas. Price: UK £16.99. Publisher: Moa Beckett, Auckland ISBN: 186958015X**

This is sub-titled: The Career and Philosophy of a Rugby Revolutionary and is the story of John Hart, the former All Blacks coach.

If you want to know why New Zealand rugby is struggling to maintain its role as the premier country in the world, read this challenging and controversial book. But take it with a pinch of salt even though this reviewer couldn't put it down. **280pp; high quality production throughout.**

Carling: A Man Apart **by Peter Bills. Price: UK £14.99. Publisher: Witherby, London ISBN: 0854932305**

This sold so well that it is appears up-dated and as a paper-back in October. Bills' account of Carling though it found no favours with the subject matter was more or less spot on. The boy simply cannot captain on the field; his results prove it: no Grand Slam in 1990 and no World Cup win in 1991; wretched decision making in 1993 and 1994 Five Nations games; a poor Lions tour in 1993; why is he the darling of the media ponders Bills, why indeed?

256pp; no colour pics only black and white and then in sections; wasted back jacket. Sensible price.

So Close to Glory: The Lions in New Zealand 1993 **by Ian McGeechan. Price: UK £9.99. Publisher: Queen Anne Press, Harpenden. ISBN: 1852915323**

Presumably, the sponsors, Scottish Life, had committed to this book before the final Test was lost and with it the series. They will not be only the only ones who kicked themselves because of the result of the first Test which is a pity because this is another beautifully produced book with lavish colour photographs throughout.

Since ITV took to covering the Lions Tours and since the broadsheets now give it such breadth with colour photographic support, where is the market for this book?

96 pp; good results section; no index; poor cover.

Rugby for Threequarters **by Peter Johnson with Richard Hill. Price: UK £9.99. Publisher: A&C Black, London. ISBN: 071363782X**

This is a disappointing book – not in terms of content which is fresh and original – but in terms of design which is quite simply appalling. **116pp; too expensive; should have been a video.**

Rugby **by Terence O'Rorke. Price: UK £8.99. Publisher: Wayland, Hove. ISBN: 0750208686**

Terence O'Rorke is former All Sport picture researcher turned writer; this book is aimed at boys and girls who want to learn about the game. The words are too large but the drawings and photographs are all in colour and are a joy. **48pp, poor cover; user friendly design**

The Game The Goal: The Grant Fox Story by Alex Veysey. Price: UK £14.99. Publisher: rugby press, Auckland. ISBN: 0908630395

This was a book first published in New Zealand in the late 1992 but did not surface in the UK until Grant Fox's decision not to travel with the 1993 All Blacks to England and Scotland and then subsequently to retire from the game. As such it came out a year early missing the 1993 Lions Tour as well.

This is a cracking read and goes way beyond the normal dull and repetitive life of a rugby player as he makes his way up the ladder. Good pieces about his childhood and the way in which he practised kicking goals with his bare feet. Any would-be child star out there who fancies himself should read these early chapters as a lesson in mental discipline. Congratulations to Alex Veysey and Grant Fox.

216pp; poor covers – especially the back; colour pics and colour sections, plenty of black and white; no index; good statistics section.

Bath: Ace of Clubs **by Brian Jones. Price: UK £16.95. Publisher: Breedon Books, Derby. ISBN: 1873626452**

This is a book that will have sold well in and around the Recreation Ground. It charts Bath's success from the late 1970s through to the end of the 1992-1993 season.

The large format lends itself to a better design and far better use of photographs but it is aimed at the popular market not the cognoscenti. Even so, it looks like a book from the mid-1970s. Shame.

Still, it does leave the market open for a definitive book on Bath like those done on London Welsh, Harlequins and Leicester Tigers.

256pp; photos littered throughout but no colour; dreadful cover

---

The Five Nations Championships 1947-93 **by John Griffiths. Price: £12.99. Publisher: Methuen, London. ISBN: 0413359611**

This is an odd book which was immediately out-of-date the moment it was published. It gives in a piecemeal way a sort of popular history of the Five Nations since 1947, why then?

John Griffiths is one of the two established statisticians in the game and this book follows in someway the format of his other "history" of the British Lions.

It just doesn't work as a book.

178pp large format; black and white photographs throughout but no colour; bizarre cover; badly designed.

The Complete Book of Mini Rugby **by Don Rutherford. Price UK £8.99. Publisher: Partridge Press, London. ISBN: 1852251964**

This is a peach of a book set to be the standard for some time. It's full of sensible advice, well laid out, plenty of diagrams and the odd joke to boot.

Who is it aimed at? Coaches not children – what's wanted now is a Super Mario Guide to Mini Rugby on gameboy and other platforms including cd-rom.

254 pp; quality production, great price hence no colour; no index

Upfront: The Jeff Probyn Story **by Barry Newcombe. Price: UK £14.99. Publisher: Mainstream, Edinburgh. ISBN: 1851585540**

Jeff Probyn has been of the great characters of the Front Row Union and his "autobiography' is laced with judicious, and occasionally acrid, comment particularly about Will Carling. In the end, Probyn will be known as the player who won more player awards on the Lions Tour to New Zealand in 1993 without playing.

192pp; 8pp colour section; classy cover; no index; keenly priced

The Whitbread Rugby World '94 **Edited by Ian Robertson and Nigel Starmer-Smith. Price; UK £9.99. Publisher: Lennard Queen Anne Press, Harpenden. ISBN: 185291534X**

This is a classy product with two colour sections and black and white photographs interspersed throughout the text. The book is a series of essays from the great and the good until it runs out of steam threequarters of the way through and then appears to settle for a sort of ghetto mix of articles that do not fit the overall flavour. Pity.

128pp inc 2 x 8pp colour sections.

Bill Beaumont's Rugby Masterpieces **with Neil Hanson. Price: £12.99. Publisher: Sidgwick & Jackson. ISBN: 0283061847**

Sub-titled Classic Tales From the Pitch, this is the paperback version of the hard-back and follows hard on the heals of Godfrey Smith's Take the Ball and Run, another rugby anthology. Nevertheless, this volume is all together more comprehensive drawing as it does on the world of rugby literature.

You can dip and dive into this book, leave it in the loo or read it at your other leisure. The problem with anthologies is that there's nothing really to get your teeth into – this is more a reflection on newspaper sports editors who seem to want smaller and smaller sound bites than on the editors of this tome.

Nice paper, good print and the large format gives value for money.

317pp inc 8pp black and white photographic section

Rugby Stories **by Peter FitzSimons. Allen & Unwin Australia distributed by Cassell UK £5.99pb. ISBN 1863734406**

Peter FitzSimons played rugby for Australia and spent four more years enjoying a swan song in France. The good thing is he writes better than he ever played and this is his first collection of journalism drawn from the Sydney Morning Herald, The Sunday Times, The Independent and the London Daily Telegraph. Most pieces embrace his love of the game and a fierce sense of humour lacking in much rugby writing at present.

The Guinness Sports Yearbook 1994 **by Peter Nichols. Guinness and Sportspages £11.99 pb. ISBN 0851127452**

Bumper book – 416pp – but rugby union receives ten pages. Most of the information can be found in other publications including this one! As an overview of the year it is quite outstanding.

Great Moments in British Sport **Edited by John Lovesey. Price: UK £15.99. Publisher: Witherby. ISBN 0854932291**

Only four mentions for rugby – Obolensky's try in 1936, the Lions victory in New Zealand in 1971, Wales's seventh Grand Slam in 1976 and England's own Grand Slam in 1991. **192 pp, largish format but could have been larger still; expensive.**

Action Replay: A Media Memoir **by David Parry-Jones. Price UK £9.95. Publisher: Gomer Press. ISBN: 185902016X**

This is an eminently readable autobiography of David Parry-Jones best known outside Wales for his rugby commentaries but that it only half the man though to be sure rugby was important to him. **198pp; paperback; poor quality photographic reproduction.**

A Question of Sport 5 **Compiled b Mike Adley & John Knight. Price: UK £5.99. Publisher: BBC. ISBN: 0563369809**

From the BBC TV series now into its dotage; this book includes rugby players – Will Carling, Jeremy Guscott, Jonathan Davies, Craig Chalmers, Jonathan Webb and Rob Andrew. **128pp; accessible and fun**

Books For Christmas 1994

1. Nick Farr-Jones by Peter Fitzsimons
Arrow A$12.95 ISBN 0091829631
The paperback of the best-selling hard back; published first in Australai in July, 1994. Includes, bravely, two colour photo sections and an up-date to include his return against the South Africans at the end of last year.

2. High Balls and Happy Hours
by Gavin Hastings with Clem Thomas
Mainstream £14.99 ISBN 1851586458

3. Smelling of Roses by Stuart Barnes
Mainstream £14.99 ISBN 1851586407
Written by Barnes himself and thought to have the potential of Nick Hornby's Fever Pitch.

4. The Official History of the Melrose Sevens by Walter Allen
Mainstream £14.99 ISBN 18515866001

5. The Scottish Rugby Union Yearbook 1995 Edited by Derek Douglas
Mainstream £9.99 pb ISBN 1851586296

6. My Greatest Game – Rugby by Bob Holmes and Chris Thau
Mainstream £12.99 ISBN 1851586342

7. At the Centre by Jeremy Guscott with Steve Jones. Pavilion £14.99
This book has been held over

8. Rugby Skills Will Carling and others
Lennard £9.99 pb ISBN 1852915552

9. The Whitbread Rugby World '95
Edited by Nigel Starmer-Smith & Ian Robertson
Lennard £10.99 pb ISBN 1852915528

10. A Game and a Half by Rob Andrew with Chris Rea. Hodder & Stoughton

11. The Save and Prosper Rugby Union Who's Who 1994/5 Edited by Alex Spink. HarperCollins £9.99pb ISBN 0002185393

12. Rothmans Rugby Union Yearbook 1993-94 Editor Stephen Jones. Headline £5.99

13. Michael Jones – The Authorised Biography by Robin McConnell Rugby press NZ$39.95 ISBN 09086630441

14. Real Men Wear Black by Trevor McKewen . Rugby press NZ$39.95 ISBN 090863045X

15. The Great Little All Black Signature Book by Margot Butcher Rugby press NZ$14.95 ISBN 0908630468

12. More Rucking Fun by Stu Wilson & Phil Kingsley-Jones. Moa Beckett NZ$24.95

17. Men in Black 1988-1993 (supplement) by R.H. Chester & N.A.C. McMillan Moa Beckett NZ$34.95

18. Men in Black 1903-1993 (complete) by R.H. Chester & N.A.C. McMillan Moa Beckett NZ$59.95

19. Jeff Wilson – The Natural by Pat Booth Moa Beckett NZ$24.95

20. Fronting Up – the Sean Fitzpatrick Story by Steven O'Meagher. Moa Beckett NZ$39.95

21. Rugby – The International Game by Pat Booth. Photographer Colin Whelan. Moa Beckett NZ$39.95 *Available in UK from Lennard Books £14.99*

1994 Books in Print

In last year's *Almanack* we published as up-to-date list as we were aware of rugby books in print. We asked publishers in New Zealand, Australia, and South Africa to correct or add to our list. Here are their additions and some extras from the UK:-

1.The Game The Goal – The Grant Fox Story with Alex Veysey ISBN 0908630395 (rugby press New Zealand)

2. 100 Great Rugby Characters by Joseph Romanos & Grant Harding ISBN 0908630344 (rugby press New Zealand)

3. Grizz – The Legend by Phil Gifford ISBN 0908630360 (rugby press New Zealand)

4. Rugby – a tactical appreciation by J.J.Stewart (rugby press New Zealand)

5. John Gallagher – the Million Dollar Fullback by Chris Brown ISBN 0908630387 (rugby press New Zealand)

6. Lock, Stock 'n' Barrel by Andy Haden ISBN 090863028X £9.95 (rugby press New Zealand 1988)

7. Poidevin with Jim Webster ISBN 0733301487 £13.50 (ABC Enterprises reprinted and up-dated 1992)

8. The All Blacks by T.P.McLean ISBN 0283060786 £14.99 (Sidgwick & Jackson 1991)

9. A Life in Rugby (Danie Craven) by Ted Partridge ISBN 1868123553 £14.95 (Southern)

10. The Year of The Rose Edited by Barrie Fairhall ISBN £14.99 1851584412 £14.99 (Mainstream)

11. Cornwall Rugby Champions by Colin Gregory ISBN 1852251662 £9.99 (Partridge)

12. Carling's England by Barry Newcombe ISBN 0002721309 £14.99 (Harvill)

13. Old Heroes by Warwick Rogers ISBN 0340554851 £14.99 (Hodder & Stoughton, NZ)

14. Sports Skills Rugby Union by Gill Lloyd & David Jefferis ISBN 0750207000 £8.50 (Wayland)

Publishers and authors are asked to keep us informed about any changes.

UK Rugby Magazines

Rugby World **Edited by Peter Bills. Price: £2 monthly. Publisher: Mark Jones, Harmsworth Active. Circulation: Edging 50,000**

The magazine is hardly recognisable from the dreary being it was a year ago. Bigger, fatter, more colourful, up-to-the-wire coverage, excellent use of Apple software, becoming more design conscious, *Rugby World* dominates the market place like never before.

Rugby News **Edited by Richard Bath. Price: £1.90 monthly. Publisher: Chris Pilling. Circulation: estimate 12,000 and improving**

Richard Bath moved from *Rugby World* to *Rugby News* and he has also done a respectable job improving the look of the magazine and increasing the depth of its articles. He could never have expected *Rugby World* to become so responsive so quickly and this may irk him somewhat.

He copied the front page logo of *Rugby World* for one edition which may have landed him in hot water. Sales are up but break even must be nearer 20,000 if the magazine is to survive.

Rugby Monthly **Edited by Nigel Melville. Price: £2 monthly. Publisher: Nicholas Alexander. Circulation: estimate 5,000**

It's hard to see what the market is for this publication. It is designed like something from the 1960s and if it is to pick up sales it needs a major editorial re-appraisal; unlikely to survive.

Ruck & Maul **Edited by Randall Northam. Price: £1.95 frequency uncertain. Publisher: David Over. Circulation: not available**

The first issue was in early 1994 and as there hasn't been a further issue we must presume that it did not score at the box office. Its design was lamentable even though there was some interesting articles.

Scottish Rugby **Edited by Kevin Ferrie. Price: £2 monthly. Publisher: Scotrun Publications Ltd. Circulation: not available**

Scottish Rugby continues to survive though the regional supplements in *Rugby World* cannot have helped its cause.

More worrying is that to build sales it needs a strong national side to act as a focus....

Rugby '94 **Edited by Greta Bourke. Price: £2.50 annual. Publisher: Kevin Harrington, Sporting World Publications. Circulation: not available**

This normally reaches the bookstalls in January and acts as a guide to the Five Nations. Its moved its editorial feel to embrace more club rugby – well Bath and Leicester and overseas tours – but were these just fillers?

International Magazines & Newspapers

AUSTRALIA:
International Rugby Review
(Tel: 010 61 2 319 1888);
Rugby News
Tel: (010 61 2 957 6652)

CANADA:
The National Rugby Post *six issues a year*

FRANCE:
L'Equipe – *daily especially good on Saturdays*
(Tel: 010 331 4969 0418)
Midi-Olympique (Tel: 010 61 41 11 49)

ITALY:
La Gazzeto dello Sport – *pink weekly newspaper, gives previews on Sunday and reports and results on Monday*
Il Mondo del Rugby – *monthly magazine*
(Tel: 010 39 45 5777266)

NEW ZEALAND:
Rugby News – *weekly newspaper*
(Tel: 010 64 9 443 0250)

SOUTH AFRICA:
Rugby – *a monthly magazine*

SPAIN
La Revista de Rugby – *monthly magazine*
(Tel: 010 341 541 4978)

USA:
Rugby – *a tabloid style monthly newspaper*
(Tel: 0101 212 787 1160)

Also received:

The Official Yearbook of the Rugby Football Union 1994 Edited by Barrie Fairall. Published by RFU

> Books, video, software, magazines and newspapers for review should be sent to:
>
> **The Editor**
> **47 Mount Pleasant Villas**
> **London N4 4HA**
> **Tel 44 81 292 0249**
> **Fax 44 81 292 0257**

COLLECTING RUGBY BOOKS

by John Whittaker

"Francis G Richings (editor). Illustrated Souvenir of the Springboks Tour 1931-1932. G Mitchell & Co Ltd 1931. 64pp/ Well illustrated. Limp covers. Page size: 21cm x 14cm. A detailed pre-tour publication. Includes biographical details and photograph of each of the tourists (three per page), full-page photographs of the Springboks of 1906, 1012 and 1921, All Blacks of 1905, 1924 and 1928 and the British teams of 1924 and 1930. Much written material also. Preface by Paul J Roos. A very good, clean copy of this scarce publication. £30"

This was item 217 in a specialist bookseller's catalogue in 1989. You would have to pay a good deal more for this now, certainly more than £50. Why is this? The reasons are many and various. One is the growing interest in collecting rugby books (and many rugby collectors are clearly well-heeled). Another is a growing realisation of what is or is not available. There is nothing like a definitive bibliography of rugby books (although the enthusiast would find David McLaren's *A Handbook of Rugby Literature* invaluable). It now seems clear that Richings' publication is one of just two on the South African tour of the British Isles. The other is Lowenstein & Hayes' *National Souvenir of the Springbok Rugby Tour of the UK 1931-1932*, another pre-tour publication.

Where, however, do you find rarities such as these for sale? The answer is on the shelves of a specialist bookseller. It is, of course, possible for a rugby gem to be located in a general secondhand bookshop. My experience is that most general dealers shy away from books about rugby football. Some don't know what their stock includes and request for directions to the rugby section can evoke responses such as "I think there is something on sport in that pile behind the electric fire", or "Rugby. Now let me think, that's Warwickshire isn't it?"

Perhaps this is a bit unfair. There are many booksellers who keep high-quality stock, know what they have got and know about values. Almost certainly, however, if you come across a rugby football rarity which you want, it will cost a fraction of the price you would have to pay in acquiring it from a specialist. There is always a chance that *The Complete Rugby Footballer on the New Zealand System* (Metheun, 1906) by D Gallaher and W J Stead in immaculate condition can be found for a fiver in this way. I would charge something like £150 for the same thing. Condition is a major factor in determining price. The Yorkshire Rugby Football Union *Commemoration Book 1914-19* and *Official Handbook Season 1919-20* in fine condition would sell for something around £60. In worn covers, loose at the spine, grubby inside and with page-edge tears, it would still command a price of £10 because it is much in demand and there are not many copies around. A book in top-class condition would fetch nothing at all if nobody wants it, no matter how scarce it is. In the end, the price of a book is determined by how much customers are prepared to pay.

There is not enough room to list here a comprehensive guide to secondhand rugby book prices. What follows is an approximate pricing under various headings. Other specialist dealers will disagree with my valuations but not by much. There are not many of us around, however. In England the Courage League comprises more than 1,000 rugby clubs. Twickenham holds about 70,000 specators. In the UK there are just three specialist rugby book dealers.

The listing is of publications in extremely good condition – very clean inside and out, complete and tightly-bound and with very nice dust wrappers where appropriate.

Early 'Classics'

Rev F Marshall (editor). *Football. The Rugby Union Game.* Cassell & Co 1892. 512pp. 157 illustrations. Hard blue cloth with title, etc in gilt.   **£100**

Harry Vassall. *Football: The Rugby Game. With Chapters on Professionalism, Refereeing, and the Northern Union by Arthur Budd.* George Bell & Sons, 1898. 78pp + 8pp. of plates + 8pp. of advertisement pages. Hard decorative cloth.   **£60**

G H Dixon. *The Triumphant Tour of the NZ Footballers.* Geddis & Blomfield, 1906. 176pp. Illustrated.   **£200**

R A Barr. *With the British Rugby Team in Maori Land.* Otago Daily Times & Witness Newspapers Co Ltd, 1908. 168pp. Illustrated.   **£150**

Football: A Weekly Record of the Game Vol 1 1882-3. A bound volume of 28 consecutive weekly editions of this periodical. Oct 4, 1882 to April 11, 1883. 424 pages in all. Index. Hard, blue cloth covers. All edges gilt. Deals with association football as well as rugby football.   **£225**

Brinley E Matthews. *The Swansea Story. A History of the Swansea Rugby Football Club 1874-1968.* Swansea Cricket & Football Club, 1968. 102pp. Frontispiece and 12 pages of plates.   **£15**

Dublin University Football Club 1854-1954. Published by the club, 1954. 93pp. + advertisements. (i to xxii). 9 plates. 3 full-page caricatures. Pages 1 to 38 are on the history of the club. These are followed by facts and figurespages. Hard blue cloth with title in gilt. **£20**

Old Merchant Taylors Rugby Football Club. Records of Twenty Seasons 1882-1902. 264pp. 10 photographs. Hard red cloth with title in gilt. **£50**

The Bristol Football Club Jubilee Book 1888-1938. 102pp. 4pp. of photographs. Limp illustrated covers. A history of the club. Written by W T Pearce, C H Reed and six others. **£40**

Ross McWhirter & Sir Andrew Noble Bt. *Centenary History of Oxford University Rugby Football Club.* OURFC, 1969. 212pp. + 84pp. of biographies + 7pp of records. Page size: 31.5cm x 20.5cm. Illustrated. Complete with folding chart of Oxford v. Cambridge results. **£40**

C D Stuart. *West of Scotland Football Club 1865-1965.* Glasgow, 1965. 117pp. Illustrated. **£15**

Gosforth F C 1877-1977. 16pp. within illustrated card covers. Illustrated. The club's centenary publication. **£6.50**

Tour Accounts

Terry McLean. *Kings of Rugby. The British Lions' 1959 Tour of New Zealand.* Baily Bros & Swinfen Ltd, 1960. 248pp. Illustrated. **£15**

John Hayhurst. *The Fourth All Blacks 1953-1954.* Longmans, Green & Co, 1954. 267pp. Illustrated. **£12**

Denis Lalanne. *La Melée Fantastique. The French Rugby Tour of New Zealand 1961.* Reed, 1962. 207pp. **£20**

Biographies, Autobiog's etc

Edward Bagnall Pulton. *The Life of Ronald Poulton.* Sidgwick & Jackson Ltd, 1919. 410pp. + frontispiece plate + 16pp other plates. **£50**

W W Wakefield & H P Marshall. *Rugger.* Longmans, Green & Co, 1927. 491pp. Illustrated. Pages 3 to 107 form the rugby autobiography of Wavell Wakefield. **£20**

R W H Scott and T P McLean. *The Bob Scott Story.* Herbert Jenkins, 1956. 209pp. Illustrated. **£8.50**

Alex Veysey. *Colin Meads All Black.* Collins, 1974. 256pp. Illustrated. **£15**

Gerald Davies. *An Autobiography.* Allen & Unswin, 1979. 160pp. Illustrated. **£6.50**

Roger Uttley. *Pride in England.* Stanley Paul, 1981. 189pp. Illustrated. **£8.50**

Gordon Brown. *Broon from Troon.* Stanley Paul, 1983. 220pp. Illustrated. **£6.50**

Willie John McBride & Edmund Van Esbeck. *Willie John.* Gill & Macmillan, 1976. 160pp. Illustrated. **£15**

Rowe Harding. *Rugby. Reminiscences & Opinions.* The Pilot Press, 1929. 154pp. Frontispiece and 16 other pages of plates. **£40**

W J Townsend Collins ("Dromio"). *Rugby Recollections.* R H Johns, Newport, 1948. 182pp. 99 illustrations. **£28**

Miscellaneous

Ompax. *Rugby – The Game.* James Hedderwick & Sons Ltd, Glasgow, 1927. 152pp. **£10**

Gerald Holmes. *Midland Rugby Football.* Littlebury & Co Ltd, Worcester. 1949. 102pp. 16pp. of plates.   **£15**

Winston McCarthy. *Haka! The All Blacks Story.* Pelham, 1968. 348pp. Illustrated.   **£12.50**

O L Owen. *The History of the Rugby Football Union.* Playfair Books for the RFU, 1955. 368pp. Illustrated.   **£15**

Bill Beaumont. *Bedside Rugby.* Willow Books, 1986. 88 large pages. Hard covers.   **£5**

Northumberland Rugby Union Official Handbook 1972-73. 125pp. Card covers.   **£1**

Fylde Rugby Union FC USA Tour 88. 32 large pages. Limp covers. Brochure.   **£1**

Manhattan Rugby Football Club, New York City, USA Home Countries Tour 1970. 32pp.

Illustrated. Card covers. Brochure.   **£5**

The Evolution of Rugby Football. Nonsense Verses by A Podmore. Drawings by Francis Brown. Lettering by E W Brown. Ashley & Smith Ltd, 1911. 30 large pages. Card covers.   **£25**

Robert Anderson (editor). *Heard in the Scrum. A Lighthearted Look at the Game of Rugby.* Stanley Paul, 1964. 132pp.   **£6.50**

Reference: D McLaren. *A Handbook of Rugby Literature. Second Edition.* Published by the author:- *219 High Street, Dunedin, New Zealand.*

Rugby specialists*: Malcolm Spark, Oval Books, Graylings, Niddside, Darley, Nr Harrogate HG3 2PW. Tel: 0423 780792.*

D P Richards, Rugby Relics, 61 Leonard Street, Neath, W Glamorgan SA11 3HW. 0639 646725.

John M W Whittaker, 51 Western Hill, Durham City DH1 4RJ. 091 384 3202

COMPUTERS, FILM & VIDEO

Computer Games

There has been no major breakthrough in this area for rugby. It isn't perceived as an international game, the problem is that as America is the major first market, the game has to mean something there. Also, though there are national heroes, there is no single dominant world personality to hook into. The two games still in circulation are:

International Rugby Challenge
by Domark for IBM, PC and Compatibles, and Commodore, Amiga and Atari ST.
Price £29.99

World Class Rugby
by Anco for Super Nintendo
Price £44.99

Film

We published every rugby film in the British Film Institute's National Film and Television Archive in The *International Rugby Almanack 1994.* Since then there have been some addition to the 1993 list:

18.4.93
Rugby World Cup Sevens: The Final. ITV. 156 mins

26.6.93
South Africa v France. ITV. 113 mins

21.5.94
Natal v England. ITV

25.5.94
Western Transvaal v England.
ITV

28.5.94
Transvaal v England. ITV

31.5.94
South Africa B v England

4.6.94
South Africa v England 1st Test, ITV

7.6.94
Eastern Province v England. ITV

12.6.94
South Africa v England
2nd Test. ITV

Contact at BFI: Simon Baker
Tel 44 71 255 1444
Fax 44 71 580 7503

We will publish a complete up-date in next year's Almanack.
We would also welcome news from other national arcive libraries on their rugby footage.

Video – listing compiled by Clive Fortnum

Title	Distributor
100 Years of All Black Rugby	Quadrant Video
101 Best Tries with Cliff Morgan	BBC Enterprises Video
60 Year with the British Lions	Karussell Ltd
All Blacks, A Decade of Rugby, the Eighties	BBC Enterprises Video
All Blacks vs Springboks, their toughest rivals	Pickwick Video
All Blacks vs Wallabies, their greatest encounters	Pickwick Video
Barbarian – The Final Challenge	BBC Enterprises Video
Barbarians vs the All Blacks 1973	BBC Enterprises Video
Bath's golden decade – Never in Doubt	First Independent Video
Battle of the Giants – New Zealand v South Africa 1986	Duke Marketing
Bill Beaumont selects The Best of BBC Rugby	BBC Enterprises Video
British Lions Tour of Australia, 1989	Video Collection Int Ltd
Century of the Barbarians, A	ATerry Blood Dist
England's Glory Years	BBC Enterprises Video
England's Grand Slam 1991 – the Five Nations Championship	BBC Enterprises Video
Five Nations Championship, 1988 – Wales vs Scotland	BBC Enterprises Video
Five Nations Championship 1994	BBC Enterprises Video
Five Nations Championship 1993 – Wales 10 England 9	BBC Enterprises Video
Great Match, The – England vs Ireland 1982	BBC Enterprises Video
Great Match, The – Scotland vs Wales 1971	BBC Enterprises Video
Greatest Rugby Moments	BBC Enterprises Video

Greatest Hits and Dirty Bits – Presented by Mick 'The Much' Skinner	Pickwick Video
Hong Kong Sevens 1990	Quadrant Video
Hong Kong Sevens 1991	Quadrant Video
Hong Kong Sevens 1992	Quadrant Video
Hong Kong Sevens 1993	Quadrant Video
Hong Kong Sevens 1994	Quadrant Video
Pilkington Cup story 1994, The	Visionsport International
Power Play – All Blacks, How they became world champions – The Official Film of the 1987 World Cup	Screen Entertainments Ltd
Pride and passion, The – Official highlights of the 1993 British Lions Tour of New Zealand	Pickwick Video
Return of the Dragon, The – Welsh Triple Crown 1988	BBC Enterprises Video
Rugby Master Class	Visionsport International
Rugby World Cup – Australia vs England	Pickwick Video
Rugby World Cup – Campese, Wizard of Oz	Pickwick Video
Rugby World Cup – Flowers of Scotland	Pickwick Video
Rugby World Cup – Gold Rush, the World in Union	Pickwick Video
Rugby World Cup – Greatest Tries	Pickwick Video
Rugby World Cup – Swing Low Sweet Chariot	Pickwick Video
Scotland's Grand Slam	BBC Enterprises Video
Sevens Heaven – Rugby World Cup Sevens 1993, The Official Highlights	Pickwick Video
Sweet Victory – England vs the All Blacks 1993	BBC Enterprises Video
Try, Try again – A Welsh Rugby Union coaching series, Vol 1	Quadrant Video
Try, Try again – A Welsh Rugby Union coaching series, Vol 2	Quadrant Video
Try, Try again – A Welsh Rugby Union coaching series, Vol 3	Quadrant Video
World Cup Rugby 1987	Quadrant Video
World's Greatest Rugby Players, The	Vision Video Ltd
World's Greatest XV, The	Karrussell Ltd

Clive Fortnum, Videolog, Cherryholt Road, Stamford, Lincs PE9 2HT.
Tel (44) 780 64331. Fax (44) 780 55006.

A PLEA FROM BIG SISTER

Keep in touch with the latest news – and communicate information – on rugby via
BBC Ceefax, says Annie Briggs

COMMUNICATE AND DELIVER

Rugby has been part of the sports coverage on Ceefax since the early days of the BBC's teletext service. It has always been a popular sport with viewers and, as the output expanded, more space was made available for rugby news.

Rugby was eventually given a section of its own a couple of years ago and an index is carried on page 370 (currently on BBC2 only on weekdays but on BBC1 as well at weekends and on Bank Holidays).

Rugby Union often provides some pretty good news stories during the week, particularly when tours are approaching and there are players struggling to be fit, big names being ousted from the squad by young pretenders and the on-going debate over professionalism (ie cash) creeping into this amateur sport.

Then there are those dastardly players who 'defect' to rugby league, big sponsorship announcements and the inevitable banning of players caught misbehaving on the pitch.

By Friday there is usually some team news about for Saturday's major clashes and a huge number of weekend fixtures are listed. Five Nations matches get special treatment, not surprisingly. The World Cup will command even greater coverage. Yet this sport, which has such a vast and enthusiastic band of followers has, in my opinion, little or no idea how to encourage media interest – at least at a club level.

Ceefax is a terrific medium for promoting any sport. Teletext TVs are in use in millions of homes and, in seconds, news of a postponed match or a result can appear on the fixture pages. Yet every week Ceefax faithfully carries lists of club fixtures, any number of which may have been called off weeks before. The first our sports desk will know of it is late on Saturday afternoon when a fruitless search

of a long list of results shows no sign of the match, or that the home fixture has become an away fixture.

Why should this be? We rarely miss a football cancellation, even those in the non-league Beazer Homes or Northern Premier. We receive faxes informing us of re-arranged basketball and hockey matches, telephone calls when speedway meetings are waterlogged and re-arranged. But updates to our rugby club fixtures? Rarely ever.

Scottish Championship news is also conspicuous by its absence. Perhaps those promoting the sport there are unaware that each week Ceefax carries a set of McEwans National League results and two divisions of tables.

We had a very interesting letter from Brenda Hobday, press officer for the Middlesex County RFU. She had faxed us some news of a last minute injury which had resulted in a player being called up for the County semi-finals at lunchtime on the Friday. He failed to inform the Richmond 1st XV until Saturday morning but this was not a problem. "We know, we saw it last night on Ceefax," he was told..

Brenda went on: "A similar event happened when Middlesex recalled Martin Hobley. The selection was made at training on Wednesday night and faxed through to you. Harlequins had agreed he could play but Hobs himself had not cried off to the 2nd XV coach. However, he saw it on Ceefax at about 11am on Thursday!

"Some rugby players are not too sharp on their communication," she concludes. "But a lot of people must refer to Ceefax at all times of the day." So, rugby clubs and promoters. It is over to you... ∎

The author is Ceefax Sports Editor

7. Issues in Rugby

Edited by Nick Keith and Derek Wyatt

LAWS: REFEREEING

The rugby referee's lot is not an easy one in a game with complex laws. PETER BROOK (below) says that national unions must get together to adopt a truly international approach so that there is a uniform standard of refereeing, and consistency of interpreting the law

WHISTLE A COMMON TUNE

The big challenge in refereeing is for decisions to be uniform and for consistency in application of the laws. This is not a question of the Northern Hemisphere v the Southern Hemisphere; or one nation's interpretation against another's; or how good or bad a law may be. We must have uniformity of interpretation from one referee to another so that the players can concentrate on playing the game to the laws rather than to the referee.

The trouble is that this uniformity has only been addressed once every four years at the time of a World Cup; and we have not been able to maintain this subsequently, when the national unions tend to go their own way.

In the 1991 World Cup, I was a member of the Referees' Appointments Panel and we assembled, with the referees in Cardiff, a week before the start of the World Cup. There was nothing revolutionary in our discussions. We went through the laws with them and we stressed this necessity for uniformity of interpretation, with particular reference to two simple points:

- Players should play on their feet
- Players should stay onside

We then told all the teams and their managers that the referees would be strict on interpret-

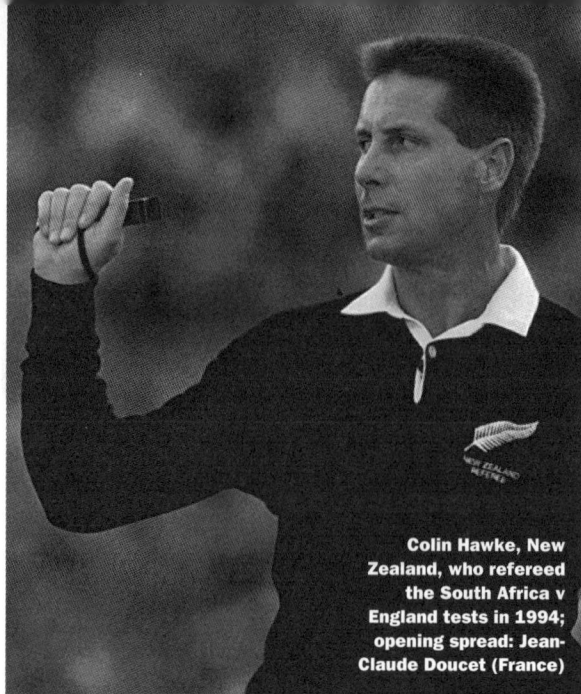

The complex laws of the game are often criticised for causing most of the problems in rugby. But uniformity and consistency in interpreting the laws would do much to alleviate this

ing these two points and that they should make their game plans accordingly.

After the first pool games the referees came in for some criticism because, to achieve this uniformity, they had to blow a fair amount of whistle. But by the quarter finals we had established a uniformity which had been rarely achieved before. Then people told us: "At last we are getting a lead from the top". (Incidentally I noticed that the soccer referees in the 1994 World Cup came in for the same criticisms about inconsistencies after the early matches in the US; so consistency of refereeing is an issue in sports other than rugby).

The sad thing is that this uniformity soon disappeared after the 1991 World Cup. The Rugby World Cup provides the authority for a short time but many people see the organisation of the game as being in the hands of the individual unions. That is what the International Rugby Football Board is up against – although, of course, it is argued that the IRFB should establish its own authority.

Whether you like it or not, you have to remember that the International Board (IRFB) is an amateur body, and some of these issues need a large amount of time and effort to be resolved. There are criticisms of the

IRFB as the ultimate international administrator and law-maker. The membership of the Board is constantly changing: some only stay for a few years while others remain on the Board for 20 years or more.

The future is going to be exciting. If people want to get things done on the Board, they will have to stand up and be prepared to be counted. The IRFB are trying to get there, but changes need to be made. For one thing, the Board does not yet have a referees' sub-committee.

The complex laws of the game are often criticised for causing most of the problems in rugby. But uniformity and consistency in interpreting the laws would do much to alleviate this. I have recently been chairing a working party on the laws for the Rugby Football Union. Members of the panel included players such as Jeff Probyn and Rob Andrew; plus Paul Ackford, the England and Lions lock; Bob Taylor, the former England loose forward; Steve Hill, a coach from Kent; Robert Horner, chairman of the RFU laws subcommittee; and Ed Morrison, the current English international referee.

On the whole we did not favour much change in the law. The key thing is to have a period of stability to achieve common understanding of the laws between the players, referees, coaches and the like. In the past the Southern Hemisphere countries have been more pro-active in campaigning for changes in the law – although not necessarily acting in unison.

We must establish uniformity of refereeing standards. I would start by changing the way referees are appointed. At the moment the appointment of referees is done by country, on a rotational basis. So we tend to get a repetition of Englishmen refereeing in Dublin, Welshmen at Twickenham, and Irishmen in Paris. Referees should be appointed on merit rather than as a result of where they were born.

Hand in hand with the appointment of the referee should go the appointment of the touch judges. On major international tours with eight or more matches there should be a panel of three referees and touch judges – all from one country. They would take it in turns to referee and run the line at all the matches on that tour.

The purpose of this is that referees must have total confidence in touch judges. If there is violence or an off the ball incident and the touch judge puts up his flag, the referee should be able to go to him and ask these simple questions: What did you see and which players were involved? Should I send them off? The referee must have full confidence in his touch judges' decision and award the appropriate penalty accordingly.

The problem of appointing officials was highlighted on England's tour to South Africa in 1994. For the Tests, the referee Colin Hawke (opposite page) was flown over from New Zealand; and touch judges came from Wales and from Namibia. No disrespect to the touch judges, but this does not seem to me the ideal platform for creating confidence in a team of three officials. It is important to the success of the referee that he knows the competence and capability of the touch judges well beforehand.

However, I don't agree with those who argue that there should be two referees, as I prefer to have one person in charge (with assistance from his two touch judges). But I do favour giving more responsibility to touch judges to help the referee to adjudicate off-sides.

We have experimented in England with wiring up the referee and the touch judges for sound and having them telling the referee about off-sides on the intercom. Players in an experimental game – including England scrum half Kieran Bracken – welcomed the experiment and said that it created more space from marauding flankers who could have been "fringing" in an offside position.

Whatever happens, the touch judges should be allowed to give more advice. However, the decision must be made by the referee. We also need a panel of independent assessors of referees, such as the Five Nations have implemented recently. Similar systems should be used worldwide on a zonal basis. A database will be established and information exchanged between the zones so that all the best referees are monitored and classified. This will help to get the best men refereeing the best games.

This already happens, to some extent, in Britain for incoming tourists: all the games of an All Black tour to, say, England will be refereed by a neutral from Scotland or Wales or Ireland or whichever. While some may argue that this system of neutral referees is easy to apply in Britain, worldwide travel is much simpler today and Unions think

> **We have experimented with wiring up the referee and the touch judges for sound and having the linesmen telling the referee about off-sides on the intercom... Players welcomed this**

English referees have recently had the benefit of fitness training at Loughborough University. This included tests on their physical flexibility. As a result they were given personal exercises to help avoid injuries such as hamstrings

Referees take a humourous stance with dark glasses and white sticks at the Cathay Pacific Hong Kong Sevens

nothing of flying a referee across the world.

For instance, as I write in June 1994, Ed Morrison will leave England in August to referee the Bledisloe Cup between Australia and New Zealand. And he's not going for a quick visit, because he will spend some time acclimatising and getting completely fit. The question of time pressures applies as much to referees as to players.

The number of internationals will increase progressively. There will be more qualifiers – and more qualifying matches – for the 1999 World Cup when only four teams will qualify automatically (the finalists, the winners of the play-off for third place, and the hosts; if one of these has dual qualification, there will be only be three qualifiers).

Referees must also be given help and advice on preparing themselves to keep up with the modern game. It has long been true that there is a vast difference in speed and thought and action between club rugby and internationals.

Backs are as big and powerful as forwards used to be and forwards have the speed and skills of backs in the old days.

So there is a need to educate referees on what players and coaches are striving to achieve and how best to prepare physically and mentally for the modern game.

English referees have recently had the benefit of fitness training at Loughborough University. This included tests on their physical flexibility. As a result they were given personal exercises to help avoid injuries such as hamstrings.

In sum, there is still much to be done to bring referees up to the standard required from the modern game. Make no mistake, the referees are every bit as keen as the players and they need all the help and guidance we can give them ■

The author is a former international referee, who joined the IRFB in 1993 as one of the two Rugby Football Union members.

LAWS: OPTIONS

The laws of rugby, and their interpretation, produce heated argument wherever the game is played. As rugby has moved towards being a truly world-wide game, DAVID LAWRENSON asks whether the rules will hinder its progress and suggests some options

CHANGE AND DECAY?

A book could be written on the recent decision by the International Board (IRFB) to amend the ruck/maul law and most of that would be made up of the outpourings of various coaches throughout the world. Meanwhile for the last decade followers have been bemoaning the dominance of the kickers and the dearth of tries in the modern game.

Rugby has been famous (or notorious) for going its own sweet way. As an amateur game it has not needed to kow tow to the demands of paying spectators or the media – "this is our game, like it or lump it". But if it really wants to be a serious world game then it will have to take heed of these criticisms.

Law changes seem to be introduced by the IRFB without any serious consultation with clubs, coaches and players. The result is constant farce. Witness the ruck/maul law, which after just one season had to be amended and still is not universally liked. But there are areas in which the game could be improved. Penalties disrupt the flow of play; there are far too many of them; and they favour the kicker.

Take the line-out for example. The number of possible offences at this particular set piece are legion, and at any given line-out the referee could blow his whistle for at least one.

This is one facet of play for which the differing interpretations, particularly between Northern and Southern Hemisphere referees, assume ludicrous proportions What is acceptable in one country is totally unacceptable in another and the line-out becomes a farce. In some countries the referees give up altogether and, as long as the ball comes out, they are happy. Despite referee exchanges between the hemispheres, the problem persists, so something has to be done.

The time has come to simplify matters in the line-out, apart from foul play which has to be penalised. For a start, let us allow lifting and the use of either arm. This might mean that teams without giants could work on techniques to secure line-out possession and it would reduce the number of penalties given.

The mark – a throwback to the old days – disrupts the flow of play. How often have you seen play stopped dead when a full back has caught the ball and made a mark before hoofing it into touch? If he didn't have this luxury the attacking side would have more chance and, if the full back did make a clean catch in space, he would be kicking under pressure. Gone would be the stop/start element associated with this facet of play and there would be more continuity.

Another big bugbear over the last few years has been the points scoring system. The law makers have tried to encourage more tries by increasing the value to five points, but as long as drop goals and penalties remain at three points we'll continue to see games decided by kickers. I have always believed that three points for a drop goal is out of proportion to its importance and three points for a penalty is somewhat excessive.

Certainly dropping goals requires skill, but how many times have you seen a fly half in a good attacking position opt for a drop goal rather than trying to instigate a move which might lead to a try? Why take the risk when you can settle for a comfortable three points?

These days the first name on any team sheet is likely to be the kicker. Without a heavyweight points scorer teams simply can't complete in modern day rugby. And it can have a huge influence on selection. Although Ian Hunter is one of the best full backs in the country, England were reluctant to pick him because he wasn't a recognised goalkicker – although in Andrew and Barnes they had top class kickers at fly half. It took a spate of injuries in South Africa before England were forced to play the highly skilful Paul Hull, who added another dimension to their play.

The game at all levels has been littered with kickers whose other skills were sadly lacking. Grant Fox may have been like a metronome with his boot but how many breaks did he make? Simon Hodgkinson was another points scorer who would probably never have played international rugby but for his goal kicking.

From the first class game to local junior rugby inevitably you'll come across sides who possess one player with a mighty boot and often he'll have the cleanest shirt in the team.

The value of penalty goals and drop goals should be reduced to two points. Critics would argue that such a reduction for the penalty goal would lead to teams conceding penalties at will in order to thwart the opposition and deny them scoring opportunities.

I don't believe this would be the case. The

John Eales rises above the pack, with a little help from his friends...

nearest equivalent sport, Rugby League, has a two point penalty and there is little evidence that they are freely given away. Admittedly, there's perhaps more opportunity to offend in Rugby Union, given the ruck and maul situation and there's also the problem of the so-called "professional foul".

Of course anyone committing such a foul should be sent off but perhaps there's a case for keeping penalties given for foul play to three points; either that or let the kicker take it from under the posts.

Any tinkering with the laws always provokes criticism, but it should be remembered that the basic framework of the current game was formulated when the pitches, as well as the balls, tended to be heavier. In the old days it was extremely difficult to kick soggy leather balls huge distances, but with the current synthetic balls, and the addition of aids such as kicking tees, this has become commonplace.

Let's make the game easier to watch and more exciting to play, perhaps Rugby Union will make even greater strides ■

The author is Deputy Editor of Rugby World. *His book on Martin Offiah was published by Methuen in 1993.*

PROFESSIONALISM

The great divide between Rugby Union and Rugby League is still gaping wide nearly 100 years after the Northern Union suceded on the grounds of broken time payments. They set up the professional 13-a-side game which has flourished as Rugby League. The division has never healed and Union players who turn out under the League code after the age of 18 – even as amateurs – are banned from playing Union. DAVID HINCHCLIFFE MP explains why the rift should be healed and discrimination by Union against League brought to an end

THE GREAT DEBATE

t is hard to explain to the unconverted how my own personal well-being has been intimately tied up with the fortunes of Wakefield Trinity Rugby League Club and with the game in general. Those who don't understand may gain a better idea of what I mean by reading a book called *When Push Comes to Shove*. It is a unique celebration of the Rugby League community – the people who live and love the game. It is their own explanation of a passion for what some would say is far too modestly described as The Greatest Game.

From my childhood, blessed with the privilege of being born into Rugby League country, I have also played, watched and loved the game, sharing in its ups and downs. When a parliamentary colleague from Geordieland described me as a 'one sport man', I pleaded guilty. I readily confessed to an abiding passion for a sport that to me offers everything – speed, personal courage, unbelievable skills, finesse and, on occasions, sheer brutality.

I have always felt a political affinity with a game that emerged from the day to day struggles of working people in the industrial North. It has suffered numerous attacks from the sporting establishment in the 99 years of its existence.

Like many of my era, I was banned from Union for committing the cardinal sin of playing amateur Rugby League after reaching the age of 18. As an MP many years later I have seen first hand how the prejudice against Rugby League remains alive and well at the most senior levels of government, civil service and the media.

Fighting this prejudice was one of the main reasons why – in the very room in which Cromwell signed the death warrant of Charles I in 1649 – the parliamentary Rugby League Group was born in 1988.

In 1995 it is the centenary of the League; it is time to end the rift and outlaw the blatant discrimination imposed by the Union. Next year would be a very appropriate time to end this nonsense once and for all. My views were outlined in a debate in the House of Commons in April 1993; and in June 1994 I introduced a Private Member's Bill★.

One fundamental question is how amateurism is defined within the regulations of the Rugby Football Union. This affects the relationship between union and league players, amateurs as well as professionals. In fact, the vast majority of Rugby League is

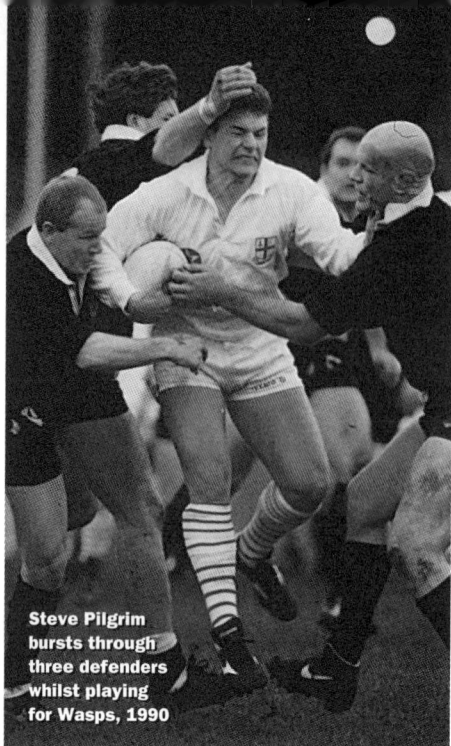

Steve Pilgrim bursts through three defenders whilst playing for Wasps, 1990

played by amateurs, and the professional game is a small part of the sport. It annoys many of us interested in League to hear it described as a professional code.

The case of Steve Pilgrim highlighted the unfairness of the Union "amateur" rules. Pilgrim played rugby union for Wasps in London and for England B, and he went for an unpaid amateur trial at Headingley with Leeds Rugby League Club. As a result he was automatically banned from playing rugby union football for two years.

The interesting point is that, if Pilgrim had gone to the other side of the Headingley ground, for a professional trial for Yorkshire cricket, he would not have been banned. Had he gone to Elland Road, and been paid for playing soccer for Leeds United, he would not have been banned. Had he been playing professional tennis, professional golf or even American football, he would not have been banned. Unfortunately, he played Rugby League. He has not received a penny for doing so, although he has had trials since then with the Halifax rugby league club. Neither club has signed him on, and he is now between the

devil and the deep blue sea – not signed on the Rugby League but banned from his previous sport. In the view of many decent, thinking people in sport as a whole, including many in the sport of Rugby Union, that is unacceptable in this day and age.

HOW THE RIFT STARTED

In 1895 the northern rugby union split away from the rest on the issue of broken time payments. In the industrial north, and elsewhere, working-class people could not afford to miss time from work to play Rugby Union; therefore, young men were paid to cover the money that they could not earn in their normal course of employment because they were playing rugby. The result was the development of Rugby League.

Unfortunately, since 1895, some in the 15-a-side code have attempted, right up to the present day, to kill off the game of Rugby League – both the amateur and the professional games. Many who have been involved in both rugby codes feel that that is unacceptable in this day and age. It is some measure of Rugby League's strength and popularity that, despite all those attacks over nearly a century, the game continues to thrive and prosper, at both the amateur and professional levels.

It is some measure of rugby league's greatness that – despite the obvious prejudice of the establishment, the media, the education system and the armed forces against the 13-a-side code – as a professional sport it is second only to association football as the most popular spectator team sport in Britain. In terms of spectators, it is more popular than Rugby Union and cricket.

Some years ago, when I played both codes, I took part in a game of Rugby Union at a club in Otley. When I entered the club house, I noticed a painting of the team that had won the Yorkshire Rugby Cup two years before the 1895 breakaway. A number of the faces had been blanked out. They were players who had, after 1895, moved from northern rugby to play in the new northern union. They have never been forgiven. I want to see the day come, before too long, when the faces of those players are painted back into that picture, and an end to the nonsense of the past 100 years.

As an amateur league player, I was banned from playing Rugby Union. Many of my friends in Wakefield still have the letters that they received from local Rugby Union clubs saying that they were no longer welcome because, after the age of 18, they had played rugby league. We were considered sporting lepers. I will never forget that experience for as long as I live. Sadly, that attitude still prevails.

There have been attempts to build bridges but I could give one example after another to show how they have failed. In Reading, for instance, an attempt was made to form the Unity Rugby Club, to play both codes under the same banner. Plenty of clubs play cricket and rugby, or soccer and rugby. Why should not Rugby League and Rugby Union use the same facilities, pitches and equipment? It would be sensible. However, permission could not be obtained from Twickenham, simply because, they were told, they were playing Rugby League. Had it been cricket, soccer, or any other sport, there would have been no problem.

There have been many examples of what can only be described as blatant discrimination in

It is absolute nonsense to suggest that Rugby Union is an amateur code

the armed forces against people who want to play the game of Rugby League football. We have been told that the armed forces could not afford to fund Rugby League although the same balls, jerseys, shorts, boots, socks and other items that rugby players wear are used in both code. It is high time that we did something about that prejudice.

"SOME UNION PLAYERS ARE PROFESSIONALS"

The rules differentiating amateurs and professionals appear to apply only to those concerned with Rugby League, although some union players are, to all intents and purposes, professionals. We know for a fact that Rugby Union players are paid and that they receive rewards often far in excess of what is payable in the rugby league game.

In France – which is a party to the International Rugby Board's rules on amateurs, which forbid professionalism in rugby – entire Rugby League teams have transferred to playing union because they can get more money. In New Zealand and Australia payments are commonplace. Can anyone tell me that David Campese is truly an amateur? Does he go to Italy every winter to play for nothing? Of course he must be paid and so, in reality, he is a professional, and rightly so. He is an excellent rugby player, so why should he not be rewarded for his skills and for the fact that he, like many others, entertains vast numbers of people?

Payments are also commonplace in South Africa. Recently, my own team, Wakefield Trinity, was in the process of signing a Springbok Rugby Union player called Albertus Einslin. He pulled back from signing the deal because he had been offered £200 a match and a job playing "amateur" Rugby Union in South Africa. It is absolute nonsense to suggest that Rugby Union is an amateur code. Many of us are annoyed that the South African Rugby Union has attempted to stamp on the development of Rugby League in the black townships on the basis that its amateur code there will lead to professionalism although, as everyone knows, the South African Rugby Union is semi-professional, if not wholly professional.

In this country, the Pugh Report considered the Welsh Rugby Union players who went on the so-called centenary tour of South Africa against the advice of the various home unions. The Pugh Report, which has been

Jonathan Davies sporting his professional colours. The journey North was one-way

suppressed, suggested that those players received about £30,000 each. Let us remember that that was in an "amateur" game.

Week In Week Out, a BBC Wales programme, recorded a player saying that, to his knowledge, payments were made to Wales in the dressing room, in front of a Welsh Rugby Union official, and the same WRU banned Jonathan Davies from commenting for the BBC at Cardiff Arms Park because he had gone north to play for Widnes Rugby League Club.

The parliamentary Rugby League Group has about 70 members and we have become rather impatient. We contacted the International Rugby Football Board (IRFB) to ask it to explain its rules on amateurism. At one time we met Dudley Wood, the secretary of the Rugby Football Union, and Bob Rogers, the chairman of the English Rugby Football Union Amateurism Committee. They had a fairly hot reception.

They conceded that there were problems in certain unions – not the English union – due to the interpretation of amateurism, not the principle. They insisted that, although there were problems in Wales, France and here, there and everywhere, in England everything in the garden was fine. They said that there was no evidence of any payments to players in the English Union.

There have been one or two developments since. Soon afterwards the IRFB met in Edinburgh and decided that Rugby League professionals who have never played Union would be allowed to play Rugby Union within two years of making known their desire to switch codes. However, Union players who have turned to league are still banned from returning to union. That reads like a Monty Python script.

...a BBC Wales programme recorded a player saying that, to his knowledge, payments were made to Wales in the dressing room, in front of a Welsh Rugby Union official, and the same WRU banned Jonathan Davies from commentating for the BBC at Cardiff Arms Park because he had gone north to play for Widnes...

Alan Watkins wrote in *The Independent* that the lack of equality between the codes means that "While Jonathan Davies cannot return to Llanelli, or Martin Offiah to Rosslyn Park, there is nothing to prevent Ellery Hanley, say, from signing on for the Harlequins, playing a couple of seasons at the Stoop, and then returning to Leeds or some other Northern club to see out the autumn of his days."

What absolute nonsense – yet that is the present position. At there same time there was a report in *The Times* with the headline:

"RFU finds breaches of amateurism rife".

According to the article, a report circulating in English Rugby Football Union clubs:

"has forced the RFU to confront a situation it denied existed to any serious extent. It reveals numerous illustrations of disregard for the amateur principles which officials at Twickenham insisted had more to do with imagination than reality.

"A working party set up by the RFU to investigate growing allegations of financial benefits for amateur players has found the claims to be substan- tially true. Its report.... says many examples of such payments have been received."

So much for assurances that everything in the garden was lovely in the English Rugby Football Union.

There appears to be some inconsistency between the official position and reality. The official position is clearly in conflict with what we know and what the union, too, knows is happening. The worry is that the rules of amateurism as administered by the RFU apply only to those who have contact with the game of rugby league. It seems that anything is allowed to go on in rugby union.

I emphasise again that many of us have no objection to Rugby Union players receiving payments. We have no wish to prevent funding from going to Rugby Union clubs. I have two – Sandal and Wakefield – in my constituency. I played discreetly for both teams many years ago as a Rugby League player. I have friends who are involved in both clubs. They are two excellent Rugby Union clubs which are a credit to the game of rugby as a whole. I have no wish to see them deprived of funds that may accrue from the national lottery.

As the League Express newspaper put it: "The Union authorities have no moral, legal or any other right to pronounce on the sport of Rugby League, or prevent free men and women playing whatever sport they like. No amount of window-dressing will alter the fact that their game is continuing to use unjust and illegal discrimination against a sport they perceive as a competitor to their own."

There is great anger on the issue. We hope that the Government will grasp the nettle and end this nonsense once and for all ∎

This article is adapted from a speech made by David Hinchcliffe, Labour MP for Wakefield, in the House of Commons in April 1993. In June and July, a sports (Discrimination) Bill proposed by David Hinchcliffe very nearly reached the statute book.(see appendix)

The story of Gareth Savin, paralysed at 18 after the collapse of a scrum, is a chilling reminder. TED AVES recounts how Gareth has pulled through with great courage, and with the help of the rugby community

LIFELINE FOR GARETH

Midway through the second half of an under-19 fixture between Richmond and Lewes the scrum collapsed. It had been a well-refereed, good-spirited contest which Richmond were comfortably winning. All the players got back to their feet except two; one was badly winded but was soon able to resume.

The other, Gareth Savin, remained on the ground with a broken neck. By the evening he was in Stoke Mandeville Hospital where it was confirmed that, as a result of the near total severing of his spinal column between the fourth and fifth vertebrae, Gareth was paralysed from the neck down and would never walk again.

Gareth had joined Richmond earlier that season, two months before his 19th birthday.

He had shown a lot of promise and maturity as a tight head prop. John Kingston, Richmond's current premier squad coach, then responsible for the under-21s, had selected him for several games at that age group where he had always shown great commitment and enthusiasm. On the day before the Lewes match he had helped his Air Training Corps team win the Corps championship and on the strength of his performance had been selected for the England ATC XV.

Gareth's injury will probably rate as every sportsman's greatest nightmare. The prospect of spending a lifetime in a wheelchair makes you shudder and turn to other thoughts. Gareth's team mates and recently-made friends were stunned. Nothing like it had ever happened to them before.

Knowing what to do and how to respond was made easier by Gareth himself who within hours of the accident sent back a message with his first visitors that, more than anything, he wanted to see his rugby mates. He wanted to talk rugby, hear about the last game and discuss the next. He wanted to feel he was still part of the squad. Visits from John Kingston for talks on training and the team's progress meant a lot to him.

Perhaps the greatest lift he got in those first days was when his hero, Jeff Probyn, gave him his England shirt signed by other members of the Grand Slam team. This was proudly displayed to all Gareth's visitors until he was told that through too much handling the signatures were beginning to fade. Gareth had the shirt carefully wrapped in a polythene bag and stored safely away in his locker.

In every tragedy like this, there is usually an instant surge of sympathy, often accompanied by acts of kindness and donations. Peter Bray, Richmond's under-19 manager, and Andy Quigley, Chairman of Youth, lost no opportunity to cash in on Gareth's behalf. Under-19 and under-21 players took buckets along to matches wherever there was a sizeable gate. Fortunately, Richmond Athletic Ground often hosts large representative fixtures including those for England B. These were a good source of funds.

London Irish and London Welsh, Richmond's neighbours and arch rivals in mini and youth rugby, made generous collections; as did Lewes. Rosslyn Park, another famous neighbour, paid out £1,000 from their own Injury Trust Fund. Mini rugby players carried out sponsored "pass-athons" and fathers clubbed together to arrange evening entertainments of food, booze and strippers – all in a good cause.

There were many spontaneous acts of charity in the early days that put some funds in the kitty and made Gareth's accident more widely known. But what was needed was a sustainable campaign that could effectively cater for his longer term needs.

Richmond's chairman, Tony Hallett, promised within a week of the accident that the club would "seek to provide on-going support and help in every way". The club secretary, Peter Quinnen, headed a committee that aimed to establish a Gareth Savin Charitable Trust "to improve the quality of Gareth's life and pay for items which he would not otherwise have and which would help him live a full and active life". Andrew Hill, solicitor and manager of Richmond under-13s, was the treasurer of the funds and responsible for executing the Trust Deed. Vinny Codrington, director of rugby, whose numerous tasks included the preparation of the Richmond Newsletter, used the magazine as the vehicle for keeping club members and friends up-to-date on the progress of Gareth and the Trust.

Peter Quinnen was probably Gareth's most regular visitor during his six months at Stoke Mandeville. In that time he learnt a lot about the young man and his ambitions. Gareth had demonstrated in many ways a great determination to make something of his life. Because he was planning a career in the RAF, he transferred allegiance from the Boys Brigade (which he had joined at seven) to the Air Training Corps where he had risen to the rank of corporal. He had completed the silver stage of the Duke of Edinburgh's Award Scheme and was in sight of gold. He had passed the entrance tests for the RAF but, because there were no immediate vacancies, had decided to join the Fire Brigade. All of this had lain ahead.

The reports from Stoke Mandeville confirmed that Gareth had expressed a strong wish to be independent, live in the community and, of course, be as mobile as possible. With this brief, Peter Quinnen's committee agreed that the funds, which were slowly building, should be used for buying a state-of-the-art wheelchair and a van capable of being driven by a tetraplegic. The committee also agreed to find accommodation and adapt it to his needs. In this

Gareth's injury will probably rate as every sportsman's greatest nightmare. The prospect of spending a lifetime in a wheelchair makes you shudder and turn to other thoughts...

respect they were greatly helped by the Richmond Council.

When all that had been costed, it became clear that the current funds needed a serious boost. Steve James, the club's newly elected president, circulated a letter to every member seeking a minimum of £10 from each in exchange for being listed in the club's match programmes. "If guts and determination to overcome the most devastating blow imaginable are worthy of your support, both financial and moral, nobody could have exhibited them in greater quantities than Gareth," the letter said.

The appeal, regularly fuelled by publicity from the Newsletter, was well supported. It was the Newsletter that kept Gareth's plight in mind. In it we learnt that, after two months in Stoke Mandeville, Gareth had movement "in one arm and the other shoulder" and that, miraculously, from these small tokens of mobility he was able to propel a wheelchair. Even more astonishing, we learnt that after only four months Gareth, plus attractive physiotherapist, had made an appearance in Richmond's famous watering hole "The Sun", where he was seen downing a pint with only limited help from his friends.

After six months, Gareth was fit enough to be discharged from Stoke Mandeville and to take up residence at the Royal Hospital Putney for occupational therapy. To mark this occasion, a Charity Rugby Match was held at the Athletic Ground. Billed as the "Clash of the Titans". It pitted Gareth Savin's Select XV against the Audi International XV and was settled with a drop goal in the final minutes by none other than Jeff Probyn – the first drop goal in his long and illustrious career.

Another match was held in Gareth's honour, England's under-21s, who had just returned from a highly successful tour of Australia, turned out to meet Richmond under-21s, Gareth's team. Richmond had completed an unbeaten season, collecting the scalps of all the country's leading clubs. England

proved too strong on the day but the takings from the gate, the programmes, the barbecue and carvery more than compensated.

As it happened, Gareth missed the match, which was played in a heavy downpour throughout. While the under-21s skidded about in the mud, he was watching a match in South Africa's sunny veldt, courtesy of the Richmond and Capetown Rotary Clubs.

It is rare for Gareth to miss a home fixture, let alone an event held on his behalf. The club has organised marathons, celebrity dinners, auctions, raffles and more to raise funds for the Gareth Savin Trust Fund that provides not just for Gareth but for others who have been seriously injured in sport. He is a great ambassador for the Trust and the game for which his enthusiasm is undiminished. Each fundraising event says a lot about the comradeship and spirit that is so special to rugby.

It was a tribute to that spirit and Gareth's courage when Richmond's chairman, Tony Hallett, presented him to the Queen on the afternoon in March 1994 when Twickenham's new East Stand was officially opened and the outcome of the Five Nations Championship was decided. For Gareth, the only pity was that Jeff Probyn was not wearing the no. 3 shirt for England ∎

The Author manages Richmond U21 XV and is a former Oxford Blue at athletics

INJURIES: PREVENTION

**How the English Rugby Union has attempted to prevent injuries in the game.
IAN BEER explains what is happening and recommends the work of SPIRE**

HEALING HANDS

It was in the late seventies that I began my interest in rugby injuries and about that time that I asked the Rugby Union if we might start a working party to look into the prevention of injury in the game. So was born the Injuries Prevention Working Party which this season has now been replaced by a proper Sub-Committee renamed The Player's Safety Sub-Committee dedicated to making the game as safe as possible for all players.

During the period that the Working Party on Injury Prevention was in operation we attempted to record all injuries within certain selected clubs. For a period of time we were fairly successful and were able to publish good statistics for a limited number of sides. However, we were never able to stimulate the support of a sufficient number of clubs to make the results statistically significant. The Safety Sub-Committee is now concentrating on returns only for injuries which keep players out of the game for a period of three weeks or more, but are still finding it difficult to get the co-operation of a large enough number of clubs.

In the early eighties it did become apparent that there were a growing number of serious neck injuries. In England the Injuries Working Party introduced changes in the Laws of the game for players under the age of 19 and almost at once the serious 'epidemic' of neck injuries ceased. At the same time southern hemisphere countries were also experimenting with similar law changes so that the following year the International Board made changes for all rugby to make it safer. Since then the process has continued and many of the Law changes since 1983 have been related to increasing the safety of playing the game.

In the last two years there has been a slight increase again. These neck injuries are not related to any particular position on the field, but they are related to the process of tackling. The injured person is so often the tackler or the tackled. Quite often this is related to incorrect technique; hence the emphasis in recent seasons from the Rugby Football Union to teach the correct technique of tackling to all players. In my mind it is also related to the commitment of the tackler or, sometimes, the tackled player. Although the definition of a tackle is clearly defined in the Laws, the purpose of a tackle is not; that is solely in the heart and

> **The injured person is so often the tackler or the tackled. Quite often this is related to incorrect technique; hence the emphasis in recent seasons to teach the correct techniques**

... but today not all players, coaches or spectators seem to have 'right minds'. What is the meaning of the cry 'take him out', or 'destroy him', or – as many of us have heard, sadly especially at junior rugby – 'kill him'?

mind of the tackler. Does he tackle to deprive his opposite number of the ball, or to prevent his forward progress, or encourage him not to want to receive the ball next time, or to hurt him, or to remove him from the field of play either temporarily or permanently? Those of us in our right minds know where the line is drawn but today not all players, coaches or spectators seem to have 'right minds'. What is the meaning of the cry 'take him out', or 'destroy him', or – as many of us have heard, sadly especially at junior rugby – 'kill him'? These expressions, and the motivation behind them, are aspects of the modern game, maybe modern society, which we have to watch and eradicate if we are to preserve our game.

How often does such serious injury occur? As far as we can tell with the numbers of players playing the game today in England it concerns only 0.002% of the playing population.

The latest figures which we have from the Spinal Injuries Association record that of all the serious neck injuries in the UK which result in tetra- or paraplegia, only 2% are related to rugby, whereas 4% are attributed to horse riding, 8% to swimming and diving; 15% to all sports and 37% to traffic accidents. These figures help keep the dangers of rugby in proportion but one broken neck in our game is one too many, so we continue to do all we can to minimise injury through coaching and Law changes.

For the person who does break their neck there is insurance cover. All clubs have to insure their players as a condition of being a

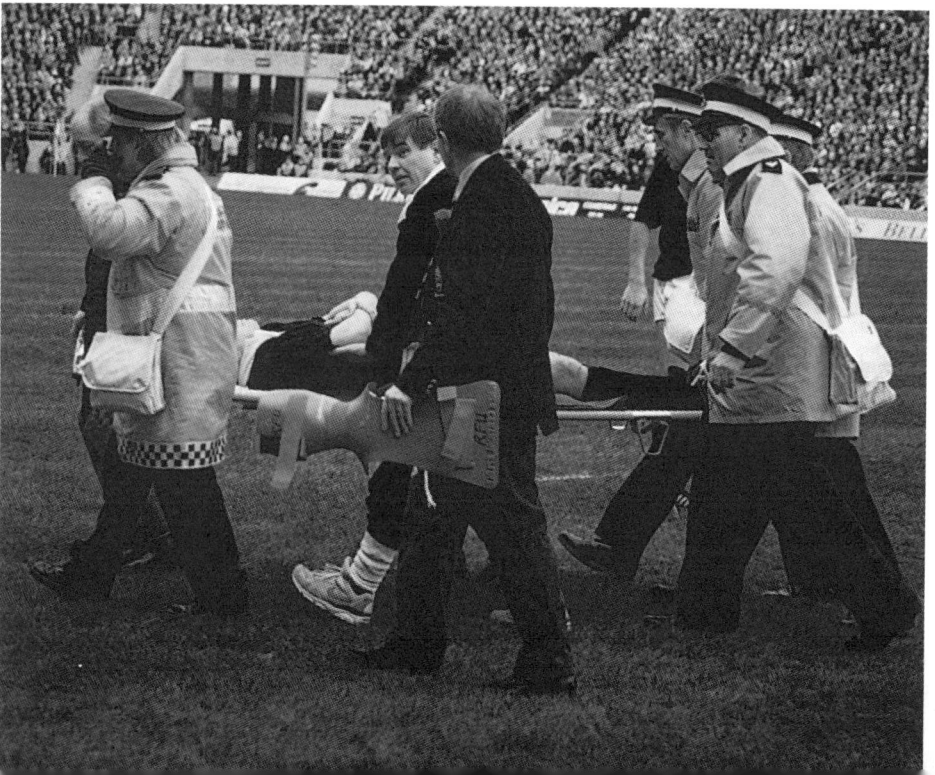

member of the RFU. The Premium is paid for our of club subscriptions but now money is also being put in to the cover by the RFU from sponsorship money. The schools who pay a registration fee of £10 have their insurance paid for by the Wavell Wakefield Charitable Trust. Many schools also have another private cover with the brokers Holmwood. Some players may take out their own cover. The cost of insurance is, however, fairly high so that the RFU scheme brings to the injured player only £125,000 and the Holmwood scheme something like £350,000. For someone who becomes tetraplegic we calculate they will require something in the region of £1,125,000 for the rest of their life.

It was for this reason that I decided to create SPIRE (Support Paraplegics in Rugby Enterprise). The Rugby Football Union Charitable Trust had been helping some players very well but they did not have enough capital to cope. The Wooden Spoon Society was doing a brilliant job to help the RFU create better facilities for wheelchairs at Twickenham but we needed a special fund just to help the lifestyle of our ex-players who were in these wheelchairs. SPIRE is there to build up a charitable capital fund, the income of which will go to support the wheelchair victims. They are the responsibility of the game; they are few in number but we owe it to them not to forget them.

Alongside the monetary fund we have, through The Players Safety Sub-Committee, also triggered off our whole concern for the short term care when the injury occurs and

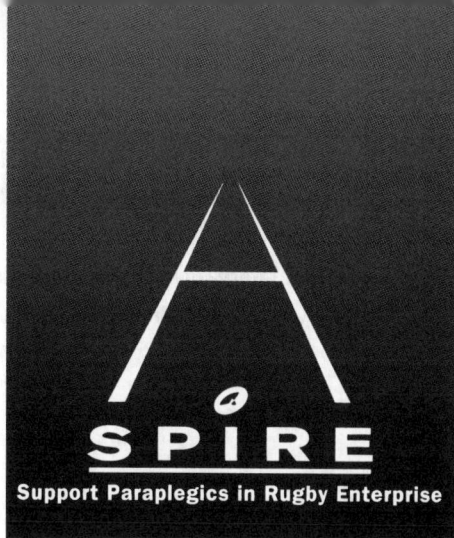

SPIRE
Support Paraplegics in Rugby Enterprise

the long term care of the ex-player. We are in the process of putting all these gentlemen in touch with each other if they so wish, of having meetings to find out their requirements and concerns. Before this year we did not even know how many there were, nor who they were. We now have 83 on our register and one of the things we could certainly do to help is to see that all those who want a job, and have the ability, are found a job. I feel ashamed that we do not employ anyone in a wheelchair at Twickenham... I hope that we shall be able to correct that before too long. And some of the clubs who seem to be able to find an up-and-coming player a job can do just that for one of our disabled.

So I am pleased that in a short presidential year we have been able to create something for the future which cares for people in the way that teaches those who join our game to care for each other. I am grateful to the thousands who have helped raise well over a £250,000 so far, but I want a capital fund of something like £2 million to do justice to the cause. Between us all we will do just that for SPIRE in the SPIRIT of RUGBY FOOTBALL IN ACTION... and the spirit of Rugby Football is alive and stronger today than it has ever been ■

The author is the immediate Past President of the Rugby Football Union (England).

...one broken neck in our game is one too many, so we continue to do all we can to minimise injury through coaching and Law changes

MEDIA: TELEVISION

Television turns international sports into global sports. Without it, sports cannot survive. Anyone who thinks otherwise it just waking from a sleep begun in the 1920s, DEREK WYATT reports

STAYING TUNED?

Think about it, the International Olympic Committee with only one bidder for the 1998 Nagano Winter Olympics still extracted US$480million from the NBC network in America. Earlier this year, the Murdoch players at the Fox Network in Los Angeles, bid US$1.5 billion for a four year NFL deal which broke all records.

Two years before that the Murdoch people in London surprised everyone by winning the rights to the Premier Soccer league for £305 million. Ouch. What's going on? And is nothing sacred? Is there no public service requirement left for sport to be available to the largest audiences rather than the largest pay-cheque?

Tom Pendry, Shadow Minister of Sport for the Labour Party in the UK, wants sports programmes such as the Five Nations to be protected and, in effect, only to be available to terrestrial broadcasters. The French Federation was asked to move its Tests against New Zealand (a first) to Sundays so that the TVNZ could show other more local rugby on the Saturday. The French were incensed but you could understand the broadcasters logic, driven as it was by commercial considerations.

Everywhere you look, television rules. It will not always rule as the SuperHighways are laid down over the next 20 years but for the moment it is king. The SuperHighways of optic fibres will allow 500+ different types of communication channels to be in every home in the land. Some of these channels may be shopping mall channels, others might be their marketing equivalents trying to sell or service your bank or insurance portfolio, some will be educational, and maybe as many as 50 will be broadcast, video or computer-game oriented channels.

Change is in the air; perhaps the most fundamental change we have ever experienced.

As television signals become compressed, "digitised" is the in-word, it will be possible for the consumer at home to call up their favourite television programmes as and when they want. Most television programmes are already pre-recorded or bought in and just waiting for a schedule to be agreed. Only sport and news would become the premium shows because they are live. Live events keeps afloat many a broadcast station.

The reason Murdoch has been hoovering up sports rights and trying to establish a global news channel (via Star TV in Hong Kong) is because he knows that when he switches these to pay-for-view, he will win in spades. A grand slam indeed. Take a bow Ted Turner for showing us the way with your CNN news channel and TBS equivalents.

So, if sport is to be one of the two driving forces in the future of broadcasting, rugby will benefit like never before. It wasn't always the case. For a spell I was a member of the Oxford committee. It was Varsity Match television rights discussion time and we had to talk to our counterparts at Cambridge. No-one was certain who owned the rights to the television matches.

Some aficionados believe that television rights for rugby really took off only after the 1991 World Cup...

Letters were despatched and Bob Weighill, then the Secretary at the RFU, finally agreed that the two committees owned them but that the RFU had been selling them on their behalf. Selling them would be a slight euphemism... giving then away might be more appropriate.

Cliff Morgan, then in charge of BBC Outside Broadcasting, would lunch or dine Weighill every three years and I imagine over a bevy or two would slip in the fact that the Varsity match would be welcomed again on BBC and should we have the same arrangements as before? As before, in this case, meant a paltry £7,500.

The lovely thing about this story is of course that the RFU in its infinite wisdom, and we're only talking of the middle 1980s, banked this money and kept the change. Now the Varsity Match weighs in at £100,000 which, considering its overseas sales, is still slight.

Some aficionados believe that television rights for rugby really took off only after the second World Cup in 1991. Only took off because, of course, the live TV audience for the first World Cup was small. Small not because the rugby viewing audiences of Australia and New Zealand were tiny, which they are, but because the main audience would have been in the Five Nations and they were all asleep when the matches were relayed live.

There is some truth in the fact that the second World Cup helped the rugby explosion. Fortunately, the ITV coverage was, after a few gremlins in the opening rounds, a considerable improvement on that of the BBC, the traditional home of Rugby Union.

The selling of the TV rights beyond the Five Nations countries was a brilliant success except in one matter. The organising company of the 1991 world cup, CPMA, would not entrust TSL, the television sales company responsible for selling the rights, with the Japanese territory, preferring to keep them themselves. Presumably, they thought the Japanese rights with the attendant sponsorship deals would be more lucrative.

Thus CPMA set about selling the television rights themselves. They sold them not to the most commercial channels, nor via a sponsor did they barter them. They sold them to NHK, the BBC's equivalent public service broadcaster. That's right, to a broadcaster who didn't take advertising. I'm sure there was a logic in there somewhere.

The other point that was missed was that ITV was able to take its own TV sponsor and pocket the money. As they paid close to £3.5 million for the 1991 rugby rights and then persuaded Sony to part with just over £2 million for the broadcast sponsorship rights, you can understand why ITV executives were keen to buy even more rugby. Indeed, to be fair to them, they have done the public service bit better than the BBC. They have shown the Lions tours (1989 and 1993) and all of the Four Home Unions overseas tours.

You could understand the gloom that descended over ITV Network Centre when they learned that the BBC had outbid them by a mere £250,000 for the rights to the next three years of the Five Nations championship. ITV bid £27 million; the BBC bid £27,250,000.

Where was Murdoch's Sky in all this? Surely they would want the rights à la NFL/Premier League? In the best kept secret of the year, Sky did not bid. Instead, they made a play for club rugby which they won for £7.5 million, plus they will be able to show the Five Nations – but not live. Murdoch will wait until 1997 and then bid and win the Five Nations rights for 1998 onwards. By then he will have established his global sports network.

In the meantime, the poor British viewer is left knowing that he and she will have to put up with some of the worst commentaries and production values left in sports coverage. It was no real surprise that, in acknowledgement of this, the BBC decided to allow its Rugby Special programme to go to an independent production company outside of the BBC.

The Five Nations contract was not a five-country, but a four-country, affair. The French contract is out of kilter with the Four Home Unions, Where it runs from 1994-1997. The current broadcaster, France 2, paid FF37 million (US$6.4 million) which was 13 times more than she paid for the 1991 Rugby World Cup.

There was much acrimony over the Four Nations bid when the RFU asked for more of the cake. Previously, it had been split equally. The RFU rightly pointed out that the majority of the audience is English and therefore was entitled to the lions share. In the end the international matches were split equally but the RFU receive most of the Sky rights money for club rugby.

As the Celtic fringe were very unhappy that the old deal was challenged, they might care to analyse the National Lottery Act 1993. For sport, which will receive 20% of the moneys, it will be distributed via the respective sports councils as follows:

83.3% to England & Wales, 8.9% to Scotland and 2.8% to Northern Ireland

Proof, if it was ever needed, of the RFU's strong case.

The discussions in the latter part of 1993 to move the 1995 Rugby World Cup from South Africa to the Four Home Unions was really only a debate about television time and therefore the maximisation of commercial revenues. South Africa is one hour ahead of the Four Home Unions and therefore, had the World Cup been switched, most of the sponsors and advertisers would have been more than satisfied ■

TOP RUGBY PROGRAMMES ON UK TELEVISION 1993-94

(BBC1 unless stated)

1. England v New Zealand 6.36 m
2. England v Wales 6.11
3. Scotland v England 6.08
4. England v Ireland 5.65
5. Wales v Scotland 4.70
6. France v England 4.68
7. Scotland v New Zealand 4.54
8. Barbarians v New Zealand 4.21
9. Scotland v Ireland 4.07
10. Grandstand Bath v Leicester Pilkington Cup Final 3.23
11. International Rugby ITV England v South Africa 1st Test 3.00
12. Five Nations Preview 2.89
13. Rugby Special BBC2 England v NZ 2.66
14. Grandstand Harlequins v Bath Pilkington Cup semi-final 2.59
15. International Rugby ITV England v South Africa 2nd Test 2.34
16. Rugby Highlights ITV 7 June 1.98
17. International Rugby ITV 28 May 1.96
18. England A v NZ BBC2 1.77
19. International Rugby ITV 7 June 1.46
20. Varsity Match 1.23

Rugby Special – magazine programme: BBC2 Sundays

1. England v New Zealand 2.66
2. London Counties v New Zealand 1.73
3. Oxford v Cambridge 1.50
4. South West v New Zealand 1.48
5. Barbarians v New Zealand 1.48
6. 30/1 1.42
7. Wales v Japan 1.38
8. Scotland v New Zealand 1.36
9. Scotland A v New Zealand 1.33
10. 9/1 Five Nations preview 1.28

Sky Sports, UK – Astra satellite

figures in thousands

1. 7/4 59k. 2. 9/4 56k. 3. 21/12 51k.
4. 23/4 50k. 5. 2/1 7s 42k. 6. 5/5 42k.
7. 11/5 40k. 8. 18/5 31k
9. 7s 2/1 30k. 10. 8/4 30k. 11. 31/3 28k.
12. 14/4 27k. 13. 25/10 26k

Source: BARB/DG&A

AN END TO RACISM?

DILLON WOODS (below) reports from South Africa how England's summer tour signalled the acceptance of a new era when sport can help end the myths of racial hatred

TOUR DE FORCE

The contrast between the images of the old era and the spirit of the new nation were everywhere in Pretoria and Cape Town. Driving to the first Test at Loftus Versfeld, I saw flag sellers with the old orange, white and blue flag, the new multicoloured flag and a couple of the old "vierkleur" Transvaal flags, echoing the days of the Boer War.

Tension was already evident following Stuart Barnes' widely read article "Escape from Bloemfontein" about the hostility the English had received in the predominantly Afrikaner capital of Bloemfontein. The announcement of the arrival of the new President, Nelson Mandela, was respectfully greeted, though not as rapturously as the arrival of the second Deputy President, F W de Klerk.

The first Test I saw as a 10-year-old was against the 1974 Lions who later came to my home town of East London to play my local heroes, Border. I was perplexed as to why the supporters in the non-white section were "disloyally" supporting Willie John McBride's boys. My father's reply had little to do with rugby but explained why a certain cricket fan named Nelson Mandela had admired Neil Harvey for resisting the all-white Springbok cricket team in 1950.

Entering the stadium, I noticed the new flag was greatly outnumbered by the orange, white and blue symbol of the old regime. Embarrassing thoughts of the new anthem being hissed or booed flew through my mind. The tension was somewhat alleviated when dancers took to the field with a positive representation of all the races. Accompanying me was a loyal English supporter and a progressive Afrikaner who had previously worked in the foreign office and was now embracing his new administration with equal vigour.

After my English friend had given a proud rendition of "God Save the Queen", I, as an ANC supporter, sang "Nkosi Sikelel 'iAfrika" (with no support at all within earshot) and then "Die Stem" thundered out over the stadium in this heavily Afrikaner city. I was pleasantly surprised there was no disrespect for any of the anthems – an attitude enhanced by the loud and patriotic helicopter fly-past featuring the new flag and the Cross of St George.

Although the old flag predominated in the crowd, there were encouraging cries of: "Come on Chester, GO!" during South Africa's first genuine attack. After the match, the president of the Orange Free State RFU presented Stuart Barnes with a small memento as a peace offering following the England fly-half's outspoken criticism of the behaviour of some of the Free Staters during the England visit to Bloemfontein.

The only fixture between the two Tests was marred by blatant stomping on English heads by some of the Eastern Province pack. This occurred in the first few minutes of the game and was repeated twice before any punching started. Before the two players were sent off, Jonathan Callard was badly gashed above his eyes and his remark that he and Phil de Glanville could form a "Cyclops" club was a wry comment on the obvious good fortune of both players in retaining their eyesight despite the mauling they had received.

The other two cases of stomping could easily have resulted in fractured skulls or worse. The refusal of the referee to intervene until too late is characteristic of the standard of refereeing in South Africa. The fact that veteran referee Freek Bruger had to sit down with the South African team between the Tests and explain why so many decisions had gone against them at Loftus was further testimony to this, not to mention the low standard of coaching as well.

South Africa is as full as it ever was of rugby talent, and there's certainly enough of that commodity to win the World Cup, but not if coaches around the country fail to control indiscipline and breaches of the laws of the game. With the financial stakes growing as they are in world rugby, and the consequent need to look after players better, I believe it is only a matter of time before television umpires are used to penalise intentional and premeditated foul play.

Abdullah Ibrahim's "The Mountain" would have been a suitable tune for the setting for the second Test at Newlands, but the sound system packed up. Nevertheless the Cape Town Crowd reserved their wrath for the introduction of the SARFU President, Louis Luyt, who was greeted with widespread booing. This time, several hundred joined in for "Nkosi Sikelel 'iAfrika" which may have inspired the new South African combination for the final clash.

The English hardly got out of their own 22 for the first 35 minutes, but the South Africans were unable to convert their pressure into points. However, their initial unwillingness to pass the ball was superceded by two flowing tries which were triumphantly executed by Hennie le Roux and Andre Joubert, the former charging straight over Rob Andrew. However, South Africa must surely hold the all-time record for selecting a penalty kick instead of a run from such a short distance – just six inches. The mind-set for the future of rugby can now only be jolted with six or seven points for a try.

For me the nicest feeling of the tour was being able to sing "Nkosi Sikelel 'iAfrika" and supporting the national team as well, for the first time in 20 years.

The success of the tour can be measured by the fact that it took place so soon after a period of high tension during the April election. This bodes well for next year's World Cup and the possibility of hosting the Olympic Games in 2004.

It also signals acceptance of a new era by those who previously would never have been seen cheering on black players like Chester Williams. Ubogu, Ojomoh and Hull showed the way for future South African stars who will surely play their own part in breaking down further the myths of hatred. In the words of the noted American civil rights lawyer from Alabama, Charles Morgan: "It was the success of the black sports stars in the South that brought white crowds to their feet and to their senses" ■

> **...I, as an ANC supporter, sang "Nkosi Sikelel 'iAfrika" with no support at all within earshot...**

Dillon Woods works for the British Defence and Aid Fund

8. Appendix

Appendix 1

SELECT COMMITTEE ON SPORTS SPONSORSHIP AND TV COVERAGE

Sport and Politics have been uneasy cousins. In 1994, the UK government began an inquiry into aspects of sport sponsorship and television coverage. This took place in the National Heritage Committee Select Committee. The members were Gerald Kaufman, Chairman; Joe Ashton, Dr John Blackburn, Jim Callaghan, Michael Fabricant, John Gorst, Bruce Grocott, Toby Jessel, John Maxton.

The committee sat throughout March, April and May and heard evidence from: 10 March 1994 - The Sports Council & The Central Council of Physical Recreation; 17 March 1994 - Guinness plc/United Distillers; Alan Pascoe Associates and Tobacco Manufacturers Association/Gallaher; 24 March 1994 - Sir Paul Fox CBE & Donald Trelford; Football Supporters Association and Brass Brewers; 14 April 1994 - IBM UK/Comark Communications; British Paralympic Association; British Olympic Association and British Athletic Federation; 21 April 1994 - Test and County Cricket Board; Football Asscociation; Lawn Tennis Association and the *Rugby Football Union (Dudley Wood, Secretary)*

We print below the complete interview with Dudley Wood, Secretary, Rugby Football Union.

21 April 1994
Examination of Witness

MR DUDLEY WOOD, Secretary, Rugby Football Union, examined.

Chairman

626. Mr Wood, I would like to welcome you to the Committee and before we proceed to questioning, I wonder if you have an opening statement you would like to make to us?

(Mr Wood) *No, sir, I do not think so really, except to say that we in rugby football are running an amateur sport for people playing in their spare time which is the way we want to keep it and we are a self-funding, a self-financing sport. Sponsorship and television are quite important to us, but we would survive without them. They enable us to do things we would not otherwise be able to do in terms of the development and promotion of our sport.*

627. Could you just enlarge a little on that last point that you made that sponsorship enables you to do certain things that you would not be able to do without it?

(Mr Wood) *Our big requirement for funds is for the development of our sport, that is to encourage young people to play, and we spend a very significant proportion of our income on that. We*

have teams of youth development officers around the country teaching people to play. We have been brought to that decision by the fact that team games are not played in the schools in the way in which they used to be and we decided we had to do something about it ourselves and so that is a very significant proportion of our expenditure. The other major item is the improvement of our facilities and Twickenham is a case in point where we are spending over £60 million on rebuilding a national stadium which we believe is prestigious for the country, although it does not attract any help in financial support from other sources, so these are the main two items on which our television and sponsorship monies are used, quite apart from the general day-to-day running of the sport and our competitions.

Mr Maxton

628. Can I unusually start by congratulating you and your fellow colleagues in the Union on ensuring that the BBC kept the Five Nations' Championships rather than it going to BSkyB which was, I think, a real possibility. Do you think that will help you to continue the development of the game?

(Mr Wood) *Yes. It was not a possibility as far as I was concerned, but in fact we were lucky in the sense that we had two terrestrial channels and a satellite channel all bidding which obviously increased the value of the contract considerably and we were most anxious to keep them all in the hunt, but yes, we are very pleased that we have retained our television on BBC, which is where in fact our supporters expect to find it.*

629. Can I also, and this is, I can assure you, the last point of congratulation, congratulate you and the game of rugby, because I come from Scotland, on the youth programmes you have carried out because I do think that unlike most other sports rugby actually has spent a lot of money on ensuring that young players are brought on and developed and I hope you can continue that. Now, I can move on. Is there not a great danger, however, that the popularity of rugby on television is having two effects? Firstly, it is commercialising it. It is all right saying you are an amateur sport, but when we read in the newspapers that Mr Will Carling is now earning £100,000 a year from rugby – you shake your head.

(Mr Wood) *Not from rugby. It is because of his fame at rugby, but he does not take any money out of our game.*

[**Mr Maxton** *Cont*]

630. But how long will it be before that happens?

(Mr Wood) *Well, it is a very commercial world and times are changing and we have to change with them and learn to cope with them. We certainly believe that it is worth trying to retain the amateur status of our sport, but we recognise that because there is a lot of money in the sport, there will be abuses of the amateur code. We deal with those as we can, but that will happen, but when you say players in this country, and I can only speak for England, are earning a lot from the game, they are earning a lot* because of the fame and popularity of the sport, but I know of no cases where they are actually taking money out of the game that would otherwise be in the game.

631. But is this not just a first step? At one time you could not even earn money from rugby in other ways. In other words, even if you wrote your memoirs as an ex-international, you immediately barred yourself from not only playing the game, but from going to a club and coaching the game, so is this not just the first step in a move towards a professional sport?

(Mr Wood) *Yes, it is. When the proposal was made at international board level that players should not be denied the possibility of earning money from non-rugby-related activities, we supported that. We could not see what right we had to prevent a player, a private individual from earning money from the fact that he had become popular and was in the public eye and if he, for example, was required to speak at a Barclays Bank annual dinner for a fee of £500, we felt we had no right to stop him.*

632. Right, but then the next step, which is already happening or it appears to be happening, is that a rugby club like Bath and maybe four or five other top clubs in England are obviously now attracting the cream of English rugby to the detriment presumably of other clubs. How are they doing that if it is not by financial reward?

(Mr Wood) *Well, I do not believe it is, although of course they can pay legitimate expenses which junior clubs could not afford to pay, but the fact is that those players want to play for England and they believe that their best chance of gaining national selection is to join one of the top clubs and it is not just Bath, but to join one of the top clubs is the best way to be selected for England and I am bound to say that they are proving to be right because if you want to play for England, you have got to play at the top level week in, week out.*

633. Are you telling me that there are not companies attached or related to these top clubs who are essentially giving these people jobs "to ensure they play for that club"? Are you assuring me that does not happen?

(Mr Wood) *I believe that there are companies which are supporting clubs and I believe that in the freemasonry of rugby, players have always been able to find jobs because it opens doors. It always has. As long as I have been involved in the game, it has always opened doors. If a player is offered a better job to move clubs, then that is a contravention of our regulations.*

634. That is a contravention?

(Mr Wood) *Yes, and we would try and do something about it.*

635. I gather you are, however, now moving to a system of registration of players.

(Mr Wood) *We have a registration for our competitions.*

636. Is there not a great danger with the popularity of rugby in the televising of the sport that you are going to have to change the laws of the game you will notice I used the correct terminology—in order to make it more popular with the non-rugby-playing population?

(Mr Wood) *I think there is pressure to do so, particularly from other parts of the world. It is pressure that we try to resist. We believe that the game is really primarily for the players and we*

are delighted that people want to watch it. We are not seeking to take over the premier position in winter sports and we are very happy with the position we are in at the moment and the popularity we enjoy. We believe that there could be a benefit if there were changes to the law to improve the game, but not for the purpose of attracting more public support.

637. As rugby union becomes more and more commercial, when are you actually going to get together with rugby league and sort it out so that we only have one game of rugby in this country?

(Mr Wood) *I would regard that as an unmitigated disaster and my reason for that is that if you do that, then a player has to decide whether he is going to play rugby or pursue a career and we do not have that position. All our players are in full-time employment and are able to follow a full-time career. The best example I can always give is Jonathan Webb, an England full-back who qualified and practised as a surgeon whilst playing rugby for England. I regard that as a tremendous advantage and any one is available to play. If you have time I will develop this sir. If you look at cricket; cricket, because of the end of the amateur, is now restricted merely to those players who come out of schools who are prepared to give up any full-time career pretensions they may have in order to play on empty county grounds week in, week out and we lose so many potentially good cricketers for that reason and I have talked to many of the old stagers about it and I am afraid that is a loss we do not want to see in rugby. In rugby league I think you have a few hundred players to choose from. In rugby union any one of our 500,000 players could play for England if he is good enough. He does not have to give up anything. He has to train hard.*

638. I hope you will not mind me saying so but that is a very English rugby view. Welsh rugby union players come from a much broader class spectrum than rugby in either England or, can I say, Scotland, but we have got a full Welsh Fifteen now playing rugby league and we cannot keep them because they have to make a living and they cannot make a living from playing rugby.

(Mr Wood) *I do not accept for a moment there is any restriction on a class basis in playing rugby union and I could demonstrate that quite easily. Our players come from a very wide spectrum of society. I think the Welsh have found themselves in a difficult position with a number of players coming to expect very high price offers. I think we are lucky in that we have not found ourselves in the same position.*

[Mr Maxton *Cont]*
639. Lastly, as rugby becomes more professional— and it is going to become more professional, I think, and I think it is unfortunate—is it not a game that is far too dangerous with its present laws to be played for money?

(Mr Wood) *No I do not believe that. In fact, I believe the rate of injury for a physical contact game is relatively containable, but one of the factors which we are weighing up very carefully is that people are becoming bigger, faster and fitter, and that does create, I believe, more injuries and we do have working parties on that subject studying all the time how the laws might be amended to reduce the dangers, but, no, I do not believe statistically it is a very dangerous game to play and I know in terms of serious injuries, and the figures are there, that other activities* such as riding and trampolining and diving are far more dangerous than rugby or football.

640. I said if it becomes more professional. The ability to foul and to injure deliberately in rugby are very, very apparent to anybody else.

(Mr Wood) *As a professional sport, I would pay a compliment to rugby league, I believe they have contained that situation extremely well.*

Mr Maxton: By changing the laws to obtain that and therefore again the game can begin to merge.

Chairman: I think that we are moving slightly tendentiously away from the subject of the inquiry, interesting though this stroll down a philosophical byway has been.

Mr Maxton: Sorry, Mr Chairman, professionalism in rugby is coming as a result of pressure from the televising of the sport which makes it popular.

Mr Fabricant

641. While Mr Maxton was switched into congratulatory mode he said how pleased he was that the Five Nations' Championship has been retained with the BBC and you, in responding to him, mentioned that this was despite quite energetic competition from presumably Independent Television and BSkyB. I am just curious to know whether the BBC put in the highest bid?

(Mr Wood) *No.*

642. So what made you choose to go with the BBC? Let me ask you, was BSkyB the highest bid?

(Mr Wood) *No.*

Chairman: We are proceeding by a process of elimination, Mr Wood!

643. So it was a question—that is an interesting one—then of competition between two terrestrial channels? It has to be.

(Mr Wood) *Yes. BSkyB having started the negotiation read the signs and decided that they were not going to bid for the main contract and in fact we achieved with them a back-up contract mainly based on repeats and so we have a very satisfactory contract with BSkyB as well, but, no, the decision was made to take the BBC's offer.*

644. Let me go into my "subjunctive mode", as I call it, so if BSkyB had put in the highest bid, though, would you have still preferred to have gone with the BBC? In other words, I think the Committee really has been questioning people and we have been looking at the trade-off between maximising audiences with maximising income and I am wondering whether the Union takes a view on this?

(Mr Wood) *I must make it clear that these things are not my decisions. I am involved, but they are not my decisions. There are many other people involved. I do not believe that the committee concerned would have accepted a higher **offer from BSkyB** had they made it. I think the view is that **BSkyB or satellite** do not, at the present time, have the sufficient coverage through cable and dishes to justify giving them the major contract. **Certainly,** it would have been extremely unpopular with our supporters.*

Chairman

645. Is then the consequence of your answer to Mr Fabricant that what those responsible for negotiations were looking to was not a maximisation of income but a maximisation of television audience?

(Mr Wood) *Yes, I think that is the major factor. It is a combination of factors. Of course, you want to be satisfied that you are going to get the quality of production that you feel you need. You certainly want the coverage, the audience exposure, but, of course, we all have a need for money as well. Those are the factors which you have to weigh up.*

646. In the kind of rough sport that Mr Maxton has been indicating you are in, it seems to me you are extraordinarily fastidious.

(Mr Wood) *We have been called many things, sir.*

Mr Fabricant

647. There was an article in *The Independent on Sunday* which talked about the influence of television on the game and Mr Mr Maxton has already raised the possibility of changing the rules, and I am conscious of the fact that Australian Rules Football, which I suppose has more similarity with rugby than it does with soccer. It is partly a response to the television audience. We have seen, for example, the influence of Kerry Packer on cricket. In this article in *The Independent on Sunday* it talks about going to see a football match at 5 pm on a Sunday. It says: *"The game had been moved to such an unlikely hour"* – I do not know why it is so unlikely – *"to accommodate the live television broadcast of another game at 3 pm."* I am wondering to what degree the timing, if not the rules, of your matches are dictated by television?

(Mr Wood) *They are not at all and we have resisted any pressure to make us change the time to the extent that we have, of course, in the Five Nations' Championship two international matches on the same day. The television people tell us it would be logical to play one at two o'clock and the other at four o'clock, but we refuse that and they still play at the same time.*

Mr Ashton

648. But you have no floodlights, so how could you?

(Mr Wood) *That has not influenced it. Other national grounds already have floodlights and floodlights will be installed at Twickenham at the end of 1995.*

[Mr Ashton Cont)

649. But the other clubs have no floodlights, so you cannot.

(Mr Wood) *No. Well, I think he was referring to international matches, but no, I take your point. A lot of clubs do have floodlights, but we are not normally influenced over this by the television, but I would not rule it out in the future.*

Mr Fabricant: May I compliment you on your monastic purity!

650. Could I ask you, you talked about the best clubs, but how do you define the best clubs?

(Mr Wood) *Well, we now have a league structure which we claim, possibly wrongly, to be the largest of any sport in the world, which has 108 leagues in it.*

651. In one league?

(Mr Wood) *In one league. There are 108 separate leagues with promotion and relegation and so a club in the 108th league by winning year in, year out could proceed to the top.*

652. But why do we not get this intense excitement that there is now in football at the end of the season, which Mr Grocott referred to, where it is a financial disaster as well as a playing disaster if you get relegated? You do not think that would enhance the tension and enlarge the newspaper coverage and the number of people who will take an interest in it if you had that sort of promotion and relegation system?

(Mr Wood) *We have, and it does.*

653. But it does it among a very small circle of friends.

(Mr Wood) *The league is based on two clubs up and two down and you are right, it is a disaster for a club to be relegated.*

654. Yes, it is a disaster for a club, but in other sports it is a disaster for the town or the city and they feel that the city has lost some prestige by not being in the top rank and even the local council go into mourning and things like that and I have no doubt it does to a certain extent in rugby, but it does seem as though you are not bothered about widening the audience or whether people take an interest.

(Mr Wood) *I do not think that is true, but it would be regarded as a disaster, I am sure, in a rugby town if a team is relegated. Even, for example, Redruth – when they go down at the end of the season – which is devoted to rugby, there is no question that there is no significance in that and they will regard it as a disaster when their team is demoted and it will affect the financial viability of the club, but really I think the answer to what you are saying is that we do not enjoy the status of our national sport, football, which I fully accept.*

655. Is it because there is an elitism about it or that it tends to be in smaller rural areas or certain types of schools where rugby is pushed? Basically I think football is popular because it costs nothing for kids to play. They can put two coats down in the park and get a ball and it costs them nothing, but they have to pay to go on to the tennis courts, and it spreads the game. Now, I would imagine that in certain areas, certainly I have seen many working class kids in rugby league areas playing rugby league and it is very, very popular in coal-mining areas in Wales, as we have said, but the English rugby union people seem to want to keep everybody else at a distance and they are not interested in sponsorship like other sports, and why should that be?

(Mr Wood) *Again I do not think that is true, but I do not think that rugby football is really a game that can be played on a casual basis with coats being put down in a public park. I would be very unhappy about that from the point of view of control of the sport, making sure that the laws of the game are obeyed and that it did not get out of hand, bearing in mind that it is a violent game, so I would not be happy with that. Also it is not a simple game. I do not see that personally as a disadvantage. I believe that sport should be complicated. I like, for example, cricket where people are constantly discussing tactics and why they did this and why they do that*

and I do not particularly want rugby to be a simple game.

656. You mentioned the violence which is giving your game a bad image on television. Surely when there is violence, if you are paying the players and they are registered, that is the thing that stamps it out? When football has a violent element, the referee sends them off and they lose two weeks' wages because they are not able to play for the club and the club has been deprived of their services and that tends to keep it down. It is the loss of the wages rather than the thump in the eye that tends to stop it. Now, would it not be a good thing if that was introduced in your game?

(Mr Wood) *Well, that would not be a good reason for introducing it, but it is true, we do not have that sanction. We cannot dock a player's wages because of violence. We can suspend him and we do suspend players. The referee has all the powers in the world and we have the back-up disciplinary system to deal with them and we can do that, but truly we do not have the same sanction of hitting their pockets.*

Mr Jessel

657. Mr Wood, I ought to know, but I was not quite clear whether you said there was or there was not any kind of commercial sponsorship for rugby union.

(Mr Wood) *Yes, we have a whole range of sponsors who put money into the sport, yes.*

658. Could you please be kind enough to give the Committee an idea of what industries and what are the principal firms involved, if it is not commercially sensitive?

(Mr Wood) *No, not at all. Our main sponsors of international matches are Save & Prosper and of our competitions it is Pilkington Glass for the Pilkington Cup, Courage for the League competition, CIS Insurance for the Divisional and County Championships. There are a whole range of other sponsors, but of the leading ones who are putting in really substantial money, the biggest is Courage who have put in £7 million over four years and Pilkington who have put in a couple of million and so on. Those are the biggest, Save & Prosper, Courage and Pilkington.*

659. And could you kindly confirm that they never include any tobacco companies?

(Mr Wood) *No. One of my small successes was to remove the one tobacco company we had soon after I arrived at Twickenham.*

[Mr Jessel Cont]

660. May I please congratulate you on that. I said earlier, before you arrived, to the Committee that I have no bias against your game.

(Mr Wood) *Thank you. In view of your constituency, sir, I would hope not!*

Chairman

This has been a very happy session and it has ended in a roseate glow, Mr Wood. I am very grateful to you. We seem to be encountering in this, of all games, the last of the gentlemen. Thank you very much indeed!

Printed in the United Kingdom by HMSO
19585 CS 5/94 157465 PP

Appendix 2

SPORTS DISCRIMINATION

A Bill to

"Make it unlawful for any administrative rule-making body for a sport to discriminate against persons who have participated, are participating or are expected to participate in any other lawful sport, and for connected purposes.

Be it enacted by the Queen's most Excellent Majority, by and with the advice and consent of the Lords Spiritual and Temporal, and Commons, in this present Parliament assembled, and by the authority of the same, as follows:-

1. This Act shall apply to any sport or game which is played in public and to which the public is or may be admitted, whether or not on payment of a fee.

2. It shall be unlawful for any association (whether incorporated or unincorporated) which has responsibility for administering or making rules for the conduct of any sport or game, or any club affiliated to such an association, to discriminate against any person by reason solely of either - **(a)** his past or present participation, or **(b)** a presumption (whether reasonable or not) that he intends to participate - in any other lawful sport or game, whether as a player or otherwise.

3.(1) A claim by any person that an association has committed an act of discrimination against him which is unlawful by virtue of section 2 of this Act may be made the subject of civil proceedings in like manner as any other claim in tort or (in Scotland) in reparation for breach of statutory duty.

(2) Proceedings under subsection (1) above - **(a)** shall be brought in England and Wales or in Northern Ireland only in a county court; and **(b)** shall be brought in Scotland only in a sheriff court.

4. For the purpose of this Act, to "discriminate" means either to treat any person less favourably than any other person or to make any rule which has the effect of so doing.

5. This Act may be cited as the Sports (Discrimination) Act 1994."

Presented by Mr David Hinchcliffe.
Supported by:-
Mr Ian McCartney, Mr Gary Walker, Mrs Elizabeth Peacock, Mr Allan Rogers, Mr Terry Rooney, Mr Neil Gerrard, Mr Norman A Goodman, Ms Liz Lynne, Mr Alan Williams, Kate Hoey and Mr Tom Pendry
Ordered by the House of Commons to be printed, 12 June 1994

Editor's note: *This Private Member's Bill was given a first reading in the House of Commons in June 1994. It was the only Bill to be given an unopposed Second Reading.*

On Wednesday 13 July the Bill went to Committee Stage. Two days later, the Bill was scheduled for Third Reading. It was the fifth and final Bill on the Order Paper. If the day's Parliamentary business had made it possible for the Bill to start, it would have needed to have been finished by 2.30pm or it would have fallen, and the Bill would have been lost.

This was likely to happen as Sir Peter Fry (MP for Wellingborough) had tabled 11 amendments – with the apparent intention of defeating it. However, David Hinchcliffe, know-

ing this, asked for the Third Reading to be delayed until the next session of Parliament. It is now scheduled for a Third Reading on 21 October and has a very strong chance of becoming law. If this happens, the RFU will have been forced to concede the argument that former Rugby League players will be allowed to play Rugby Union and that UK citizens will be allowed to play both Rugby League and 'amateur' Rugby Union at any time.

CHANGES TO THE LAWS 1994

1. LAW 3: NUMBER OF PLAYERS
1.1 Amend 3(4) (b) to read:
Exceptions
"Up to seven players may be replaced..."
1.2 Amend 3(4)(b) to read:
"A player who has been permanently replaced must NOT resume playing in the match"
1.3 Add new Note (i) after Section 3 (4):
"(i) When a team names seven replacements four of the seven replacements must cover the following positions: Loose head prop, Hooker and Second row forward"

2. LAW 4: PLAYERS' DRESS
Amend Section (2) to read:
"(2) Shoulder pads of the "harness" type must not be worn nor braces nor supports including rigid or reinforced material. The wearing of thin pads of cotton wool, sponge rubber or similar soft material may be permitted provided they are attached to the body or sewn to the jersey."

3. LAW 6A: REFEREE
3.1 Delete the last paragraph of 6A (7) and substitute:
At half time the referee shall allow the coach of each team on to the playing area to attend their teams."
3.2 Re-write 6A(8)(d) to read:
"(d) A player who has an open or bleeding wound must leave the playing area until such time as the bleeding is controlled and the wound is covered or dressed. Such a player may be replaced once only, on a temporary basis, until the wound is covered or dressed, but after 10 minutes the replacement becomes permanent. The 10-minute period commences when such a player leaves the playing area."

4. LAW 10: KICK-OFF
Amend Section (4) to read:
"If the ball crosses the opposing team's goal line from a kick-off, without touching or being touched by a player, the opposing team has the option of grounding the ball, making it dead, or playing on. If the opposing team grounds the ball or makes it dead or the ball becomes dead by touch-in-goal or by touching or crossing the dead ball line, they will have the option of either having a scrummage formed at the centre of the half-way line, with the put-in, or having the other team kick-off again."

5. LAW 14: IN-GOAL
Amend Section (4) to read:
"Except where the ball is knocked on or thrown forward in the field of play or In-goal, if an attacking player kicks, carries, passes or charges down the ball from an opponent's kick

and it travels into his opponent's In-goal, either directly or having touched a defender who does not willfully attempt to stop, catch or kick it, and it is there grounded by a defending player, or goes into touch in goal or over the dead ball line a drop-out shall be awarded".

6. LAW 17: KNOCK-ON
To the penalty provision add: "A penalty try may be awarded."

7. LAW 18
Amend Section (1) (a) to read: "A tackled player must immediately: pass the ball or release the ball and get up or move away from the ball".

8. LAW 21: RUCK
8.1 Insert a new Section (3) in place of Experimental Variation: "(3) When the ball in a ruck becomes unplayable a scrummage shall be ordered and the ball put in by the team moving forward immediately prior to the formation of the ruck. When neither team was moving forward or where the referee is unable to determine which team was moving forward, the ball shall be put in by the attacking team."

8.2 Add a new Note (ii) after Law 21 (3): "(ii) Before whistling for a scrummage the referee should allow a reasonable time for the ball to emerge from the ruck particularly if either team is moving forward. If the ruck becomes stationary or in the opinion of the referee the ball will probably not emerge from the ruck without delay, he should order a scrummage."

9. LAW 22: MAUL
9.1 Amend the first paragraph of the Definition to read; "A maul, which can take place only in the field of play, is formed by one or more players of each team on their feet and in physical contact closing around a player who is in possession of the ball."

9.2 The Experimental Variation, Law 22 (4) (a) is adopted and amended to read: "When a maul becomes stationary or the ball in a maul becomes unplayable a scrummage shall be ordered and the ball shall be put in by the team NOT in possession at the commencement of the maul, except where the referee is unable to determine which team was in possession then the ball shall be put in by the team which was moving forward prior to the stoppage or, if neither team was moving forward, by the attacking team."

9.3 The Experimental Variation, Law 22 (4) (b) is adopted and amended to read: "(b) If a player catches the ball direct from a kick by an opponent, other than from a kick-off or from a drop-out, and is immediately held by an opponent so that a maul ensues and the maul becomes stationary or the ball becomes unplayable his team shall put in the ball at the ensuing scrummage."

9.4 Add a new Note (i): "(i) Direct from a kick means the ball has been caught without having bounced off the playing surface or without having touched or been touched in flight by another player."

9.5 Re-write Note (i) to become Note (ii) and amend as follows: "(ii) When the maul becomes stationary but the ball is being moved and can be seen by the referee, he should

allow a reasonable time for the ball to emerge but not permit the maul to start moving again. When the ball in a maul becomes unplayable the referee should not allow prolonged wrestling for the ball and should order a scrummage."

10. LAW 23A: TOUCH
Delete in Section (3) "or touch in goal" in the second line.

11. LAW 23B: LINE-OUT
11.1 In Section (5) (a) delete "taken" and substitute "awarded".
11.2 Re-write Sections (7), (8), (9) and (10) as follows:
(7) "The ball may be brought into play at a formed line-out or by a quick throw-in which can only be taken before the line-out has formed. If a quick throw-in occurs after the line-out has formed, it is void and the ball is brought into play at the formed line-out by the same team.
(8) At a formed line-out the ball must be thrown in at the place indicated in (5) so that it first touches the ground or touches or is touched by a player at least five metres from the touch-line along the line-of-touch; otherwise the opposing team shall have the right, at its option, to throw in the ball or to take a scrummage."
(9) (a) At a quick throw-in, the ball that went into touch must be used and, after going into touch, it must have been touched only by the player throwing it in; otherwise the ball shall be thrown in at the place indicated in (5) by the same team.
(b) At a quick throw-in the throw must be straight along the line-of-touch for a distance of not less than 5 metres; otherwise the opposing team shall have the right, at its option, to throw in the ball or to take a scrummage at the place where the quick throw-in occurred.
(10) If, on the second occasion, the ball is not thrown in correctly, a scrummage shall be formed and the ball shall be put in by the team which threw it is on the first occasion.
11.3 In note (xi) replace 23B (8) (a) with 23B(8)
11.4 Experimental Variation 23B(16) is adopted.
11.5 In Penalty (a) delete (8)(b).

12. LAW 24: OFF-SIDE
12.1 Amend Law 24C(1)(d) to read:
(a player is off-side if he:)
"(d) unbinds from the ruck or leaves the maul and does not *immediately* retire behind the off-side line or once he is on side, if he rejoins the ruck or maul in front of the hindmost player of his team".
12.2 Amend Law 24C(1)(b) and Law 24C(2)(b):
(a player is off-side if he:)
"(d) joins in front of the hindmost player of his team."

13. LAW 24(1)
Amend 1st pica dot by deletion of "without infringing Law 24A(2)."

(ITEM 8) TO RECEIVE AMENDMENTS TO THE REGULATIONS RELATING TO AMATEURISM adopted by the International Rugby Football Board pursuant to the following Bye-Law 4

BYE-LAW 4. AMATEUR PRINCIPLES
(i) The Game is an Amateur Game. No Person is allowed directly or indirectly to: (a) receive payment, benefit or other material reward, or (b) accept promise of future pay-

ment, benefit or other material reward, for taking part in the Game except as provided for by the Regulations Relating to Amateurism.

(ii) Pursuant to Bye-Law 3(b), the Council shall adopt Regulations Relating to Amateurism which shall be binding on all Unions.

(iii) A Union may frame additional Regulations Relating to Amateurism provided they are not in conflict with the Council's Regulations. Such Regulations shall have effect only within the jurisdiction of that Union.

REGULATION 3

3.1 Personal and Communication Allowances
Amend to read;

3.1.1 Personal and Communication Allowances may be paid to cover personal requirements not otherwise provided by the Unions, but shall not be more than such daily amount as the Council shall determine at the Annual Meeting.

3.1.2 The Personal and Communication Allowance may be paid to the players and nominated officials of National Representative Teams while assembled as such and on such special occasions as the Council by Resolution may

from time to time determine.

3.1.3 The Personal and Communication Allowance is normally a charge to the Visited Union while on tour, but, when mutually agreed, may be paid by the Visiting Union.

3.1.4 The Personal and Communication Allowance may also be paid by the Visited Union to referees who are appointed by their Union to officiate in overseas matches designated by the Council.

3.1.5 The players and nominated officials to whom and the tours to which provisions of this Regulation may apply are defined in Resolution 2.

REGULATION 9.6
Amend to read:

9.6.3 Any form of logo, trademark or advertising, other than that of Unions or their affiliated Clubs as defined in Regulation 1.1 is prohibited on: (a) the playing area as defined in Law 1 of the Laws of the Game (b) touch judges' flags, goal posts and cross bars.

(Note: The prohibition in respect of goal posts does not apply to padding and protectors up to a height of two metres from the ground).

ADDENDUM

FIRA RESULTS 1993-94

Federation Internationale de Rugby Amateur (FIRA)
Formed 1934
Headquarters: 7 Cite d'Antin Paris 9 (same as French Federation de Rugby). Tel 010 331 48 74 84 75. Fax 010 331 45 26 19 19

FIRA has six leagues which operate throughout the season:

Group A, Pool 1
Spain, France, Italy, Romania & Russia

Groupe A Pool 2
Germany, Belgium, Morocco, Portugal & Tunisia

Groupe B Pool 1
Andorra, Holland, Poland, Czech Republic & Sweden

Groupe B Pool 2
Austria, Croatia, Hungary, Slovenia & Ukraine

Groupe C Pool 1
Georgia, Latvia, Luxembourg & Switzerland

Groupe C Pool 2
Bulgaria, Denmark, Lithuania & Moldavia

RESULTS
A1
France 51 Romania 0
Russia 19 Italy 30
Italy 16 France 9
France 49 Spain 3
Spain 9 Russia 16
Spain 3 Romania 11
Romania 30 Russia 0
Italy 62 Spain 15
Romania 26 Italy 12
Russia 9 France 11

A2
Tunisia 15 Germany 6
Germany 32 Belgium 16
Belgium 18 Morocco 14
Germany 35 Morocco18
Belgium 10 Portugal 8
Portugal 18 Germany 20
Morocco 20 Portugal 15
Portugal 16 Tunisia 18
Tunisia 16 Belgium 16
Morocco 25 Tunisia 10

B1
Sweden 25 Andorra 6
Czech R 19 Poland 18
Holland 42 Czech R 6
Czech R 34 Sweden 7
Holland 31 Sweden 6
Poland 30 Andorra 10
Andorra 10 Holland 49
Poland 13 Holland 10
Czech R 56 Andorra 0
Sweden 18 Poland 25

Sweden 6 Holland 44
Andorra Sweden n/a

B2
Hungary 3 Ukraine 41
Austria 11 Slovenia 14
Hungary Austria n/a
Croatia 41 Austria 12
Croatia 77 Slovenia 10
Croatia 13 Ukraine 23
Ukraine 41 Slovenia 26
Slovenia 28 Hungary 17
Austria 72 Ukraine 0
Hungary 5 Croatia 31

C1
Luxembourg 10 Georgia 10
Latvia 10 Switzerland 0
Luxembourg 10 Latvia 25
Luxembourg 8 Switzerland 17
Switzerland Georgia n/a
Georgia Latvia n/a

C2
Lithuania 6 Moldavia 22
Bulgaria 9 Lithuania 9
Bulgaria 11 Denmark 9
Moldavia 42 Bulgaria 3
Denmark 69 Lithuania 6
Denmark Moldavia n/a

In the light of the International Olympic Committee's recognition of FIRA we shall include a separate and comprehensive analysis of the work of FIRA in next year's *Almanack*.

WESTERN SAMOA TOUR TO AUSTRALIA
July-August 1994

v Victoria, won 60-26
Date: 23 July

v Capital Territory XV, won 39-13
Date: 27 July

v Queensland, won 24-22
Date: 30 July

v New South Wales XV, won 21-18
Date: 3 August

v Australia Test, lost 3-73
Date: 6 August
Venue: Sydney

A near flawless performance saw Australia rout Western Samoa.

P	W	D	L	F	A
5	4	0	1	147	152

SOUTH AFRICA TOUR TO NEW ZEALAND
June-August 1994

No other country but South Africa could afford to spend eight weeks away on an overseas tour especially as the schedule of matches reads like a Lions tour. The good thing is though that the Test series is the best of three matches and this must be the way forward. Either side plays a one-off or they play the best of three. A two-Test series, which usually ends up with the series being shared, satisfies only those best interested in compromise.

The South Africans perceived that as they had dismantled England in the second of their two-Test series that they were going to New Zealand to prove they were, after Australia, the second best side in the world for 1994.

v King Country, won 46-10
Date: 22 June

v Counties, won 37-26
Date: 25 June

v Wellington, won 36-26
Date: 28 June

v Southland, won 51-15
Date: 2 July

v Hanan Shield XV, won 67-19
Date: 6 July

v New Zealand First Test, lost 14-22
Date: 9 July
Venue: Dunedin
Referee: B Stirling (Ireland)

A dour match which NZ had to win to prevent them from "achieving" three losses at home for the first time in their history. Place-kicking again let the South Africans down and in the first five minutes they wasted a three-man overlap.

John Kirwan created a new NZ record in winning his 58th cap; for good measure he scored his 35th try which is also a record for his country.

v Taranaki, won 16-12
Date: 13 July

v Waikato, won 38-17
Date: 16 July

v Manawatu, won 47-21
Date: 19 July

v New Zealand Second Test, lost 9-13
Date: 23 July
Venue: Athletic Park, Wellington
Referee: B. Sterling (Ireland)

John Le Roux bit off more than he could chew and was sent home after an ear biting exercise with Sean Fitzpatrick. This was a desperately close match and one NZ were glad to win and with it the series.

v Otago, lost 12-19
Date: 27 July

v Canterbury, won 21-11
Date: 30 July

v Bay of Plenty, won 33-12
Date: 2 August

v New Zealand Third Test,

Drew 18-18
Date: 6 August
Venue: Auckland

South Africa scored two tries to nil and still couldn't win.

P	W	D	L	F	A
13	9	0	4	445	241

In the end this was a disappointing tour for South Africa but probably much more important to their world cup preparation than the two-Test series at home against England. Violence still permeates her game and stronger endorsement of the laws is required in her own domestic rugby before there can be changes at the top.

For New Zealand after the French whitewash there was relief all round.

UK PHONE DAY

In the UK the national code change will take place on 16 April 1995. This means you must:
● insert the numeral 1 after 0 in area codes;
● use new codes for Sheffield, Leeds, Nottingham, Leicester and Bristol;
● use 00 for international access.
Thus London becomes 0171 or 0181 and International access changes to 00 (from 010).
Other UK code changes:
Bristol to 0117-9 (from 0272)
Leeds to 0113-2 (from 0532)
Leicester to 0116-2 (from 0533)
Nottingham to 0115-9 (from 0602)
Sheffield to 0114-2 (from 0742)
These five cities change both their city code and then add either a 2 or a 9 to existing local numbers; thus they become seven digit numbers (instead of the exisiting six digit numbers).
From overseas, callers will dial for London 44 171 + number and for Leeds 44 113-2 + number.
Emergency Services, Operation Services and Directory Enquiries remain unchanged.
Mobile 'phone numbers and special numbers such as 0500, 0645 and 0800 remain.
Don't forget to up-grade telephone memory numbers ■